D0000605

The Best American
Sports Writing
2017

NO LONGER PROPERTY OF
ANYTHINK LIBRARIES/
RANGEVIEW LIBRARY DISTRICT

GUEST EDITORS OF
THE BEST AMERICAN SPORTS WRITING

1991 DAVID HALBERSTAM
1992 THOMAS MCGUANE
1993 FRANK DEFORD
1994 TOM BOSWELL
1995 DAN JENKINS
1996 JOHN FEINSTEIN
1997 GEORGE PLIMPTON
1998 BILL LITTLEFIELD
1999 RICHARD FORD
2000 DICK SCHAAP
2001 BUD COLLINS
2002 RICK REILLY
2003 BUZZ BISSINGER
2004 RICHARD BEN CRAMER
2005 MIKE LUPICA
2006 MICHAEL LEWIS
2007 DAVID MARANISS
2008 WILLIAM NACK
2009 LEIGH MONTVILLE
2010 PETER GAMMONS
2011 JANE LEAVY
2012 MICHAEL WILBON
2013 J. R. MOEHRINGER
2014 CHRISTOPHER MCDOUGALL
2015 WRIGHT THOMPSON
2016 RICK TELANDER
2017 HOWARD BRYANT

The Best AMERICAN SPORTS WRITING™ 2017

Edited and with an Introduction
by Howard Bryant

Glenn Stout, *Series Editor*

A Mariner Original

HOUGHTON MIFFLIN HARCOURT

BOSTON • NEW YORK 2017

Copyright © 2017 by Houghton Mifflin Harcourt Publishing Company
Introduction copyright © 2017 by Howard Bryant

ALL RIGHTS RESERVED

The Best American Series® is a registered trademark of Houghton Mifflin Harcourt Publishing Company. *The Best American Sports Writing*™ is a trademark of Houghton Mifflin Harcourt Publishing Company.

No part of this work may be reproduced or transmitted in any form or by any means, electronic or mechanical, including photocopying and recording, or by any information storage or retrieval system without the prior written permission of the copyright owner unless such copying is expressly permitted by federal copyright law. With the exception of nonprofit transcription in Braille, Houghton Mifflin is not authorized to grant permission for further uses of copyrighted selections reprinted in this book without the permission of their owners. Permission must be obtained from the individual copyright owners identified herein. Address requests for permission to make copies of Houghton Mifflin Harcourt material to Permissions, Houghton Mifflin Harcourt Publishing Company, 3 Park Avenue, 19th Floor, New York, New York 10016.

hmhco.com

ISBN 978-0-544-82155-2 (print)   ISBN 978-0-544-82156-9 (ebook)
ISSN 1056-8034 (print)   ISSN 2573-4822 (ebook)

Printed in the United States of America
DOC 10 9 8 7 6 5 4 3 2 1

"Almost There" by Roger Angell. First published in *The New Yorker.* Copyright © 2016 by Condé Nast. Reprinted by permission of Condé Nast.

"Hit Man" by Dan Barry. From the *New York Times,* October 30, 2016, copyright © 2016 by the *New York Times.* All rights reserved. Used by permission and protected by the Copyright Laws of the United States. The printing, copying, redistribution, or retransmission of this Content without express written permission is prohibited.

"(Long) Gone Girl" by Jon Billman. First published in *Runner's World.* Copyright © 2016 by Rodale Inc. Reprinted by permission of Rodale Inc.

"Why Steve Kerr Sees Life Beyond the Court" by John Branch. From the *New York Times,* February 25, 2016, © 2016 by the *New York Times.* All rights reserved. Used by permission and protected by the Copyright Laws of the United States. The printing, copying, redistribution, or retransmission of this Content without express written permission is prohibited.

"Some Very Dirty Tricks" by John Colapinto. First published in *Vanity Fair.* Copyright © 2016 by John Colapinto. Reprinted by permission of John Colapinto.

"Lost in America" by Luke Cyphers and Teri Thompson. First published in *Bleacher Report.* Copyright © 2016 by James D. "Luke" Cyphers and Teresa D. Thompson. Reprinted by permission of James D. "Luke" Cyphers and Teresa D. Thompson.

"Hooked for Life" by George Dohrmann. First published in the *Huffington Post.* Copyright © 2016 by George Dohrmann. Reprinted by permission of the *Huffington Post Highline.*

"Sucker Punch" by Tim Elfrink. First published in the *Miami New Times*. Copyright © 2016 by the *Miami New Times*. Reprinted by permission of the *Miami New Times*.

"The Shooter and the Saint" by Sean Flynn. First published in *GQ*. Copyright © 2016 by Sean Flynn. Reprinted by permission of Sean Flynn.

"Four Years a Student-Athlete" by Patrick Hruby. First published in *Vice Sports*. Copyright © 2016 by Vice Media LLC. Reprinted by permission.

"Kaepernick Is Asking for Justice, Not Peace" by Bomani Jones. First published in *The Undefeated*. Copyright © 2016 by ESPN, Inc. Reprinted by permission of ESPN.

"Barry Switzer Laughs Last" by Pat Jordan. First published in *Men's Journal*. Copyright © 2016 by Pat Jordan. Reprinted by permission of the author.

"26.2 to Life" by Jesse Katz. First published in *GQ*. Copyright © 2016 by Condé Nast. Reprinted by permission of Condé Nast.

"Why One Woman Pretended to Be a High-School Cheerleader" by Jeff Maysh. First published in *The Atlantic*. Copyright © 2016 by Jeff Maysh. Reprinted by permission of *The Atlantic*.

"Today, Her Whole Life Is a Free Skate" by Terrence McCoy. From the *Washington Post*, February 26, 2016, © 2016 by the *Washington Post*. All rights reserved. Used by permission and protected by the Copyright Laws of the United States. The printing, copying, redistribution, or retransmission of this Content without express written permission is prohibited.

"The Away Team" by Alexis Okeowo. First published in *The New Yorker*, December 12, 2016. Copyright © 2016 by Alexis Okeowo. Reprinted by permission of The Wylie Agency, LLC.

"Too Fast to Be Female" by Ruth Padawer. First published in the *New York Times Magazine*. Joint copyright © 2016 by the *New York Times* and Ruth Padawer. Reprinted by permission of Ruth Padawer.

"The Longest Run" by S. L. Price. First published in *Sports Illustrated* and *Time*. Copyright © 2016 by *Sports Illustrated*. Reprinted by permission of *Sports Illustrated*.

"The Outsized Life of Muhammad Ali" by David Remnick. First published in *The New Yorker*. Copyright © 2016 by Condé Nast. Reprinted by permission of Condé Nast.

"The Most Successful Female Everest Climber of All Time Is a Housekeeper in Hartford, Connecticut" by Grayson Schaffer. First published in *Outside*. Copyright © 2016 by *Outside* magazine. Reprinted by permission of *Outside* magazine.

"A Wonderful Life" by Dave Sheinin. From the *Washington Post*, February 12, 2016, © 2016 by the *Washington Post*. All rights reserved. Used by permission and protected by the Copyright Laws of the United States. The printing, copying, redistribution, or retransmission of this Content without express written permission is prohibited

"The Spirit of a Legend" by Kurt Streeter. First published in *ESPN: The Magazine*. Copyright © 2016 by ESPN, Inc. Reprinted by permission of ESPN.

"William Perry" by Rick Telander. First published in *Sports Illustrated*. Copyright © 2016 by *Sports Illustrated*. Reprinted by permission of *Sports Illustrated*.

"Serena Williams, Andy Murray, and a Political Wimbledon" by Louisa Thomas. First published in *The New Yorker*. Copyright © 2016 by Condé Nast. Reprinted by permission of Condé Nast.

"The Secret History of Tiger Woods" by Wright Thompson. First published in *ESPN: The Magazine*. Copyright © 2016 by ESPN, Inc. Reprinted by permission of ESPN.

"Welcome to the Big Time" by Don Van Natta Jr. First published in *ESPN: The Magazine*. Copyright © 2016 by ESPN, Inc. Reprinted by permission of ESPN.

"Andrew Cuomo Would Have Blacklisted Muhammad Ali" by Dave Zirin. First published in *The Nation*. Copyright © 2016 by *The Nation*. Reprinted by permission of *The Nation*.

Contents

Contents

Foreword

WHEN I LIVED in Boston in the 1980s and early '90s and trudged through Kenmore Square on the way to work or to see some band in some bar, the sidewalk was often littered with flyers for a local psychic. Usually distributed by some college student who stuffed them in your hand as you passed, they were often discarded as quickly as they were delivered, leaving the ground covered with tiny chartreuse or hot pink ad cards that breathlessly read in bold: "THOUGHTS HAVE WINGS!"

I threw my share to the ground, but even then I loved the idea, the metaphor—thoughts flying off in all directions, destination unknown, influence unpredictable, impact unforeseen. When I found one of these flyers in an old book the other day—I must have used it as a bookmark—I was thrilled, and soon followed the memory path back to that sidewalk. Thoughts *do* have wings, and that one had been carried forward for more than three decades before, improbably, landing here. As the late, great, and now nearly forgotten Dominican pitcher Joaquín Andújar once wisely observed: "There is one word in America that says it all, and that word is, 'You never know.'"

This brings me around to this book, sports writing, and writing in general. As I have learned, not only do thoughts have wings, but so too do words, and so does this book. Over nearly three decades, *The Best American Sports Writing* has been carried to places hard to imagine and to writers of all backgrounds who have in some way found it either instructive or even formative.

Just today, as I type this, a writer sent me a note asking if I had seen a particular story written by someone else, because she thought it might be something for the book. I had, and that led me to send her a copy of something else that appeared in this book 15 years ago ("Her Blue Haven" by Bill Plaschke), a story I still can't forget, one that I don't think anyone who has ever read it ever will.

And just now, I swear, another writer just posted on Facebook a photo of a letter to the editor from a magazine. It referenced a story she wrote that the letter writer had encountered in an earlier edition of this book—the photographer had been the writer's high school sweetheart and met her again through her story.

I've lost count of the number of times a writer has told me that this book, a story they read in these pages, or a writer they first encountered here changed their lives. This duplicates the same experience I wrote about in a long-ago foreword in which I recounted how my writing obsession was first lit by a poem by Langston Hughes. And only a few weeks ago I was contacted by a writer, an academic researching the early history of the black press, about my first mentor, Mabray "Doc" Kountze. She had first learned of him from my foreword to the 1994 edition of this book.

Words really do have wings.

Their reach is not confined to this country, or even to the Americas. While *The Best American Sports Writing* has always been open to writers in both American and Canadian publications (I'm a Canadian citizen myself), for years I have heard from writers in Europe, Australia, South America, and Africa bemoaning the fact that there is no similar collection for their home country. Many note that the kind of sports writing they find in this book doesn't even exist in their own culture. In other places the genre is usually confined to sports reporting or argumentative debate and doesn't take the more nuanced, thoughtful, and thought-provoking approaches one finds here.

Outside of the United States, the notion that sports writing might have "literary merit" (the publisher's loose criterion for inclusion in this volume) is almost an alien concept. I do know that there was once an annual *Best Australian Sports Writing* collection, and there is apparently a *Best Canadian Sports Writing* collection in the works. There have been many comprehensive anthologies of historical sports writing from other nations, such as India and Germany, and some overseas websites (such as the Irish-based *The*

42) regularly curate sports writing, but I am aware of no other similar annual collection. As a result, in other nations this book has become the de facto volume to which many English-reading sportswriters, particularly younger sportswriters, turn for inspiration. I regularly hear from readers in Australia, Ireland, England, the Philippines, Germany, and other countries with a significant English-reading population. They order the book (often at great cost depending on the currency rate), ask friends and relatives in the United States or Canada to send it to them, or scour used-book shops for older copies abandoned by tourists. (It makes great plane, bus, or train reading.) I myself have placed copies on "share-a-book" shelves in the Caribbean, leaving the pages to be scattered by the winds.

The way each of these volumes finds its way into a reader's hands creates its own story. One Kenyan reader, Bill Ruthi, an extremely talented younger writer I admire and now consider a friend, came across his first copy of this book a few years ago at a streetside used-book vendor in Nairobi. He recognized some of the writers from his online reading. Although he has yet to find the book in a Kenyan bookstore or library, he keeps finding "more and more editions" for sale on the street, he writes, and now has a fairly complete collection. When his Kenyan friends ask why he bothers reading about American sports, he tells me that he answers simply, "Here are some of the best writers I know of." I have no doubt that he could discuss the merits of various *BASW* contributors better than many readers in this country.

A young Texas woman, Rachel Goodman, recently copied me on a tweet that read "Best graduation present just completed the move to Philly . . . all 27 of them @GlennStout. I guess I'll call this place home now!" Attached was a photograph of her windowsill lined with all 26 previous editions as well as *The Best American Sports Writing of the Century*. I thanked her, and she wrote back that she had "stumbled upon the 2013 edition just wandering around the sports section of a book store my freshman year of college. I've always been interested in how sports speak to bigger issues happening around us, so *BASW* was perfect for me. And one of my sports reporting professors in college, Kevin Robbins [a senior lecturer at the University of Texas], used 2015 as our 'textbook.'" I then asked if the collection really was a graduation present. She answered, "Yes, from my parents! And a few from a childhood

friend . . . It is no exaggeration to say that *BASW* has influenced
the trajectory of my life and career . . . and hope to end up in
BASW one day. Looking forward to the next one!" Well, Rachel,
next time your name appears in this book, I hope it's in a byline
atop your own story.

Last spring I received a letter from a man incarcerated in a federal prison in Pennsylvania. He had come across an earlier edition
of the book in the prison library. He asked: If he were to publish a
story someday, even from inside prison, would it be eligible for this
book, which he has found helpful in his current situation? I told
him that of course it would, and offered to send additional copies
of previous editions to the prison library. He wrote back that he'd
been told it was "too much of a hassle" for the library to accept
donations. Then he added, "I'll send you a copy of my story when
it appears." I look forward to it, and nothing would make me happier than to see it earn its way into these pages.

I meet many younger writers and am sometimes embarrassed
—a few years ago, at the Mayborn conference, one extraordinarily
talented young writer blurted out upon meeting me, "This is surreal!" I felt the same way hearing him say *that*. My influence on
this volume is often overstated by people who don't bother to do
even a modicum of basic investigation into the process—such as
reading the foreword, where the selection methodology has been
described for 27 years. I don't know how many times or in how
many ways I've had to explain that this is in no way "my book," just
as none of the other *Best American* volumes is the province of the
series editor. We're all freelancers who work year to year, and in
27 years I have not selected a single story for inclusion on my own.

Every year I read widely and put out a call to readers, editors,
and writers to submit work of merit. Literally anyone on the planet
can submit a story that fits the publisher's criteria. My role, beyond
the merely custodial, is to assist the guest editor by forwarding perhaps 75 stories for initial consideration. (As a professional in the
field, each guest editor presumably reads hundreds of stories, if
not thousands, on his or her own as well.) I forward these stories
blind: each is reduced to a Word file identified by neither author
nor source, and given the volume of stories I consider, I often
know nothing whatsoever about the author. In the interest of full
disclosure, there is one story in this volume in which I played a

minor editorial role in advance of publication, but it too was submitted blindly to the guest editor.

In general, submissions are representative of the larger industry: wide and varied, but also narrow in some ways, reflecting this time of continuing contraction in the print industry and new media struggling with its commitment to journalism. If that prisoner in Pennsylvania writes something good enough that I read it twice, and if the guest editor concurs, he has as good a chance of having that story put forward as any freelancer or staff member for any publication or online outlet in the United States or Canada. The guest editor is under absolutely no obligation to select a single story I put forward, but most do. After all, many of the very best stories in any given year not only stand out immediately but are often widely known and discussed. Still, I always make certain that guest editors feel welcome to make as many of their own selections as they care to.

That has been the case again this year with guest editor Howard Bryant, who made several wise picks of his own. I have known Howard as a friend since he covered technology for the *San Jose Mercury News* nearly 20 years ago, and working with him on this project was a real pleasure. We first spoke when he called me to discuss a project he was working on, one that eventually sent him to the baseball beat and became his first book, *Shut Out: A Story of Race and Baseball in Boston*. Three and a half hours later, I hung up the phone and had a feeling we'd be talking again. It's been a real pleasure to watch his career grow and flourish at the *Bergen Record*, the *Boston Herald*, the *Washington Post*, and now at ESPN, and to read a series of increasingly important books he's written, including his account of the PED era of baseball, *Juicing the Game*, and his biography of Henry Aaron, *The Last Hero*. For a number of years I've been hoping my publisher would invite Howard to serve as guest editor (that decision has never been mine to make), and I was elated when it finally happened. The words of our initial conversation took wing and now, almost two decades later, have finally landed us as partners in these pages.

Each year I read hundreds of sports and general-interest newspapers and magazines in search of work that might merit inclusion in *The Best American Sports Writing.* I also look for high-quality writing across a wide variety of online outlets and make regular stops at aggregators such as *Longreads.com, Longform.org,* and other similar sites where significant sports writing is often noted. I also make periodic open requests through Twitter and Facebook and contact editors and writers from many outlets to request submissions. As always, and because this book really belongs to the reader, I encourage submissions from anyone who cares about good writing —including readers. The process is open to all. And for the 27th time, not only is it okay to submit your own work, but it is actually encouraged. Neither the guest editor nor I can consider work we do not see.

All submissions to the upcoming edition need only adhere to the publisher's criteria for eligibility, which also appear here each year, on my own website (www.glennstout.net), and on the Facebook page for *The Best American Sports Writing.* Each story:

- Must be column-length or longer
- Must have been published in 2017
- Must not be a reprint or a book excerpt
- Must have been published in the United States or Canada
- Must be postmarked by February 1, 2018

All submissions from either print or online publications must be made in hard copy (submission of only a link or a bibliographic citation is not acceptable), and each should include the name of the author, the date of publication, and the publication title and address. Photocopies, tear sheets, or clean copies are fine. Readable 8½ × 11 reproductions are preferred. Submissions of newspaper articles should be a hard copy or a copy of the article as originally published—not a printout of the web version. Individuals and publications should please use common sense when submitting multiple stories. Owing to the volume of material I receive, no submissions can be returned or acknowledged, and it is inappropriate for me to comment on or critique any submission. Magazines that want to be absolutely certain that their contributions are considered are advised to provide a complimentary subscription to the address listed below. Those that already do so should extend the subscription for another year.

All submissions must be made by U.S. Mail—midwinter weather conditions often prevent me from easily receiving UPS or FedEx submissions. Electronic submissions of any kind (email, Twitter,

URLs, PDFs) are not acceptable—some form of hard copy only, please. The February 1 postmark deadline is real, and work received after that date may not be considered.

Please submit either an original or clear paper copy of the story, including publication title, author, and publication date, to:

> Glenn Stout
> PO Box 549
> Alburgh, VT 05440

Those with questions or comments may contact me at basweditor@yahoo.com. Previous editions of this book can be ordered through most bookstores or online book dealers. An index of stories that have appeared in this series can be found at glennstout. net. For updated information, readers and writers are encouraged to join *The Best American Sports Writing* group on Facebook or to follow me on Twitter @GlennStout.

I thoroughly enjoyed working with guest editor Howard Bryant, and appreciated the opportunity to do this book with a friend and colleague whom I not only admire, but who has helped shape this series and my own story sensibilities for so many years, and who takes his duties and responsibilities as a writer so seriously. Thanks also to those at Houghton Mifflin Harcourt who have helped with the production of this series, to Siobhan and Saorla for their unwavering faith, and to the many, many friends and writers over the past year who have expressed their understanding and support and continue to produce such vital work in a time that too often favors dogma over discourse. Your words prove otherwise.

GLENN STOUT
Alburgh, Vermont

Introduction

AFTER A WORKOUT SESSION in Goodyear, Arizona, the spring training home of the Cleveland Indians, a colleague told me he was happy I attended the morning media session with Terry Francona, the Cleveland manager. The reason, he said, was that Tito and I were so familiar with each other that the manager was more relaxed, his interview session was more engaging, and the stories he told were better. Francona and I have known each other now for a decade and a half, from when he served as the Oakland A's bench coach under Ken Macha in 2003 to being together in Boston during the big years, when the Red Sox won it finally, not once but twice. Journalism is a game of facts but also one of relationships, and when I met Terry for the first time, it was Macha, his longtime friend from their mutual hometown of Pittsburgh, who vouched for me. Once in, I obviously had to prove to Tito I could be trusted, but Macha's imprimatur gave Tito an initial level of trust toward me that wouldn't have been there otherwise. I came with good recommendations.

Steroids and performance-enhancing drugs were never far from what I wrote about, which made some people less inclined to talk to me. The only thing treated more like Kryptonite in baseball than being directly associated with PEDs was anyone asking about them. One day at the Red Sox spring training facility in Fort Myers, Florida, Dave Wallace, the Sox pitching coach, introduced me to Sandy Koufax. Naturally, I hung out after the workout to bask in the presence of a legend, and after Koufax left, Francona came over. We sat on a picnic table, and he said, "Tell me about steroids. I swear to you, I'm not paying attention to this stuff. I don't know what they are, or what they can do. Let's talk." And we did. No pen. No pad. No recorder.

When the regular season starts, Sundays are always different from the rest of the week. They are slower, usually a getaway day for at least one team and sometimes both teams in an upcoming series. To accommodate television, baseball has largely shifted from its traditional weekend schedule—a Friday night game followed by Saturday and Sunday day games—to Saturday night games, so everybody on a Sunday morning is just a little more bleary-eyed than usual. One Sunday morning, Tito and I were talking in his office when a nervous Red Sox staffer appeared in his doorway, making frantic signals. There seemed to be a problem with Manny Ramirez, both his best player and biggest headache. Francona got out of his chair.

"Wait here."

He returned, his olive-skinned face pinkish and reddening.

"Shut the door."

I did.

"You know what?" he said. "At 7:05, when the game starts, in between the lines making pitching changes, all the stuff the fans drill you for? That's the easy part. This bullshit? This is the fucking job. Right here. This is what managing is. Putting out fires. Pain in my ass."

During spring training, Francona conducts his interviews with the writers in the intimacy of the media work room, and my history with him contributed to a lively morning session that day in Goodyear. He was animated and funny about the presidency, hobbled now with two titanium knees, recovering from hip surgery days after the World Series ("I thought we won I was on so many pain killers"), and poignant about time and age ("When I have to pee, which is frequently now, I gotta give myself a pep talk just to get out of bed").

A colleague and I left the Indians complex, and walking back to the car, we talked about how different the daily sports job is today from when I left the business technology pages of the *San Jose Mercury News* and became a full-time baseball writer in 1998. I thought about the night in Kansas City when the A's lost a tough one to the lowly Royals and Oakland's gentlemanly manager, Art Howe, who had just undergone laser eye surgery, got so upset he tossed the entire press corps out of his office.

"All right, everybody outta here," he said. "I've given you enough to write a fucking book."

I remained.

"What are you still doing here? I thought I told you to get out of here."

"Art, I just wanted to let you know your left eye is bleeding."

Embarrassed by his cursing, his temper, and the temporary loss of his customary civility, Howe asked me to stay. He cracked open two beers, the Dominican brand Presidente. One for him, one for me. He apologized, and we engaged in an impromptu therapy session at nearly 11:00 p.m. He went on about his too young, under-talented roster and his despotic general manager, Billy Beane, who tormented him every night. I listened.

I thought about Francona, who, like Art Howe (yet another Pittsburgh guy) before him, is one of the great characters and people in the game but who, like virtually every manager in the league, now conducts both his pre- and postgame interviews with the writers at a remove. No longer in his office, as in the old days, Francona fields questions from a podium, with a public relations man nearby. The session is videotaped and broadcasted and live-tweeted, and when it's over, the manager slips out the door. Gone are the days when the camera lights shut off and the writers and manager just talked, off the record, pens down, recorders off. It was there in those golden sessions, which once were available twice a day, eight months a year, that the players became people and the writing process actually began.

Without those sessions, the job of knowing and understanding and feeling and learning is that much harder. Declining access is the eternal condition of sports writing, but a certain level of access —enabling the great *Boston Globe* writer Bob Ryan, for instance, to tell enviable stories about interviewing Wilt Chamberlain one-on-one by the pool before a Lakers-Celtics game—is gone, and it's never coming back.

How, then, in a time of podium interviews and fewer chances to drink a beer in the manager's office while his laser-repaired eye fills up with blood can writers attain the level of access, trust, and *feel* required to write the types of stories that have populated *The Best American Sports Writing* collections for more than a quarter century? Good question. That is the challenge, and the answer is basic: Work harder. Work the room, get those cell numbers, send those texts, and build those relationships, because next-level writing with the kind of space and detail that we all wish we could produce cannot happen without next-level access.

My colleague that day in Goodyear was Dave Sheinin, the terrific *Washington Post* writer whose profile of Dusty Baker, "A Wonderful Life," is featured in these pages. It is the detail that makes the story —Dave sitting in Dusty's kitchen at his home in Sacramento, far removed from the dugout and the field and the grind, as he makes lunch—but it is also the access that separates Sheinin's story from any other attempt to write about the Nationals' manager. If Dave isn't in that kitchen, smelling firsthand the aroma of Dusty's cooking, the scene fails and the words never find the page.

This distance is reflected in the types of stories selected for a book that celebrates the best American sports writing of the last calendar year. It is ostensibly a book about an industry punctuated by buzzer beaters, sweat, emotion, and reflection, and yet only two selections—Sheinin's and John Branch's terrific work on Golden State Warriors coach Steve Kerr—are in-depth stories of active members of one of the four U.S. professional sports, and both are coaches. None of those in-depth stories are about active players on the field. The players, whether because they've chosen to connect directly to the public through social media or *The Players' Tribune* or because of distrust or lack of interest, now often wall themselves off from the kind of access that was once a standard of in-season writing and is vital to writing about people in full dimension. The payoff still exists, but at least in this year's edition of the book it had to wait for players to retire, as shown by both Rick Telander's hard and frustrated look at William "Refrigerator" Perry and Pat Jordan's account of his raucous days with Barry Switzer. The people are still there. The stories and spirals are still there, and the writing awaits, but the barriers grow taller.

Yet, this is only a partial lament. It's supposed to be hard.

Despite the ubiquity of the phrase "stick to sports," sports has never quite known how to stay in its lane, never allowed itself to be relegated to the kids' table, even when newspapers would derisively refer to it as the "Toy Department." Online commenters and fans may rage when the First Amendment collides with first-and-goal, but sports has always told us more about who we are and where we're going than most care to admit. Some of us want to dip our nachos and watch home runs, while others want athletes to be citizens of the world. In the five years since the death of Travyon Martin and the unrest in Ferguson, Missouri, after the killing of Michael Brown at the hands of the police, some athletes (especially some black athletes) have repudiated the old Michael Jordan standard of being apolitical as the commercial dollars roll in, being inoffensive to the mainstream consumer, being oblivious to the black athletic heritage of activism. The year 2016 continued the post-Ferguson awakening on the part of athletes, and Colin Kaepernick's escalation of that protest, linking the failed relationship between police and the African American community to the failing of the ideals embodied in the American flag, defined a divided country and sports industry. The image of Kaepernick and the other players who followed him taking a knee during the National Anthem was clear, but writing about it was a difficult task that no writer did as well as ESPN's Bomani Jones in "Kaepernick Is Asking for Justice, Not Peace."

Where we are now is a scary time: we're not just living in a dangerous world but in an America that isn't quite sure if America still means what we once collectively believed it did. The question of who we are also stands at the center of another wonderful piece, "26.2 to Life," Jesse Katz's story of the annual marathon within the walls of the federal penitentiary at San Quentin. In this country of mass incarceration and mandatory prison sentences, the question of whether we are a nation of jailers or rehabilitators hovers over Katz's piece so ubiquitously that he never needs to directly ask it.

Our borders may be open—but then again, they may soon be closed. The notion of America providing a fresh, free new start for citizens from other parts of the world may be an outdated one, but throughout my reading of the submissions to this book it was impossible not to think about the implications of American attitudinal uncertainty for the athletes around the world who view sports as a pathway to America, to the better life, even if sports only provides the springboard to the next phase in a person's

journey. Two stories in particular, the *Time/Sports Illustrated* dual
publication of S. L. Price's "The Longest Run" and Luke Cyphers
and Teri Thompson's "Lost in America" from *Bleacher Report,* un-
derscore the new arena of America and the refugee, in which the
once-clear happy ending to the story is no longer a given. Reading them anew, it was hard not to wonder if America is still that
place of refuge. The journeys of these young basketball and soccer
players force us to recalibrate the assumption of America as a welcoming destination, leading us into the different, dystopian space
of asking what happens to people arriving in an America that no
longer wants them.

It's not only a dangerous world but a complicated one, and if
using sports to cross borders and tell larger truths about survival
and spirit has always been part of the appeal of the game, its simple notions of meritocracy have also been part of its foundation.
Such a notion in a world where identity is addressed with science
rips apart those narratives and twists their morality from ostensibly
simple to very complicated. Ruth Padawer's "Too Fast to Be Female" describes another complicated space: sports in a transgen-
dered world. Her story is fascinating for its questions of fairness
and ethics and science as sports shifts along gender definitions,
but it also reveals something less complicated and more persistent:
the aggression and demeaning attitudes toward women practiced
by the governing bodies of sport.

There is genuine and legitimate reason to fear for the roots that
attracted so many of us to the writing business, and one of the
revelations in selecting these pieces was recognizing the economic
universe in which they were written. As always, contraction and
changes in the media business leave long-form writers vulnerable,
especially in a world obsessed with small screens and left-swiping
and so much talking on the television screen that we've forgotten our primary job as journalists is to listen. When I worked in
newspapers and talk of layoffs or buyouts would surface, one piece
of advice remained universal: "Stay busy. Make sure you're in the
paper." That was simple code to produce in volume. "Be in the
paper" meant being visible, of not giving the impression that your
position—and by extension you—were expendable as the economic guillotine was rolled out of storage. It takes time to write
a 4,000-word profile or investigative narrative, time that requires

not being in the paper. Thus, profiles and investigative narratives soon were disappearing, not necessarily because the bosses valued them less, but because of your fear that *you* were valued less, your fear of not having a byline as the list of expendable names was being compiled by your potentially soon-to-be ex-supervisors. In such a climate, the skills and attitude of a beat writer become very marketable: being able to produce daily bylines (*be visible!*), with no aspirations beyond writing the requisite game story and notes, is both a commodity and a source of cost-efficiency. Beat writing is certainly visible, but it's also a dead-end job for a writer who's no longer able to transfer years of relationship-building into, for example, sitting on the front porch with Barry Switzer.

Equally chilling is another consequence of a contracting business: writing with the understanding that your subject may soon be your employer. As the number of news outlets shrinks, the biggest employers of reporters may soon be the leagues themselves. MLB.com, NBA.com, NHL.com, and NFL.com are inundated with beat writers and columnists and national take-out writers who once vowed to never work for these league sites but who also made another vow: to feed their families and make sure their children had clean clothes and money for college. In the case of baseball, MLB. com has become a viable, mainstream destination. Its writers are now part of the Baseball Writers' Association of America, which makes them eligible to vote for the Hall of Fame, even though they are drawing a paycheck from Major League Baseball, and it is well known that MLB tightly controls tone and the subjects that writers are allowed to explore. Knowing that MLB.com could very well be their next employer undermines the willingness of writers to be tough in their coverage, whether the subject is labor or PEDs, the ongoing demand that public money be spent for private stadiums, or MLB leadership taking the game in the wrong direction. Certainly you might think twice before writing a hard profile of Roger Goodell or Rob Manfred, knowing you may one day need to work for the NFL or MLB. Through the simple act of self-protection, writers might resist taking on stories critical of sports executives. Leagues could reward the best writers for their courage by forever refusing to hire them. A 30-year-old with a family, doing the math of wanting to write for the next 35 years, might not be so willing to be unpopular with the powers that journalism is supposed to hold accountable. The power wins, and it receives a free pass.

The leagues certainly are aware of their growing position, which is why it is gratifying to see ESPN's Don Van Natta Jr. consistently being unafraid to do the work. Because of the television-induced shrinkage between journalism and celebrity, investigative writing has been under threat, but "Welcome to the Big Time," his story of the latest bubble in sports—daily fantasy sports—represents the kind of month-to-month, minute-to-minute storytelling mastered by some of the best newspaper and magazine writers whose writing reads like espionage thrillers (the late, two-time Pulitzer winner J. Anthony Lukas being one of the best examples). Beyond the game on the field, certain architects and elements of a sports world worth tens of billions of dollars may try to live in the shadows. Thankfully, because of writers like Don, they do not.

There are so many ways to write well, and the joy of selecting the pieces for this collection was in being reminded that, as much as writing cedes ground to left- and right-swiping and the small and big screen (the apocalypse keeps announcing the arrival of *The Emoji Movie*, which need not be presented with extended comment for anyone who cares about words), and the seeming impatience with thoughts beyond 140 characters, there are wonderful writers whose gifts on full display remain compelling. The submissions, just over 100 in total, also served as a reminder that taste is highly personal and writing is not math: coming up with a different solution doesn't make us wrong, and we like what we like. I found myself gravitating toward stories that I began to categorize as "sideways"—stories of how it all went wrong, of how pathways that had once seemed clear were anything but. I loved the moments before sunset, the stories and profiles that stare at a life that sits in the rearview mirror as the years pile up and the road ahead is no longer limitless. Time is shortening, and the deadline for reconciliation is no longer infinite. Kurt Streeter's excellent "The Spirit of a Legend," on the controversial burial place of the great Jim Thorpe, might best exemplify this theme.

For all of the complaining that writers and journalists love to do, this experience was for me restorative. I also am aware of my limitations, and next year's editor will discover his or her own preferences as a reader. I found myself falling not only for stories but also for styles. I love kinetic writers, and there is none better than Roger Angell, whose piece "Almost There" reminded me of what the great saxophonist John Coltrane once said of Stan Getz: "We'd all like to sound like that—if we could." Angell was born in 1920. He saw Ruth and Williams, Robinson and Koufax, Reggie and Cal, Bonds and Trout. He saw them all live, firsthand. The one thing even he did not see, until now, was a Chicago Cubs World Series victory. Angell is able to accomplish perhaps the most difficult writing task: to describe not only the high drama on the field but the actual movements of the players, and their importance, while sounding like a poet instead of a kinesiologist. His powers of description create an indelible image of the game, while also conveying his own joy in being there. He is a marvel.

Angell's *New Yorker* colleague Louisa Thomas writes about tennis in a similarly kinetic way, watching the body work, capturing the detail and personality of physical movement, what emotional wrestling with the pressurized circumstances at hand creates the movement, and how each looping backhand and tremoring forehand builds the points and the score, simultaneously creating the pieces of a jigsaw puzzle she constructs with a signature beauty that is not aloof. Thomas is a master at being present as a writer, yet she is so gifted that her characters and the action—on the grass in "Serena Williams, Andy Murray, and a Political Wimbledon"— are always presented ahead of her. Like the spectators at Centre Court, Thomas watches, feels, and thrills for the participants and the drama, yet for all the shuddering excitement, she somehow makes no distracting noises. We'd all like to sound like that—if we could.

Sometimes the best writing resembles a gangster film—direct and Spartan scenes where one tough picks up another by the lapels and hurls him through a storefront window—while other times the best writing reads like a family history, a heavy dynastic arc of legends as sweeping as a fictional saga. Dave Zirin of *The Nation* gives us the former kind of writing and *The New Yorker*'s David Remnick the latter in their dual postscripts on Muhammad Ali, the most towering American athlete of his time and, many would say, of any time. Zirin's pugnacity is especially vibrant and essential in today's world, where we use terms like "postfactual" so casually (as if its long-term dangers are akin to simply surviving a bad winter), and his insistence that Ali not be co-opted in death sends a larger message: truth is not something the powerful can blithely massage into something less sturdy, into *opinion,* to be believed—or not. Try it and, as happens to New York governor Andrew Cuomo in "Andrew Cuomo Would Have Blacklisted Muhammad Ali," expect Zirin to toss you through the glass.

Remnick's words in "The Outsized Life of Muhammad Ali" are as much about us, the road under America's feet, as about Ali. He tells us our story as we shifted and grew and matured as a country around our famous son—sometimes authentically, sometimes cynically, and not nearly so heroically, Remnick concludes, as to merit any virtuous claim on an American original who became so (and here Remnick deftly uses a well-known detail) because someone stole his bicycle when he was 12.

Back in 1980, Angell wrote "Distance," a wonderful piece of writing on the pitcher Bob Gibson for *The New Yorker.* As the money increases, distance is what the sports world seems intent on creating between itself and the rest of the world. Yet what ties together the 27 stories in this edition of *The Best American Sports Writing* is how the writers navigate the gulf between themselves and their subjects and show us, the readers, the beating heart that does not always want to be found. Sometimes the result tests the reader's ability to keep reading without flinching, especially as some of those subjects make choices that hasten their demise, such as in "Sucker Punch," Tim Elfrink's haunting piece from the *Miami New Times* on the avoidable turning fatal, or Jeff Maysh's heartbreakingly sad "Why One Woman Pretended to Be a High-School Cheerleader" from *The Atlantic.* Sometimes the writers are looking for people uninterested in advertising their personal quest for discovery, like Wright Thompson stalking the steps of Tiger Woods, without Tiger's permission or cooperation, in "The Secret History of Tiger Woods."

The common theme here is clear: all of these pieces find a way to close the space between writer and subject by turning obstacles into allies and by remembering, even as so much journalism morphs into punditry, that listening is always better than talking. Whether encountered at a podium or a picnic table, the beating heart is always there. We just have to work harder these days to find it, and that is what the writers in this collection do. The result is a cross-section of pieces, spanning several sports, disciplines, and styles, that move me, each in its own way, closer still to my lifelong joy in words, in reading them—and in writing more of my own. I hope this collection moves you too. Enjoy.

HOWARD BRYANT

The Best American
Sports Writing
2017

William Perry

FROM SPORTS ILLUSTRATED

WE CAN START with this: everybody loves the Fridge. William Perry could have been called the Car or the Shed or the Washing Machine or even the Water Heater. But he wasn't. The Refrigerator it was—Fridge, for short—ever since his days as a 300-plus-pound nosetackle at Clemson. Because it fit. Nicknamed for that most wonderful of American kitchen appliances—the one with the good stuff inside that keeps us alive and happy and sometimes fat—Fridge in his heyday was as well liked as that leftover piece of apple pie, wrapped in cellophane, just behind the mayonnaise and cold chicken.

"If you didn't like Fridge," says Mike Ditka, his coach in Chicago, "you didn't like anybody."

When the world champion Bears started to pull in endorsements and celebrity gigs following Super Bowl XX, in 1986, and Perry, just a rookie, hauled in more than anyone—more even than Walter Payton or Jim McMahon or even Da Capitalistic Coach himself—"it would have been easy for us to resent him," says Dan Hampton, Perry's defensive linemate. "But we loved Fridge."

There was a role—convivial Southern goofball—that the swollen, gap-toothed Perry played in that magical season, and he played it well. Some of it was artifice, from mythology and expectation and the media's need for simplicity. Fat equals jolly, you know. But much of it was Perry, for real. He was as easygoing as you would expect given his Deep South roots, in Aiken, South Carolina. He did have 11 siblings; seven brothers and four sisters. He, indeed, had his front tooth shot out by a BB gun as a lad. He had drunk a couple cases of beer after one college game. He could eat like a shark, guzzle like a horse, take off like a rabbit, jump like a lion. Yes, at 6'2"-and-change he could dunk a basketball. I saw him do it. My guess is that he weighed 330 at the time. We were at the Multiplex Fitness Club in suburban Deerfield, Illinois, a couple of years after his rookie season, playing pickup ball. The rim survived.

His fame started when Ditka put him in to block for Payton and then to tote the rock himself against the defending champion 49ers in week six of that rookie year. San Francisco's coach, Bill Walsh, had used 275-pound guard Guy McIntyre in the backfield the previous season, in an NFC championship game victory over Chicago, and Ditka had remembered.

But Fridge's notoriety really exploded, like a grenade in a tomato patch, when he lined up and ran for a touchdown on October 21, 1985, in a Monday night game against the Packers. Much of America was watching as he became the heaviest man in NFL history to score off a set play. All the overweight, Barcaloungered, chip-dipping, vicariously living fans across the country were mesmerized and thrilled. *Hot damn!* This was entertainment.

Back then, you have to remember, 308 pounds was a crazy-big deal, like something from a tent show. Fridge was the "best use of fat since the invention of bacon," one sportswriter wrote. But now there are hundreds of players in the NFL Fridge's size or larger. Many high school teams have one or two. Looking back at the video from when Fridge went on *Late Night with David Letterman* in 1985, it is stunning how slim he appears compared with what we're used to seeing on the field these days.

Humor was maintained that night on *Letterman* with some gags about eating, and when Fridge saw 43-inch, 36-pound teenage actor Emmanuel Lewis in the green room, he told a reporter, "Man, last time I was that small was when I was born."

So who could dislike this fellow? As long as he wasn't played for a complete yokel or freak, he could get along with anybody. And as long as you weren't lined up opposite him, then he posed no danger to anyone or anything. As Fridge, 53, says now, "I'm not doing anything bad. That's not in me, not in my family—we weren't raised that way. I do things in a correct way, a respectful way."

But not, alas, in a healthy way. And not—if we're thinking of life as a brief moment to be tended to with diligence and care—in a proper way. Fridge drinks. Too much. That he drinks *at all*, really, is a problem. He has physical and mental issues that demand sobriety. ("I'm sure he's got traces of CTE," says younger brother Michael Dean, himself a former NFL defensive lineman.) In 2011, just 11 years after he flashed his famously imperfect smile for the cheery cover of *Sports Illustrated*'s first "Where Are They Now?" issue, Fridge declared publicly that he is an alcoholic. He has been to rehab. He's been told by doctors to stop drinking. He's been told by family members.

None of it matters. He's got drinking buddies. Alcohol's his special pal. He's back in slow, sleepy Aiken and, by God, he's doing what he wants to do. Even if it causes pain and divisiveness in his family, as members watch him slowly implode and are at a loss to help him.

"I'm home and I'm happy," Fridge says. "I ain't got no plans. I'm just gonna relax and take my time."

So the love and support he receives from others is dead-ended by his stubbornness. Perry can barely walk, and only then with a walker. He's at least 150 pounds overweight—around 430, even 450, according to friends and family. He doesn't work with physical therapists or wear the compression socks or orthopedic shoes that he should. His hearing is terrible, but he won't wear his aids, so he ends up virtually reading lips unless you are close to him and speaking loudly. He has four children, and he doesn't see them much, or at least not as often as one would expect. Both of his ex-wives are out of the picture. He lives alone in a retirement facility.

What does one do? Let him be? He has diabetes and the residual effects of a nasty thing called Guillain-Barré syndrome, which hit him in 2008. Tellingly, one of the concerns with the mosquito-borne Zika virus is that researchers believe it can cause not only birth defects but also Guillain-Barré syndrome, which creates neurological problems that can leave victims paralyzed and sometimes on life support. Its effects can diminish or last forever.

Fridge was nailed by it, possibly because of a severe dental infection, and at one point in 2009 he was near death. He couldn't move and was wasting away in bed, dehydrated beyond recognition, without any family near. Willie, one of his older brothers, says that when he found Fridge, he looked like a gaunt war-camp victim, down to 190 pounds. Look at Perry now, and you might guess that his skeleton alone weighs 190 pounds.

Oh, and the millions of dollars that Perry made over his 10-year NFL career are long gone too. So is his Super Bowl ring—at size 25, believed to be the largest ever made—auctioned off a year ago for $200,000, without Fridge getting anything for it.

It's all a mess, it seems, from health to finances. And sadly, in a sense, the people suffering the most from Fridge's demise are his children (three girls and a boy) and family members, who all claim to want to help him, but who are too busy fighting among themselves to enact any change. Michael Dean, who lives in Charlotte, was named by a judge as guardian and conservator of Fridge's affairs when William was first incapacitated, in 2008. But Perry's son, William II, told a Chicago TV reporter last year that he has doubts about Michael Dean's stewardship and legal control. "It's a bad situation," he said. "Hopefully we can get guardianship over [my dad] and go forward, and get him removed so he can do the right thing and be independent."

Willie is more desperate than that. "Jealousy," he says, is why Michael Dean keeps Fridge under his power. "When William was messed up, it made sense, but not now." Willie claims that Michael Dean, who lives 150 miles away from Fridge, is only giving his brother the "minimum care" that he needs; he suggests that Fridge doesn't see the necessary doctors or attend certain autograph and celebrity outings where he could make much-needed money. This Michael Dean finds hilarious; he says that he was the one who nursed Fridge back to health in 2009, that his sister Patsy is now in Aiken taking care of their brother, and that William's own stubbornness explains his missing appointments. He also claims that Willie wants to pry guardianship away so he can use Fridge himself as his "cash cow."

If this makes no sense, so be it. The Perry family is tight but torn, with age difference, gender, and competitiveness all leading to a big, interwoven, fractious ball of domestic dysphoria. Willie claims that Michael Dean profits off Fridge's minimal income (from Social Security and from his NFL pension; public records show Perry with total equity of $35,245 and net income of $13,921 for 2015), pointing to an annual $1,250 "caretaker/conservator" fee in his records. But Michael Dean flat out denies any improprieties; any money, he says, goes toward accounting and bookkeeping. "I'm getting rich off Fridge?!" he asks, incredulous. "I don't want anything to do with the mess! He still owes a couple hundred thousand to the IRS. Everything you put in place, he fights. I can't babysit him for the next 20 years. I've tried to get rid of the guardianship and conservatorship. I'd give it up to anybody—*except Willie.* Anybody but him."

Fridge is in his office—that is, he's in his white Hummer H2, parked in the driveway of a ramshackle house on Ridgewood Lane in Aiken. It's 6:00 p.m., early April, 72 degrees outside, and 10 or more people hang around the SUV as if it's a tiki hut on a beach. Fridge is tipping back a beer and appears to be a tad inebriated, louder than usual, more demonstrative.

Hanging by the driver's window is a hefty guy in a white T-shirt, smoking a menthol, drinking vodka from a plastic cup. His name is Darrell Epps. Both Willie's and Fridge's sometimes manager—a mysterious woman from Aiken who goes by Jaye, whose email begins Perrymediamgt and who occasionally finds Fridge paying gigs —feels that Epps is the worst enabler around. What she wants to tell all these friends is, "You're sitting there watching him die!" Willie says simply of Darrell, "He's William's leech." Again, fingers point across the divide like daggers. Epps says that Jaye is the real fraud in all of this; "a b—!" Michael Dean, meanwhile, paints Jaye and Willie as trying to make money off it all, "trying to drain [Fridge]."

Despite all the tumult, this is pretty much what Fridge does every day now: hang out with people who lack apparent jobs or places to be, shoot the breeze, and drink. He's got his own vodka cup. Maybe it's not that much different from what high-class retirees do at the 19th hole of country clubs, calling it socializing rather than wasting away. The thing is, Fridge can't move from his driver's seat. His car reeks of urine because he sometimes can't control his bladder, sometimes doesn't care. And there's not a medical journal on diabetes or the central nervous system anywhere that recommends alcohol consumption of this frequency for good health.

"I'm his best friend," says Epps, cordially pouring a little vodka for a visitor. "Listen to me. *I'm his best friend!*"

I remember the good old days back in Lake Forest, Illinois, when the Bears practiced at the original Halas Hall on the east side of town and the Ditka-led circus was the wildest, craziest thing ever to hit the NFL. Before the 1985 Bears went on to outscore their foes 91–10 in the playoffs, before the regular season was even over, half the team filmed an arrogant rap video called *The Super Bowl Shuffle*. Their coach got a DUI on the way home from one game. Their star QB mooned a New Orleans news helicopter on the eve of the Big Game.

And that's not even mentioning the amazing Fridge, who was once penalized for attempting to throw Payton over the goal line. Fridge would sometimes walk over to my house, a block from the training facility, just to see if I wanted to play basketball. Once he sat in my kitchen and watched, mesmerized, as Manute Bol, his physical opposite, played hoops on TV. Who would have guessed that a decade and a half later Perry would box the 7'7" Dinka Dunker in as absurd a Las Vegas fight as has ever been seen? "What a great visual image!" announcer Chris Rose said that night, not long before Fridge—looking like a truck tire inflated 10 times past its limit—almost collapsed from exhaustion and lost a unanimous decision to the human pencil.

Back in the mid-1980s, Perry was a naïf. Maybe he still is, though the world has taken its toll on his innocence. He has lost several Aiken houses, one of which went into receivership and is starting to rot, another of which is occupied by his first wife, Sherry. Perry has been diagnosed with mild cognitive impairment, perhaps from the Guillain-Barré, perhaps from headbanging. "Nah," he says when I ask him about football-related brain trauma. "I didn't get concussions. I gave 'em." Funny line. Maybe only half-true.

The thing about Fridge is that early on he was a rare physical talent, not simply lard. He was a very good swimmer, a former lifeguard at the park pool just a couple hundred yards from his childhood home. His short-burst running speed was shocking, his basketball jumper deadly, his raw strength unworldly. "On the D-line, all of us—me, Richard Dent, Mike Hartenstine, Steve McMichael—could power clean 370 pounds," says Hampton. "But Fridge just did it like he was picking up a cat. We called it goofy strength."

"He was a different individual when I had him, at 308 pounds," says Ditka. "He was a hell of an athlete, with a great attitude. Most of it now has to do with alcohol. You think you're invincible, nothing can hurt you . . . I know. I've been through it."

The William Perry that I see here in the spring dusk, in his car, doesn't look invincible in the least. He simply looks like a man trying very hard not to think about anything at all.

The following night we meet at an Applebee's. That the actual intersection of Whiskey Road and Easy Street is nearby tells you something about this town that is by parts pretty and decrepit, with Civil War memorials, gas costing 1.37^9/_{10}$ a gallon, and a place that's still referred to as the Aiken Colored Cemetery. Nearby, off Willow Run Road, there's a weedy field where a black fellow named Harry McFadden, an acquaintance of Willie Perry's, was reportedly lynched in 1978.

Fridge comes in with Epps, placing his walker next to the table. He doesn't eat much, just nine wings. "Not like the old days," he says. But he has four double Jack Daniels and Cokes, and once he has hobbled back to his car, he asks Epps to go back and get him some pecan pie and a brownie to go.

A couple of months before this I had visited Fridge at Northwestern Memorial Hospital in downtown Chicago. He had come to town for a 30-year reunion event celebrating Super Bowl XX, with his brother Willie and Jaye escorting him. But after being roundly cheered at halftime of a Bears-Lions game at Soldier Field, he'd become ill with a leg infection related to his diabetes. He told me he could no longer feel from the shin down and that his hands were numb too.

That night there was talk that he might need to have a foot amputated if things didn't improve. Lying in his bed with a hospital gown on, catheter in place, Fridge didn't frown or complain. He'll never say he's hurting. Former Bears trainer Brian McCaskey remembers when Perry came to the sideline during a game, held his forearm out, and said, "What do you think?" "It was bent down and up," recalls McCaskey, amazed, "broken all the way through."

The doctor comes in. He says that for some reason Perry has been taking pills he wasn't prescribed; meanwhile, he's *not* taking the ones he *should* be. Willie and Jaye think this shows, again, how little Michael Dean is caring for his brother. They think it might be damn close to poisoning him. Which Michael Dean finds bewildering; guardian though he is, he points out that Patsy is the one who now oversees William's medicine intake.

But when it comes down to it, shouldn't a grown man take care of himself? Especially one who in 2014 was declared by a doctor, cognitive issues and all, to be capable of managing his own affairs and no longer in need of a guardian?

"When I'm ready, I'll take [Michael Dean] back to court and

I'll get my guardianship back," Fridge says. But he's done nothing. And it's likely he never will. He's slip-sliding away. He seems tired of any struggle whatsoever.

"Talent can be a curse," says Hampton. "At 14, Fridge was the biggest thing in Carolina. Everybody expected him to play football. It's almost like he was a reluctant participant. He didn't have to sell out to be the best, and now he doesn't have to care."

Ditka, whose Gridiron Greats charity has helped pay for some of Perry's debts, finds it all heart-wrenching. "It's a great life wasted," he says. "There's no reason it has to happen. A bad deal? *No, he got a great deal!* In life you gotta help yourself. It's tragic. I think he's given up. And the question in my mind is, Why?"

The air is clear and fresh at 1:00 p.m. on a Wednesday in Aiken; it's 78 degrees, bright sun. The Masters will start soon in nearby Augusta, Georgia, and flowers will start opening from south to north, like popcorn seeds cooking in a pan.

Fridge is in his car, parked under a shade tree near some men playing checkers. Two months from now he'll be hospitalized briefly for what Willie describes as a ministroke, his second in a short period. Michael Dean will deny that either ever occurred. But for now the big man is at ease, drinking beer from his cooler, his buddy Epps nearby, smoking and drinking, wiping away sweat with a white towel draped over his shoulder. We're barely two blocks from where Fridge was raised, and that seems relevant.

"I'm home," he says. "And I'm happy. I can't say everything is peachy keen, but I'm still enjoying life. I love Chicago, but there's no place like home."

The acrid stench from his car interplays with the fragrance of apple blossoms drifting in the breeze. He's making a stand right here. A declaration.

"I'm my own man," he says, seemingly tired of people trying to improve him. "It's simple. I ain't never trying to be famous. I never, ever try to be extravaganza. I'm just a plain old country boy!"

As if that explains it all. Or anything, really.

PAT JORDAN

Barry Switzer Laughs Last

FROM MEN'S JOURNAL

BARRY SWITZER AND I are driving through the Oklahoma University campus in his black Mercedes on a sunny day in September. He slows the Benz, lowers his window, and calls out to a coed in a miniskirt and high heels: "You wearin' some beautiful shoes, girl." She smiles and says, "Thank you, Coach." I ask if he knows her. He says, "Hell, no!"

Traffic is backed up downtown because of tonight's game against Tennessee. A skateboarder darts out from behind a parked car. Switzer yells at him, "Get outta the fuckin' way!"

We finally park and step into Louie's Too, an OU dive bar. It's deserted at noon, except for a young woman wearing an impressively tight-fitting black T-shirt with LOUIE'S TOO written across her chest. She's sitting at the bar, her legs thrown over the legs of some guy, her arms around his neck. Switzer says, "You workin' here, girl, or you just workin' on him?" The woman blushes and hustles behind the bar.

We sit at the bar, chatting up the barmaid, whose name is Lisa. She says she works nights in a hospital giving ultrasound tests. Switzer grins and asks her how old she is. "Thirty-two!" he says. "You damned near too old for me, girl." Switzer is 78.

Lisa laughs, then notices the Super Bowl ring on Switzer's left hand. He takes it off and hands it to her, saying, "We goin' steady now." Lisa puts the ring on her finger and strikes a pose, placing the flat of her hand against her cheek, flashing the ring with a coquettish smile and a flutter of eyelashes. Then she gets us two more drinks.

"I dunno, girl," Switzer says. "One more drink and I'll need a nurse."

"I'm not a nurse," Lisa counters.

"You're close enough," Switzer says.

Lisa goes down the bar to show the guy the ring, leaving us to talk. When I ask Switzer about his coaching career, he suddenly grows serious. "I had a great run," he says. "College was my game. I liked my pro players, but I didn't have relationships with them. You don't recruit pros, get to know them, their parents, their personal problems. If they can't play, you get rid of their ass. You recruit a kid in college, he's yours for life."

Switzer pauses. When he continues, it's with uncharacteristic modesty. "Hell," he says, "I was just as good a college coach as the other guys. The magic is always in the players."

Switzer is one of only three football coaches to win both an NCAA championship and a Super Bowl. Between 1973 and 1988, his Oklahoma Sooners won 157 games, lost 29, and tied four. Until this year Switzer held the highest winning percentage, .837, of any major college coach of 150 games or more. He won three championships, and he would have won more if his teams hadn't been constantly flirting with NCAA probations. Then, in his four years coaching in the pros, he led the Dallas Cowboys to a Super Bowl victory over Pittsburgh in 1996. And he did it all on his terms. Switzer spoke his mind and played by his own rules. He was described as the coach in the black cowboy hat, the outlaw coach who played it fast and loose. NCAA rules were for the other guys, stiffs like Penn State's Joe Paterno, Texas's Darrell Royal, Nebraska's Tom Osborne. Switzer didn't have many rules for his players. He treated them, he says, like "grown men" who could "carry their own water."

Stories about Switzer's drinking and womanizing were legendary, maybe apocryphal. The $100,000 bar tab during Super Bowl week of 1996. The stewardesses he banged two at a time. The Sooner coeds whose cars were parked outside his house in the morning. The very public affair he carried on with the wife of one of his assistant coaches. These stories endeared Switzer to Sooners fans. Even the school president told him he could smoke dope as long as he won national championships.

Switzer never shies away from the peccadilloes of his past. "You bet that damned bar tab was the truth," he says. "I kept getting the damned bill for three months. Hell, there was a $3,500 bottle of Louis XIII cognac on it. I was worried gangsters would come after me." Jimmy Johnson, the Cowboys coach whom Switzer replaced, told him to give it to the team's owner, Jerry Jones. "But wait until he's in a good mood," Johnson said. Finally Switzer handed the bill to Jones, who was less than happy—but, says Switzer, "I never got another bill."

After his pro career ended, Switzer moved back to Norman, Oklahoma, where he is treated as a kind of coach emeritus, an éminence grise. Parents bring their kids to his house to meet the legendary coach, sometimes by appointment, sometimes unannounced. Switzer will tousle some youngster's hair while regaling them with stories of some legendary Texas-Sooners game. Before home games he stands on a stage on campus to have his picture taken with an endless line of fans. In restaurants women take selfies with him, and men sit down and propose business deals.

He doesn't really drink anymore, not heavily, anyway. As for the women, he plays his flirtations for laughs now, the harmless old lech. One night at dinner, he says to our young blond waitress, "You look familiar."

"I use-ta be a Sooners pom-pom girl, Coach."

"Use-ta?" Switzer replies. "How old are you?" Twenty-two, she tells him.

He smiles and says, "That's about right."

"When Barry was coaching the Sooners, his moral lines were broader than most other coaches'," says Brian Bosworth, or "The Boz," who played linebacker for Switzer in the mid-1980s. "To his players he was the lord of lords. We idolized him because he loved to have fun. Even now his fuel is meeting people. He needs that. It's his life's purpose. Coach was always the prettiest girl in the room."

Switzer drove moralistic, straight-arrow coaches to distraction. He broke all the rules and still beat Darrell Royal's Longhorns like a drum. Royal accused Switzer of paying his players and demanded he take a lie-detector test. Switzer told him, in essence, to go fuck himself. College coaches liked to say that Switzer's players had to take a pay cut when they went to the NFL. Joe Paterno, who treated his players like his children, considered himself the moral conscience of college sports until, of course, the world learned differently. When asked in the 1980s if he'd ever retire, Paterno

said, "I can't leave the college game to the . . . Barry Switzers of
the world."

Before I headed to Norman, Switzer and I spent an hour on the
phone. It wasn't long before we began strutting our bona fides. He
works out every day. So do I. His sport is football, mine baseball.
He drinks scotch. I drink bourbon. We both smoke cigars, carry
guns, love dogs, and women too. We both have been arrested in
airports with guns in our bags. He was fined $75,000 and shortly
afterward lost his job with the Cowboys. I spent eight hours sleeping on a concrete floor in the Broward County, Florida, felony
holding tank.

It gets deeper. Both of our mothers died of their own free will:
his shot herself, mine pulled the feeding tubes from her arm in a
hospital. My father was a gambler, con man, and grifter. His father,
he tells me, was a "rounder, womanizer, drinker, bootlegger, and
atheist." And Switzer carried on the tradition — "a rogue who lives
on the edge," he says. "Just like my daddy."

Louie's Too is crowded now. We're constantly interrupted by students and alums who want their pictures taken with Coach. He
obliges them all. It becomes impossible to talk, so we hop into the
car and drive to Switzer's house.

Along the way, Switzer makes a business call. He has his fingers
in a lot of pies: oil, banks, real estate, a Napa vineyard, and storage
units called Switzer's Locker Room. He says into the phone, "You
gotta get the governor to get that guy off that commission so he
can appoint our guy and the deal will go through." He hangs up
as we pass the liquor store he owns, Switzer Wine and Spirits, the
only one close to campus. The parking lot is filled with cars whose
owners are stocking up for tonight's game. Switzer grins and says,
"I always thought that if I ever needed a job, I could become a
bootlegger like Daddy."

Frank Switzer sold his liquor mostly to African Americans in the
tiny town of Crossett, Arkansas, where Switzer grew up in a ramshackle house that lacked, until the 1950s, glass windows, running
water, a telephone, and electricity. As a young boy, Barry led his
mother through the backyard at night to the outhouse. He carried
a flashlight to light the way and a pistol to shoot copperheads.

In high school Switzer was a handsome, rawboned football
hero, 6'1", 180 pounds, yet no respectable white girl in town would

date him, a bootlegger's son. "So I hung with blacks," he said. "I identified with them. I'd get on my school bus and wave to them waiting for their bus. When their bus broke down one day, I told them to get on our bus. Our driver said, 'Sit your ass down, boy, and shut up.'" Switzer was raised by the same black nanny who had raised his father, because his mother, Mary Louise, lacked the will or the energy to raise Barry and his younger brother, Donnie. She preferred to escape from her loneliness and despair into a fantasy world of novels, liquor, and barbiturates.

In 1954, when Barry was 16, Frank Switzer was sentenced to five years in the Arkansas State Penitentiary for selling untaxed liquor. He was released five months later on a legal technicality, just in time to watch his son pack his jeans and T-shirts into an empty Early Times box and head to the University of Arkansas on a football scholarship.

In August 1959, the summer before his senior year at Arkansas, Switzer came home for a visit. As usual, Frank was gone, who knows where, and his mother was sitting in her favorite chair, blissed out on booze and pills, reading a book.

"My mother had no life," he tells me. "She was deep in the country, alone, no phone, no car. It was a terrible existence for a woman who had been the valedictorian of her high school class." Then one night Barry was asleep and Mary Louise woke him. Her eyes were glazed over and she was smiling her blissed-out smile. He said, "Mother, I would rather not ever see you again than see you like this." When she leaned over to kiss him, he turned away. Moments later he heard a shot.

"For 30 years I felt her suicide was my fault," Switzer says now. "I should never have said what I said. Then years later my brother showed me a suicide note she had written. I asked him why he never showed that to me before. He said Daddy wouldn't let him." His mother, it turned out, had come to say good-bye to her oldest son. "I realized she'd had a plan that night that had nothing to do with what I'd said to her," he says. "It finally removed my guilt."

Thirteen years later Frank Switzer died at 64. "He was shot and killed by his 28-year-old girlfriend," Switzer tells me, "when she caught him with another girlfriend."

After his playing career, at Arkansas, Switzer became an assistant coach at his alma mater. Then, in 1966, his former defensive coordinator at Arkansas, Jim Mackenzie, was named the head coach at OU. The first assistant he hired was Switzer. In 1973, he took over the top spot.

Unlike many college coaches, Switzer got close with his players. When one got married only to have all his wedding gifts stolen from his apartment, Switzer personally replaced the items. It was in violation of NCAA rules—"but that's the way Barry was," says former coach Merv Johnson. When a running back's mother died, Switzer bought the kid an airplane ticket home—another NCAA rules infraction, but to Switzer it was the right thing to do. His players never forgot his kindness, and years later, when their parents died or they died, Switzer did not forget them either. "He doesn't just remember me," says Jon Phillips, a former offensive lineman. "He knows my telephone number, my parents' names." Adds Merv Johnson, "Not a soul in Oklahoma has given more eulogies than Barry Switzer."

Switzer was an outstanding recruiter of talent, especially when it came to young African American players, with whom he had no problem connecting. In the South of the 1970s, this was a rare quality. Switzer would walk through the hallways of black high schools, "flashing his big, long fur coat and all his championship rings on his fingers," said Charles Thompson, a former quarterback from Lawton, Oklahoma, who was recruited by Switzer in 1987. "Texas and Oklahoma were full of great black players, but the Longhorns didn't recruit them," Switzer says. "So I did." No wonder he was known by his players as "the Sooners' first black coach."

I ask Brian Bosworth if Switzer was as close to his white players as he was to his black ones. "Barry put a lot more effort into the problems of his black players," Bosworth says. Still, athletes of all races loved playing for Switzer because he played it loose, with few rules. "I never muzzled them," Switzer says. "I let them have their own personalities." Thomas Lott, a quarterback who went on to play for the Atlanta Falcons, wore a goatee and a do-rag; running back Little Joe Washington wore silver cleats; Bosworth cut his hair into a Mohawk and painted his uniform number on his scalp. Other players wore earrings, Afros, had gold teeth and tattoos. Some were black militants; some, like The Boz, were just white-boy egomaniacs. Says former offensive lineman Terry Webb: "People didn't come here to play for the University of Oklahoma. They came to play for Barry."

Not all players responded to Switzer's flamboyant style. When Troy Aikman came to Oklahoma in 1984, he was a serious, disciplined quarterback who was discomfited by Switzer's style. A drop-back passer, he left the Sooners for UCLA after only a year. He was replaced by Jamelle Holieway, who took the Sooners to the NCAA championship, something Aikman never did. Curiously, 10 years later Aikman would be Switzer's quarterback with the Cowboys, leading the team to the 1996 Super Bowl victory. Holieway, meanwhile, was cut after just one year with the Oakland Raiders.

This was not uncommon for the Sooners, largely thanks to Switzer's wishbone offense. In four years with the team, for example, Holieway completed only 117 passes but ran for 2,713 yards and 32 touchdowns. Unfortunately, NFL coaches weren't looking for running quarterbacks. They wanted drop-back passers like Aikman. Switzer's players did not make the transition easily. "Even our offensive linemen were at a disadvantage," Bosworth says. "They weren't prepared to be pass blockers, because all they'd ever done in Oklahoma was run block."

Bosworth, for example, was considered one of the greatest linebackers ever in college football, a two-time All-American. In 1987, he was drafted by the Seattle Seahawks, who awarded him the largest rookie bonus ever—$11 million over 10 years. But in the pros, The Boz was unable to back up his outrageous persona with accomplishments on the field. Before one game against the Raiders, Bosworth told reporters that he was going to shut down star running back Bo Jackson. The first time he hit Jackson, Bo carried The Boz over the goal line. Bosworth was cut after just two years. ESPN called him the sixth worst NFL flop ever.

Bring up the spotty NFL performance of former Sooners, and Switzer gets defensive. Bosworth's career, he says, was cut short by a shoulder injury, not by any coaching deficit. He turns the conversation toward players who excelled in the NFL—and later in life. "Lee Roy Selmon was an NFL Hall of Famer," Switzer says. "Billy Sims was a Heisman Trophy winner, a college Hall of Famer, and an NFL Rookie of the Year. Little Joe Washington was his team's MVP. He's now a financial adviser for Wells Fargo, for chrissakes."

Still, by the late '80s, Switzer was becoming an anachronism. The college game was changing, from a plodding, four yards off-tackle running game to a wide-open passing game more like the pros. The University of Miami's Hurricanes became the NCAA's alpha dog, winning championships under coaches Howard Schnellenberger and Jimmy Johnson. Miami players like Michael Irvin and Vinny Testaverde, rather than Sooners, went on to dominate the NFL. "The program began unraveling," Bosworth says. "The new players were less disciplined. It all happened so fast. Coach didn't see the disease spreading."

In 1988, the NCAA began investigating the Sooners program for 16 NCAA violations. Most were typical, picayune charges. Somebody had bought a player dinner, loaned a player a car, given him a few bills to buy clothes. Others were more substantial, including recruits being offered cash to come to Oklahoma and no-show jobs once they arrived. The Sooners program was accused of lacking institutional control. In 1989, quarterback Charles Thompson was arrested for selling cocaine, set up by a friend. That same year a player shot a teammate, and two Sooners raped a woman from Oklahoma City. Then the coke-dealing quarterback convinced his friend the snitch to rob Switzer's house of his championship rings —and then ratted *him* out.

Switzer says this kind of behavior snuck up on him. "You have to understand, the early eighties is when the drug culture hit," he says. "When I played it was beer. Then, in the seventies, you had marijuana. But in the eighties it was street drugs, cocaine. When that hit everything changed. I had four kids who committed felonies in a very short time. Hell, I didn't think I had to tell my players, 'Don't rape anyone, don't shoot each other, don't sell drugs.'"

Thompson spent 17 months in a federal prison on the cocaine charge, where he wrote a book, *Down and Dirty: The Life and Crimes of Oklahoma Football.* In it he celebrated Switzer as a coach who "identified with his black players," and "had a good heart," and couldn't "say no to kids from a broken home." But at the same time, he wrote, Switzer was "a supreme bullshit artist who let his coaches be the bad guys." The coach, Thompson wrote, supplied his players with "beer and booze. He [Switzer] was always high on booze and primo [cigarettes sprinkled with cocaine]. He drank us all under the table." When I asked Switzer about this, he denied it.

By the spring of 1989, everyone with an interest in Sooners football—players, fans, alumni, administrators, the media—had had enough. On June 19, 1989, Barry Switzer resigned from the "only job I ever loved," he told me. He'd never coach college football again.

Switzer always said he had no interest in coaching in the NFL. But in 1994, a bitter and longtime feud between Dallas Cowboys owner Jerry Jones and head coach Jimmy Johnson came to a head, despite two Super Bowl wins. Switzer had been out of the game for five years, but Jones, who played for the Razorbacks while Switzer had been an assistant coach, gave him a call. "So just before Jerry and Jimmy got divorced, Jerry calls me and asks if I want to coach the Cowboys. I said, 'I didn't know the job was open.' He said, 'It's fixin' to be.' The next day he fired Jimmy. Why me? He wanted to have people around him who were loyal, who he knew. I'm the guy he turned to."

His mandate was not to overcoach, not to fuck up a sure thing. Switzer ditched his vaunted college wishbone offense and ran Johnson's passing offense behind quarterback Troy Aikman. In his second season, the Cowboys won the Super Bowl.

But Switzer resigned after only four seasons in the pros. His heart, he says, just wasn't in the pro game. "I liked the kids, you know?" he says. He could never get close to the pros like he could his college players. What's more, at OU Switzer was the star of Sooners football. In Dallas the players were the stars. "I quit," he says. "It wasn't fun anymore." Two years later Switzer came back to Oklahoma and assumed his new role there: elder statesman, lovable anachronism, the Grand Old Man on campus.

Switzer pulls the Benz into the circular drive in front of a big, faux-stone Tudor house that is a shade short of a mansion. We go into the garage, where he keeps three German shepherds in wire kennels. One of them snarls at me and bares his teeth. "Don't go near him," Switzer says. "He'll tear your ass up. He was abused. They kept him in a kennel for his first eight months. So I adopted him. He didn't know how to socialize, but I turned him around. Now he loves me and my wife."

We go to the backyard. Unreal green grass, swimming pool, a big cabana open on one side. "Watch out for dog shit," Switzer says. "He'll only shit on concrete 'cause that's all he knows." Switzer gets a pooper scooper and picks up dog shit on the tile around the pool. I tell him he has a beautiful lawn. "AstroTurf," he says. "When it snows I just sweep it off."

Inside the cabana are sofas, easy chairs, and a circular bar with stools. This is where Switzer does his weekly webcast, *Coaches' Ca-*

bana, streaming live every Saturday during the games. His guests are usually retired players and coaches, Sooners from the glory years of the '70s and '80s. They watch the game on television and chitchat in that way of ex-jocks in a bar.

We go inside to the kitchen, where Switzer introduces me to his wife, Becky, a petite blonde of 60 who looks younger than her age. She is Switzer's second wife, a former gymnast, trained by Béla Károlyi, who went on to coach the Sooners. His first wife, Kay, the mother of his three children, divorced him in 1981, after 18 years of marriage. When I ask Switzer about the divorce, he just says, "Kay left me for the right reasons. I was an asshole." When I press, he explains what he means. "I made mistakes," he says. "I was undisciplined, immature. My daughter says I was a great father but a terrible husband."

On game day I drive to Switzer's house at noon. Becky is carrying in groceries from her car. I help her in an awkward silence. Finally I ask her how she deals with all the people who want her husband's time. "We have eight beds upstairs," she says. "On game days most of them are occupied. Barry loves it."

I go outside to smoke a cigar at a small table overlooking the front yard and the street that leads to the campus. Cars pull into the driveway and people come over to me to ask if "Coach is home." I say no. They are sure to tell me their names—a fan, an alumnus, a player from 35 years ago—and add, "Tell Coach I stopped by to say hello."

When Switzer gets home, he sits with me outside in the cool afternoon sunlight. Soon we are talking again about our fathers. I tell him of the time my dad took me on a fishing trip: two blocks down the street to a golf course with a water hazard, a stagnant pond. I sat there for hours with a stick and string and a safety pin for a hook, hoping to catch—what, a Titleist?—while the old man was booking bets in the bar across the street. "At least your father took you hunting," I say. I had seen an old photo of a four-year-old Switzer with a dead squirrel in one hand and a rifle over his shoulder. His father kneels beside him, smiling.

Another car pulls into the driveway. A handsome young man wearing sunglasses comes over and sits down. Switzer introduces him as "Ryan, my computer guru."

Ryan is holding an envelope stuffed with $100 bills. He counts out 45 C-notes and hands them to Switzer. "Not in front of the old fiction writer," Switzer says. "He'll think I'm a bookie." Then he grows serious. "Are you sure you don't need it?"

Ryan hesitates. "I said I'd pay you back."

"You were gonna use it for a down payment on a house."

"Well, my granddaddy passed a while ago and he left no money for his funeral. I was grateful I could pay for it."

"Now you can't buy the house?" Switzer asks. Ryan nods. "How much do you need?" Ryan says $3,000. Switzer counts out 35 bills. "You always need extra," he says.

"I can't be in your debt again, Barry."

"Take the money and buy the fucking house. It'll come back to you."

"I don't know how long it'll take me to pay you back."

"I don't care! But the next time I see you, you'd better own that fucking house."

Ryan takes the money and gets up to leave. "Barry, you bring tears to my eyes."

After Ryan leaves we sit in the sun, not talking, a little embarrassed. Switzer checks his messages. "Come on," he says. "I gotta make an appearance at this guy's house." We drive through campus, passing flocks of people walking toward the stadium. Switzer finds a small ranch house and we go inside. There are more than 30 people partying inside and out by the pool. The redneck crowd is drinking beer, eating nachos and wings, singing Sooner fight songs, cheering, and yelling at one another already, four hours before the game. Switzer works the room like a Vegas shill, shaking hands, slapping backs, hugging women, posing for selfies, telling stories—another ancient Longhorns-Sooners game, which, in his telling, always ends the same, with a Sooners victory.

A short man smoking a cigar, belly protruding from his T-shirt, approaches. Switzer introduces me. The man pumps my hand and asks if he can take a picture of Barry and me with his daughter. "We'd be so proud," he says. His daughter is a pretty blonde in a tight miniskirt. She stands between Switzer and me, with our arms over her shoulders. Her father, beaming, takes the picture.

Back in the car, Switzer says, "He's a good ol' boy—a millionaire 200 times over, yet he's not pretentious. I like him."

By 7:30, back at Switzer's house, about 50 people crowd the pool area and cabana, eating from a buffet of chicken wings, drinking at the bar. Switzer tells me to enjoy the party and heads to the cabana to host his show. Tonight's guests are former players Billy Sims and Thomas Lott. The two men look prosperous and a good distance from their playing weight. In fact, Sims's life after football was a series of catastrophes: failed business ventures, bankruptcies, divorce, jail time, charges of domestic violence. In 2001, he was forced to sell his Heisman Trophy for $88,000. Now he's back on his feet with a chain of 46 Billy Sims Barbecue restaurants. Lott, meanwhile, hosts a sports radio show.

I watch the three men from a chair by the pool, but it's hard to hear much over the noisy crowd. They're hunched together almost conspiratorially, oblivious to the pool party. It's a bond often seen among veteran athletes, as well as cops and soldiers—men who have fought together and know things the rest of us do not.

After a couple of hours, I get up to leave. I look back at Switzer, sitting with his former players on the sofa, gabbing about the game. No one, I notice, seems to be paying attention to them. Their voices go unheard, except by one another. It's the coach and his players—all Barry Switzer ever needed.

DAVE SHEININ

A Wonderful Life

FROM THE WASHINGTON POST

GRANITE BAY, CALIF.—The pale California sun makes its midday bend toward the southwest, drenching the freshly pruned vineyards of Baker Family Wines out behind the house with nurturing sunlight. It sends bright-colored beams through the stained glass windows atop the vaulted ceilings. And it radiates upon the massive solar panels at the edge of the property, filling them with the energy that courses into the house and illuminates the recessed lighting of the gourmet kitchen, where Dusty Baker is standing at the stove making collard greens.

You can learn all you need to know about a man from his collard greens.

Baker grew his own in his backyard garden because that's how his daddy taught him, from heirloom seeds he got from his friend, blues legend Elvin Bishop. So already you know this about Johnnie B. "Dusty" Baker Jr.: He is his father's son, from the ground up. But it's the blues that nourishes him.

He cooks his collards with low-sodium chicken broth and boils the salt out of his ham hock before dropping it into the pot. So you know this too: the new manager of the Washington Nationals is deeply aware you only get so many trips around the sun, and at age 66, after surviving both prostate cancer and a stroke, he isn't taking any of them for granted.

"Doctor says I'm supposed to watch that sodium," Baker says, scraping the minced garlic and chopped bell peppers into the pot.

You would need more hours than there are in the day—and more collard greens than there are on the green earth—to know the totality of Dusty Baker, if it can be known at all. But here is a taste:

Aside from being a vintner, a gardener, a solar-energy entrepreneur, and a cancer survivor, he is also a published author, a motivational speaker, and an outdoorsman of some renown. He has been, at various times in his life, a prep basketball star, a journalism student, and a Marine Corps reservist. He once smoked marijuana with Jimi Hendrix on a San Francisco street corner. He counts among his friends a tribal elder of the Northern Cheyennes, the artist behind the hit single "Fooled Around and Fell in Love," and the president of the United States of America.

His preferred denomination of walk-around money is $50 bills, and he is generous with his tips.

"He's like everybody ought to be," said Bishop, the songwriter and blues guitarist who befriended Baker after they met years ago at John Lee Hooker's house. "He treats everybody with respect and an open mind. He's just a beautiful person. If the Martians ever land here, this is the guy I want to send to go talk to them—to represent the human race."

Baseball is perhaps the least interesting thing about him, and all other things being equal, he would have rather made his name in music. ("You can do music," he says, "till you die.") But his baseball life is still rich enough to deserve its own accounting, and so:

He played 2,039 games for four big league teams without ever going on the disabled list. He once shared a dugout with Satchel Paige. He was in the on-deck circle, kneeling, when Hank Aaron broke Babe Ruth's career home run record in 1974 and in the dugout, managing, when Barry Bonds broke Mark McGwire's single-season record in 2001. He may have accidentally invented the high-five on October 2, 1977.

It has been an extraordinary life, and its evidence is displayed on the walls of the house Baker shares with his wife, Melissa, and their 17-year-old son, Darren: guitars autographed by the likes of B. B. King and Buddy Guy; photos of the Bakers with all manner of athletes or celebrities or both ("There's one of my mom with Tony Orlando and Dawn—and Roy Campanella"); letters to Baker from Bob Hope, Gerald Ford, and Frank Sinatra.

"Those some bad dudes, huh?" Baker says, grinning.

His collection of baseball memorabilia—old uniforms and bats, his Gold Glove and Silver Slugger trophies—fills several walls' worth of custom-made lockers and is so vast it needs its own itemized inventory list.

"I can't even get in this one," he says, pointing to an exclusive case filled only with balls signed by Hall of Famers. "Maris. Brock. Yogi. Feller. Koufax. Oh, those some baaaaad dudes."

Still, a man's walls only show you what he wants to show. For the truth, you need the collard greens. Back at the stove, Baker adds some vinegar to the pot. Just a few shakes. The bottle goes on the table, so you can add more yourself if you would like. Taste, see, is a personal thing.

"If you like me, fine," he says at one point, referring to the way he seems to engender deep affection from many people in baseball and deep disdain from others. "If you don't, fine."

Which brings us to this observation: Baker hasn't once used a measuring cup or spoon or turned on a timer.

That's right. He's not going by the recipe book. That can mean only one thing:

He's going—wait for it—with his gut.

Old school—but not the one you think

One evening in 2007, a handful of close friends was summoned to the home of Bill Walsh, the revered architect of the 1980s San Francisco 49ers dynasty, for dinner. The guest list included four of Walsh's favorite players from that era—Joe Montana, Dwight Clark, Bill Ring, and Eric Wright—and Dusty Baker.

Everyone knew Walsh was battling leukemia, but his condition had worsened. As the group told ancient stories and relived ancient glories, no one spoke of what was really going on. But shortly afterward came the grim confirmation: Walsh passed away July 30 of that year at the age of 75.

"That night," Baker says, "was his Last Supper."

Baker still doesn't know exactly why Walsh took to him so strongly, their paths having first crossed in 1981 when a mutual friend introduced them. But one day in 1993, when Walsh was coaching at Stanford and Baker had just been named the Giants' manager, Walsh invited him to his office and handed him an oversized accordion file stuffed with manila folders. Inside the folders were Walsh's handwritten notes—scribbled on large pieces of easel paper—about how to run an organization.

Essentially, it was Walsh's blueprint for how he built one of the NFL's greatest teams. He wanted Baker to have them.

"Look—he had everything mapped out," Baker says now, pulling out pages from folders marked with headings such as "Training Staff," "Pre-Camp Coaches Meeting," "Fine Schedule," "Team Travel," and "Public Relations."

All the folks who deride Baker as an "old-school" relic are right: he's straight out of the 1980s. But it's the 1980s NFL.

"He used to talk to me about the importance of having balance in your life as you got older," Baker says of Walsh. "He said you should always be open to new ideas."

About that "old-school" label. It's true: Baker is a mostly observational leader in an increasingly analytical era. But it's an oversimplification, one that has been used to demean him for years. It is impossible for his critics to acknowledge he is brilliant in the ways of managing men because it is not something that can be measured with numbers.

"How did I win all those games?" he says sarcastically. "I guess it was luck."

This is why the collard greens are important: they're perfect. He doesn't need a recipe. This is why the blues are important: within the rigid structure of those 12-bar verses are an infinite number of patterns and modulations. This is why Bill Walsh is important: Baker still embraces new ideas, even at 66 years old. Especially at 66.

"I believe in the new school big time," he says. "There've always been analytics in baseball. It just didn't always have a name."

A long time ago, Baker rode some pitchers hard. In some pockets of Chicago, he always will be blamed for shortening the careers of Kerry Wood and Mark Prior—a notion that still chafes him. But baseball is not a static enterprise. The sport has gotten wiser about pitch counts, arm fatigue, and elbows, but somehow it is only Baker who is still blamed for the way he used his pitchers in a different era.

"How he handled pitchers 15 years ago? The game has changed, and he's changed," Bob Miller says. "Look around. Some pitchers are ridden hard, and some are treated with kid gloves. And they almost all get hurt."

Miller was an assistant general manager in Cincinnati for the entirety of Baker's stint there as manager from 2008 to 2013, moving to the Nationals' front office in November 2014. When the Nationals fired Matt Williams a year later, general manager Mike Rizzo leaned heavily on Miller's experience with Baker in evaluating the man the Nationals eventually would hire.

"My biggest [role] was to tear down the negativity people have about him," Miller says. "He was very open to ideas from the front office [in Cincinnati]—as much as we wanted him to be. He's still an old-school guy, and he's still going to go by his gut and listen to his players.

"But he believes in sabermetrics more than the sabermetrics people believe that these are humans playing the game and that some things can't be measured."

His George Bailey moment

The sun is lower now, its deepening light filling the window-lined nook where the kitchen table sits, perhaps the sunniest spot in the whole house. The greens are served, alongside elk-and-venison sloppy joes. "I eat wild," Baker explains.

This is the Bakers' dream home—a compound, really—built to their specs in this Sacramento suburb seven years ago. There's a basketball court, a covered batting cage for Darren, and a detached garage/man cave/fishing lodge with its own kitchen and shower.

Baker loves being home, even if he never intended to be home so much lately. It wasn't as if he was pleased to get fired by the Reds after the 2013 season—after a 90-win season that the franchise hasn't come close to matching—but it did afford him the chance to watch his son play a lot of baseball these past two years, and it meant he could be there to walk his daughter, Natosha, from his first marriage, down the aisle on a summer Saturday in 2014.

"The time off did me some good," he says. "I didn't think it would. But it gave me the time to get everything back together—my mind together, my spirit together, and my body together."

A most curious picture hangs behind Baker's head as he talks between forkfuls. In a house where everything has its own logical place, he has chosen this spot, above the kitchen table, for a black-and-white photo from the classic Frank Capra film *It's a Wonderful Life*.

The photo, showing Jimmy Stewart as hard-luck building-and-loan man George Bailey, is from one of the darkest scenes in the film, when Bailey—whose selflessness and honesty go perpetually unrewarded—explodes at his family on Christmas Eve following a disastrous day at work, when he lost the last of his money. A couple of scenes later, devoid of hope, he is about to jump off a bridge to commit suicide when an angel intervenes.

"His whole world was upside down," Baker says softly. "I've been there. I know what it's like to lose hope."

The words come haltingly. "There was a time, at a down moment, I was tired of it all," he says, pausing. "Man, some of this stuff I've been holding on to for 20 years."

In the mid-1980s, Baker's life was falling apart. Divorce. The end of his playing career. Worst of all, the IRS had begun coming after him for millions of dollars in back taxes, interest, and penalties after it determined a series of tax shelters he had used for years—at the direction of his brother, Victor, who managed his money—were disallowed. The IRS was asking for $4 million, Baker says, and at one point when he was managing the Giants on a $900,000 salary, his paychecks were being garnished, leaving him $4,500 a month to live on.

Baker's relationship with money has always been a deep one. As a boy, he remembers helping his dad at his second job, mowing neighbors' lawns. He didn't get a dime. "You see those big old shoes on your feet?" his father would tell him. "You see that food on your plate? That's your pay."

As a young man, Baker says, he aspired to be "the richest black man in America." And like George Bailey, he had always tried to do right by people, sharing his good fortune with those he cared about. He delighted in setting up scholarship funds for his nieces, nephews, and literally dozens of godchildren. "You don't owe me nothing," he would tell the kids. "Just be something."

The mere insinuation that he was a tax cheat was as painful as the actual dollar amount.

"I ain't no tax evader," he says now. "I've never evaded anything in my life."

Some friends suggested to Baker he should declare bankruptcy, but that was never an option. "Being African American," he says, "that was more of a sign of failure than it was for Donald Trump or somebody else. It's a business move for him. But with us, it was always viewed as: 'You dumb athlete—you squandered your money.'"

At his lowest moment, Baker says, he was George Bailey on that bridge, his money gone, his hope depleted, his demons unconquerable. In the movie, the angel jumped into the water first, knowing Bailey would jump in to save him, thus reminding himself of the value of life. Baker's angel came barging into the room where the same demons had placed a gun in his hand.

"If it hadn't been for God or my daughter . . ." he starts to say.

What do you mean?

"She was eight years old," he says. "She came in and said, 'Daddy, what are you doing?' I was sitting there with my gun in my hand."

What if she hadn't walked in?

A long pause. "I don't know, man."

It took years—and the tireless efforts of a tax-crisis lawyer—for the mess to be straightened out, with the IRS ultimately acknowledging Baker should not have been charged for penalties and interest. Still, the episode left Baker shaken and bitter, never more so than when the story was leaked to ESPN shortly after he left the Giants in 2002.

"What I saw," the lawyer, Karen Hawkins, recalled in a telephone interview, "was a man whose honor and reputation are everything to him [and] somebody who was very angry because he had been so straightforward and honest [and] others wouldn't treat him the same way. He's a very, very honorable man. They don't make them like him anymore as far as I'm concerned."

The Bakers' beautiful house, full of mementos and, at this very moment, the comforting aroma of collard greens, is a testament to a lesson learned, a fortune rebuilt, and a life renewed.

"I've been from the top to down near the bottom and back up again," he says. "But you never forget what you went through. I don't know if that contributed to my cancer—they talk about the stress being a factor—or my stroke . . . That's why all that stuff people say about me, none of it matters."

Baker wasn't sure he would manage again. For a long time, teams weren't calling him about their open jobs. In late October, when it appeared the Nationals' job would go to Bud Black, he opened up to a reporter about baseball's checkered history of minority hiring, at a moment when there were no African American managers in the game. (Baker's eventual hiring and the Dodgers' subsequent hiring of Dave Roberts brought the number to two.)

"I don't know how much more backwards we can go," he said then. "You wonder if it's by accident or design."

And now: "There were things a lot of us felt that you couldn't easily say for fear you would never work again," he says. "But after a while you get tired of being PC and sugarcoating things. What I said was true."

When the Nationals came back to Baker with the job offer, he took it to his family, with Darren telling him, "It's the chance of a lifetime, Dad."

"Wrapping up [his career] on his terms. That's what this is about," Melissa says. "After all he's accomplished, I think he deserves that."

So he took the gig, even though his two-year contract guarantees him only about half the $3.5 million annual salary he made in Cincinnati, with additional incentives based on performance.

"Yeah, it bothered me somewhat," he says of the low contract offer. "But that's all right. I'll make the rest of it up in incentives."

A couple months after joining the Nationals, closer to Christmas, Baker settled into his spot on the leather sofa and watched *It's a Wonderful Life,* as he does every year, and he thought about life, and about ringing bells and angels' wings, and he cried a little, as he does every year.

DAVID REMNICK

The Outsized Life of Muhammad Ali

FROM THE NEW YORKER

WHAT A LOSS to suffer, even if for years you knew it was coming. Muhammad Ali, who died Friday, in Phoenix, at the age of 74, was the most fantastical American figure of his era, a self-invented character of such physical wit, political defiance, global fame, and sheer originality that no novelist you might name would dare conceive him. Born Cassius Clay in Jim Crow–era Louisville, Kentucky, he was a skinny, quick-witted kid, the son of a sign painter and a house cleaner, who learned to box at the age of 12 to avenge the indignity of a stolen bicycle, a $60 red Schwinn that he could not bear to lose. Eventually, Ali became arguably the most famous person on the planet, known as a supreme athlete, an uncanny blend of power, improvisation, and velocity; a master of rhyming prediction and derision; an exemplar and symbol of racial pride; a fighter, a draft resister, an acolyte, a preacher, a separatist, an integrationist, a comedian, an actor, a dancer, a butterfly, a bee, a figure of immense courage.

In his early career, when he declared his allegiance to Elijah Muhammad's Nation of Islam, rid himself of his "slave name," and lost his heavyweight title rather than fight in Vietnam, Ali was vilified as much as he was admired. Millions hated Ali; he threatened a sense of the racial order; he was, in his refusal to conform to any type, as destabilizing to many Americans as he was to the many heavyweights who could not understand why he would just not come to the center of the ring and fight like a *real* man. He was, for many years, a radical figure for many Americans. For years, many refused to call him by his new name. "I pity Clay and abhor what he represents," the columnist Jimmy Cannon wrote. Even Red Smith, the most respected of all sports columnists, compared Ali to the "unwashed punks" who dared to march against the war. But in recent decades, as Parkinson's disease began to overwhelm his gifts for movement and speech, and as the country's attitudes changed, Ali became a focus of almost universal affection. The people who encountered him at charity dinners, in airports, at sporting events approached him as they would a serene Pope Francis or the Dalai Lama, and, if he could summon a whispered joke or flirt for a moment or just widen his eyes in that old vaudeville way of his, people left with a sense of having met a source of wonder.

Cassius Clay lived in a modest house on Grand Avenue, a relatively pleasant street with other black families, not in "Smoketown," the poorer black neighborhood in southwest Louisville. It was middle class, "but *black* middle class, black *Southern* middle class, which is not white middle class at all," Toni Morrison told me when I was working on a book about Ali. (As an editor at Random House, Morrison had worked on Ali's autobiography, *The Greatest.*) Cassius was named for a 19th-century Kentucky abolitionist and military commander who inherited 40 slaves and then freed them when he came home from the war in Mexico. He was, for a while, Abraham Lincoln's emissary to Russia, but he soon returned to Kentucky to work again for the abolitionist cause. Cassius—the boy, the fighter—was told stories about his great-grandfather who was raised on the abolitionist's farm, "but not in a slave capacity. No, sir!" as Clay Sr., Ali's father, once said.

Louisville, when Cassius was growing up in the 1940s and '50s, was a Jim Crow city. American apartheid. Not quite as virulent as in Jackson or Mobile, but plenty bad. At movie theaters like the Savoy, whites sat in the orchestra, blacks in the balcony; most other theaters were for whites only, and so were the stores downtown. There were white schools, white country clubs, white businesses. Blyden Jackson, a black writer from Louisville, who was in his forties when Clay was growing up, wrote, "On my side of the veil everything was black: the homes, the people, the churches, the schools, the Negro park with Negro park police . . . There were two Louisvilles and, in America, two Americas." It was a childhood in which Cassius saw his mother turned away for a drink of water at a luncheonette after a hard day of cleaning the floors and toilets of white families. These were daily scenes, the racial arrangements of Louisville.

Cassius's father was a man of thwarted dreams. He distrusted whites, and felt he was prevented from becoming a painter of canvasses rather than of signs and billboards. He drank too much, and his bitterness sometimes tipped into chaos. He was, one of Ali's friends said, the source of a great deal of pain in the family. His mother, Odessa, was usually the object of Cassius Sr.'s fury and fists, and she was the boy's comfort. Odessa was the first to know that her son was hyperverbal and quick with a left hand. As she once recalled, "He was always a talker. He tried to talk so hard when he was a baby. He used to jabber so, you know? And people'd laugh and he'd shake his face and jabber so fast. I don't see how anybody could talk so fast, just like lightning. And he never sat still. He was in the bed with me at six months old, and you know how babies stretch? He had little muscle arms and he hit me in the mouth when he stretched and it loosened my front tooth and it affected my other front tooth and I had to have both of them pulled out. So I always say his first knockout punch was in my mouth."

As an athlete and as a performer, Clay learned from, and copied, a multitude of sources: the braggadocio of the professional wrestler "Gorgeous" George Wagner, the footwork and boxing style of Sugar Ray Robinson. But no public figure affected him more deeply than Emmett Till, a boy from Chicago, who, on a visit to family in Money, Mississippi, was murdered for the alleged sin of "reckless eyeballing." The story was that Till, who was 14, dared to call a white cashier "baby." A few days later, white men turned up at the house where he was staying, dragged him out of his bed, shot him in the head, tied barbed wire attached to a bulky cotton-gin fan around his neck, and threw his corpse in the Tallahatchie River. The horror that Cassius experienced looking at the pictures of Till's brutalized face in the pages of the black press helped convince him of the limits of his possibilities as a black kid in the South.

"There wasn't nothing to do in the streets," he told one writer, recalling his own stunted growing up. "The kids would throw rocks and stand under the streetlights all night, running in and out of the juke joints and smoking and slipping off drinking, nothing to do."

At Central High, Cassius's marks were so bad in the tenth grade that he had to withdraw and then come back and repeat the year. A career in professional football or basketball seemed to require college, and that, he felt, wasn't going to happen. Boxing was the path. He daydreamed in class, shadowboxed in the hallways. He trained at first in the gym of a local police officer named Joe Martin and, even as a teenager, he showed uncommon skill. He was incredibly disciplined even then, waking at dawn and running through Chickasaw Park.

And the preternatural confidence was there from the start. He was The Greatest practically before he entered the ring. Even in those days, Clay was using doggerel verse, like a pugilistic Ogden Nash, to predict an opponent's demise: "This guy must be done / I'll stop him in one." At school assemblies, he got up in front of the student body while the friendly principal, Atwood Wilson, introduced him as the "next heavyweight champion of the world! This guy is going to make a million dollars!" He struggled in class, finding it hard to read a book, but he was intelligent, absorbing things through other means. As an aspiring fighter, he tore through Golden Gloves competitions, leading his mentor, Wilson, to say, "The truth is, the only thing Cassius is going to have to read is his IRS form, and I'm willing to help him do it."

But, while he eventually became an Olympic champion, he did not so much impress boxing writers as bewilder them. Even A. J. Liebling, the finest of all boxing writers, and no one's idea of a reactionary or a hack, was confounded by the young man's loose-limbed style. Clay's refusal to exchange punches with his opponent in the traditional manly fashion, his way of dancing, of circling an opponent, flashing lacerating jabs that came lashing up from the hip . . . this was not proper, somehow.

At the 1960 Rome Olympics, Clay won the gold medal with a victory over a lumbering opponent from Poland. Liebling offered only qualified praise. "Clay had a skittering style, like a pebble scaled over water," he wrote. "He was good to watch, but seemed to make only glancing contact. It is true that the Pole finished the three-round bout helpless and out on his feet, but I thought he had just run out of puff chasing Clay, who had then cut him to pieces."

Even after Clay turned pro, Liebling never quite warmed to him. Witnessing Clay's battle with a persistent heavyweight named Doug Jones, Liebling focused less on Clay's narrow decision and more on his bragging before and after his bouts. He called Clay "Mr. Swellhead Bigmouth Poet." Others called him Gaseous Cassius. Pete Hamill, another white liberal who would eventually come to adore the fighter, wrote in the *New York Post*, "Cassius Clay is a young man with a lot of charm who is in danger of becoming a dreadful bore."

History will record that the athletic career and the American life that unfolded in the coming years were the very opposite of a bore. Muhammad Ali was a central excitement and provocation in the midst of civil rights, Vietnam, and Black Power. Between 1964 and 1980 came a story, Ali's story, that no one book could quite take in. Too many triumphs, too many crises, endings, false endings, comebacks, comic outrages, trials, tragic scenes.

The only thing ordinary about the boxing career of Muhammad Ali was that he stayed too long and ended up damaged. Everything else was outsized: the upset victory in 1964, to win the title from Sonny Liston ("I'm King of the World!" he shouted to the reporters at ringside), the friendship (and falling out) with Malcolm X, the embrace of the Nation of Islam, the blaze of brilliant fights in the mid-sixties, then the draft, the acceptance of a potential jail term, the stripping of his title, the years in exile. Ali was not to be mistaken for a political leader or a thinker, but he had political importance as a symbol of refusal, of black pride. And, along with his importance as a symbol, particularly to young people facing the draft or marching in the streets, there was a level of glamour without parallel even among the rock gods of the time. When Ali fought Joe Frazier for the first time, at Madison Square Garden, in March 1971, the ringside photographer for *Life* was Frank Sinatra. When Ali went to Zaire to fight, and defeat, George Foreman, half of PEN seemed to follow, and Norman Mailer's account, *The Fight*, is the writer at his comic-epic best, describing the final knockout with precision:

> Foreman's arms flew out to the side like a man with a parachute jumping out of a plane, and in this doubled-over position he tried to wander out to the center of the ring. All the while his eyes were on Ali and he looked up with no anger as if Ali, indeed, was the man he knew best in the world and would see him on his dying day. Vertigo took George Foreman and revolved him. Still bowing from the waist in this uncomprehending position, eyes on Muhammad Ali all the way, he started to tumble and topple and fall even as he did not wish to go down . . . He

went over like a six-foot sixty-year-old butler who has just heard tragic news.

Ali's athletic feats were outsized, not least because they were performed at the risk of terrible physical harm. Watch the third fight with Joe Frazier, in Manila. The two men nearly destroy each other. Ali admitted afterward that it was the "closest I've come to death." And Frazier, who despised Ali for mocking him, for calling him a gorilla and an Uncle Tom, said, "I hit him with punches that would have knocked a building down." Ali, who had won after Frazier's cornermen determined that he was too swollen, too blinded to go on, admitted that both he and Frazier were never the same after that third fight. "We went to Manila as champions, Joe and me, and we came back as old men," he said.

Ali was not blind to the hypocrisies and brutality of the "game" that had been his professional life. The source of his fame was a sport in which race was often an ugly element of its history, a contest in which one man tries to beat another senseless, tries to inflict temporary brain injury (a knockout) on another. Ali reaped millions of dollars from the fight game, and yet he was, at times, ambivalent about that history and the lurid spectacle of one man fighting another, particularly one *black* man fighting another. Ali had the capacity to enjoy the fruits of the game and the riches it brought, but he also knew the history of the sport—John L. Sullivan refusing to fight black challengers and Jim Jeffries telling the world he would retire "when there are no white men left to fight." Ali was schooled in the history of Jack Johnson's pride and persecution—the band at ringside struck up "All Coons Look Alike to Me" when Jeffries finally dared to face Johnson. He knew well how Jack Dempsey avoided black fighters after taking the title. Ali had seen how fighters before him had been sponsored, managed, and exploited by Mafia thugs. He remembered from childhood how Joe Louis's handlers gave him a set of rules to avoid alienating white America.

"They stand around and say, 'Good fight, boy: you're a good boy; good goin','" Ali said, in 1970. "They don't look at fighters to have brains. They don't look at fighters to be businessmen, or human, or intelligent. Fighters are just brutes that come to entertain the rich white people. Beat up on each other and break each other's noses, and bleed, and show off like two little monkeys for the crowd, killing each other for the crowd. And half the crowd is white. We're just like two slaves in that ring. The masters get two of us big old black slaves and let us fight it out while they bet: 'My slave can whup your slave.' That's what I see when I see two black people fighting." It was almost as if Ali, at the height of his fame, was hinting that we were all complicit in something fallen and dubious, even as we were rooting him on.

What modern athlete, much less one at Ali's level, has ever talked with such political complexity, ambiguity, or engagement?

When I was doing the research for my book on Ali, I interviewed one of his main early antagonists in the ring, Floyd Patterson, who was clearly suffering from trauma-induced dementia. Patterson could barely string a few sentences together. Sonny Liston, his other early rival, had died years earlier with heroin on him. Ali, for his part, was living with his wife, Lonnie, at their farm, in Berrien Springs, Michigan. He was suffering from Parkinson's, and it was hard to believe that the accumulation of punishment (from Frazier, from Earnie Shavers, Ken Norton, Larry Holmes, from a lifetime of beatings) had not been at least partially responsible for his condition. But he refused any note of regret. We watched films of his fights with Liston and couldn't help admiring his younger self: "Sooo pretty!" More than a generation after his retirement, and now, after his passing, Ali and his story remain known everywhere in the world. How many today know the name of his current inheritor, the heavyweight champion of the world? The story of Muhammad Ali will long outlast the sport he took up, 62 years ago in Louisville, to avenge the theft of his beloved red bicycle.

One last thing: at the Greek Theatre in Berkeley tonight, Paul Simon was singing "The Boxer." Pausing before the final verse, he told the audience, "I'm sorry to tell you this, but Muhammad Ali just passed away."

KURT STREETER

The Spirit of a Legend

FROM ESPN: THE MAGAZINE

IN A CLEARING on a grassy hillside near a two-lane highway in eastern Pennsylvania lie the bones of Jim Thorpe, the man considered by many to be the world's greatest athlete. Fashioned of polished stone the color of red riverbank mud, his tomb is oblong and almost six feet tall. A truck rumbles past, then another. The rustle of wind blows low across the glade and through a line of trees. Few people stop to pay respect to this legendary Native American.

The crypt is at the edge of a small town Thorpe was never known to visit, a place with which he had no known connection. The community, Jim Thorpe, Pennsylvania, took his name to claim his body, and its residents think their town has won a decades-long battle to keep his remains as a tourist destination. Thorpe's sons, the last of his living children, think his spirit wanders the earth in sorrow because he has never had a proper ceremony for the dead. They say they will fight for his remains until they can return him to his original home in Oklahoma.

One thousand four hundred eighty-two miles southwest of Thorpe's grave, his son Richard walks slowly through the living room of his small home, tucked off a narrow, gravel road near Waurika, in the stillness of southern Oklahoma. Richard Thorpe is 83, thin and halting. His grip is weak. His voice is low and rounded, as if his words are flowing over pebbles stuck in his throat. For 63 years, he says, the spirit of his father, Wa-tho-huck, "light after the lightning," has been wandering the earth without peace. Richard Thorpe and his brother, Bill, who is 87, want to bring him back to these dusty hills and give him a proper burial where he wanted to be: with his family, where he was born.

"He lives with me each day from the moment I wake," Richard says, motioning toward one wall of his cream-colored living room. He stares through thick eyeglasses at a photo of himself and his father, taken in black and white in the mid-1930s. Richard was a bashful boy at the time, standing on a front porch, wearing a Native American headdress. The wide hand of his father lies across one of his narrow shoulders. Richard Thorpe struggles to speak; not long ago, he suffered a stroke. "To everyone else, he was this famous man. He'd walk into a room, and everyone would turn and look," he says. "To us, he was Dad. Just plain Dad."

On other walls in the room are more images: paintings and lithographs of Jim Thorpe, with his rugged face, his wide neck, and his quick, sinewy muscles. He is motionless, yet full of energy, as he plays college football in the thick woolen uniform worn at the Carlisle Indian Industrial School in Pennsylvania, as he races down a track at the 1912 Olympics, and as he gets ready to bat for the New York Giants. On a bookshelf in Richard's living room are medals and statues, each inscribed with the name JIM THORPE.

One hundred twenty-five miles farther south, Richard's brother Bill sits in his living room in Arlington, Texas, also surrounded by paintings and photographs of their celebrated father. Bill, a former parts-supply supervisor in the aeronautics industry, and Richard, a retired purchasing agent for the state of Oklahoma, share Jim Thorpe's flinty eyes, his determined jaw, and his sturdy shoulders. The sons are not given to emotion, but when they speak of their father's soul, they are stricken, particularly when they recount a cold spring night in April of 1953, which still has the sharp sting of a fresh wound. That was the night their father's body was snatched away during his funeral.

"Time is getting short," Bill says, speaking about himself and his brother. They want to be alive to see their father come home. If they hope to win the battle for his bones, they must do it now. "His spirit isn't rested," Richard says. He forces the words to come. "The people of his tribe never finished the burial the way it must be done. He was taken from us. We never finished."

*

In the low, rolling hills just outside Shawnee, Oklahoma, a bulky, dark casket lay on a blanket-covered bench in the middle of a ceremonial hut covered with canvas. Inside the coffin was Jim Thorpe, his head pointed to the west, where the spirits of the properly buried go to live.

Under his wire-rimmed glasses, blue paint swirled around his eyes. He was dressed in a buckskin jacket and leather moccasins. "He had beadwork draped around his shoulders," Bill Thorpe says. He clutched tobacco that had been blessed by the tribe. Next to his body lay an eagle's wing. Food would be placed inside his casket before it was closed, enough to keep his spirit nourished on its long westward passage to the other side.

The sons and others remember that it was dark. The hut was filled with family and members of the Sac and Fox tribe. Smoke floated in the air. Metal pots hung over a fire. The pots were brimming with beef, chicken, venison, corn, and pumpkin.

Tom Brown, a tribal elder, started the prayers. Patsy was Jim Thorpe's third wife, and she had shown little interest in, and sometimes even disdain for, tribal tradition. She wouldn't have been permitted inside for long regardless; a spouse is not allowed to spend much time with a deceased loved one, as it can disturb the spirit. "All of this must be done properly, in the traditional way," says Sandra Massey, the tribe's historic preservation officer. It has been this way since before white men set foot on North America. It is important to feast on the stew bubbling in the pots, and then to sit with the body in the darkness past sunrise. Sometime before noon the next day, Jim Thorpe's coffin was to be carried out of the hut through a door facing west.

His body would be taken to a mausoleum while details were completed for a memorial on a family burial plot nearby. Meanwhile, Thorpe's spirit would travel on an extensive journey where it would be tested. His spirit would have to fend off distractions, and it would be asked to give an accounting of his life. According to Sac and Fox beliefs, failing to complete a burial observance has terrible consequences. "If you don't [finish], he is earth-bound," Massey says. "He is stuck here, stuck on this plane."

As Brown prayed, Patsy burst into the hut.

Richard and Bill and the rest of Jim Thorpe's living offspring looked up, startled. They were the children of his previous two wives. Patsy's relationship with the four sons of Thorpe's second wife, Freeda, was strained. "A royal piece of work is what she was," Richard says. "To me, that woman, she seemed just mean, all the time." Adds Bill: "The way she looked at it, people answered to her. She didn't answer to anyone."

Patsy had brought the police and a few men in suits.

"He's too cold!" she declared. She ordered the men to take the coffin.

"You can't do this!" Bill shouted. "No! Absolutely no."

Jim Thorpe's daughters, Grace, Gail, and Charlotte, yelled: "No! No!"

So did other members of the tribe.

But the police, Bill says, stood nearby "while the hearse people took the body and the casket."

Neither Richard nor Bill remembers Patsy saying more.

The two sons recall a sense of sheer helplessness. Patsy was white. Whites held virtually unquestioned authority on native land, especially in places like rural Oklahoma. The tribe members in the ceremonial hut had been conditioned to acquiesce.

"The feeling was like this," Bill says. "'What can we do?'"

Jim Thorpe's children and members of the tribe never saw him or his coffin again.

"The way it happened that night—hell yeah, I'm still angry," Bill says. "That kind of hurt doesn't go away."

The battle of Little Big Horn and the Nez Perce conflict were over, but the Massacre at Wounded Knee was still to come, when Jim Thorpe was born on May 28, 1887, in a wood cabin near Shawnee, on what was called an Indian allotment.

The United States was suppressing Native American religious practices, banning reservation residents from leaving without permission, putting agents in charge of the welfare of their children, and sending them to Indian boarding schools hundreds of miles from home to forcibly assimilate them into white culture.

Hiram Thorpe, Jim's father, was part Sac and Fox and part white. Charlotte Vieux, Jim's mother, was part white and part Potawatomi. As sometimes happened to Native American children, Jim Thorpe was baptized a Catholic and given a Christian name, Jacobus Franciscus. But he came to identify as a Native American and followed Sac and Fox ways as much as he could.

"Dad was connected to the land," Richard says. "It gave him peace. Made him strong."

By age eight, he was an expert fisherman and hunted deer and turkey. By 10, he was breaking wild horses. He liked to spend days alone, studying the movements of animals.

Apart from athletics, little came easy for him. His twin brother, Charlie, died of smallpox as a child. By his midteens, Jim had lost both his parents. He was sent away to a series of Indian schools. "Relentless and brutal places," says Philip Deloria, a professor of history and American culture at the University of Michigan. "They were trying to beat the Indian out of these kids, and the kids were often paying with their lives."

Thorpe gained national attention at the Carlisle Indian Industrial School in Pennsylvania, where he played football for Glenn "Pop" Warner. In the first game of his breakout sophomore season, Thorpe, a pounding defender and slashing back, scored six touchdowns in two quarters. In 1912, Carlisle played Army at West Point, where George Custer is buried. "Your fathers and grandfathers fought their fathers," Warner told his team. "These men playing against you today are soldiers. They are Long Knives. Tonight we will know if you are warriors."

The game was a demolition. Carlisle won, 27–6.

"Standing out resplendent in a galaxy of Indian stars," reported the *New York Times,* "was Jim Thorpe, recently crowned the athletic marvel of the age. At times the game itself was almost forgotten while the spectators gazed on Thorpe, the individual, to wonder at his prowess."

Thorpe, 6'1" and 185 pounds in his prime, went on to become the nation's biggest draw in the early days of professional football. He played baseball as well, including six seasons in the major leagues. He batted .252 in his career with the New York Giants, Cincinnati Reds, and Boston Braves, including a .327 season in 1919.

But it was during the 1912 Olympics that he gave people reason to regard him as the world's best athlete.

He hardly trained. When he traveled to Stockholm aboard the SS *Finland,* he was relegated to sleeping in steerage while others on the U.S. team enjoyed upper-level staterooms. But he won a gold medal in what was then the pentathlon, which combined a long jump, javelin throw, discus throw, 200-meter race, and 1,500-meter race. Except for finishing third in the javelin, he placed first in each event.

He took a second gold in the decathlon, to this day considered the ultimate test of overall athletic ability. He beat his closest challenger by nearly 700 points, setting a world record of 8,412 points —a record that would stand for 20 years.

Few knew it at the time, but just before the decathlon's 1,500, Thorpe had reached into his bag and found his shoes were missing. He went to the locker room and found a replacement shoe for his left foot. Then he dug in a trash can and found one for his right. In this mismatched, ill-fitting pair, he won the race.

"He could really move," Richard Thorpe says, looking up at a painting of his father in Stockholm. "He was too old to show it by the time I came around, but sometimes you could see it. He could still have that ease."

Jim Thorpe's dominance at the Olympics, together with his feats in football and baseball, turned him into an icon. Deloria calls him "the first pop star" in American sports. In 1951, the Associated Press asked sports reporters and broadcasters to pick the greatest athlete of the half-century. Babe Ruth was second. The winner, by a large margin, was Jim Thorpe.

When he won his gold medals, Thorpe was not yet an American citizen (most Native Americans didn't receive full citizenship until the 1920s) and he struggled to balance white expectations with his identity as an Indian. He was "part of the outside world, but he always felt a distance from it," Bill Thorpe says. "When you grow up the way he did, that's just the way it was."

Thorpe drank too much. He worked to control it, but Bill says the combination of alcohol, bars, and a nettlesome public sometimes led to fights. His first child, Jim Jr., contracted polio at age three and died in his arms. He and his first wife, Iva, had three more children—daughters Gail, Charlotte, and Grace—before she divorced him, citing desertion. He had four sons with Freeda: Carl, Bill, Richard, and Jack.

Richard and Bill remember good times with their father. Roughhousing, fishing off the piers of Southern California, trips to San Diego. But he "wasn't easy," Bill says. "I think I still have a few scars on my butt from when he took a belt to us." After 15 years, Jim and Freeda were divorced in 1941.

For much of his adult life, a shadow hung over Thorpe. In 1913,

the Amateur Athletic Union (AAU) retroactively deemed him a
professional (he had left Carlisle for a short time to play semipro
baseball) at the time of his Olympic competition and famously
stripped him of his medals. He was an easy target: Native American, and not well educated.

Thorpe's playing days extended into the late 1920s. Afterward,
he bounced around. He lived in California, Nevada, Michigan, Illinois, and Florida. He coached, sold cars, joined the Merchant Marine, and became a security guard at a Ford plant. He owned bars,
judged dance competitions, and dug ditches. He drove a Model T
across the country, hunting dogs at his side, and delivered speeches
extolling physical exercise. He dressed in Native garb and lectured
schoolkids and community groups on the history and potential
of his people. In Hollywood during the 1930s and '40s, he found
his steadiest foothold, playing bit parts alongside Errol Flynn, Mae
West, and Buster Keaton.

In 1945, Thorpe married Patsy, a dark-haired nightclub singer.
She boasted of playing piano in one of Al Capone's Chicago bars.
Kate Buford, author of *Native American Son: The Life and Sporting
Legend of Jim Thorpe,* says Patsy was intelligent and witty but "also an
alcoholic who was manipulative, mercurial, predatory, and some-
times cruel and unbalanced."

Jim and Patsy Thorpe had a stormy relationship, full of hard
drinking and sometimes fights. She managed his business affairs
aggressively: booked his speaking engagements, negotiated with
movie studios, and badgered reporters to write about him.

But they had trouble holding on to money.

By the early 1950s, they were living in a trailer on the flats of suburban Los Angeles. He underwent surgery for lip cancer. "We're
broke," Patsy told reporters at a news conference afterward. She
thanked doctors for operating free of charge.

"Jim has nothing but his name and his memories," she said.
"He spent money on his own people and has given it away. He has
often been exploited."

Thorpe suffered a series of heart attacks. His children prepared
for the worst. One afternoon, Jim Thorpe began speaking about
what the family should do with his body if he died. Bill says his
father "wanted to make sure he was buried in Oklahoma. On Sac
and Fox land." Bill and Richard Thorpe say he repeated the request to others.

Jim Thorpe died on March 28, 1953, of another heart attack.

The family—including Patsy, Bill says—agreed to take his body home to the plot near Prague, close to the Indian allotment where he was born. There would be a traditional Sac and Fox rite, then a Catholic Mass. Afterward, his body would be kept in a mausoleum until Oklahoma built a Jim Thorpe memorial, which was being proposed by a state commission for construction on or near the burial site.

When Patsy Thorpe left the hills of Shawnee with her husband's body, she went ahead with the Catholic Mass, then took him to a local mortuary. Plans for a Jim Thorpe memorial were falling through. It was budgeted to cost at least $25,000 in public money, but Gov. Johnston Murray said the state couldn't afford that much and refused to fund it.

Without consulting her husband's children, Patsy began to look elsewhere.

"Moving my father's body around like some sort of commodity," Bill says.

Biographer Bob Wheeler, author of *Jim Thorpe: World's Greatest Athlete,* interviewed Patsy during the late 1960s, a few years before her death. Wheeler says Patsy told him she began shopping the body when Oklahoma refused to pay for his memorial. "She was so incensed that she just lost it," Wheeler says. "It would take a master psychologist to ascertain her motivations. Her personality was extremely complex."

Patsy looked east. There might be money in Pennsylvania, where Thorpe had gained his initial fame playing football for the Carlisle Indian school. Town fathers picked out a location for a memorial but their plans fell through. The head of a local committee has since said Patsy's dollar demands were too steep.

Next, Patsy went to Philadelphia, where she hoped to persuade NFL commissioner Bert Bell to help. Watching television in a hotel room, she saw a report about two towns some 80 miles to the northwest: Mauch (pronounced "Mok") Chunk and East Mauch Chunk, from Native American words meaning "bear mountain." The towns, split by the Lehigh River, were locked in an intense rivalry. One was mostly German, the other Irish. "When they weren't getting along, one side would cut electricity to the other side because they had the transformer," says Danny McGinley, a local bartender and historian. "The other side had the water, so they would cut the water off over there." If a blaze broke out in one town, fire-fighters say, trucks from the other refused to help without special orders. Both towns depended upon railroads hauling coal, and both had boomed in the 1800s, attracting East Coast tycoons who built mansions and even an opera house. By the 1950s, coal was declining and the towns were economically depressed.

The TV report said Joe Boyle, editor of the *Mauch Chunk Times News,* was urging the towns to save money by combining. Boyle had established a fund to build infrastructure, lure employers, and revive fortunes. He was asking all Chunkers to contribute a nickel each week. The Nickel a Week Fund caught Patsy's eye. She went to Mauch Chunk and sat down with Boyle. They cut a deal. Patsy would hand over Jim Thorpe's body if her dead husband was honored with a tomb and a public memorial. The towns would combine and rename themselves Jim Thorpe, Pennsylvania. The name, she said, would draw tourists and restore the economy.

Boyle died in 1992 and never revealed the terms of the arrange-ment. Neither have any other leaders among the Chunkers, many of whom are no longer living. Wheeler says Boyle told him that Patsy was paid, but only to reimburse the cost of her travel and lodging.

Not everyone in Jim Thorpe, Pennsylvania, was happy with the agreement. Joe Boyle's daughter, Rita, now living in Texas, says, "Daddy took a lot of heat for it because of the name change. My daddy's life was threatened."

Some residents started calling the town "Jim Chunk."

Still, when the pact was put to a vote in May 1954, the Chunkers approved consolidation and the tomb by a landslide. The body of Jim Thorpe was sure to create a renaissance. Maybe the NFL would build its Hall of Fame in Jim Thorpe, Pennsylvania. Maybe developers would invest in accommodations for a huge influx of tourists, perhaps even a hospital. Maybe there would be an ath-letic field and a manufacturing plant for sporting goods—all with good paying jobs. Patsy talked of constructing a hotel with a Native American theme: Jim Thorpe's Teepees.

While a memorial was constructed, Thorpe's body sat in a mau-soleum in a local mortuary. At one point, a rumor surfaced that his body hadn't actually been inside the casket that Patsy deliv-ered. Joe Boyle and a group of other residents opened the crypt.

Onlookers saw that Thorpe was indeed inside, his head wrapped in a plastic bag.

In 1957, Thorpe's body was placed in the new tomb. Etched on the sides of the red stone monument were pictures of Jim Thorpe playing football and baseball and running track, along with the words spoken by King Gustav V of Sweden at the end of the Stockholm Games: "You, sir, are the greatest athlete in the world." Thorpe's children did not attend the dedication.

There would never be a hall of fame or a hospital, no Jim Thorpe's Teepees. To this day, people on the streets of Jim Thorpe, Pennsylvania, recite a remark by a city leader, in a *Sports Illustrated* story from 1982: "All we got here is a dead Indian."

The tomb and its surroundings fell into disrepair. In the 1990s, Richard Thorpe, along with his daughter, Anita, and her two children, visited the Pro Football Hall of Fame in Canton, Ohio. They drove farther on, to Jim Thorpe, Pennsylvania, where Anita recalls Richard's shock at seeing his father's memorial. Alongside the road, she said it looked like a place where people might stop to "relieve themselves." "Dad was talkative and cheerful the whole way. Then he saw it, and the moment he did, and from then on all the way back, he hardly said a word," she says. "It bothered him, the look of it, as if no one even really cared. The whole thing really hit him, how far away his father was from home."

Bill visited the roadside crypt in the 1960s. "I was saddened to my core," he says. "At that particular time, they didn't even have a sidewalk in front of his plaque. I was there by myself, and I just wanted to spend some time. I stayed for, I don't know, 30, 40, 50 minutes. I was upset. The place looked like—you know, it looked like hell. The lawn wasn't mowed. Weeds were there, and everything else, you know.

"But I stayed around, and I visited [with Dad]. We talked."

His voice quivers, and tears appear behind his wire-rimmed glasses. "It was just, you know— [I was] sorry to see him go. I can't remember what I said or anything like that, but it was—it was emotional. Actually, we talked."

Bill says he got a feeling that his father "wasn't in the right place."

Jim Thorpe's other children shared the feeling. At first they were united. All of them wanted their father's body returned. In time, however, his daughters came to accept Jim Thorpe, Pennsylvania. In 1998, Grace presided over a rededication of her father's tomb. "I want to thank the community for all that you've done," she said. "I know my dad is happy to rest here."

At one point, son Jack seemed to agree. He wrote a letter to the town saying, "I now feel that the remains of Jim Thorpe are in a good place, and he is at peace." But then he changed his mind and rejoined his brothers in demanding that their father be brought back to Oklahoma. The presence or absence of Jim Thorpe's bones, the sons said, would not make or break the town of Jim Thorpe, Pennsylvania.

On June 24, 2010, Jack Thorpe, who by now had served for several years as chief of the Sac and Fox tribe, mounted a legal attack. Patsy had died in 1975, so Jack sued the town.

His lawsuit, filed in Pennsylvania federal court, cited the Native American Graves Protection and Repatriation Act, passed by Congress in 1990, requiring the return of Native American remains and sacred objects. The law, known as NAGPRA, gives tribes and families a way to repatriate Indian remains from museums, which it defines as any agency or institution that receives federal funds.

Over the years, hundreds of thousands of native people have been dug from their graves for storage or display at museums, universities, and an array of gallery exhibitions across the country. At a 1987 congressional hearing, Robert McCormick Adams, secretary of the Smithsonian Institution, testified that 42.5 percent of the 34,000 human remains in its collection were from Native Americans.

The federal government itself has exhumed Native Americans. In 1867, the Army surgeon general ordered military medical officers to send him Indian skeletons to study. The goal was to build research collections that aimed to prove white superiority by demonstrating that Indians had smaller craniums. The directive encouraged widespread looting. Medical officers, soldiers, and sometimes civilians collected skulls from battlefields and waited for funerals to finish, then raided burial sites for skulls and bodies to send to Washington.

Using NAGPRA, the 4,000 members of the Sac and Fox tribe already had won the return of nearly 100 bodies. Suzan Shown Harjo, a Cheyenne and Muscogee who helped develop the act and get it passed, says bringing Jim Thorpe home would be important not just for the Sac and Fox but for all Native Americans. "It would send a message that our people are not being stepped on," she says. "It would show we are not going to be kept as collections or roadside attractions anymore. We are going to stand up to that."

The suit enraged the Thorpians, as residents had come to call themselves.

"The state of Oklahoma wanted nothing to do with Jim Thorpe, and a community took him in—our community," says Michael Sofranko, the longtime mayor. "This is the place that took Jim Thorpe in. [We] changed the name of the community, and we have held up our end of the contract. We have done everything we were asked to do."

Six decades after the arrival of Thorpe's body, the fortunes of Jim Thorpe, Pennsylvania, have, indeed, picked up. Divisions have melted. The economy is strong for a town of only 5,000 in a region still being buffeted by the recent recession. Now, when Mayor Sofranko sits on the second-floor deck at the well-appointed Inn at Jim Thorpe, he sees Broadway bustling with people. Many are tourists. Some pedal red and yellow mountain bikes. Others amble along in stylish hiking boots, passing art studios and coffee shops.

The mayor concedes that few of the visitors have come to see Thorpe's tomb. They are there to play in the surrounding hills and on nearby rivers, which have become a hot spot for hikers, bikers, and whitewater rafters. But Jim Thorpe's tomb and monument has played a part in this, Sofranko says. "To get things going." And residents are proud to possess Jim Thorpe's body. To suggest this might be worth reconsidering, if only on moral grounds, makes the Thorpians dig in. Oklahoma had its chance, says Ray Brader, sitting in the back of his gift shop on Broadway. Mention the spiritual claims of the Sac and Fox, and Brader grows indignant. "Jim Thorpe the Olympian was brought here, not Jim Thorpe the Native American." Thorpe smiles from posters and photos on streetlights and restaurant walls. His image is on T-shirts and coffee mugs. Students go to Jim Thorpe Area High School, home of the Olympians. "The movie about him with Burt Lancaster [*Jim Thorpe: All-American*, released in 1951], is required viewing when you grow up here," says Brandon Fogal, manager of a whitewater

rafting business. "You see that film again and again. You can't escape hearing about him. It's hard to find people of any age who
don't feel an attachment."

Each spring, Jim Thorpe, Pennsylvania, celebrates the birthday
of its namesake. At his tomb, a local troupe of Native Americans
dance, pray, chant, and beat drums. Improvements are noticeable.
The tomb is well kept and has additions: a bronze statue of Thorpe
throwing a discus, another of him holding a football. Plaques describe his feats. A metal sculpture of a lightning bolt reminds visitors of his Native American name.

At a firehouse in a neighborhood called The Heights, volunteer
firefighter Jay Miller and his colleagues are suspicious. Miller says
Oklahoma didn't care about Jim Thorpe until his Olympic medals were restored in 1983. Other townspeople have heard a rumor
that the tribe wants to put Thorpe's bones in a casino to boost
business. They seem to see little irony in the fact that they have
used his bones to build their own economy. Ninety-five percent
of the residents of Jim Thorpe, Pennsylvania, are white. By count
of the latest census, the percentage of Native Americans in town
is nearly zero. But its residents do not accept the view that Jim
Thorpe is a stranger. They say he belongs with them.

In court, the Thorpians fought back.

Their attorneys argued that the town was not a museum, even
under the most expansive definition of the law. Moreover, they
said NAGPRA was not meant to apply to "modern remains such as
those of Jim Thorpe." His wife and the town had signed a contract.
"He was merely laid to rest," one court document read, "in accor-
dance with his faith."

The town's case was helped by the fact that Jim Thorpe had
never made a will. In the oral tradition of Native Americans, there
are few written wills. The town's response also was strengthened
by a legal brief from John Thorpe, the 59-year-old son of Jim's
daughter Charlotte. In 2005, John, a Lake Tahoe disc jockey, had
abandoned his father's surname, Adler, so he could take his grandfather's name instead. "I am extremely proud of my heritage," he
says. Nonetheless, he favored leaving his grandfather's body in
Jim Thorpe, Pennsylvania. He filed his brief after attending a Native American sun dance in Bastrop, Texas, where he went to a
sweat lodge. In the steam and the smoke from burning cedar, John

says, a spiritual healer "told me that he had made contact with my grandfather, and these were his words: 'I am at peace, and I want no more pain created in my name.'"

As the court battle waged, Jack Thorpe died of cancer at age 73. Bill and Richard Thorpe and the Sac and Fox tribe joined the lawsuit in his place.

On April 19, 2013, Judge Richard Caputo of the U.S. District Court of the Middle District of Pennsylvania ruled in favor of Jim Thorpe's sons and the tribe. NAGPRA, Caputo said, superseded contract law. Congress, he said, had "recognized larger and different concerns in such circumstances, namely, the sanctity of the Native American culture's treatment of the remains of those of Native American ancestry."

Bill Thorpe remembers thinking: "This is all going to be done with soon. Justice."

Nearly 300 angry Thorpians packed a town hall. "We had an open discussion on what to do," Ray Brader says. "It was very emotional." Speakers included members of the Jim Thorpe High School history club. "It was beautiful," adds his coworker, Anne Marie Fitzpatrick. "The last thing they said was: 'Please leave our namesake alone.'"

The town decided to appeal.

On Oct. 23, 2014, a three-judge panel of the U.S. Third Circuit Court of Appeals overturned Caputo and ruled in favor of the Thorpians. The reversal was based on what is known as the "absurdity doctrine," which judges can use when they think the results of a case have gone against congressional intent.

Chief Judge Theodore McKee said Thorpe's burial accommodated the wishes of his wife and was therefore lawful. In addition, McKee said, Jim Thorpe, Pennsylvania, did not meet NAGPRA's definition of a museum, even as broad as the definition was.

"We find that applying NAGPRA to Thorpe's burial in the borough is . . . a clearly absurd result . . . contrary to Congress's intent to protect Native American burial sites," McKee wrote. Therefore, Jim Thorpe, Pennsylvania, "is not subject to the statute's requirement that his remains be 'returned' to Thorpe's descendants."

In Pennsylvania, there was joy, mixed with relief.

In Oklahoma, misery. "It felt like this was the same old story, the same old raw deal that Indian people have always gotten," says

attorney Stephen Ward, who represented Thorpe's sons and the
tribe. "It felt like the courts just don't work well for Indian people."

Bill and Richard Thorpe appealed to the U.S. Supreme Court.
On Oct. 5, 2015, the court declined to hear the case without
comment.

Bill Thorpe heard the news over the phone. He could barely
speak. "It hurt bad," he says. "The worst part of it is that we felt like
we were not being heard. Not even given a listen, a chance to tell
our story. It's as if you don't count or exist. But then again, we've
gotten used to this sort of thing. It's the Indian way, maybe. We've
had to get used to it. Disappointment. Bitter disappointment."

The bones of Jim Thorpe do not rest easy.

Bill and Richard Thorpe and the Sac and Fox tribe believe that
Jim Thorpe, Pennsylvania, wouldn't be harmed by giving up their
father's remains. "What difference could it possibly make?" Richard says. "The town can keep its name and everything else. Just
give Dad back."

There has been talk, however vague, of suing in state courts,
of a boycott, of getting help from a wealthy Oklahoma oilman,
"someone like T. Boone Pickens," says Massey, the Sac and Fox
historic preservation officer.

More concretely, Bill Thorpe has engaged Tom Rodgers, a
Washington lobbyist who was a key whistleblower in the 2006 case
against Jack Abramoff, the D.C. power broker sent to prison for
defrauding Native American tribes. Rodgers, a member of the
Blackfeet tribe in Montana, is working pro bono.

He plans to meet with the civic leaders of Jim Thorpe, Pennsylvania. "I am going to appeal to their sense of ethics and morality,"
he says. "You are displaying a man's remains and making money
off of it. Jim Thorpe may be buried there, but that is not his home.
I will remind them of history: how the white man took our land,
our children, and then they came and took our spirits and our
bones. Failing that, we will go another route."

Rodgers won't say on the record what that route might be.

Meanwhile, the burial land waits. Thorpe's daughters are in-
terred near Cushing, Oklahoma, surrounded by gentle hills in every direction. His first wife is laid to rest there, too. Behind her
is a gray, leaning stone topped by a rounded sculpture of a baby
lamb. Buffeted by a century of hard weather, its inscription is so

worn that only part of it can be read: "James, Son of Jim / May 1915"—the toddler who died in his arms. Near Stroud, there is a plot in a circular memorial park for military veterans, across the highway from a small casino and a few dozen paces from the tribal headquarters, a police station, and grounds used for sacred tribal gatherings. And there is a flat, rectangular cemetery near the North Canadian River and a school that Jim Thorpe attended before he went to Carlisle. It is easy to imagine him as a boy there, chasing horses in the distance, hunting rabbits and squirrels. In one corner, by a low fence, near a leafy tree, lies his father, Hiram.

Bill reflects on the possible sites and thinks of his own father, Jim Thorpe.

He curls his right hand into a fist.

"We are not giving up."

26.2 to Life

FROM GQ

THE RACE BEGINS on the west side of San Quentin's lower yard, just before the sun creeps over the walls. Two dozen men surge forward. With few exceptions all are murderers, most at least a decade into their sentences, including the early leader, a lifer named Markelle Taylor, who has run this course before but never for as long or as fast as he hopes to today.

With mesh gym shorts hanging to his knees and a cotton tank that soon droops with sweat, Taylor springs over a patchwork of gravel and pavement and grass scorched by the California drought. He makes his first turn at the laundry room, where inmates in V-neck smocks and denim jackets exchange their prison blues, then jabs right at the horseshoe pit and climbs a tight concrete ramp—a pivot so abrupt it has a name: the Gantlet. He swings east across blacktop, past the open-air urinals, past the punching bag and chin-up bars, past the clinic that treats the swell of aging convicts, all while staying within the spray-painted green lines that are supposed to remind the 3,700 non-runners housed here not to wander into his path. On the north side, Taylor guides the pack downhill toward the base of a guard tower, then makes a final 90-degree turn—his sixth—where convict preachers thump Bibles in a cloud of geese and gulls.

That's one lap. Today there's a marathon. Behind these walls, that means 104 to go.

Once a year, the runners of San Quentin do this—stretch their tatted limbs, hike their white crew socks, and attempt to extract under the worst of conditions something that resembles the best of themselves.

"You're seeing people escape from prison," says Rahsaan Thomas, sports editor of the inmate-produced *San Quentin News,* who is 12 years into a 55-to-life sentence for shooting two armed men. "Here," says Thomas, who is helping pass out water, "you can only be free in your own mind."

If running a marathon is as much a test of mental rigor as of physical endurance, then doing 26.2 miles at California's oldest prison, home to America's largest death row, is the ultimate internal contest. On the outside, marathons are movable celebrations that engulf and delight entire cities. The Los Angeles Marathon follows a glittery path from Dodger Stadium, via the Sunset Strip and Rodeo Drive, to Santa Monica Beach; the New York Marathon traverses a five-borough jamboree to the cheers of a million spectators. In the lower yard, a four-acre box on San Quentin's sloped backside, the only way to re-create that distance is to run the perimeter—round and round, hour after hour—going nowhere fast.

Sometimes even that exercise in confinement will grind to a halt. No matter the day, alarms punctuate life at San Quentin, signaling fights or medical emergencies, often in corners of the prison unseen from the lower yard. In those moments, every inmate must drop to the ground—runners included—and wait for guards to restore order. During last year's race, the marathoners had to stop four times.

Perched on the redwooded fringes of San Francisco Bay, about 12 miles north of the Golden Gate Bridge, San Quentin is an anachronism: a moldering castle that dates from the Gold Rush days, now commandeering 432 acres of waterfront property in California's richest county.

Charles Manson and Sirhan Sirhan have passed through these iron latticed gates. Johnny Cash has performed here, earning a Grammy nomination and inspiring a young burglar named Merle Haggard. So many bebop greats did time for heroin that San Quentin used to field its own jazz band. Crips leader and Nobel Peace Prize nominee Stanley "Tookie" Williams (played by Jamie Foxx in *Redemption*) was executed here. Wife slayer and cable-news obsession Scott Peterson (played by Dean Cain in *The Perfect Hus-*

band) awaits his turn. So do 725 other men, their fate likelier to be
decided by old age, or their own hand, than by the state's glacial
appellate machinery.

Despite its notorious name and medieval atmospherics, the Q is
known within the American penal system as a rehabilitative showcase, the place to be if you want to do something productive with
your time—and not, as the old heads will say, let your time do you.
The prison hosts at least 140 programs, from Wall Street investing
to Shakespearean theater, sustained by thousands of volunteers
from the Bay Area's prosperous burbs. Which is how Frank Ruona,
then the president of an elite Marin County running club, ended
up receiving a call in 2005 from a prison administrator seeking a
coach. Ruona—a veteran of 78 marathons who was also an executive at Ghilotti Bros., a ubiquitous highway contractor—didn't see
himself ministering to felons, but when he forwarded the request
to his hundreds of fellow Tamalpa Runners, he got no response.
"So, I said, 'Yeah, I'll come over,'" Ruona recalls. "I wasn't sure
what to expect."

The 163-year-old prison, for all its educational offerings, was a
cold, clamorous tangle of concrete cellblocks, five stories tall and
ringed by razor wire—"an environment that's very degrading, very
demoralizing," Ruona had to admit—and yet he discovered that
it had also bred a small brotherhood of would-be runners "trying
their best to pay for whatever errors they've made."

His first order of business was to outfit them in decent shoes,
a task complicated by the prison's strict, sometimes cryptic dress
code. Even though he was shopping for a racially diverse bunch,
men who did not seem caught up in the gang rivalries or affilia-
tions of the segregated yard they trained on, Ruona's donations
kept getting rejected for their potential to create division: no blue
swooshes, no orange stripes, no air-bubble soles. Black shoes were
okayed, then nixed. Lately the only colors he can push through
the bureaucracy are white and gray. "I've had a couple times where
guys gave me their size, I brought in the shoes, and they didn't
fit," says Ruona, who trains with the inmates every other Monday.
"Then I found out they didn't know what their size was."

The marathoners face other obstacles, reminders of their cap-
tivity. On days when the fog rolls in, clinging to the yard like a pelt,
the track is off-limits; the sharpshooting guards in the watchtowers
need a clear view. Health scares can trigger lockdowns—chicken

pox in 2012, Legionnaires' disease in 2015—as can shank-swinging melees, the sort that have to be quelled with pepper spray and foam projectiles. Says Ruona, now 70 and hobbled by a bum knee, "You kind of roll with the punches."

On this crisp Friday morning in November, the eighth running of the San Quentin Marathon, there is no ceremony or fanfare. The only prize is a certificate, made on PowerPoint, for each participant. The men who have signed up for the race, who have submitted to the risk of injury and exhaustion and failure, did not ask for anyone to come document their efforts. A few have dates with the parole board on the horizon, but many have no illusions: they will die inside these walls.

"I'm trying to be the best person I can be, with what I have left," says 49-year-old Darren Settlemeyer, a repeat offender who will be 99 when he is eligible for release. He tried to kill himself, he says, when he first got to San Quentin. "You will do stuff in here that you wouldn't normally do, and some of it's really not good for a person to be doing." Settlemeyer stayed on meds for a decade until he started running last year. "You run the track," he says, "and you just let everything go."

The marathon was scheduled to begin at 8:00 a.m., but already Eddie DeWeaver has been trotting around the yard for an hour. He has a class to attend after lunch, "Guiding Rage into Power," and does not want to be late. "I used to think, when something happened to me, it was the end of the world," says DeWeaver, his long twisted locks glistening as if dusted with diamonds. "Now I know: just stay in the moment, focus on what you're feeling in that moment, focus on why you feel that way, what need are you not having met that has you feeling this way. That's part of the power right there: you look inside yourself for the answers."

"We're going in four and a half minutes, four and a half," Ruona hollers, checking his watch. Armed with a clipboard and spreadsheets, a Ken-Tech digital clock, and several bottles of Succeed! electrolyte capsules, he is not a "Kumbaya"-singing coach. He barks at the runners to hydrate and pace themselves, a challenge if you're emerging from a two-man cell the size of a walk-in closet. Last year an old-timer named Lee Goins ignored that advice; he collapsed at the 22-mile mark and had to be revived intravenously.

"Guys will say, 'Man, slow down, you're going too fast,'" says Michael Keeyes, who is 68 and entering his 43rd year of incarceration.

His response is a punch line: "I've got Dobermans on my heels!" He ran his first marathon in 2014, finishing in a respectable four hours and 29 minutes. To improve on that today, he has an Ensure nutritional shake poured into a plastic horseradish squeeze bottle.

"All right, good luck, gentlemen," Ruona says. "We're going in ten, nine, eight, seven, six, five, four, three, two, one—you're off!"

From the start, all eyes are on the leader, Markelle Taylor, who is loping along like a spaceman on the moon. A chiseled 43-year-old former nurse, he went to high school south of here, in Silicon Valley, and ran track on some of the very courses Ruona has trained on. But those were all sprints compared to this—his first marathon. "They call him the Gazelle," shouts an inmate who's been watching from a patio the Native Americans claim. "The Gazelle of San Quentin."

As the hours tick by, the morning grows warm. "There are a number of guys who aren't going to make it all the way," says Ruona, studying the hitches and grimaces. Defending champion and course record holder Lorinzo Hopson, 61, who has been running bare-chested with a Rambo headband torn from a T-shirt, drops out at 13 miles. "I still got it," he says, explaining that he merely wanted "to give the others a chance." Also stopping halfway is Chris Schuhmacher, an Air Force veteran who has been devising a fitness app for addicts, like himself, to help guide their recovery.

"It's getting tough, Coach, it's getting tough," moans Andrew Gazzeny, a lifer who was denied parole this year, as he lumbers around his 17th mile.

"Nice and easy," Ruona says.

After three hours, it's clear that Taylor is living up to the hype. He's got slender legs and powerful arms, and he's still running gracefully, in sodden gear, on an institutional diet, over a crazy, knotted course. Until, on his 104th lap—mile 25.75, at the crest of an astounding performance—it happens: an alarm. With one extended, gurgling blast, like a balky game-ending buzzer, it turns the marathon into an emergency drill.

"Oh hell, no!" one of the lap counters groans.

There is no sign of commotion, no explanation for the shutdown and none expected; the inmates know the routine. As Ruona anxiously watches the clock, each runner has to stop in his tracks and sit his butt on the ground, including Taylor, so close to completing the longest race of his life. He rests his hands on his knees, compliant and chagrined, for a full minute and 20 seconds. "Getting up," he says later, "oh man." But he does it, peels himself off the earth and, in one last burst of mettle, finishes what he started. Ruona, subtracting the stoppage, is almost giddy: 3:16, a new course record. Out in the free world, Taylor would have come within a minute of qualifying for the Boston Marathon.

As he walks stiffly around the yard in search of dry clothes, his neck still encrusted in salt, I ask Taylor what he'd been thinking about. "Thinking about my family, my kids, running for everybody . . . uh, my victims, everybody," he says. I inquire about his crime. He sighs and shakes his head. "I foolishly and selfishly took a life," says Taylor, who was denied parole 13 years into his sentence for second-degree murder, just weeks before the race. "I still have shame for that. That's one of my motivating factors to get out there and run."

He doesn't elaborate, and I decide for the moment not to probe. It seems almost unfair to insist that a man who has just completed such a monumental feat, who has expended everything he has, relive the most horrendous thing he's ever done. The same goes for the others: Mike Keeyes, who shaved half an hour off his time; Darren Settlemeyer, who broke down at 17 miles last year but finished in 4:04 this year; Lee Goins, who made it to 25 miles today before once again collapsing. "I never ask what they did," Ruona says. "I feel like it's not really any of my business. We all make mistakes, and some people make worse mistakes than others."

Later, when my curiosity sends me digging, I discover why it's sometimes better not to know. Almost to a man, their crimes are jaw-droppingly atrocious, the stuff of headlines and horror shows. Some of the particulars—unknown to San Quentin's general population—are so stigmatized within the prison world's peculiar hierarchy of misdeeds that to identify each runner's offense, to point out who was the child molester and who killed his own baby, would make those men targets. Several have committed crimes that the California Department of Corrections and Rehabilitation, as a matter of policy, refuses to publicly confirm.

Out on the track, there was a man who stabbed his wife, set her on fire, and blamed it on a voodoo curse—"the most heinous crime I've ever seen," said the sentencing judge. Another runner raped and strangled a young lady selling encyclopedias door to door—

"the most vicious criminal I have encountered in my career," that judge said. One marathoner tortured a friend over some stolen weed, handcuffing him to a guitar amplifier, then stripping him naked and beating him with a pool cue before stabbing him with a kitchen knife and dragging his body, rolled up in a blanket, to the trash. Less outlandish but no less violent is the man who killed two people in a mindless head-on crash—a decade after falling asleep at the wheel and causing the deaths of two others.

None of them got off easy. They have all been sent away for a very long time, to a place that could have—and, some will no doubt say, should have—broken them. And yet each woke up this morning with enough of his spirit intact to try something difficult and potentially uplifting, even if nobody else is watching or cares.

To talk about running is often to talk in platitudes, about pain and courage and limits that inevitably turn out to be self-imposed. To prove you have it in you to run 26.2 miles at San Quentin, where the limits are so tangible, is an achievement of another sort, one whose rewards, I'm inclined to believe, transcend any medal or finish-line photo. "You have to have love for yourself," Taylor tells me. "Treat yourself, take care of yourself, watch yourself, what you do, what you eat, how you act. Before, I didn't love myself. That's why it was hard for me to express that love toward other people. But I love myself now."

With the race over, San Quentin's marathoners limp from the sunshine of the yard back to the prison's warren of dank cells. Behind iron bars, they hang their drenched clothes on the webs of twine they've rigged as drying racks. Whatever approximation of freedom they've experienced today, an uncomfortable reality awaits: to save water in this unprecedented shortage, the state has limited all inmates to just three showers a week. A few of the runners, those who showered yesterday, will have to wait until to-morrow.

Lost in America

FROM BLEACHER REPORT

THE CALLS CAME around 11:00 p.m. on a cold January night in 2015, first to the Serbian boy with the little Samsung Android phone, then to the Cameroonians. "You ready? I'm gonna come tonight," the voice on the other end of the line said. "Pack your stuff."

Within hours, four teenage basketball players had hurriedly filled their gym bags with their scant possessions, including the clothes that now hung off their tall frames like cheap drapes, the result of months of having to scavenge for food from a nearby sub-urban Atlanta strip mall. They sneaked out of the drab townhouse apartments where they slept jammed into small rooms, usually on the floor and often without heat, and silently piled into a rented gray van.

They had never heard of Lake Wales, Florida, the place where the driver of the van, Gordon Gibbons, an assistant coach who had taken pity on them, was delivering them. They didn't care. It couldn't be worse than the place they were fleeing in the middle of the night—Stockbridge, Georgia, and Faith Baptist Christian Academy North. They were sure they had been conned there, and they'd had enough.

Their tribulations began as soon as they set foot in America. Rostand Ndong Essomba, a quick, 6'0" point guard from Yaounde, Cameroon, was told back home that Faith Baptist North was of-fering him a full scholarship. He jumped through all the bureau-cratic hoops, procuring a coveted I-20 form that grants permission for international students to apply for a non-immigrant visa to enter the country and study in the U.S.

But when Rostand arrived at Hartsfield-Jackson International Airport in Atlanta in October 2014, he says Faith Baptist North's founder, George Flint, took one look at him and told the 17-year-old African he was too short. Rostand says that Flint told him that if he wanted to stay in America, he had to cough up $2,000. "Where's the money?" Flint allegedly asked his new recruit.

Franck Tsoungui, Rostand's slender, sharpshooting 6'7" countryman, had left a stable situation at a prep school in Maine five months earlier, enticed by Flint's promises of a new program playing a powerhouse schedule that would expose his talents to Division I coaches. What Franck got was a merry-go-round of missed meals and canceled games.

Mahmadou Ngoucheme had only been at Faith Baptist North for six weeks, but he packed plenty of suffering into that time. He was seven feet tall, but that was about the only thing he had going for him as a U.S. hoops prospect. He was raw, which was a nice way of saying he possessed few offensive skills, and he had a gentle disposition off the court—and on it.

What he really wanted was an American education, but after arriving in December 2014, Mahmadou had yet to attend a single class. Faith Baptist North had held no classes since mid-November.

Stefan Nakic-Vojnovic grew jaded early. The 6'5" shooting guard from Belgrade, Serbia, had been in Georgia the longest, since July, meaning that he had heard more broken promises than any of them. First there was the matter of the Faith Baptist North campus. There wasn't one, despite the brochure Faith Baptist North circulated to starry-eyed teens around the world via the Internet, with photos of a beautiful lakeside compound and state-of-the-art athletic facilities.

The real Faith Baptist North was a football field and a rented gym housing a few unused classrooms behind a small church in Stockbridge, south of Atlanta. Stefan lived first in the basement of Flint's two-story home in Conyers, a few miles from Stockbridge, with as many as 20 other boys, then in a run-down apartment building, where he and some Serbian players pooled what money they had to buy a tiny electric heater to fend off the cold.

During the few weeks of classes held in the fall, Stefan says he took math tests for football players and laughed as Flint lectured students on avoiding bad people. Much of the rest of the time, he says he slept on cold floors and scrounged for food and free Wi-Fi hotspots. He sums up Faith Baptist North in three words: "a big nothing."

The van ride promised something better. For a little while, anyway. About five hours into the seven-hour trip to Lake Wales, a town in central Florida, Stefan received another call from a Serb who was at Faith Baptist North. Flint now was aware of the getaway, and in response, the founder who referred to himself as a preacher and a man of God had apparently told people he'd canceled the four teens' I-20s, rendering their student visas invalid.

"We knew that we were basically illegal now," Stefan says. The boys all had the same thought: "What are we gonna do?"

Over the past six months, a *Bleacher Report* investigation into Faith Baptist Christian Academy North has revealed how the startup school ended up crushing dreams, squandering families' savings, and disrupting lives. The four boys who fled Faith Baptist North for Lake Wales are now witnesses in a widening federal investigation into human trafficking, allowed to remain in the country under the Trafficking Victims Protection Act.

Their flight that January night set off a chain of events that led to the resignation of the Lake Wales High basketball coach and federal raids of Faith Baptist North, which has since closed, and its sister campus, Faith Baptist Christian Academy in Ludowici, Georgia, a four-hour drive southeast of Atlanta.

In a letter sent by the U.S. Department of Homeland Security to the federal Citizenship and Immigration Services agency on behalf of one of the boys, Faith Baptist's south campus in Ludowici was described as an Immigration and Customs Enforcement (ICE)–certified school that "worked in conjunction with a noncertified northern campus to recruit, exploit and defraud hundreds of international and domestic students."

George Flint, who founded Faith Baptist North, declined multiple interview requests from *Bleacher Report* by telephone, text, and mail, saying in a text message in late May, "I really have no comment at this time."

However, he has denied any wrongdoing to others interviewed by *Bleacher Report,* including Matthew Sellars, the athletic director at Faith Baptist's south campus in Ludowici. Sellars recalls seeing Flint at a JUCO jamboree in October 2015, seven months after

Faith Baptist North closed. "The first thing out of his mouth was, 'I had nothing to do with that; whatever it is they said, it isn't true,'" Sellars says.

Bleacher Report has learned that the probe, which includes agents from Homeland Security's Atlanta, Savannah, and Tampa offices, has expanded its scope beyond Faith Baptist Christian Academy's two campuses to include potential trafficking cases elsewhere in the Southeast.

On May 16, law enforcement officials in Alamance County, North Carolina, arrested Aris Hines, a former Flint associate who sometimes coached players from Faith Baptist North and worked briefly with Flint in a failed attempt to start another prep school, on state law charges of obstruction of justice and obtaining property by false pretense.

Alamance County Sheriff Terry Johnson told *Bleacher Report* the charges are part of an investigation into human trafficking of athletes. He said the FBI, ICE, Homeland Security, including Homeland's Atlanta office, and the U.S. Department of State have entered the investigation, which involves a 15-year-old Nigerian basketball and football player and three girls from the Dominican Republic whom Hines allegedly attempted to enroll in a North Carolina high school with false documents and expired visas.

The sheriff's office said the search warrants in the case are sealed and police reports are not available to the public because of the investigation. Hines, who did not return messages left by *Bleacher Report,* denied wrongdoing in an interview with WTVD, a North Carolina TV station.

Depending on the source, the Faith Baptist fiasco was either a cascading failure that started with good intentions or a corrupt, cynical grab for money and sports glory at the expense of gullible foreign athletes and their families. It also reveals that in the U.S., there are still Good Samaritans willing to help kids in trouble. Thanks to the actions of the Lake Wales community, and one family in particular, the four Faith Baptist North players still have a chance at an American education.

Anyone familiar with modern prep school sports agrees the system is rife with problems. A number of American prep schools effectively operate as AAU teams with a "school" around them, coaches say.

For decades, the NCAA has tried to crack down on "diploma mill" prep schools designed to make academically struggling athletes eligible for college ball. The incentives to run such programs are strong. Successful programs not only enjoy prestige for winning and turning out star players, they also can earn money from sneaker company sponsorships.

There are also age-old stories of prep and AAU coaches paying handlers for access to players and getting kickbacks for sending players to certain colleges or steering them to certain professional agents. But the international component has added a new dimension—a massive, global pool of athletes to be exploited.

"This whole prep school thing is an absolute scam," says one veteran basketball coach who asked not to be identified. "There are literally hundreds of these bad situations throughout the country."

These situations can appear attractive. "Corrupt schools can put up a front; they may look credible on the surface, but once we peel back the layers, we find irregularities," says Lou Farrell, director for the Student and Exchange Visitor Program (SEVP), the arm of ICE that certifies and monitors U.S. schools that enroll international students on an F or M visa. "Schools and individuals who try to manipulate the student visa system for personal gain are being held accountable for their actions."

While human trafficking cases involving sexual exploitation of women are well documented, trafficking of athletes is a subset of labor exploitation that has only recently shown up on the radar of activists and government agencies. But it is a crime nonetheless, says Katherine Kaufka Walts, director of the Center for the Human Rights of Children at Loyola University in Chicago.

"It's the recruiting, it's the moving, it's the harboring and financially benefiting from the involuntary servitude, debt bondage, peonage, or slavery of another person by force or by coercion," Kaufka Walts says. "The common thread is the economic exploitation of someone else's body, whether it's to perform labor in a field or to perform labor on the court."

At the heart of the U.S. athlete trafficking issue is the quest for I-20s, the necessary form for student visa status. The latest quarterly statistics released by SEVP reveal 1.2 million international students studying in U.S. elementary schools, high schools, colleges, and vocational schools. It is unclear how many are athletes—students aren't required to reveal their athletic ambitions to immigration agents—but prep school rosters across the country are dotted with, and sometimes laden with, international players.

The come-ons prep schools use to attract these players can be comical. Until recently, the website of the Evelyn Mack Academy, or EMA, a Charlotte prep school stocked with international athletes, featured a photo of an imposing domed structure fronted by Ionic columns. The building didn't belong to EMA but to MIT —the Massachusetts Institute of Technology.

But serious national security issues come into play. Even before 9/11, when some of the foreign nationals who brought down the Twin Towers trained to fly planes in the U.S. due in part to improperly issued visas, security experts worried about bogus student visas being a portal for terrorists.

There are also health concerns: some players arrive in the country without proper immunizations, and their schools never bother to vaccinate them. Mahmadou, Rostand, Franck, and Stefan didn't receive their mandated shots until they arrived at Lake Wales High.

Those are worst-case scenarios, but the everyday abuses are bad enough. Whether through incompetence, ambition, or, as several international students allege, corruption, schools like Faith Baptist North can leave aspiring athletes out on the street in a foreign land, disillusioned, vulnerable, and illegal.

The Georgia school is rare in that it has precipitated a federal investigation, but as the North Carolina investigation reveals, there are other schools and individuals allegedly abusing the I-20 system, potentially leaving students in deplorable conditions with little or no way out.

"I would try every day to get back in my country," says Mahmadou. "Because in Georgia, I didn't go to school. I didn't sleep good, eat good. Nobody to tell me how I would do. My first plan was to get back to my country. Because I was . . ."

He pauses, struggling to find the word. "Lost."

As dawn broke over the citrus groves in Lake Wales on April 22, 2016, Lora Watts Donley was in an urgent care office pleading for antibiotics and anything else that would knock out the walking pneumonia the doctor had diagnosed. She felt like hell, but there was no time for coddling a 102.7 degree fever. Lora rarely failed to complete a task, and this one was no different.

It had been more than a year since the four young basketball players, basically homeless in a foreign country, had landed in the Donley home near Lake Wales. Now, Lora was literally reversing their course, taking Mahmadou and Stefan to a junior college showcase in the Atlanta suburb of Norcross, nine hours away.

Things had gone well for the most part in the year since the boys had fled Faith Baptist North. The Donleys took them in because they believe in helping others in need, and because they have the resources to do it. They go to church, and it's right to share blessings.

David, Lora's husband, runs a family citrus-growing operation and owns land throughout central Florida. Lora's family lives nearby and owns a blueberry packing house and floral manufacturing business.

Thanks to the Donleys, the boys were finally living the kind of American life they had seen on television and read about on the Internet. They had their own space in a beautiful home, nice clothes, plenty of food, good schools to attend, and sports teams to play on. The Donleys' generosity included helping arrange for Stefan's mother to come to Florida from Serbia to visit her son.

"Those kids lucked out," says Donna Dunson, the Lake Wales High principal.

But the kids were still witnesses in a federal investigation, allowed in the country as long as investigators found them useful. Homeland Security agents told Lora the investigation could last two years, but nobody knew for certain, and their witness status was set to expire at the end of March 2016. After that, they would be vulnerable, much the way they were in the van the year before, when George Flint claimed to have canceled their I-20s.

Lora and David were keenly attuned to any change in the boys' behavior, and it was clear that the ordeal they had endured in Georgia—the lack of food, the threats of deportation, the alienation—had taken a toll. The boys were homesick, yet worried about whether they could continue their educations in the U.S. "They were crashing on me, losing morale," Lora says.

Lora figured the surefire way to keep the boys on track was to find them college scholarships and the I-20s that came with them. That way, even if the government dropped the investigation and no longer needed them as witnesses, they wouldn't be deported.

Lora had already succeeded with Franck, who had graduated

from high school by the time he arrived in Lake Wales and earned a JUCO basketball scholarship from State College of Florida in Bradenton.

For Rostand, Mahmadou, and Stefan, however, time was running out, and tensions were high.

Propped up by antibiotics, massive doses of ibuprofen, and a sackful of vitamins, Lora loaded Stefan and Mahmadou into the SUV along with Stefan's mother, Lola, and Lora's daughter, Kaylee, and began the long drive north. The destination: the All-American Showcase, an event for unsigned high school, prep, JUCO, and international prospects.

As they checked into their hotel and the boys registered for the tournament, Lora described her mission in a Facebook post:

> ✓ *Basketball Showcase weekend: must get the boys a scholarship.* ✓ *Three days of being sick: bed is not an option.* ✓ *Predawn urgent care trip: 2 shots in my butt and a bag of prescriptions.* ✓ *9 hour road trip through a monsoon with fever: we have arrived.* ✓ *God please send the right people this weekend. You know what everyone has gone through to get here.*

Rostand landed in America on October 24, 2014, at exactly 3:35 p.m.; he checked his phone to mark the moment. He arrived with a small suitcase, two pairs of shoes, and an inconspicuous belt bag his mom had given him in which he kept his documents and $150 in cash. But he felt rich. This, he thought, would be the start of a new life, a chance to gain an education in the United States (annual per capita income, $55,230, according to the World Bank) and rise above his station in Cameroon (annual per capita income, $1,350).

Rostand's first love wasn't basketball. Soccer mattered more. He grew up playing it, and by the age of 14, a local manager offered to take him to Europe to try out with a professional club. But African kids are well aware that unscrupulous managers have promised soccer contracts in Europe and then discarded the kids with no way for them to get back home.

"My dad said no," Rostand recalls. "He didn't want it to happen."

Basketball in the U.S. was different. "I didn't think anything could happen like that in the United States—never," he says. "If you have a chance to go to the United States, you should take it."

American basketball had bestowed opportunity on dozens of players from Cameroon in the past decade. A guy Rostand knew, Landry Nnoko, was playing at Clemson University on a full scholarship. Joel Embiid was the third overall pick in the 2014 NBA draft. And it was another Cameroonian success story, former UCLA star and NBA veteran Luc Richard Mbah a Moute, who helped pave Rostand's path to Atlanta that October afternoon.

Rostand shone at Mbah a Moute's annual summer camp in Cameroon the previous year, earning him an invitation to the NBA's 2013 Basketball Without Borders Camp in South Africa. Out of 64 players, Rostand says he was among 20 chosen for the all-star game. He met and took a photo with his idol, Cleveland Cavaliers point guard Kyrie Irving, and heard some coaches say he had "a good chance" to play and get an education at a U.S. university.

For nearly a year, though, Rostand heard nothing more. That's not surprising. In the hunt for international talent, big men are the priority. For whatever reason, the U.S. high school system is producing few quality post players. And those rare top-tier prospects—such as Anthony Davis and Jahlil Okafor—are quickly gobbled up by NCAA powerhouses.

Meanwhile, the non-elite college programs have begun spanning the globe for height, with Africa being a favorite focus. Many prep schools also jumped into the fray, stocking their rosters with tall international players in hopes of moving them up the ladder. But African backcourt prospects are rare.

Rostand didn't know this, of course, when a Cameroonian teacher who would teach briefly at Faith Baptist North asked him if he would be interested in a scholarship to the new prep school. He leaped at the chance.

The teenager's American dream lasted about as long as the walk to customs. Officials told him his I-20 wasn't in their files. For six hours, he waited in the airport, not knowing if they were going to put him right back on a plane to Africa.

When Rostand finally cleared immigration and met his new coach face-to-face, he says Flint turned to a colleague and said, "Really? Look at him. He's not even tall."

Not long after, Rostand says Flint demanded $2,000. "I opened my bag and showed him the full scholarship that I have," Rostand recalls in his French-accented English. He insisted he wasn't supposed to pay anything. Flint's response, according to Rostand: "Okay, that means you want to go back to Cameroon, right?"

Rostand's parents had all but liquidated their savings for their son's plane ticket, but the teenager relented. "I was just getting out of the issue with my papers, and I was so afraid," Rostand says. "I say, 'Okay, okay, okay. I will give you the money.'"

He contacted his family, who somehow rounded up and wired $500, enough to appease Flint. As bad as Rostand's first day was, his stay in the States was about to get much worse. He was not alone.

Over the past 15 years, dozens of sports-centric prep schools have opened in the U.S. Increasingly, these "Bootleg Prep" schools, as one coach calls them, seek to fill seats by attracting top athletes from overseas, who in turn attract less skilled players and regular students who are willing to pay hefty tuition.

The goal is to become the elite Montverde Academy, near Orlando, Florida, which helped propel Australia's Ben Simmons to the top of the NBA draft board and which has a significant number of international students paying the annual boarding school tuition of $49,600.

While Montverde was founded in 1912 and has a solid academic reputation to go along with its top-level sports program, Faith Baptist North was the new school on the block in the summer of 2014. And to the four federal witnesses, it looked like a perfect opportunity.

The photos in the Faith Baptist North web brochure were the clincher. "It was beautiful," says Stefan. "When [Flint] said that he offers me a full ride and he sent me the pictures of the 'campus,' it didn't take my family long to say yes."

The boys did whatever it took to get there, and Flint obliged them. In addition to offering them full scholarships, Flint supplied them with I-20s signed by officials from Faith Baptist's south campus in Ludowici. After the African teacher helped recruit Rostand, the player headed for the U.S. embassy in Yaounde with his I-20 in hand. He was interviewed by officials there and granted a student visa.

Franck came via a different route. He was already in the U.S., playing at Lee Academy in Maine. But he wasn't on any college's recruiting list. Gibbons, a former Division II college coach who had retired in the Stockbridge area, had agreed to help coach at

Faith Baptist North in its inaugural season, and he was looking for players on short notice. Gibbons saw potential in a video of Franck, and soon the player was headed south.

Mahmadou had played against Rostand in some Cameroon national tournaments, but he was just learning the game. He was a seven-footer, though, so Faith Baptist North got in touch with him through one of the "handlers" or "recruiters" who help a player find a school, or vice versa, and coordinate the player's passage to America. The Cameroonian recruiter asked Mahmadou to go to the embassy and get a visa.

It didn't matter that it was already December and the season was well under way. On December 6, Mahmadou landed at Washington Dulles International Airport, and even though he spoke almost no English, he found his way to a bus station and took a 20-hour ride to Atlanta.

Stefan's decision was a family affair—and a family sacrifice. His older brother, Filip, was also a good basketball player, but the family could afford to send only one of the boys to the States. The other would have to stay in Belgrade to help with the family business, a café.

At Filip's insistence, they sent Stefan. "I can never be grateful enough for him giving me the chance to try to succeed in what I love to do," Stefan says of his brother.

With help from a Belgrade-based recruiting agency, Stefan received his I-20 from Faith Baptist. On July 3, his mom's birthday, he was on a plane to the U.S. to meet George Flint.

Flint is a stocky, round-faced 42-year-old with an undeniable love of sports, an entrepreneur's persistence, and, when he wants to talk, a preacher's eloquence.

In recent years Flint, who now runs a business called Goshen Financial Services, Inc., in suburban Atlanta, has focused on his son's fledgling basketball career. Flint coached his son's AAU teams throughout the boy's teens and kept moving him to different high schools in hopes of helping him land a Division I scholarship.

Jonathan Morgans, an Iraq War veteran, got to know Flint on the AAU circuit. Morgans had coached as an assistant at Faith Baptist in Ludowici in 2012 and '13, and says Flint frequently discussed taking an even bigger role in his son's career.

By the spring of 2014, Morgans says Flint started talking about opening a school and surrounding his son with top-flight talent. He asked Morgans for help. In May 2014, Morgans set up a meeting between Flint and his former employers at Faith Baptist's Ludowici campus.

Flint was interested in starting up a "sister campus" in Atlanta and using Faith Baptist's certification to issue I-20s to international players. In the previous few years, the Ludowici school had begun to take in foreign students, mostly baseball and basketball players from the Dominican Republic, plus a few from Africa, says Matthew Sellars, the athletic director at Faith Baptist's south campus and the son of the school's founder, Pastor Terry Sellars.

"Basically, we had been playing several schools in some national events, and it just seemed like every team we played, the kids on the other team weren't speaking English," Matthew Sellars says. "I was like, 'What's going on?' And so I started talking to some of my coaching friends, and they said, 'Yes, well we started getting exchange students.' . . . So we started it here."

Now, Flint offered a chance to expand that mission. "I didn't know Flint from Adam," Matthew Sellars says, but he introduced him to his dad. "And they kind of hit it off because [Flint] was pretending he was a pastor and all this Christian aspect."

While Matthew Sellars says Flint "was trying to do something good," he says his dad was taken advantage of. "He is trusting until obviously you bury him," he says. "He wants to be friendly, and he got conned." Pastor Terry Sellars declined to comment for this story, referring *Bleacher Report* to his son.

Soon, Flint and the Sellars family were in business together. It didn't matter that Flint had no school building, no curriculum, no teachers, no place to house students, no experience running a prep school, and no SEVP certification. It didn't matter that it was May, and he wanted to open the school in September. He had an AAU team, and he had access to I-20s. In a few months, he had eager teenagers from around the world coming to play for him.

In July and August, Stefan practiced with Flint's AAU team, played some games, and heard assurances from Flint that the school was going to be great as athletes trickled in. But when it came time for school to open, classes weren't held at the gleaming, whitewashed campus in the brochures.

Instead, Flint leased the gym, playing field, and some classroom space behind New Hope Christian Ministries in Stockbridge.

While football and basketball practices started on the site in August, classes did not. "They said school starts September 1," Stefan says, "and like three weeks passed, and we still didn't go to school."

There was no permanent lodging either. In the fall, several basketball players, including Stefan, stayed at Flint's house. The rest bunked at what was then an EconoLodge in Stockbridge. "He populated like half the hotel," Stefan says. Flint's house and the motel were 30-minute drives to the makeshift Conyers "campus" at New Hope, longer when traffic was bad.

When classes finally started in late September, players shuttled between their lodging and the gym in a cast-off yellow school bus Flint had somehow picked up from Canada.

The student body formed a motley crew: more than two dozen basketball players, most from overseas; 35 or 40 football players, mostly American, but including Chidi Valentine-Okeke, a Nigerian-born blue-chip offensive line prospect who now plays at LSU; a couple of Serbian soccer players, who, when they realized Faith Baptist North wouldn't field a soccer team, joined the football team to place-kick and punt; and three girls—a Serb and two Nigerians who left home to play hoops for a team that never materialized.

Scheduling was a joke. Practices would be delayed, and delayed again, and finally called off. The football team's coaches were replaced in October, and the squad kept canceling games before the season ended.

School was no better. Some days the busload of students would get all the way to the New Hope building and then turn around, students and coaches say. No school today. Once, they canceled school because it was raining, other times because the heat didn't work. Another time, according to Morgans, they halted classes for a couple of weeks because the three teachers Flint had brought in walked off the job.

"One of the teachers, he said, 'They ain't paying us,' and then it just spun out of control from there," Morgans says. "And then they came back, and the kids were in school again."

At first, there was food. And maybe even some hope that the whole school idea might work. "It was exciting," says Morgans, who often shuttled players between lodging and practices. "We were living in that hotel in Stockbridge. We had three meals a day. Everything was good."

After several weeks, though, "The food started slacking off," Morgans says. "It wasn't the same quality; it started to become bologna-and-cheese sandwiches, stuff like that."

Within a couple of months, Morgans says, Flint could no longer afford the motel, especially after several of the football players left mid-semester. So in November he moved a group of Nigerians to a house several miles away, and another group of Africans and Serbs, including Stefan, into three townhouse-style apartments behind a big-box retail strip in Stockbridge.

Mahmadou, in his limited English, concisely described life in the apartments: "No heat. No food."

After his insulting welcome at the airport, Rostand says he had to endure neglect every night—no bed, sheets, blankets, or heat. "I was sleeping with my head on my baggage."

In Cameroon, he says, "I lived in a normal house, sleeping in beds, like a normal kid, living a normal life."

Meanwhile, according to the boys, Flint frequently threatened to pull players' I-20s and constantly demanded money from Rostand and Stefan, despite having promised them full scholarships. (The amount, $25,680 for a 10-month term, was also noted on their I-20 forms.) After giving Flint several payments of a few hundred dollars, both say they simply refused, effectively calling Flint's bluff on threats to send them back across the Atlantic.

Mahmadou regretted his trip from Africa almost immediately. For his first two weeks in America, he lived in Flint's house with no adult there. The power went out for two days; he slept in the dark.

The French-speaking Cameroonian had little knowledge of Western appliances. One day, Stefan was on his phone and noticed black smoke billowing out of the kitchen. "He had put two pieces of bread in the microwave," Stefan says, "and he put it on like five minutes."

"I couldn't read the instructions," Mahmadou says. "They were in English." They laugh about it now, but he nearly set the place on fire.

The worst was December, when Flint and his wife, Maria, left to take Faith Baptist North's national team to play in the Under Armour tournament in San Diego and the Tarkanian Classic in Las Vegas. The boys remember the Flints dropping off two boxes of pancake mix and a small package of rice to the apartments. This was supposed to last two weeks. "It was gone in like a day," Stefan says.

Attempts to reach Maria Flint through her cell phone and her email address listed on the Faith Baptist Christian Academy North, Inc., filings with the Georgia Secretary of State were unsuccessful.

The already skinny teenagers steadily lost weight. Rostand shed 10 pounds in three months. Mahmadou dropped seven pounds in a little over a month. And Stefan saw his weight drop from 200 pounds to 175 from July through December. At one point, Mahmadou nearly passed out after a four-hour practice. "I'd only had one McChicken to eat," he says.

Aleksandar Cosic, another Serbian player who wound up leaving Faith Baptist North shortly after the Lake Wales boys, confirms the dire circumstances. "We were not getting food," he says.

Nigerian players were in particularly bad shape. "Those guys were losing weight," Cosic says. "One guy was 6'10", 240 or 250, but by the end of the year he lost 40 to 50 pounds."

The two dozen or so boys living in the cul-de-sac apartments survived by combining resources. Stefan talked his parents into sending him $30 a week, which he pooled with his fellow Serbs to buy groceries. He and Franck cooked for the group.

Then they would go to a CiCi's Pizza in a nearby strip mall and wait until closing time, when the manager would give them the leftovers from the buffet. Days were filled using the Wi-Fi at Starbucks and hanging out at LA Fitness, where the boys circulated free guest passes among the group and would sneak each other in.

Complaints about the conditions in Stockbridge and Conyers began to trickle south to the Sellars family in Ludowici throughout the fall. Dominican kids in Stockbridge began talking to their countrymen at Faith Baptist's south campus, says Matthew Sellars. The DR players in Stockbridge reported sleeping on the floor, and that the power would cut off at night, and that they weren't getting enough food.

"A lot of times, in programs like this, kids complain all the time," Sellars says, admitting that he hadn't personally visited the campus and had only seen it depicted on Flint's website. "So I played it off."

But the stories kept coming, now from Nigerians and Serbians at the north campus. Sellars says he confronted Flint about the players on the south school's I-20s, telling him, "You're treating them bad, and it's going to make us look bad." He says Flint responded by saying, "No, man. We're doing the right thing."

Pastor Sellars sent Flint a cease-and-desist letter on October 31, 2014, cutting official ties with the north campus, and relocated 15 kids out of Stockbridge to Ludowici.

Sellars says the south campus rescinded the I-20s for the students who didn't transfer to Ludowici—which would have meant the remaining teens were technically illegal from November on, long before Stefan and the boys worried about their status on the ride to Lake Wales.

"We told George, 'Look, by this date, we're terminating the I-20s,' so they probably did have a terminated I-20 as a result of his school not having SEVIS status," Sellars says of the Student and Exchange Visitor Information System the government uses to track students, adding that Flint would not have had the authority or access to SEVIS to cancel the I-20s himself.

While the living conditions and the dispute with the sister campus led to Faith Baptist North's downfall, the lack of coursework proved the final straw.

"The first problem was to go to school," Mahmadou says. "I asked Coach George every day, 'When do we start school?' And he said, 'The next week.'"

And every week, through November, December, and January, there was still no school. There wasn't much basketball either. From the end of November through mid-January 2015, the schedule grew littered with cancellations—until there were more cancellations than actual competitions.

By the second week of January 2015, two of Flint's coaches, Morgans and Gibbons, decided Faith Baptist North was untenable, both for them and the students still there. They hatched a plan to move players to schools where they could actually attend classes.

While Morgans was seen as Flint's right-hand man, responsible for driving players to and from practice and trying to maintain some order in their living quarters, Gibbons was a retired coach who had won more than 450 games at NCAA Division II schools Florida Southern and Clayton State, in Georgia, and who was inducted into the Florida Association of Basketball Coaches "Court of Legends."

From the beginning, Morgans says, Flint ignored his employees when he wasn't micromanaging them. "You've got Gordon Gibbons, who's a Hall of Fame college coach," Morgans says, "and you're telling him he don't know what he's talking about?"

Morgans says the only reason he and Gibbons stayed as long as they did was "to make sure nothing happened to them kids."

Gibbons, especially, felt a responsibility to the half-dozen students—including Franck and Cosic—whom he had recruited to play at Faith Baptist North through his web of college and high school connections. Through Franck, Gibbons had gotten to know the other Cameroonians, Rostand and Mahmadou. Gibbons didn't recruit Stefan, but he had grown close to him as he coached him on the high school team.

"We were all loving Coach Gibbons, who was a really great coach, and he was really caring about us," Rostand says. Stefan says Gibbons was the only adult in Georgia telling them the truth. So when the coach pulled Stefan aside during a practice in mid-January and said, "There's no future for you here, kid," and told him he knew a coach at a public school in Lake Wales, the player replied: "Take me tomorrow."

The Lake Wales boys weren't the only players to bail on Faith Baptist North. Just about the time the boys were leaving, a group of Serbian immigrant families in the Atlanta area banded together to take several other Serbs from Faith Baptist North into their homes. Dragan Milakovic, a mining expert who lives near Atlanta, saw the boys' living conditions.

"They got some macaroni in the morning . . . that's all for them all day. They [the Flints] didn't share heating, they didn't share nothing."

By contrast, Milakovic and his wife took in a pair of twins who came to Faith Baptist to play soccer, as well as Cosic. They helped Cosic transfer to Faith Baptist's south campus so he could graduate in the spring, and Gibbons helped him get a college scholarship to Union University in Jackson, Tennessee.

Gibbons was reluctant to be quoted for this story, saying he didn't want to criticize Flint or Faith Baptist. He says he believes Flint had good intentions.

But he does offer this explanation for pulling the kids out of the school: "My role in moving players from Faith Baptist North to other schools was simply because I thought they needed to get in school so that they could finish a second semester, and I was not sure that was going to happen," he says. "I found some schools that would take them."

Moreover, "I just felt like there wouldn't be a basketball environment for them," he says. "That was what they came here for."

When Gibbons called Randy Lee in Lake Wales and asked if he might help him out, Lee reflexively said yes. His late father, Jim, had been Gibbons's best friend when Gibbons coached at Florida Southern in Lakeland, and Randy had grown up watching Gibbons's teams and had grown close to the coach.

As the head basketball coach at Lake Wales High, a public charter school about 30 miles from Lakeland, Lee was in a position to help. He even had experience with international students.

Lee's previous job was at Tennessee Temple, a small Christian college in Chattanooga. While there, Lee and his father started a now-shuttered business called Global Prep LLC, using the college's K-12 academy as a landing spot for international players who paid tuition to hone their skills and academics.

Lee wanted to import Global Prep to Lake Wales and tried to sell Lake Wales principal Donna Dunson on the idea, presenting her with a 50-page business plan during the 2012–13 school year. Dunson listened but passed.

"I thought it could be a conflict of interest," Dunson says.

It was against this backdrop that four tall kids showed up on the Lake Wales campus, seemingly from out of nowhere.

To the boys from Faith Baptist North, Lake Wales was a vast upgrade. They went to real classes every day. Though they couldn't be part of the Lake Wales team, Lee allowed them to practice basketball. Most important, says Rostand, "People were caring about us."

But there were still big problems. When they arrived from Georgia, the boys moved into a small house leased to the girlfriend of one of Lee's assistant coaches. The boys shared the space with two single mothers, who had four young children between them. In a rough neighborhood, the house was crowded, and the boys slept in the living room.

"I was sharing a couch with a seven-footer," Stefan says. "It didn't really work."

After a week of going to class, Rostand missed the next five school days with migraine headaches. "I was feeling really bad," he says.

His absence triggered a visit by the Lake Wales High dean of students, Stacey Butcher, who immediately told them to pack their things. In a later report issued by the school, the living conditions in the house were described as "deplorable," which Lee disputes.

In any case, the boys were on the move again. Now, so was the school. A call for help went out to the Lake Wales community, and parents in the school responded immediately. One parent knew of a vacant unfurnished house; another family, the Donleys, loaded up a trailer with furniture for the boys.

What David and Lora Donley gave the boys was reassurance, something they hadn't felt in months. Rostand recalls the first day he met Lora, helping her unload the truck full of furniture and wondering about this woman who looked too young to be a mother.

"That day was funny," he says. "She wasn't knowing me, she wasn't knowing anything about us, and she said, 'Don't worry. We will do something for you guys.' And I never forgot about it. Never."

Rostand's deep voice and generally implacable facial expressions tend to hide his emotions. But they're not up to the job when he's talking about Lora. "Since that day," he says, "I felt like I met with an angel here in the United States."

A March 4 visit to Lake Wales High by Jon Morgans, Flint's former right-hand man, triggered an investigation into how the boys had ended up at the school, first by detectives from the Polk County Sheriff's Office, and then federal Homeland Security agents.

Morgans says he was only there to see how the boys were doing, and that he went to the school office and was invited into Lee's classroom. He says he chatted briefly with the boys, who Morgans says asked to see him.

Lake Wales administrators saw it differently. In the school's official report to the Florida High School Athletic Association, Dunson says, "I was alerted there was a man from the Georgia school on campus, and the boys did not want to see him."

Lora Donley happened to drop in on the boys that day. As they sat in her car eating lunch, she says, one of them slumped down in the seat to avoid being seen by Morgans, telling her, "He's probably here to get us."

Events escalated quickly. Dunson questioned "why a total

stranger from the Georgia school would show up on our campus," and why Lee would suddenly help enroll four basketball players in the school without telling her personally. Lee says he had notified other school administrators and assumed Dunson knew.

The principal wondered if Lee was trying to build his old dream of Global Prep using these students from the Georgia school. Lee denies he had any plans to use the Faith Baptist North kids as part of an athletics program. "Our goal from the start, Coach Gibbons and myself, was to get them educationally in school," Lee says.

Dunson disagreed. Less than a week after Morgans's visit, she put Lee on administrative leave, and soon after that asked for his resignation. "Randy said, 'I'm just trying to help them because this school is closing,' and it may be true," Dunson says, referring to Faith Baptist North. "But three Cameroonians and a Serbian? What's going on?"

Lake Wales had opened an in-house inquiry into eligibility issues with the new students. Within days, her school was part of a much bigger probe.

On March 9, after having been alerted by Donley to Morgans's appearance at the school and the boys' situation, the sheriff's detectives and state workers from the Department of Children and Families questioned Dunson and her staff at the high school. "I'm glad you're here," Dunson told them. "Help us solve this."

On the morning of March 25, it was Homeland Security's turn. Agents took the four boys out of school to interview them about Faith Baptist. Within hours, the federal government would step in.

Nothing much was happening in Ludowici, Georgia, on the afternoon of March 25, 2015, as Matthew Sellars coached his Faith Baptist Crusaders through a baseball practice. He noticed a couple of news crews on the street, but he thought they were there to get video of his squad, which had some talent that spring.

"And then, boom, all these cars pulled up," he says. "And these guys got out—looked like anybody you'd pass on the street. Well, they were all federal agents from Homeland Security."

Five in all, Sellars says. They searched the Ludowici campus founded by his father, the pastor, in 1979. A couple of dozen kids were living in the gym building and in adjacent rooms built onto the back. Fire officials shut down the gym for code violations and removed 30 students who were living there, placing them with the Red Cross. All with the cameras rolling.

Aleksandar Cosic, who had seen terrible conditions at Faith Baptist North, was there when law enforcement raided the Ludowici campus. Faith Baptist's south campus wasn't as bad as Faith Baptist North, but it was no picnic either. Cosic says dozens of teens lived in poorly ventilated rooms that surrounded the basketball court, and that he lived in a room that had no power for much of the day and night. Food was limited to two meals per day, according to Cosic.

On the day of the raid, Cosic spent more than two hours answering investigators' questions about both schools. "Then they made us all, like 30 to 40 of us, sit on the bleachers," he recalls. Officers read off a list of names of students who supposedly had I-20s from the Ludowici campus. "There was like 60 names, and there was only like 30 of us there."

He recognized some of the names and knew that those players were in schools in North Carolina, Florida, elsewhere in Georgia—but not in Ludowici. "I remember the agents were really surprised when they were reading the names," Cosic says. "If they read your name, you put your hand up. But there was nobody to raise those hands, because they were not there."

The agents were learning what dozens of foreign athletes already knew. An I-20 from Faith Baptist in Ludowici didn't necessarily mean you attended school there.

A week later, 240 miles to the northwest, Homeland agents were searching George Flint's home and the New Hope church property that had served as Faith Baptist North's campus.

When a call went out to find furniture for four international students who'd hit some hard times and needed help, Lora Donley answered like she always does. "That phone call changed my family's life," she says.

When they met the boys, they were all polite enough. "It wasn't until we started asking them questions that I realized something wasn't right," Lora says.

At the mention of Georgia, they shut down completely. Stefan explains: "I was very suspicious, 'cause I mean I come from a country like where everybody's corrupted, and everybody just tries to look after themselves," he says. "There's not really people like her who just help people because they love to."

The charity only grew. After Morgans's visit spooked the school, everyone decided the boys needed an adult around. The Donleys stepped up. They had a nice house, with a swimming pool and a basketball court on five acres—plus a game room with a pool table. And an iron gate at the head of the driveway that nobody could get through. It was like George Flint's brochure, only real.

Plus, there were kids. The Donleys had two teenage boys, Brandon and Chris, and two younger girls, Kaylee and Ally. Not one of them flinched at taking in the tall boys. "They had open arms," David says.

They were already a close family. Now they were just a much bigger one. Still, the boys had issues. Most pressing was their immigration status, and their role in what would soon be a sprawling investigation. But there was also the matter of their athletic careers.

Lora wanted the boys to have a chance to pursue their hoop dreams, a tricky proposition to be sure. Franck had exhausted his high school eligibility; there was no way he could play at Lake Wales, or even attend classes. He had already graduated.

"He was devastated," Lora says. "He asked me if he could just go to classes anyway because he liked school so much." To stay in the States, he had to find a college willing to take him.

Mahmadou was an even tougher case. He had no sports eligibility left at Lake Wales. He needed a prep school where he could work on his game and his English. Stefan and Rostand each had a year of high school eligibility remaining, but they needed to prove that to skeptical state high school athletic administrators.

Lora refused to hear the word no. The boys needed an AAU team to play on. She started one herself. It didn't go well, really, but the exposure helped, and the coach at State College of Florida in Bradenton gave Franck a scholarship. One down.

Mahmadou played for an AAU team in the Tampa area, and a prep school in Clearwater agreed to take him. Two down.

Rostand and Stefan required a bureaucratic battle with the Florida High School Athletic Association, but they had Lake Wales High on their side.

Dunson and the administration engaged another Lake Wales High supporter, a prominent lawyer named Robin Gibson, who also serves as the general counsel for the high school, to help build a case for both boys to stay in school and for their right to play.

"We've never seen anything like this," Gibson says. "Here they are, way on the other side of the world almost, from home. They're 17, 18 years old. They have no family, and they are wanting to play basketball in the hopes they can get an education in the United States. Now how can you fault that?"

After some back-and-forth with the FHSAA and letters from Homeland Security detailing their situation, Stefan and Rostand were declared eligible to play sports during the 2015–16 academic year. Lora was 4-for-4.

Ever since, the tall boys have grown. Rostand learned how to swim on a boat trip out on a lake. They've learned how to hunt and fish, American style. "They're becoming redneckified," jokes Lora. After coping with lean times, they've learned to enjoy the plenty that America offers too. They go to the beach. They play on the farm. They laugh a lot.

When he first got to Georgia, Rostand says, "I was shocked about the conditions we were living in, but I had always had that faith that things were going to be better."

The Donleys had faith as well. "I don't know what that's saying about us—it could be twisted the wrong way, like we didn't think it through," David says. "But we never hesitated. And everyone just got along so well, we just rolled. Plus we're obviously faithful people, so we knew there had to be a reason. There has to be."

The transition into the 2015–16 school year went smoothly, all things considered. Stefan, the most talkative of the four, thrived. He started on the basketball team, made the National Honor Society, made friends, and got his driver's license, helping immensely with the family's various commutes.

Rostand began to realize America has a lot of good point guards but not so many gifted soccer midfielders. To help ease the congestion at the Donley house, he moved into the home of Lake Wales High teacher and soccer mom June Ullman at the beginning of the school year. He also reacquainted himself with the beautiful game, starring for Lake Wales High and drawing recruiting interest from D-I and D-II schools, including North Carolina–Charlotte and Queens University in Charlotte.

He lost a love in basketball but gained a potential meal ticket.

Mahmadou was another matter. Of the four boys, he had the most problems adjusting. He was so tall, for one, and not an accomplished or confident athlete. And his English was by far the worst of the four. His stay at the Clearwater Academy, a Church of Scientology school in Clearwater, Florida, was short-lived.

The school did not have a basketball team and the courses were rudimentary, says Lora, and after a few months, Mahmadou came back to Lake Wales. Basketball was going nowhere, again. But at least he was back with his friends, safe, in school and home.

For how long, nobody knew. They were here now as government witnesses. As Lora says: They weren't legal. They weren't illegal. They would be allowed to stay in the U.S. at the discretion of federal investigators.

So far, no state or federal charges have been brought against Faith Baptist or anyone affiliated with the Stockbridge or Ludowici schools. Matthew Sellars says SEVP does little to help campuses comply with federal immigration laws but admits that his school was in the wrong by issuing I-20s to Flint's athletes at a non-SEVIS-approved school.

"We really don't have a defense," Sellars says, "because ignorance is not innocence."

He insists it's unfair to say the Ludowici campus was involved in trafficking or any kind of document fraud. He points out that the school remains certified by SEVP to issue I-20s and that he continues to bring in international students. "The way I look at it is if they didn't want us bringing any more kids in here, we wouldn't still have status."

He says that when agents asked him why Faith Baptist issued visas to postgraduate players, who technically needed no courses to be eligible to play a sport and weren't really students, "I just responded, 'Well, you approved them . . . We printed the paper off your website. We sent it overseas, and they met with your agents, and your agents approved them.'"

Six months after Homeland Security agents spoke with George Flint at his home on March 31, 2015, about Faith Baptist, Flint had moved on. By August, he was trying to start a new school, Blue Ridge Christian Academy in northern Georgia. His basketball coach? Aris Hines. The school never materialized into more than a website.

The Department of Homeland Security will say little about Faith Baptist. A public affairs officer for ICE in central and northern

Florida apologized to *Bleacher Report* for not being able to speak about the issue, "as it is an open investigation."

But Lora Donley says agents told her that investigations out of the Tampa and Savannah Homeland offices were completed and the case would be centered out of Atlanta. "They have to do something," Lora says. "Someone has to be accountable for this."

In April of this year, the U.S. Attorney in Newark, New Jersey, announced 21 arrests of people who had allegedly brokered fraudulent I-20 forms for international students. Federal agents set up a fake school, the University of Northern New Jersey, to issue bogus I-20s that were snapped up by brokers eager to sell them to foreign nationals who wanted to get into the U.S. but often had no intention of actually studying here—what's known as "pay to stay."

Such schemes "not only damage our perception of legitimate student and foreign worker visa programs, they also pose a very real threat to national security," U.S. Attorney Paul Fishman said in a statement.

It is easy to see how I-20 abuse by prep schools could create security risks; many of the students who come to the U.S. for a chance to play basketball hail from strife-torn areas that have bred terrorist groups.

But the schools only recently have become a focus of federal government attention. A 2012 Government Accountability Office report scolded ICE for lack of oversight of schools issuing I-20s as part of the SEVP program.

The GAO report was shocking given that the entire U.S. immigration system was overhauled after Mohamed Atta and Marwan al-Shehhi, two of the 9/11 attackers, had attended U.S. flight schools on visitor visas, without proper student credentials. The potential doorway for terrorism seems to have gotten Homeland Security's attention.

Whatever the reasons, trafficking of basketball players has lately attracted scrutiny. In 2015, *Harper's* magazine published a wrenching account of African boys recruited to the U.S. by unscrupulous AAU coaches, then discarded and left homeless. But abuses of young international athletes, particularly from Africa, have been going on for years, says Ed Bona.

Born in what is now South Sudan, Bona played basketball at Fordham in the early 1980s and was among the first Africans drafted by the NBA, one year ahead of Hakeem Olajuwon. He has since settled in the U.S. and helped manage the late NBA player Manute Bol's international foundation.

During the past two decades, he has helped a handful of talented Sudanese kids find opportunities to play in the U.S.—including the Deng brothers, former UConn player Ajou, and current Miami Heat forward Luol Deng.

What he has seen at some prep schools disgusts him. He recalls being called to help a Sudanese player in the mid-2000s who was stuck in rat-infested housing with no food available on weekends.

"They may as well have stayed behind in a refugee camp," Bona says. He blames corrupt flesh peddlers bringing over dozens of kids at a time in the hope that some will hit it big and kick back part of their paychecks to the handler.

That's an illusion, Bona says. He has worked with perhaps 20 African players in 20 years, some with real talent. "Only one made it to the NBA," he says, "and that was Luol."

By the second day of the JUCO showcase in Norcross, the meds had kicked in, and Lora was keeping the entire Lake Wales community informed on Stefan's and Mahmadou's progress with feverish Facebook updates.

"One and Done! Dou finished with a dunk and bucket . . . Stefan settled with 18. Success!!"

Lora had been half expecting to run into George Flint at the tournament, and she and Stefan's mother had talked about confronting the man they believed had exploited the boys. They never saw Flint, but on Sunday as they prepared to head home, they took an informal vote. Lora, Lola, and Mahmadou opted for a side trip on the way back to Lake Wales: a somber tour of Stockbridge and Conyers.

"37 mi to our first stop," Lora posted on Facebook. "The home of the man who brought our boys to the States. The man who forever changed their lives. The moms in this vehicle want to see what our boys saw. We want to know where they walked, played and prayed."

Forty-five minutes later, as they drove past Flint's house in a relatively upscale neighborhood in Conyers, the passengers were mostly silent. "My stomach's flippin," Lora said. She had flicked

on a video camera and began posting live on Facebook. Stefan
streamed the video to his "Serbian crew."

They moved on to the rough neighborhood in nearby Stockbridge and the shabby apartment buildings. "This was the Serb
house," said Stefan, pointing to a two-story brick structure in a
nondescript cul-de-sac.

Mahmadou pointed toward a neighboring house, in front of
which a pickup truck was parked. "That's where we were stealing Wi-Fi," he said softly, referring to a hotspot where the boys
could communicate with their families. Thinking back to their
time at the apartments, Mahmadou continued, "Twenty people in
there . . . No food . . . Bad memory."

They drove past the Starbucks where they took the call from
Gordon Gibbons and pointed out the CiCi's Pizza parlor. "Shout-
out to my boys from CiCi's," Stefan said. "They gave us free pizza
every night."

By now, Lola was sobbing softly in the car. She was hearing and
seeing the story of her son's journey for the first time, as was Stefan's father, who was watching the live feed back home in Belgrade.

Lora comforted Lola. "He's better now," she said.

They love America. And these days, what's not to love? The
Donleys take them to school, the playing fields and courts, the
beach, the lake, and give them every opportunity to flourish. "It
is easier than back home," Mahmadou says, his voice as gentle as
orange blossoms. "Here, the people have a lot of opportunity."

Stefan could not be more patriotic about his homeland. He
wears Serbian T-shirts, sports a flag in his room, and a Serbian
rearview-mirror ornament. "I would do anything for my country,"
he says. But in the States, "You can be whoever you want to be. The
most important thing is you have a chance. There is something
you can look forward to."

It's up to Lora to be outraged for them. "It's not fair," she says.
"This should not happen to anyone else."

Someone took their money, which their families had scrimped
and saved, selling off jewelry, even their clothes, to obtain tickets
to America. Worse, she says, people in this country "messed with
their dreams and goals. That takes it to a completely different level
—so much bigger than just the money. Such a violation."

For nearly two years, often with only each other to rely on, the four boys have seen America's all-too-corruptible sports system from multiple angles. Yet as Mahmadou plays with Ally, holding his hand above his head and challenging the spunky nine-year-old to jump up and slap a high-five, there is no bitterness to be found. None.

When Dunson asked Stefan in January to speak about his experience to an assembly at the high school, he stepped hesitantly onto the gym floor and began telling his story. "Your lives here are so good, and you don't even realize it," he told the students. "I've seen the real world, and it's not pretty. Life here, during these days at Lake Wales High, they're a blessing."

Finally, in late April 2016, the government granted its blessing on the four boys, upgrading the "deferred-action" status they had been under for a year and approving "continued presence" for another year, meaning that as victims of trafficking they are considered refugees, allowed to remain in the country as long as they are valuable to the investigation.

Just last week, as Homeland's investigation appeared to be winding down, the boys met with the special agent in charge from Atlanta for follow-up interviews. The agent had emailed Lora a couple of weeks before to schedule the meeting, thanking her "for everything you have done to push this case forward." Mostly, the agent added, she would need to develop a rapport with the boys "since they will be witnesses for me up here."

Once the Homeland investigation is complete, agents will present their case to the Atlanta office of the U.S. Attorney, which will then decide whether to accept the case for prosecution.

When the investigation concludes, regardless of where it leads, the four witnesses can apply for citizenship, a process Homeland agents told them could take up to three years. Meanwhile, the boys do not have student visas or green cards and were told by agents that leaving the country even to visit their parents could jeopardize their status.

On June 3, a warm, windy Florida night with lightning cracking in the distance, Rostand, Stefan, and Mahmadou graduated from Lake Wales High School alongside the Donleys' two other sons. The sky darkened, but the rain held off.

"God let us have that moment, and it didn't rain a single drop," Stefan says. "The setting was beautiful. Everything was so great."

Things had mostly fallen into place on the college front too.

The trips to the showcases, the endless online college applications, the phone calls to schools—all were paying off. On the day after Mother's Day, Lora loaded up the SUV again and headed for a signing ceremony at Polk State College, a JUCO in nearby Winter Haven whose coach offered Stefan a scholarship to play on the basketball team. There was a cake and platters of food, and a horde of supporters.

Donna Dunson, the Lake Wales principal, brought along just about the entire administration, along with Stefan's teammates and 15 classmates. His AAU coach, Jack Tisdale, came, and, of course, Lora, David, Brandon, Chris, Mahmadou, and Rostand were there.

"It was as if he were signing at the University of Florida," Lora would say.

Stefan made a little speech, and when his mother was handed the letter of intent to sign, she told the group that she was making room for two signatures—hers and Lora's.

"Lola cried," Lora says. "The principal cried." Lora cried too.

Things were looking up for Mahmadou too. A coach at Oakland Community College near Detroit, Terrell Polk, had seen Mahmadou play at the JUCO showcase back in April and offered him a scholarship to that school. Rostand, perhaps the most athletically gifted of the boys, was seriously considering an offer to play soccer from Warner University in Lake Wales and planned a visit to Flagler College in St. Augustine for a workout.

They all want to stay. After seeing so much of the United States, bad and good, they want to see more.

"My dad always tell me, 'Nothing's easy in life; you have to go through some bad things to get what you want,'" Rostand says. "It's really the best country in the world, but it's just humans. It's the best country, but it's just humans who do bad things."

ALEXIS OKEOWO

The Away Team

FROM THE NEW YORKER

AROUND ELEVEN O'CLOCK on the night of October 10, 2015, Samson Arefaine learned that he had been selected to play on the national soccer team of Eritrea, a sliver of a nation in the Horn of Africa. For two months, he had been in a training camp in the capital, Asmara, with 33 other men, vying for 10 open spots on the Red Sea Camels. Now the team was due to fly to Botswana in less than two hours, to play in a World Cup qualifying match. Arefaine needed to pack quickly, so he ran to his room, in a house that team officials had arranged for players to use during the camp. The house had no electricity, and he struggled to see in the dark, but he managed to throw some shirts, shorts, and sandals into a bag. On the way to the airport, he called his parents and told them the exciting news.

At 26, Arefaine is lean and wiry, with bright-copper skin, tight-cropped curls, and a narrow face with a faint beard. On the team, he was known for being outspoken and funny, a reliable source of jokes and stories, and also as sensitive and watchful. "He knows how to read faces," one teammate said. Though he played on the defensive line, at right back, he was the fastest member of the team, and he often rushed forward to score unexpected goals. His teammates described him as one of Eritrea's best players.

When Arefaine boarded the plane, he had never been outside the country. For Eritreans, this is not unusual: Eritrea is one of the few nations that require an exit visa. An isolated, secretive state of some four million people, it has been under emergency rule since

1998. The United Nations has accused its military and its government—including the President, a former rebel leader named Isaias Afewerki—of crimes against humanity toward their own people, including indefinite conscription, arbitrary arrests and torture, and mass surveillance. "There are no civil liberties, there is no freedom of speech, there is no freedom to organize," Adane Ghebremeskel Tekie, an activist with the Eritrean Movement for Human Rights, said. "The regime can do anything it wants." According to the UN, as many as 5,000 people flee the country every month, making it one of the world's largest sources of refugees. Last year, 3,800 people drowned while trying to cross the Mediterranean Sea; many of them were Eritreans.

Despite its self-imposed isolation, Eritrea wants to be seen as a normal country, and international sporting competitions are a way to present a good face to the world. Eritrean athletes—runners, cyclists, and soccer players—are sometimes permitted to compete in other countries. The Red Sea Camels are a particular source of pride; Eritrea is no less soccer-mad than Italy or Brazil. But, embarrassingly for the government, members of the national soccer team have repeatedly defected after games abroad: Angola in 2007, Kenya in 2009, Uganda in 2012.

After the last defection, the government disbanded the team. Then, in the fall of 2015, it came up with a solution. It would form a team mostly of Eritrean athletes who lived abroad and held dual nationality, and therefore had no incentive to defect. The remaining positions could be filled with loyal athletes living in Eritrea. "They have to trust you," Yohannes Sium, one of the chosen local players, said. "Trust was the main thing, not skill."

When Arefaine and his teammates landed in Nairobi for a layover, the foreign-based players wandered through the terminal, shopping and eating. The local athletes sat at their gate in hard blue plastic seats, uncomfortably eyeing one another, while their coaches and the president of the Eritrean National Football Federation sat behind them, holding their passports. The players felt like hostages. "The others can do anything they want, but you just sit and wait," Henok Semere, a striker, said. Then a representative from the Eritrean embassy in Kenya arrived at the gate and began talking with the officials. While they were distracted, Arefaine turned to Alex Russom, a baby-faced left back, sitting next to him, and told him that he wanted to escape. "He asked if I want to join him," Russom recalled. "I said, 'How did you know I was also thinking that?'"

Arefaine had been contemplating escape for years. He had kept in touch with several players who defected in Uganda, and after they resettled, in Holland, he had asked them for advice on how to get asylum. The most important thing, they told him, was to persuade the entire team to go with him. Any one of his teammates who refused to go could betray him.

It was hard to know whom to trust. Some of his teammates later confessed that Eritrean security officials had asked them to inform on the others in case of an escape plot. "There was no closeness among the ten of us—we were not friends," Arefaine said. "I just took the risk." It turned out that many of his teammates were interested. But Nairobi wasn't a good place to defect: there was nowhere to run at the airport, and they had only two hours before their next flight. Besides, his friends in Holland had given him a second piece of advice: don't escape until after the game. "If you escape without playing, no one will notice you, because you are not on the media," they explained. "You need radio, television."

After landing in Francistown, the sleepy city in Botswana where the match was being held, the team members took a nap, had practice, and went to dinner. Then Arefaine gathered the local players in a hotel room, to determine who wanted to join the escape. Everyone enthusiastically agreed, except Semere, the striker. He had another way out: as the only college graduate and the only one fluent in English, he could apply for graduate programs abroad. The idea of leaving his family and friends made him nervous, and he knew that his father, a successful farmer, would not approve. "Henok was scared at first," Arefaine said. But he was also afraid of going back. What if he didn't get accepted at a foreign university, or the government didn't allow him to go? The other option—crossing through the desert to Sudan, Libya, or Ethiopia—was too dangerous. Finally, he agreed to join. In the hotel lobby, Arefaine helped the others purchase SIM cards and exchange their money for pula, the local currency. He asked the manager to arrange for a taxi to pick them up at 4:00 a.m., explaining that they wanted to go on vacation after the match.

They lost the game that evening. "Our minds were elsewhere," Arefaine said. Back in their rooms, the team's captain, a Swedish-Eritrean, turned on some music to help everyone relax, but the mood remained tense. Eventually, one of the dual-nationality players asked what was wrong, and Arefaine revealed the escape plan. The player gave Arefaine 200 pounds, and some of the other foreign-based teammates contributed dollars and euros.

At 4:00 a.m., Arefaine and the others assembled in the hall and packed their belongings into a single bag. They moved quietly; a Botswana policeman who was escorting the team was asleep in an adjacent room. Arefaine was in a fog. He had brought T-shirts, shorts, sandals, and track pants but had forgotten his phone. "We left the hotel in a rush—we didn't want to waste time," he said.

When they got to the lobby, there was no taxi on the street. They paused, wondering if they should wait for one. A few of the players went to the reception desk and asked where they could find the U.S. embassy or the Red Cross. The hotel staff wasn't sure, but told them that they could catch a minibus into the center of town. The players decided to try to find the offices on foot. As they walked out of the lobby, security guards watched with surprise. "We told them we were just going on a walk, relaxing," Arefaine said. "When we went out, there was nothing. It was dark, dark. We didn't know where to go."

Eritreans think of their sovereignty as hard-won, and with good reason. The country's modern borders were set in the late nineteenth century, when Italy invaded a funnel-shaped area of highlands and arid plains on Africa's northeastern coast and named it Eritrea, from the Latin phrase Erythraeum Mare, or Red Sea. The colonists could not have picked a more inhospitable environment: erratic rainfall, a desertlike coast, dry riverbeds, mangrove swamps, and valleys sunk below sea level. Their policies segregated Eritreans from Italians, in a precursor to South African apartheid, and forbade them to attend secondary school, even as they were drafted to fight Italy's wars. When Italy lost the colony to Britain, in 1941, the new administrators stripped Eritrea of much of its naval, rail, and industrial infrastructure, and then, with little use left for the colony, turned it over to the United Nations.

At the time, Eritreans had high hopes that they would finally be able to govern themselves. Instead, their neighbor Ethiopia intervened. The two countries share common ethnic groups, languages, customs, and historical origins, in the ancient Christian empires of the Horn of Africa. They also share a border, and, for centuries, Ethiopians looking across the frontier have coveted the territory, which offers both fertile farmland and a pathway to the sea. Emperor Haile Selassie, who believed that the land was his by right, lobbied the UN, and Eritrea was designated an autonomous territory under the Ethiopian crown. In the coming years, Selassie replaced Eritrea's flag with Ethiopia's, supplanted the national languages of Tigrinya and Arabic with Amharic, and finally abolished the federation, erasing the Eritrean state.

"Eritreans who were living under the Ethiopian occupation never felt at ease," Abraham Zere, an Eritrean journalist who lives in exile in the United States, told me. "It has always been 'us' and 'them.'" When resistance movements formed, in the north of Eritrea, the crown's Army punished their supporters, killing villagers, burning homes, and slaughtering livestock. By 1961, Eritrean fighters had gathered in the mountains near the Ethiopian border, in a maze of underground bunkers that contained hospitals, a school, and living quarters. It was an uneven fight: Ethiopia's population was more than ten times that of Eritrea. Ethiopia had arms and equipment from the Soviet Union and the United States, while the Eritreans were forced to capture munitions from their enemies. The war affected everyone, Zere said. "My family was often hiding from the continuous bombings."

In 1991, the Eritreans, with the help of a rebel group in Ethiopia, finally defeated the occupiers. After 30 years of fighting, Eritrea had lost as many as 65,000 people in combat, and 200,000 more to famine and the effects of war. But, with almost no support or recognition from abroad, the Eritreans had won, and they emerged proud and defiant. When I visited Asmara recently, a national festival was celebrating 25 years of independence. On the sprawling Expo Grounds, among food vendors and historical displays, the government has preserved the fuselage of an airliner, which an Ethiopian fighter pilot had strafed on the runway. Across town, in a vast place called the Tank Graveyard, the rusting remains of Ethiopian tanks stand as a monument to the war.

After the victory, Isaias Afewerki, a hero of the struggle, became Eritrea's leader, and his party, the People's Front for Democracy and Justice, or PFDJ, promised to lead the country toward a constitution and democratic elections. Two years later, though, another dispute erupted between Ethiopia and Eritrea, over a border town called Badme. Both sides quickly escalated the conflict; Ethiopia cut off trade, and Eritrea's economy stagnated. When Afewerki decided to go into battle, Eritreans, accustomed to war to preserve their homeland, enlisted to fight. One of Arefaine's older brothers went, and was killed—one of an estimated 19,000 Eritreans who died in two years.

In 2002, a commission in The Hague ruled that Eritrea had legal rights to the disputed territory, but Ethiopia has continued its occupation. As the war dragged on, people around Afewerki began describing him as severe and brutish, given to autocratic tendencies. "The PFDJ is Eritrea, and I am the PFDJ," he proclaimed. After members of the Party's central council questioned his handling of the war—had there been no diplomatic alternative to the huge loss of life and the economic devastation?—Afewerki had 11 of them thrown in prison. He also shut down independent media, jailing editors. In 2010, after an *Al Jazeera* interviewer challenged him, he called her questions "a pack of lies." Then, according to Zere's reporting, he returned to his office and slapped Ali Abdu, the information minister, while his staff looked on. Two years later, Abdu defected while on a trip to Australia. Afterward, his 15-year-old daughter, his brother, and his elderly father were put in prison.

Afewerki has used the threat, real or imagined, of renewed war with Ethiopia to keep his citizens in a precarious state that they describe as "no war, no peace." Now, Eritreans say, they can be detained for crimes as slight as harboring ill will toward the government. There is usually no trial; detainees are often not told the offense, or for how long they will be held. Zerit Yohhanes, a midfielder on the national soccer team, told me that his father has been in prison for more than 25 years. The family has no idea why. Maybe he was detained by mistake.

Asmara, where Arefaine grew up, is a serene city of half a million people, set on a plateau at almost 8,000 feet. There are broad streets with peach-toned Art Deco buildings; on Harnet Avenue, lined with palm trees, people stroll past cafés, bars, bakeries, and cinemas. In the middle of the street stands a red brick cathedral, where, during my visit, teenagers sat flirting on the steps. The city is slow-paced, and crime is low. Western diplomats say, with evident relief, that Asmara is "not like an African city."

Because the government restricts permits for new construction, there is a housing shortage in the city, and people build homes in unregulated settlements on the edge of Asmara. Arefaine grew up in one of these quarters, named Godaif; a paved main street gives way to dirt roads into the neighborhood, where the homes range from pastel-painted brick houses to lean-tos with laundry hanging outside. His father, a judge, owned land there, and so he built an orange house with four bedrooms for the family—four boys and four girls. Arefaine's mother didn't go to school, dedicating herself to caring for their children. Arefaine still sometimes cries when he talks about her. "My mom is the sweetest person, because she devoted her life to us," he told me.

Arefaine's neighborhood was known for producing skilled, if rowdy, athletes. He described the local pastimes as playing soccer, fighting, and drinking *suwa*, a kind of beer made from sorghum. Arefaine wanted to be a professional soccer player from the time he could stretch his legs. His father, who was strict and controlling, pressured him to excel in school, and they argued. Arefaine wasn't serious enough, he said. He preferred the cinema and nightclubs to school, and he was always the first one on the dance floor at weddings. But his talent for soccer was evident. As early as high school, scouts began inquiring about him. He joined a club team called Tesfa, and sneaked out of the house to play matches.

School wasn't that interesting, anyway. In history classes, his teachers spent most of the time on the country's perpetual struggle against Ethiopia. In geography, Arefaine learned the names of the other countries in Africa, but that was about it. "Our knowledge about the outside world until we finish high school is very limited," he said.

Arefaine grew up surrounded by support for the Afewerki regime. During the liberation struggle, his father had spied on the Ethiopian occupiers, and then been caught and imprisoned for seven months; he never relinquished the revolutionary spirit. In Arefaine's classes, Afewerki was described as a modest, nearly omniscient man, focused on his people's well-being. On state-run media, he gives hours-long lectures, in which he spins connections among far-flung episodes in world history and politics; local channels feature him in multipart epics about the independence struggle.

At Santa Ana Secondary School, where Arefaine studied, Eritrea's national anthem is printed on a bulletin board at the entrance: "The pride of her oppressed people proved that truth prevails." But Arefaine began to see soldiers violently round up people who had been caught without identification papers. In his second year at Santa Ana, soldiers came to take the oldest students in each grade, saying that they were going to a vocational school. Instead, they were sent to military training camps.

Afewerki had instituted the camps in the mid-1990s, as part of a national program of mandatory military service. The term of service, beginning after the third year of high school, was originally 18 months. It is now indefinite, and the program has become the country's dominant employer, shuttling recruits from camps into a wide range of occupations. A fortunate few, like children of government officials and generals, can get civil service positions or white-collar jobs—though even they have to attend drills and guard government buildings. The rest are in a standing military of some 300,000, who work on government projects in construction, farming, and mining, or are deployed to the border with Ethiopia. Most are paid roughly 400 nakfa, or $30, a month. Everyone has a gun at home.

A trainee's experience is determined by his unit and location: generally, the more remote your station, the worse the conditions. "The one thing that is constant is the abuse," Yohannes Woldemariam, an Eritrean who taught international relations for a decade at Fort Lewis College, in Colorado, said. Arefaine's older siblings came home complaining about the camps; their parents told them to be patient, that everyone went through it. But Arefaine saw people he knew, students and teachers, fleeing Eritrea. Some walked to refugee camps in Ethiopia and Sudan, braving gunfire from border guards. Others paid smugglers thousands of dollars to lead them through the Sahara to Libya and then Europe. In 2012, Eritrean Air Force pilots flew a government plane to Saudi Arabia to seek asylum.

As people left the country, the regime began a more aggressive campaign of surveillance; in some cases, Eritreans told me, you could be detained for "thinking about escaping." In Arefaine's neighborhood, a woman named Saada reported evaders to the authorities, and boys avoided walking by her house. "I started being cautious whenever I talk about the government, about other things, with friends, because someone could report me," Arefaine said. Zerit Yohhanes, the midfielder, told me that, when he dropped out of school to avoid the camps, a friend's mother reported him. She even delivered the letter recalling him for duty. Yohhanes was baffled; the woman's own son had fled to Sudan in order to dodge service. "I told her, 'Your son is somewhere else. Why are you doing this to me?'" he said. She replied, "I'm just the messenger." Suspicion is so widespread that even long-acquainted neighbors can be wary of one another. "The system has created an atmosphere of mistrust among Eritreans," Ghebremeskel, of the Eritrean Movement for Human Rights, told me. "You can't trust your own brother."

In 2004, Arefaine's older brother fled through the desert to Sudan, eventually making his way to England. "He was angry because of the national service," Arefaine recalled. "That's why he left." Still, their father encouraged the other children to volunteer for service. It was their duty, he said. The government told them that the service and the roundups were necessary, because of the threat from Ethiopia, and they believed it.

As Arefaine finished his third year of high school, he wondered which camp he would be sent to. Many of his classmates would spend their last year of high school at Sawa, an enormous military complex about 170 miles northwest of Asmara. Children of the well connected were often allowed to attend Sawa because of its proximity to Asmara. If you managed to find the time amid your duties to study there, you could gain entrance to a college.

Arefaine's teammate Semere, the son of the prosperous farmer, had lived in one of the hot, poorly ventilated hangars that function as dormitories for Sawa's thousands of trainees. In the mornings, he attended a school nearby, and then supervisors took him and the other recruits to do hard labor at commercial farms, digging and plowing for no pay. "You think, I don't deserve this at this age," he said. "You come just as a child. That's why they take you at that age—you don't know anything, and you just follow them. You are terrified."

Men and women trained together; during the independence struggle, an idea had taken hold that women should be equally involved in all national activities. But Asia Abdulkadir, an Eritrean-German gender consultant for the UN, told me that the women were often abused. "The senior commander would always choose the best-looking girl and bring her to his unit to wash his clothes, cook his food, make sure his house is always clean," she said. "And there is a pressure for the girls to offer sexual services." At Sawa, Semere knew girls who had been impregnated by commanders.

The base was close to the border with Sudan, and 30 of Semere's hall mates eventually escaped. He stayed, and studied as much as he could, poring over math and physics textbooks in the hours before a 4:00 a.m. wakeup call. If trainees failed college-entrance exams, they would be immediately drafted back into service. "So you end up in the military for the rest of your life," Arefaine said. Eritrea has only seven colleges, and there is a shortage of qualified teachers, according to Tadesse Mehari, who heads the National Commission for Higher Education. The government spends $5 million a year to hire expatriate faculty, mostly Indians. It has sent students abroad for advanced degrees, in the hope that they would return to teach. But, Mehari said, "that's not faring very well, because many of the youngsters this time do not want to come back."

Those who graduate college have little assurance of working in the area that they studied; most seem to end up back in national service. One afternoon, at a breezy, secluded café in Asmara, I had tea with a young woman who had gone to Sawa and then completed a degree in engineering. The government assigned her to teach English at a school in Asmara for three years, with the understanding, she said, that "after that maybe they can put you in your field." She now worked part-time at a restaurant; other graduates she knew were working in kindergartens. "You try to be flexible," she said, laughing. "You have to, in order to live. You can even clean the streets." She went on, "Just waiting to be an engineer is losing time. I have to do my duty to my family."

Outside Asmara, I drove past a guard post manned by soldiers. There was a cluster of zinc shacks serving as a residence, but there was nothing to guard: no ammunitions depot, no intelligence post, nothing. "If you are not on a farming or a construction project, breaking stones, it's about keeping you in check," Ghebremeskel, the activist, said. In Asmara, a man who had worked for decades in the civil service told me that he was sometimes assigned to duty as a prison guard. "What's frustrating to the youth is that there is no end to national service," Woldemariam, the professor, said. "The suspense—you can't plan your life."

*

Because Arefaine was a gifted athlete, the Eritrean Sport and Culture Commission offered a deal: if he went to a remote camp in the east, called Wi'a, he would be allowed to leave after just six months and play for a club team in Asmara. He packed jam and peanut butter, a sorghum drink, a little money, a blanket, and a few changes of clothes. He felt ready to go.

To get to Wi'a, he and about 150 other recruits rode for three hours in the back of a giant truck, so crammed together that they could barely find room to stand. When they arrived, Arefaine was stunned. The camp is in a volcanic area on the Red Sea coast, a sun-blasted expanse of white sand. "There is just plain ground," he recalled. "There is no housing except for small shelters made out of sticks." Soldiers hustled the recruits out of the truck and told them to kneel, then divided them into groups. In a long shelter covered with branches and leaves, they dropped their things. A soldier was serving stale bread and watery lentil soup, ladled out from a cavernous pot. "You could barely see the lentils," Arefaine said. He ate some of the food he had brought from home, already regretting the decision to come.

That evening, the commander, a man named Jamal, laid out the rules: trainees had to obey whatever instructions their superiors gave them, and they would be shot if they tried to escape. "Immediately after the meeting, people started running," Arefaine said. Soldiers swarmed the remaining recruits, telling them to kneel. Arefaine could hear vehicles moving over the sand and guns firing into the air. No one knew if any of the runners were caught. If they were, they would be put in the camp prison, a hole in the ground that felt like a coffin.

At night, the recruits slept in the open, surrounded by a ring of sleeping soldiers. Arefaine poured water on the sandy ground to cool it, and then laid down his blanket. Each day, he and the other trainees had to wake up at 4:00 a.m., quickly stow their bedding and change clothes, and then jog to a clearing a mile away, where they could relieve themselves, under close watch by the guards. For the remainder of the day, they marched and had target practice, with a rest in the early afternoon to avoid the high sun. Every 30 minutes, a whistle shrieked, and everyone had to line up in formation. Their superiors were checking to make sure that no one had escaped.

The recruits were beaten for failing to show up on time, or for falling out of formation, or for stealing water. "You were treated like an animal," Arefaine said. At breakfast, they were given a cup of black tea, six rolls, and five liters of water to last the day. Lunch and dinner were more lentil soup. There were about 2,000 men in the camp, and every Wednesday afternoon they all went to the river to bathe. (The women went on Tuesdays.) People unfailingly tried to escape across the river, and Arefaine watched as they were shot down, their legs collapsing beneath them in the water. The ones who made it disappeared into the scrubland. Later, when soldiers dumped corpses on the ground in front of the recruits, Arefaine saw that many of them had been mauled by hyenas.

A man in the camp was tattooing recruits, using a thorn and kohl, and although religious practices were forbidden, Arefaine had a cross imprinted on his right forearm. "We were stressed and worried, and we wanted to think of our God," he said. When the tattoo became infected, he went to a medic to have it treated. The medic scolded him: "Why did you do this?" When Arefaine came for follow-up treatments, the medic beat him with a stick.

After six months, it was clear that Arefaine wasn't going to be allowed to leave early. Around that time, his parents were permitted to make a one-hour visit. His mother looked at the camp and at Arefaine, who was frighteningly thin, and sobbed uncontrollably. "I was telling her not to cry," he recalled. "From then on, whatever happened to me I kept to myself."

When his year of training was done, he was assigned to a military base in the village of Gelalo, in the south. He was often on the move, sent to man checkpoints or guard telecommunications infrastructure, or, worse, to carry out roundups. He and his platoon were dropped off in surrounding villages to look for evaders, grabbing boys who didn't have permits off the streets or from their homes. They searched under beds, in cupboards, and even took girls, herding them into a prison or a stadium for questioning. If someone resisted, Arefaine could end up having to shoot him. "I felt very bad," he said. "No one wanted to do it." He knew that, if he protested, his treatment would worsen.

Like many men in national service, Arefaine hoped that soccer would provide a way out. The club teams are owned by the military, the ruling party, and state companies, so coaches can recruit anyone they want. When he joined the service, he wrote on his entrance forms that he was a soccer player, but nothing had come of it. At last, three years into his service, he got a call telling him to come to the city of Assab to try out for a military-sponsored club team.

Arefaine wanted to play, but he was desperate to get home. If he tried out for the team and didn't make it, he knew, he'd have to go back into national service. Instead, he sought out a relative who lived in town and, with his help, bought a forged permit that said he was on medical leave. Early one morning, he heaved himself into the back of a transport truck, and, sitting on top of the cargo, rode north. When the truck reached its destination, several hours later, he got on another one, and then another, paying the drivers small bribes. At checkpoints, he showed the fake permit. When he got home, his family greeted him with happiness and surprise; he didn't tell them that his papers had been forged. He put his belongings down in his familiar bedroom, with posters of the Barcelona soccer team. He took a bath.

On Harnet Avenue, I visited an ornate, four-level theater called Cinema Impero, where people often gather to watch soccer games. In midafternoon, fans were scattered across the seats, engrossed in an English Premier League match that played on the giant screen. The fans sat in rapt silence, periodically bursting into shouts and cheers. Soccer is immensely popular in Eritrea, featured prominently on state media and dominating the discussion in public spaces. "It is a way of escape from the frustrating reality," Zere, the exiled journalist, said, "and a refuge to discuss safe issues that will not draw attention from state security."

In Asmara, there is much that critics can't comment on. The streets are filled with decades-old bicycles and cars, and the electricity goes out frequently. The state-run mobile-phone network is spotty, and people resort to pay phones. The ruling party's company, Red Sea Trading Corporation, is the country's primary legal importer, but most of what's for sale in Eritrea's small shops is smuggled into the country in giant suitcases—a practice that is tolerated, perhaps even sanctioned, by the government. On the outskirts of the city, police cars driving to Adi Abeto prison pass a thriving black market for diesel.

According to the UN Monitoring Group on Somalia and Eritrea, PFDJ officials skim millions of dollars a year from party-run companies, but the charges are difficult to investigate because the government never discloses its budget. Eritreans joke that Afewerki runs the country as if it were a small grocery store. Hagos Ghebrehiwet, the President's economic adviser, told me that the budget had to be kept secret, to protect against "economic sabotage" by Ethiopia and its supporters. A former treasury chief, quoted in Martin Plaut's book *Understanding Eritrea,* gave a simpler explanation: no budget has ever been committed to paper.

Eritrea has resources—gold, copper, zinc, and potash—but the majority of the population depends on subsistence farming. Ghebrehiwet told me that the problem was a limited workforce: "A small country with a lot of resources in agriculture, mining, and fisheries—I don't think we will have enough manpower to be able to exploit the potential here." Bronwyn Bruton, the deputy director of the Africa Center at the Atlantic Council, was more direct. "The government is broke," she said. "They can't pay people to do jobs that would normally be civil-service posts. So what they're doing is conscripting people." In 2016, the government increased the monthly pay to between 2,000 and 5,000 nakfa. But Eritreans are not allowed to withdraw more than 5,000 nakfa a month from a bank without approval. "You take it to the market and it's gone in five days," an Eritrean in Asmara told me.

Eritrean officials insist that the threat from Ethiopia forces them to divert resources to the military. Berhane G. Solomon, the chargé d'affaires at the Eritrean embassy in Washington, D.C., complained that the international community has done nothing to compel Ethiopia to withdraw its troops. "It has put the burden on us to protect our independence," he said. "Eritrea is only 25 years old. We are just crawling, trying to stand on our own feet."

Publicly, the U.S. has hesitated to criticize Ethiopia, a key ally in regional anti-terror efforts. Between 2006 and 2009, Ethiopia sent troops into Somalia to fight Islamists, including the terror group al-Shabaab. In 2009, the UN placed sanctions on Eritrea, for allegedly supporting al-Shabaab in order to undermine Ethiopia. But the UN's own Monitoring Group on Somalia and Eritrea has found no evidence to support that claim. (The group does say that Eritrea has ties to Somali arms traffickers.) When a UN report alleged persistent human rights abuses, the government called the claims "an unwarranted attack not only against Eritrea, but also

Africa and developing nations." Amid the continuing dispute, Afewerki has barred the monitoring group from the country since
2013.

Eritrea and the United States are in a kind of standoff: a Western diplomat whom I spoke to acknowledged that Ethiopia is behaving thuggishly, but thought that the onus is on Eritrea to allow
the monitoring group to inspect again. If the country were cleared
of the allegations raised by the UN, the international community
would be more amenable to helping resolve the border issue. Eritrean officials regard the U.S.'s reasoning as nearsighted. "Why
should good relations with Ethiopia mean hostility toward Eritrea?" Yemane Gebreab, the PFDJ's head of political affairs, said.

In Asmara, Arefaine knew that he had to protect himself from in-
formants, so he went to see Saada, the neighborhood spy, and told
her that he was on medical leave and going to a military hospital
in town for treatment. Without release papers from the military,
he couldn't join a club team, so he got a job at a shop in the city.
When he wasn't working, he stayed indoors to avoid the military's
sweeps for evaders. After a few months, though, he reconnected
with a high school friend, Mikal, and started going with her to
Harnet Avenue at night, strolling from café to café or going to
Cinema Hamsien, where they could watch Indian movies for a few
nakfa.

Late one night, about a year later, he heard his father shouting
for him to wake up. A contingent of soldiers had jumped the gate
of their house and announced that they were looking for him.
Arefaine recognized the men: three were platoon mates from
Gelalo, and the fourth was the platoon leader. All were holding
guns. They handcuffed him and led him out of the house, as his
mother and sisters cried.

Arefaine spent the night in a local police station, and then was
taken to a prison near his old base in Gelalo. He was confined,
along with some 60 other men, to a cell where the only light came
from small, high windows. The men weren't allowed out, so they
had to relieve themselves in a corner. They all became infested
with fleas. "I was about to lose my mind," Arefaine said. "You think
about the way you've been taken from home. You think about your
mom, your dad, how they feel."

After six months, prison authorities told Arefaine that he was being released: the military wanted him to play soccer again. It was true that he had briefly evaded service, but so did many other men. Evasion was normal, almost expected—and Arefaine was unusually talented. Arefaine immediately called his parents, who thought he had been killed, and told them that he was free. He cut his hair to get rid of the fleas.

Back in Asmara, he practiced with the team in the mornings, went to a mandatory political-education center in the afternoons, and worked as a guard at a national-service office on some nights. He made 450 nakfa, about $28, a month. "Once you go to the camp, you are the property of the government," a former journalist in Asmara told me. "Whether you work in a highly professional position or as a security guard, everybody gets 400 for life." On nights off, Arefaine bribed his commanders to let him broker houses and cars on the informal market, so that he could make ends meet.

Arefaine was sitting in a café when he got the news that he had been called to try out for the national team. He shouted so loudly that he startled the other customers. "It was a dream come true," he said. "One day, I would be able to leave the country." When he told his parents he wanted to escape, they were against it. The government has sometimes required families of national-team players to turn over the deeds to their houses as a guarantee in case their sons fled, and if Arefaine defected his family could lose their home. He assured them he wouldn't leave. But, he said, "I made up my mind—I would do it anyway."

The team members based abroad—in Sudan, Saudi Arabia, Sweden, and elsewhere—were flown in and put up in a five-star hotel. The local athletes moved into a guesthouse with no electricity and no running water, where they slept four to a room. While the foreign-based players were paid in dollars, the rest were told that they would receive nakfa—and then were given nothing. They trained for two months, and, as Arefaine and his teammates watched the coaches lavish praise on their foreign-based counterparts, they grew resentful. "There was a double standard," Minasie Solomon, the goalkeeper, said. Solomon, the oldest member of the team, had loved his country enough to volunteer for the war effort against Ethiopia, but now he was disillusioned. By the time the team got to the airport in Nairobi, nearly everyone was ready to join Arefaine's attempt to defect. "Samson is brave and smart," Yohhanes, the midfielder, said. "He knows what he's doing."

The night of their escape, after the players left the hotel, they walked for half an hour down a wide avenue called Marimavu Road. A police car drove up to them; a policewoman had recognized them from coverage of the match. "Are you okay, guys?" she asked. "What are you doing?" Semere spoke first. "We are refusing to go home because we don't have human rights," he said. All around him, his teammates began talking at once in Tigrinya, asking him to translate. "I told them, 'Keep quiet, please—give me time to think!'" he recalled. Semere asked the officer if it was safe for them to stay in Botswana. "Yes, it's safe—don't worry," she said, and then drove away.

Not long after, several police cars pulled up to the group, and officials from the team stepped out. The players backed up as if they were going to run. "Where are you going?" a coach said. "Please don't do this." The players shook their heads. "We said we are not going back—we have decided," Semere recalled. "We have been waiting for this time." As the police discussed the situation with the team officials in English, several of the players tried to convey their desperation without words. They mimed guns and made shooting sounds and grabbed the necks of their shirts.

Finally, the officers told everyone to go to the police station, a few minutes away. The Eritrean ambassador to Southern Africa, Saleh Omar, who had come to Francistown for the game, met them there. In a holding room, he pleaded with the players to return to Asmara, promising that he would protect them. "I'll take you home myself," he said. "Nothing will happen to you." When they didn't answer, he threatened that the Botswana police would arrest them if they stayed.

Filmon Berhe, another midfielder, had been quiet, listening as his teammates did the explaining. Bearded, with wary eyes, he was usually not much of a talker. But he was getting frustrated. The ambassador didn't understand what they were telling him. "Where are your children?" Berhe asked.

Omar paused. "They are living with me at the moment," he said.

"That is why you don't feel for us," Berhe said. "You don't understand what we are going through."

Omar angrily left the room and destroyed their passports. When he returned, he said, "I'm not responsible for you. You're on your own."

The mass defection was a humiliation for the government, and if the players were deported back to Asmara they could face severe punishment. (Refugees who have been forced to return speak of being tortured, and of being held for years in windowless shipping containers with little food and water.) Gebreab, the PFDJ official, suggested that the soccer team had been deliberately lured away. "How about our runners and our cyclists who compete and come back?" he said. "For me, this is cherry-picking. In Botswana, they were given cause—they said if they stay there they will be given green cards and they will be going to the United States, so most of them decided to stay. It shows that there are certain people in this country who will take any opportunity to leave."

At the police station, though, Arefaine became convinced that they had made the right decision. "It was like I was born again—I had been given a second chance," he recalled. As the teammates pleaded with the police chief, he softened, and admitted that they had the right to apply for asylum. After waiting a week in jail, they saw a Botswana lawyer, and were allowed to call their families. Arefaine told his that he was safe.

One Sunday afternoon in Asmara, I went to see Adulis, the Asmara municipal team, play Red Sea, owned by the Red Sea Trading Corporation. The players, wearing crisp uniforms in yellows and reds, warmed up on a wide green field, surrounded by a red-brown track. Old men in corduroy blazers sat on concrete bleachers, alongside boys in sweatshirts with headphones plugged into their ears. Everyone was talking and laughing with excitement.

The defection of so many good players in the past decade had left a dearth of talent. These were two of the best teams in the country, but the players' footwork was sloppy, and passes kept going out of bounds. "It's like the ball is moving on its own," one spectator said. Another, a bald man in a camel-colored blazer, looked on in disgust. "I'm not happy with this team," he said.

After halftime, Adulis scored a goal—but the ball trickled out through a hole in the side of the net. The stadium erupted. "How can that be a goal?" a bearded young man in a blue button-down shirt yelled in front of me. (The man asked not to be named, fear-ing retaliation from the government, so I refer to him as Frese-lam.) Freselam told me he had been a finalist for the national soc-cer team that had competed in Botswana but had narrowly missed the cut. Now he was playing for another club team. It was a decent life, he said: he practiced twice a week and got paid 1,600 nafka a month, along with room and board at the clubhouse.

As the game went on, the fans' frustration gave way to scuffles in the stands, and then to an all-out fracas. In the last minutes, a referee called a foul on Adulis, and Red Sea scored on a penalty kick, winning the match. Policemen wielding batons had to escort the referee out of the stadium amid fans shouting threats. "I'm going to kill you," Freselam shouted at a man who was hassling the referee. "People like you shouldn't even be here!"

After the match, Freselam headed to a pizzeria to celebrate with some of the winning athletes and fans. He had become friends with several national-team players who are now in Botswana, and had been saddened when he learned that they weren't coming back. "I was disappointed that I wouldn't see them again," he said. "But it was their choice."

When I asked about Arefaine, Freselam smiled broadly. "He was one of the strongest players, especially with his speed," he said. "He scored a lot of points."

"He's a nice guy," another player said. "We miss him a lot."

The two players said that they hadn't been surprised when Are-faine defected. It was just something that happened in Eritrea. But they were surprised to hear that he had been dissatisfied with his life there: he always seemed happy, they said. Later, Arefaine told me, "You don't want to seem to anyone that you are not happy in Asmara. Because if you do, they may arrest you."

A few months ago, Arefaine and Russom, the left back, took a minibus from the refugee camp where they have been staying to Galo Shopping Center, a fashionable mall in Francistown. An airy, light-flooded complex with an attached supermarket, it was filled with late-afternoon shoppers. The men were relieved to be away from the camp, an uncomfortable place with limited electricity and running water. "It's not what we expected," Russom said. Un-accustomed to the local food, the players had grown skinny. They had little money, scrounging what they could from sympathizers in the Eritrean diaspora and trading their food rations with local shops to buy pasta, as well as minutes for the phones they shared. They had nothing to do and nowhere to be.

"Most Eritreans—refugees and those inside the country alike —are living in extended limbo," Zere, the exiled journalist, said. "Home has turned into a source of deferred dreams and destitution, characterized by brutal dictatorship, while fleeing is becoming equally challenging." Refugees who flee the Horn of Africa face the risk of torture, rape, and murder by smugglers in the Sahara, and then a treacherous journey by sea. Yet those who make it fare much better than those who stay in Ethiopia and Sudan, who can get stuck in desolate camps. Some of the players who defected in 2008 have reconstituted their team in the Netherlands, and Arefaine and his teammates talked dreamily of their compatriots' new lives. At the camp, they ran and kicked around a ball when they could, but they were worried that they wouldn't get a chance to play professional soccer again. An official at the U.S. embassy in Gaborone, Botswana's capital, told me that the worldwide exodus of refugees, from Syria and elsewhere, had made the team a low priority for resettlement. The UN, which administers the camp, is turning it over to Botswana in a few weeks, and the government has expressed a desire to send refugees home.

A sister of one of the soccer players lives in the U.S., and she contacted John Stauffer, the president of an advocacy group called the America Team for Displaced Eritreans. Stauffer had been worried that the "astonishing" reach of the Eritrean government would thwart the team's asylum application. "The Eritrean regime strives to control the diaspora, including through agents operating out of the embassies, in order to punish refugees and defectors," he said. Refugees who wish to obtain an Eritrean passport are pressured to sign a "form of regret," admitting that they have committed an offense and agreeing to accept any punishment. They must also disclose the names of family members back home, who may become subject to fines and imprisonment. Sometimes Eritrean security forces seize refugees from camps and residences in Sudan and return them to Eritrea.

At the mall, the players tried to stay cheerful. In the parking lot, Russom gazed at the people walking toward the entrance. "I'm trying to find Samson a girlfriend," he said, laughing. But at times they still seemed disoriented by their situation. Arefaine mentioned that he had recently gone to Gaborone to meet with Eritreans living there, and they visited a huge, gleaming shopping mall called Game City. "I was confused. I thought, 'Is this Europe?'" he said, half-jokingly.

The players missed eating *injera* and *fata* and hanging out at the cafés on Harnet Avenue. They missed their friends and families. Arefaine's older sister Helen told him on Facebook Messenger to be strong, and sent him photos and updates from home. "It makes me homesick, but it's better than not having any news at all," he said. Their families have yet to experience repercussions from their defections; the players hope that the team's high profile will prevent the government from retaliating, but they can't be certain. "My family was angry I left them, and they were afraid," Arefaine said. "The government is going to do something. I am still afraid."

Outside the supermarket, Arefaine surveyed the mall: a stretch of boutiques selling clothing, shoes, books, electronics. "There's nothing like this in Asmara," he observed. "It's nice." After a moment, he corrected himself. "The cafés in Asmara are better. There's nothing nicer than the streets of Asmara." At last, though, he had managed to leave Eritrea. When I asked how it felt, he said, "We are one step ahead from where we were."

Too Fast to Be Female

FROM THE NEW YORK TIMES MAGAZINE

ONE DAY IN JUNE 2014, Dutee Chand was cooling down after a set of 200-meter sprints when she received a call from the director of the Athletics Federation of India, asking her to meet him in Delhi. Chand, then 18 and one of India's fastest runners, was preparing for the coming Commonwealth Games in Glasgow, her first big international event as an adult. Earlier that month, Chand won gold in both the 200-meter sprint and the 4-by-400-meter relay at the Asian Junior Athletics Championships in Taipei, Taiwan, so her hopes for Scotland were high.

Chand was raised in Gopalpur, a rural village in eastern India with only intermittent electricity. The family home was a small mud hut, with no running water or toilet. Her parents, weavers who earned less than $8 a week laboring on a government-issued loom, were illiterate. They had not imagined a different life for their seven children, but Chand had other ideas. Now, as she took the five-hour bus ride to Delhi from a training center in Punjab, she thought about her impending move to Bangalore for a new training program. She wondered if she would make friends, and how she'd manage there without her beloved coach, who had long been by her side, strategizing about how best to run each race and joking to help her relax whenever she was nervous. She thought little of the meeting in Delhi, because she assumed it was for a doping test.

But when Chand arrived in Delhi, she says, she was sent to a clinic to meet a doctor from the Athletics Federation of India — the Indian affiliate of the International Association of Athletics

Federations (IAAF), which governs track and field. He told her he would forgo the usual urine and blood tests because no nurse was available, and would order an ultrasound instead. That confused Chand, but when she asked him about it, she recalls, he said it was routine.

Chand had no idea that her extraordinary showing in Taipei and at a national championship earlier that month had prompted competitors and coaches to tell the federation that her physique seemed suspiciously masculine: her muscles were too pronounced, her stride was too impressive for someone who was only five feet tall. The doctor would later deny that the ultrasound was a response to those reports, saying he ordered the scan only because Chand had previously complained of chronic abdominal pain. She contends she never had any such pain.

Three days after the ultrasound, the federation sent a letter titled "Subject: Gender Verification Issue" to the Indian government's sports authority. "It has been brought to the notice of the undersigned that there are definite doubts regarding the gender of an Athlete Ms. Dutee Chand," the letter read. It also noted that in the past, such cases "have brought embarrassment to the fair name of sports in India." The letter requested the authorities perform a "gender verification test" on Chand.

Shortly after, Chand says, she was sent to a private hospital in Bangalore, where a curt woman drew her blood to measure her level of natural testosterone, though Chand had no idea that was what was being measured. Chand also underwent a chromosome analysis, an MRI, and a gynecological exam that she found mortifying. To evaluate the effects of high testosterone, the international athletic association's protocol involves measuring and palpating the clitoris, vagina, and labia, as well as evaluating breast size and pubic hair scored on an illustrated five-grade scale.

The tests were meant to identify competitors whose chromosomes, hormones, genitalia, reproductive organs, or secondary sex characteristics don't develop or align in the typical way. The word "hermaphrodite" is considered stigmatizing, so physicians and advocates instead use the term "intersex" or refer to the condition as DSD, which stands for either a disorder or a difference of sex development. Estimates of the number of intersex people vary widely, ranging from one in 5,000 to one in 60, because experts dispute which of the myriad conditions to include and how to tally them accurately. Some intersex women, for instance, have XX chromosomes and ovaries, but because of a genetic quirk are born with ambiguous genitalia, neither male nor female. Others have XY chromosomes and undescended testes, but a mutation affecting a key enzyme makes them appear female at birth; they're raised as girls, though at puberty, rising testosterone levels spur a deeper voice, an elongated clitoris, and increased muscle mass. Still other intersex women have XY chromosomes and internal testes but appear female their whole lives, developing rounded hips and breasts, because their cells are insensitive to testosterone. They, like others, may never know their sex development was unusual, unless they're tested for infertility—or to compete in world-class sports.

When Chand's results came in a few days later, the doctor said her "male hormone" levels were too high, meaning she produced more androgens, mostly testosterone, than most women did. The typical female range is roughly 1.0 to 3.3 nanomoles of testosterone per liter of blood, about one-tenth that of typical males. Chand's level is not publicly known, but it was above the 10-nanomoles-per-liter threshold that the IAAF set for female competitors because that level is within the "male range." As a result, officials said, she could no longer race.

In the two years since, Chand has been at the center of a legal case that contests not only her disqualification but also the international policy her lawyers say discriminates against athletes with atypical sex development. For Chand, who had never heard the words "testosterone" or "intersex," it has been a slow and painful education. When she was first told she was being barred because of her testosterone level, she didn't understand anything the officials were saying. "I said, 'What have I done that is wrong?'" she told me by phone in May through a Hindi translator. "Then the media got my phone number and started calling me and asking about an androgen test, and I had no idea what an androgen test was. The media asked, 'Did you have a gender test?' And I said, 'What is a gender test?'"

No governing body has so tenaciously tried to determine who counts as a woman for the purpose of sports as the IAAF and the International Olympic Committee (IOC). Those two influential organizations have spent a half-century vigorously policing gender boundaries. Their rationale for decades was to catch male athletes masquerading as women, though they never once discovered an impostor. Instead, the athletes snagged in those efforts have been intersex women—scores of them.

The treatment of female athletes, and intersex women in particular, has a long and sordid history. For centuries, sport was the exclusive province of males, the competitive arena where masculinity was cultivated and proven. Sport endowed men with the physical and psychological strength that "manhood" required. As women in the late 19th century encroached on explicitly male domains—sport, education, paid labor—many in society became increasingly anxious; if a woman's place wasn't immutable, maybe a man's role, and the power it entailed, were not secure either.

Well into the 20th century, women were discouraged from participating in sports. Some medical experts claimed that vigorous exercise would damage women's reproductive capacity and their fragile emotional state and would make them muscular, "mannish," and unattractive to men. Critics fretted that athletics would unbind women from femininity's modesty and self-restraint.

As women athletes' strength and confidence grew, some observers began to wonder if fast, powerful athletes could even *be* women. In the 1936 Berlin Olympics, the runners Stella Walsh of Poland and Helen Stephens of the United States were rumored to be male impostors because of their remarkable athleticism, "male-like" muscles, and angular faces. After Stephens narrowly beat Walsh in the 100-meter dash and posted a world record, Stephens was publicly accused of being a man, by Walsh or Polish journalists—accounts vary. German Olympics officials had examined Stephens's genitals before the event and declared her female. Four decades later, in an unexpected twist, an autopsy of Walsh revealed she had ambiguous genitalia.

In 1938, the gender of an athlete was again in dispute. The German high-jumper Dora Ratjen, a former fourth-place Olympian who won a gold medal at the European Athletics Championship, was suddenly identified as male, prompting Germany to quietly return the medal. When Ratjen's case became public years later—he claimed that the Nazis pressured him to pose as a woman for three years—it validated the growing anxiety about gender fraud in athletics. But in 2009, the magazine *Der Spiegel* investigated medical and police records and found Ratjen had been born with ambiguous genitals but, at the midwife's suggestion, was raised as a girl, dressed in girls' clothes, and sent to girls' schools. Dora lived as a female until two years after the 1936 Olympics, when police were alerted to a train traveler in women's clothes who looked suspiciously masculine. With relief so apparent that the police noted it in their report, Ratjen told them that despite his parents' claims, he had long suspected he was male. A police physician examined him and agreed, but reported that Ratjen's genitals were atypical. Ratjen changed his first name from Dora to Heinrich. But those details were unknown until recently, so for decades, Ratjen was considered a gender cheat.

By the mid-1940s, international sports administrators began requiring female competitors to bring medical "femininity certificates" to verify their sex. In the 1950s, many Olympics officials were so uneasy about women's participation that Prince Franz Josef of Liechtenstein, a member of the International Olympic Committee, spoke for many when he said he wanted to "be spared the unesthetic spectacle of women trying to look and act like men," writes Susan K. Cahn, a history professor at the University at Buffalo, in her book *Coming On Strong: Gender and Sexuality in Twentieth-Century Women's Sports.* Others were particularly bothered by women in track and field because of the strained expressions on their faces during competition. Such female exertion violated the white middle-class ideal of femininity, as did the athletes' "masculinized" physiques, prompting Olympic leaders to consider eliminating those events for women.

In 1952, the Soviet Union joined the Olympics, stunning the world with the success and brawn of its female athletes. That year, women accounted for 23 of the Soviet Union's 71 medals, compared with eight of America's 76 medals. As the Olympics became another front in the Cold War, rumors spread in the 1960s that Eastern-Bloc female athletes were men who bound their genitals to rake in more wins.

Though those claims were never substantiated, in 1966 international sports officials decided they couldn't trust individual nations to certify femininity, and instead implemented a mandatory genital check of every woman competing at international games. In some cases, this involved what came to be called the "nude parade," as each woman appeared, underpants down, before a panel of doctors; in others, it involved women lying on their backs and

pulling their knees to their chest for closer inspection. Several Soviet women who had dominated international athletics abruptly
dropped out, cementing popular conviction that the Soviets had
been tricking authorities. (More recently, some researchers have
speculated that those athletes may have been intersex.)

Amid complaints about the genital checks, the IAAF and the
IOC introduced a new "gender verification" strategy in the late
'60s: a chromosome test. Officials considered that a more dignified, objective way to root out not only impostors but also intersex
athletes, who, Olympic officials said, needed to be barred to ensure fair play. Ewa Kłobukowska, a Polish sprinter, was among the
first to be ousted because of that test; she was reportedly found
to have both XX and XXY chromosomes. An editorial in the IOC
magazine in 1968 insisted the chromosome test "indicates quite
definitely the sex of a person," but many geneticists and endo-
crinologists disagreed, pointing out that sex was determined by
a confluence of genetic, hormonal, and physiological factors, not
any one alone. Relying on science to arbitrate the male-female divide in sports is fruitless, they said, because science could not draw
a line that nature itself refused to draw. They also argued that the
tests discriminated against those whose anomalies provided little
or no competitive edge and traumatized women who had spent
their whole lives certain they were female, only to be told they
were not female enough to participate.

One of those competitors was Maria José Martínez Patiño, a
24-year-old Spanish hurdler who was to run at the 1985 World
University Games in Japan. The night before the race, a team official told her that her chromosome test results were abnormal. A
more detailed investigation showed that although the outside of
her body was fully female, Patiño had XY chromosomes and internal testes. But because of a genetic mutation, her cells completely
resisted the testosterone she produced, so her body actually had
access to less testosterone than a typical woman. Just before the
Spanish national championships began, Spanish athletic officials
told her she should feign an injury and withdraw from athletics
permanently and without fuss. She refused. Instead, she ran the
60-meter hurdles and won, at which point someone leaked her
test results to the press. Patiño was thrown off the national team,
expelled from the athletes' residence, and denied her scholarship.

Her boyfriend and many friends and fellow athletes abandoned her. Her medals and records were revoked.

Patiño became the first athlete to formally protest the chromosome test and to argue that disqualification was unjustified. After nearly three years, the IAAF agreed that without being able to use testosterone, her body had no advantage, and it reinstated Patiño. But by then, her hopes for making the Olympics were dashed.

Dutee Chand was only four when she started running, tagging along with her sister, Saraswati, a competitive runner who liked to practice sprints along the local Brahmani River. Saraswati found training boring, so she recruited Dutee, 10 years her junior, to keep her company. For years, Dutee ran in bare feet—even on the village's mud-and-pebble streets—because she had to protect the only shoes she owned: flimsy rubber flip-flops that she knew her parents could not afford to replace.

When Dutee was about seven, her parents pressed her to stop running and learn to weave instead. But Saraswati argued that with Dutee's speed, she could earn more as a sprinter. Saraswati, who has since become a police officer, reminded her parents of the benefits her own running had brought to the family. Once the district government realized Saraswati's athletic potential, she, like other athletes, was given meat and chicken and eggs, food her family had not been able to afford. And she reminded them of the prize money she brought home whenever she did well in marathons. They agreed to let Dutee run.

Not long after, Saraswati used a string to measure Dutee's foot and took a bus to the nearest city, about 60 miles away, to find an affordable pair of sturdy sneakers for her sister. The ride took three hours, frequently picking up passengers carrying goats or chickens and large bundles. When Saraswati gave Dutee the sneakers the next morning, Saraswati told me over the phone through a translator, Dutee yelped. "She asked me what can happen if she runs wholeheartedly. She asked if she would go abroad like me, and said she had never sat in a bus or a train, and asked where the money will come from for her to go abroad. I said that 'if, with these shoes, you run well, you will be sent abroad from the money that will come to you, and not just that, but you'll also get a tracksuit. So run!'"

In 2006, 10-year-old Dutee was accepted into a state-sponsored sports program more than two hours from the family's home. Food, lodging, and training were covered. She missed home but appreciated the dorm's electricity, running water, and indoor toilets. And she was happy she could send prize money to her parents.

That same year, though Dutee didn't know it, a catastrophe was unfolding for another Indian sprinter. Santhi Soundarajan, a 25-year-old from southern India, finished second in the 800 meters at the 2006 Asian Games in Doha, Qatar, all the more impressive given her roots as a member of India's impoverished "untouchable" caste. The previous decade, the IOC and IAAF yielded to pressure by the medical and scientific community and stopped sex-testing every female athlete. But the groups retained the right to test an athlete's chromosomes when questions about her sex arose and to follow that with a hormone test, a gynecological exam, and a psychological evaluation.

In Soundarajan's case, the media noted that she wasn't just fast; she also had a deep voice and a flat chest. The day after Soundarajan's race, the Athletics Federation of India drew her blood and examined her body. Some of her results were leaked to the media. Shortly after, Soundarajan was watching TV when she saw a news report that she had "failed" a sex test. Rejected by the local sports federations, stripped of her silver medal, tormented by ongoing scrutiny, and unbearably embarrassed, she attempted suicide, reportedly by swallowing poison.

As Chand began competing in national athletics, another runner from a poor rural village, this time in South Africa, burst onto the international athletic stage. When Caster Semenya blew by her opponents in the 800-meter race at the 2009 African Junior Championships, her performance raised suspicions. Shortly after, sports officials tested her as she prepared for the World Athletics Championship. Unconcerned—she assumed the investigation was for doping—Semenya won gold again. Almost immediately, the fact that Semenya had been sex-tested was leaked to the press. Instead of attending what is normally the celebratory news conference, Semenya went into hiding. The IAAF spokesman Nick Davies announced that if Semenya was an impostor, she could be stripped of her medal. He added: "However, if it's a natural thing, and the athlete has always thought she's a woman or been a woman, it's not exactly cheating."

Fellow athletes, the press, and commenters on social media scrutinized Semenya's body and made much of her supposed gender transgressions: her muscular physique, her deep voice, her flexed-biceps pose, her unshaved armpits, the long shorts she ran in instead of bikini shorts, in addition to her extraordinary speed. A story on *Time* magazine's website was headlined "Could This Women's World Champ Be a Man?" One of Semenya's competitors, Elisa Cusma of Italy, who came in sixth, said: "These kind of people should not run with us. For me, she is not a woman. She is a man." The Russian star runner Mariya Savinova reportedly sneered, "Just look at her." (The World Anti-Doping Agency would later accuse Savinova of using performance-enhancing drugs and recommend a lifetime ban.) The IAAF general secretary, Pierre Weiss, said of Semenya, "She is a woman, but maybe not 100 percent." Unlike India, South Africa filed a human rights complaint with the United Nations arguing that the IAAF's testing of Semenya was "both sexist and racist." Semenya herself would later write in a statement, "I have been subjected to unwarranted and invasive scrutiny of the most intimate and private details of my being."

After nearly a year of negotiations (the details of which are not public) the IAAF cleared Semenya to run in 2010, and she went on to win the silver medal in the 2012 Olympics. She will be running in Rio. But the federation still faced condemnation over leaks, public smears, and the very idea of a sex test. The IAAF maintained it was obliged to protect female athletes from having "to compete against athletes with hormone-related performance advantages commonly associated with men." In 2011, the association announced that it would abandon all references to "gender verification" or "gender policy." Instead, it would institute a test for "hyperandrogenism" (high testosterone) when there are "reasonable grounds for believing" that a woman may have the condition. Women whose testosterone level was "within the male range" would be barred. There were two exceptions: if a woman like Maria Patiño was resistant to testosterone's effects—or if a woman reduced her testosterone. This entails having her undescended testes surgically removed or taking hormone-suppressing drugs.

Not long after the policy went into effect, sports officials referred four female athletes from "rural or mountainous regions of developing countries" to a French hospital to reduce their high testosterone, according to a 2013 article in the *Journal of Clinical*

Endocrinology and Metabolism. The authors, many of whom were physicians who treated the women, describe telling them that leaving in their internal testes "carries no health risk," but that removing them would allow the athletes to resume competition, though possibly hurt their performance. The women, who were between 18 and 21, agreed to the procedure. The physicians treating them also recommended surgically reducing their large clitorises to make them look more typical. The article doesn't mention whether they told their patients that altering their clitorises might impair sexual sensation, but it does say the women agreed to that surgery too.

Chand was unaware of any controversy surrounding Semenya or other intersex athletes. Her gender concerns were much more immediate: she saw other 15-year-old girls becoming curvier and heard them talk about getting their periods. She asked her mother why her body wasn't doing the same thing, and trusted her answer: Chand's body would change when it was good and ready.

In 2012, Chand advanced to a national-level athletic training program, which in addition to food and lodging provided a stipend. At 16, she also became a national champion in the under-18 category, winning the 100 meters in 11.8 seconds. The next year, she won gold in the 100 meters and the 200 meters. In June 2014, she won gold yet again at the Asian Championships in Taipei.

Not long after that, she received the call to go to Delhi and was tested. After her results came in, officials told her she could return to the national team only if she reduced her testosterone level—and that she wouldn't be allowed to compete for a year. The particulars of her results were not made public, but the media learned, and announced, that Chand had "failed" a "gender test" and wasn't a "normal" woman. For days, Chand cried inconsolably and refused to eat or drink. "Some in the news were saying I was a boy, and some said that maybe I was a transsexual," Chand told me. "I felt naked. I am a human being, but I felt I was an animal. I wondered how I would live with so much humiliation."

As news spread that Chand had been dropped from the national team, advocates encouraged her to fight back. Payoshni Mitra, an Indian researcher with a doctorate in gender issues in sport who had advocated on behalf of other intersex athletes, suggested Chand send a letter to the Athletics Federation of India, requesting her disqualification be reversed. "I have not doped or cheated," Chand said in Hindi, and Mitra, who would become Chand's government-appointed adviser, translated to English. "I am unable to understand why I am asked to fix my body in a certain way simply for participation as a woman. I was born a woman, reared up as a woman, I identify as a woman and I believe I should be allowed to compete with other women, many of whom are either taller than me or come from more privileged backgrounds, things that most certainly give them an edge over me."

Mitra and others also urged Chand to take her case to the international Court of Arbitration for Sport—the Supreme Court for sports disputes—arguing that the IAAF's testosterone policy was discriminatory and should be rescinded. She agreed. Over four days in March 2015, a three-judge panel heard Chand's appeal, as a total of 16 witnesses, including scientists, sports officials, and athletes, testified.

Female athletes, intersex and not, wondered just how this case would affect their lives. At the hearing, Paula Radcliffe, the British runner who holds the women's world record for the marathon, testified for the IAAF, saying elevated testosterone levels "make the competition unequal in a way greater than simple natural talent and dedication." She added, "The concern remains that their bodies respond in different, stronger ways to training and racing than women with normal testosterone levels, and that this renders the competition fundamentally unfair."

Madeleine Pape, a 2008 Olympian from Australia, testified for Chand. Pape lost to Caster Semenya in the 2009 World Championships, Semenya's last race before her sex-test results were made public. Pape had heard runners complain that Semenya was a man or had male-like advantages, and she was angry that Semenya seemed to win so easily. "At the time, I felt that people like Caster shouldn't be allowed to compete," Pape told me. But in 2012, Pape began work on a sociology PhD focusing on women in sport. "With my running days behind me, I had the space to think more critically about all that," she says. "Until that point, I had no idea that the science of sex differences is extremely contested and has shifted over time, as have the regulations in sports, which change but don't improve as they try to get at the same questions."

Just what role testosterone plays in improving athletic performance is still being debated. At the hearing, both sides agreed that synthetic testosterone—doping with anabolic steroids—does ramp up performance, helping male and female athletes jump higher and run faster. But they disagreed vehemently about whether the body's own testosterone has the same effect.

IAAF witnesses testified that logic suggests that natural testosterone is likely to work the way its synthetic twin does. They pointed to decades of IAAF and IOC testing showing that a disproportionate number of elite female athletes, particularly in track and field, have XY chromosomes; by their estimates, the presence of the Y chromosome in this group is more than 140 times higher than it is among the general female population. Surely, witnesses for the IAAF argued, that overrepresentation indicated that natural testosterone has an outsize influence on athletic prowess.

Chand's witnesses countered that even if natural testosterone turns out to play a role in improving performance, testosterone alone can't explain the overrepresentation of intersex elite athletes; after all, many of those XY female athletes had *low* testosterone or had cells that lacked androgen receptors. At the Atlanta Games in 1996, one of the few times the IOC allowed detailed intersex-related data to be released, seven of the eight women who were found to have a Y chromosome turned out to be androgen-insensitive: their bodies couldn't use the testosterone they made. Some geneticists speculate that the overrepresentation might be because of a gene on the Y chromosome that increases stature; height is clearly beneficial in several sports, though that certainly isn't a factor for Chand.

In court, the IAAF acknowledged that men's natural testosterone levels, no matter how high, were not regulated; the rationale, it said, was that there was no evidence that men with exceptionally high testosterone have a competitive advantage. Pressed by Chand's lawyer, the IAAF also conceded that no research had actually proved that unusually high levels of natural testosterone lead to unusually impressive sports performance in women either. Nor has any study proved that natural testosterone in the "male range" provides women with a competitive advantage commensurate with the 10 to 12 percent advantage that elite male athletes typically have over elite female athletes in comparable events. In fact, the IAAF's own witnesses estimated the performance advantage of women with high testosterone to be between 1 and 3 percent, and the court played down the 3 percent figure, because it was based on limited, unpublished data.

Chand's witnesses also pointed out that researchers had identified more than 200 biological abnormalities that offer specific competitive advantages, among them increased aerobic capacity, resistance to fatigue, exceptionally long limbs, flexible joints, large hands and feet, and increased numbers of fast-twitch muscle fibers — all of which make the idea of a level playing field illusory, and not one of which is regulated if it is innate.

Bruce Kidd, a former long-distance Olympic runner, told me in May that Olympians themselves sometimes joke that they're all freaks of nature, with one or another genetic abnormality that makes them great at what they do. Kidd, a Canadian who has long pushed for gender equity in sports, noted that there are also many *external* variables that influence performance: access to excellent coaching, training facilities, healthy nutrition, and so on. "If athletic officials really want to address the significant factors affecting advantage, they should require all athletes to live in the same place, in the same level of wealth, with access to the same resources," he says. "Boy, oh, boy, there are so many unfair advantages many Olympians have, starting with who their parents are."

But the IAAF argued that testosterone is different from other factors, because it is responsible for the performance gap between the sexes. That gap is the very reason sports is divided by sex, the IAAF says, so regulating testosterone is therefore justified.

Chand's hearing, though, was about more than just testosterone. Implicitly, it questioned the decades of relentless scrutiny of female athletes—especially the most successful ones. Veronica Brenner, a Canadian who won a silver medal in freestyle skiing in 2002, told me she first learned that female Olympians had to pass a sex test when she arrived at the '98 Games in Nagano, Japan. "I said: 'Are you kidding?' I'd been competing my whole life, and my gender has never been questioned!" Brenner's test confirmed that she had XX chromosomes, and she was given what was commonly called a "femininity card" to prove she was the gender she claimed to be. But she was irked that despite the many advances of female athletes in the last half-century, powerful male athletes are celebrated and powerful female ones are suspect. "We'd hear comments all the time: 'She's really strong—she must be part guy.'"

Other critics see testosterone testing as simply the old "gender verification," the latest effort to keep out women who don't adhere to gender norms or have a standard female body. Katrina Karkazis, a bioethicist at Stanford University who is a leader of the international campaign against banning intersex athletes and who testified in Chand's case, says that if an athlete's androgen test shows she has high testosterone, she must undergo the same gynecological exam that has existed for decades. "The rationale behind the IAAF's 'hyperandrogenism regulation' is to make it sound more scientifically justifiable and less discriminatory, but nothing in those exams has changed from the old policy except the name," she says. "It's still based on very rigid binary ideas about sex and gender."

Critics of the IAAF policy argue that if sports officials were truly concerned about fairness, they would quit policing a handful of women with naturally high testosterone and instead rigorously investigate athletes suspected of taking drugs that indisputably enhance performance. They note that in the last year, the IAAF has faced bribery and blackmail charges and widespread allegations that it intentionally ignored hundreds of suspicious blood tests.

Stéphane Bermon, an IAAF witness who took part in the efforts to identify females with high testosterone, acknowledged that doping was a significant threat to fairness but said that didn't negate the need to also regulate the participation of women with naturally high testosterone who may have an advantage. He offered an analogy: "Air pollution, like tobacco smoking, contributes to lung cancer, but one should never have to choose between these two before implementing prevention measures," he wrote in an email. "As a governing body, IAAF has to do its best to ensure a level playing field . . . These two topics are different but can lead to the same consequence, which is the impossibility for a dedicated athlete to compete and succeed against an opponent who benefits from an unfair advantage."

Last July, the Court of Arbitration for Sport issued its ruling in Dutee Chand's case. The three-judge panel concluded that although natural testosterone may play some role in athleticism, just what that role is, and how influential it is, remains unknown. As a result, the judges said that the IAAF's policy was not justified by current scientific research: "While the evidence indicates that higher levels of naturally occurring testosterone may increase athletic performance, the Panel is not satisfied that the degree of that advantage is more significant than the advantage derived from the numerous other variables which the parties acknowledge also affect female athletic performance: for example, nutrition, access to specialist training facilities and coaching and other genetic and biological variations."

The judges concluded that requiring women like Chand to change their bodies in order to compete was unjustifiably discriminatory. The panel suspended the policy until July 2017 to give the IAAF time to prove that the degree of competitive advantage conferred by naturally high testosterone in women was comparable to men's advantage. If the IAAF doesn't supply that evidence, the court said, the regulation "shall be declared void." It was the first time the court had ever overruled a sport-governing body's entire policy.

Chand was thrilled. "This wasn't just about me," she said, "but about all women like me, who come from difficult backgrounds. It is mostly people from poor backgrounds who come into running—people who know they will get food, housing, a job, if they run well. Richer people can pay their way to become doctors, engineers; poor people don't even know about their own medical challenges."

Chand hoped that the ruling would prompt the IOC to suspend its testosterone policy too, so she would be eligible to try to qualify for the Rio Games. After all, the IOC policy—which also called on national Olympic committees to "investigate any perceived deviation in sex characteristics"—was based on the same science that the court deemed inadequate.

In November 2015, the IOC established new parameters for dealing with gender. But it never actually addressed whether it would suspend its testosterone policy, as the IAAF was forced to do. That ambiguity left intersex athletes in limbo. Finally, in late February, the IOC said it would not regulate women's natural testosterone levels "until the issues of the case are resolved." It urged the IAAF to come up with the evidence by the court's deadline so the suspended policy could be resurrected. It also said that to avoid discrimination, high-testosterone women who are ineligible to compete against women should be eligible to compete against men.

Advocates for intersex women were dismayed. "It's ridiculous," says Payoshni Mitra, the Indian researcher. "They say the policy is not for testing gender—but saying that a hyperandrogenic woman can compete as a man, not a woman, inherently means they think she really *is* a man, not a woman. It brings back the debate around an athlete's gender, publicly humiliating her in the process." Emmanuelle Moreau, head of media relations for the IOC, disagreed, writing in an email, "It is a question of eligibility, not gender or (biological) sex."

A separate section of the IOC gender guidelines addressed a different group of atypical women (and atypical men): transgender athletes. Unlike the intersex section, the transgender section stresses the importance of human rights, nondiscrimination, and inclusion. It eschews most of the IOC's former requirements, including that trans competitors have their ovaries or testicles removed and undergo surgery so their external genitalia matches their gender identity. In the new guidelines, female-to-male athletes face no restrictions of any kind; male-to-female athletes have some restrictions, including suppressing their testosterone levels below the typical male range. And once they've declared their gender as female, they can't change it again for four years if they want to compete in sports.

Reactions among trans advocates ran the gamut. Many trans advocates viewed the liberalized regulations as a victory. But some transwomen athletes who long ago had their testicles removed (and as a result, make virtually no testosterone) were unhappy with the policy; they argued that lifting the surgery requirement gave transwomen who still had testosterone-producing testicles an unfair advantage over transwomen who didn't. And still other advocates said that requiring transwomen to suppress their testosterone below 10 nanomoles is premised on the very same claim about testosterone that the court rejected—that naturally made testosterone is the primary cause of men's competitive advantage over women.

Without evidence that "male range" testosterone levels really do provide that advantage, some say it's premature to base a policy on speculation—especially one that requires people to transform their bodies. In May, the Canadian Center for Ethics in Sports, which manages the country's antidoping program and recommends ethics standards, issued trans-related guidelines for all Canadian sports organizations. The statement says policies that regulate eligibility, like those related to hormones, should be backed by defensible science. It adds, "There is simply not the evidence to suggest whether, or to what degree, hormone levels consistently confer competitive advantage." And yet it's hard to imagine that many female athletes would easily accept the idea of competing against transwomen athletes without those regulations in place.

Those debates are far from Chand's thoughts. Her focus now is on making the most of the window the ruling provides: allowing her to try to qualify for next month's Olympics without having to change her body. In the miserable months after her test results were revealed, Chand's training time and concentration were interrupted, and her hope of ever competing seemed out of reach. Once the ruling was issued, though, she returned to the Indian national team, and intensified her training for the 100 meters, the 200 meters, and the 400-meter relay. In addition to working out six hours a day, she tries to relax with naps and Facebook. She has made frequent trips to nations holding qualifying competitions. In May, she competed in India, China, and Taiwan; in June, in Kazakhstan and Kyrgyzstan. She has until July 11 to meet the IOC time requirement.

She is painfully aware that if she doesn't make this summer's Olympics, she may not have another chance. The IAAF may still come up with evidence that satisfies the court and would exclude women like her from competing without altering their bodies. Chand's best shot to qualify for Rio is in the 100 meters, which she must complete in 11.32 seconds or less. She remains one-hundredth of a second short.

The Longest Run

FROM SPORTS ILLUSTRATED AND TIME

THEY RAN. So goes the first act of a refugee: a scramble for food or clothing, a grab of the nearest helping hand, flight. Were the soldiers coming to take territory? Coming for forced conscripts the way they did two years before, when Yiech Pur Biel's father ran and never came back? In those first moments it didn't matter; the soldiers were coming. So Biel and his mother, two sisters, and younger brother rushed out of their home, five more drops in the human flood rushing into the scrubby forest outside the town of Nasir, in the northeast of what would soon become South Sudan.

This was 2005. What month? Biel doesn't remember. What season? He can't say. He was 10 then, an age when time means little but the loss of home feels like the earth cracking. "When they attacked us," he says, "I saw it was the end of my life with my family."

It got worse. Biel—who would grow up intent on proving, along with the nine other members of the Refugee Olympic Team at the Rio Games, that refugees "are not animals"—then took what is often the next step. He lived like an animal. Hiding in the bush, senses on high alert, no food to be had. For three days his family, sleepless, bellies screaming, foraged for fruit and climbed trees for their bitter leaves.

Finally Biel's mother, Nyagony, made a decision. The border with Ethiopia was only 19 miles away, a week's walk; maybe they could get food there. Biel was the oldest boy. There was no avoiding the cruel calculus: She could handle three children on the road but not four. "You see," Biel says, "if I am 10 years, I can survive without her, maybe."

He tried to understand. His mother placed him with a woman from their neighborhood, gathered his brother and sisters, and went. So began the refugee's third, most wrenching act, the separation endured worldwide, in some form, by more than 21 million refugees and another 44 million forcibly displaced people. Biel has not spoken to his mother and siblings since then. He doesn't know if they survived the trek, the soldiers, the years.

While relating all this in July, during a break at the Tegla Loroupe Training Center in Ngong, Kenya, about 14 miles outside Nairobi, the 21-year-old Biel speaks in a high monotone, his face giving away nothing. He says he cried the day his mother left him, but it wasn't his worst moment. That came after, when he went with the neighbor lady and her two children back to Nasir and found his hometown in ashes. "They burned everything," he says of the soldiers. "There was nothing: the village has gone. They took animals, even killed some. The army go away. All that remained were the dead people."

That's when Biel knew: he was lost. The neighbor lady would be going now, surely, and he was terrified that she too would do the math, "turn against me," and leave him behind. "I thought it was my end," he says. So for the next 24 hours, one full day, the boy waited for his dying to begin.

When International Olympic Committee president Thomas Bach announced the 10 members of the first-ever Refugee Olympic Team in June — after a yearlong global vetting by 17 national Olympic committees and the United Nations Refugee Agency and after countless tryouts in Europe and Africa that resembled nothing so much as the hunt for Willy Wonka's golden tickets — he clearly intended the impact to redound far beyond sports. "A symbol of hope to all the refugees in our world," Bach called the squad. "It is also a signal to the international community that refugees are our fellow human beings and are an enrichment to society.

"These refugees have no home, no team, no flag, no national anthem. We will offer them a home in the Olympic Village together with all the athletes of the world."

A cynic might call this a stroke of marketing genius. What with endless reports out of Rio about depleted budgets, political collapse, social unrest, the Zika virus, and the consequent withdrawal of high-profile athletes; amid striking allegations of systematic doping by traditional powers Russia and Kenya; and after making laughable bets that staging recent Olympics in China and Russia would improve those countries' human rights records, the Olympic brand has taken a savage beating. A bit of humanitarian counterprogramming, smacking of Baron Pierre de Coubertin's ideals, surely couldn't hurt.

"We need to remind [people] that sport is a unique tool to improve society," says Pere Miró, whose IOC title is deputy director general for relations with the Olympic movement. "This is . . . a kind of hope for some people that can get us back to our roots."

To be fair, Bach had been thinking about pairing the worldwide refugee crisis—the worst since World War II—and the Olympics almost from the moment he took office in September 2013. Tegla Loroupe, the Kenyan marathon legend, had been scouting and training talented South Sudanese refugees for years; Bach spoke to her that fall about expanding the work worldwide, and last September the IOC authorized $2 million in funding for the effort. "I was always wishing that I had somebody to help me," says Loroupe, whose training camp welcomed 30 refugee runners last October. "If it was not for IOC, I couldn't support these athletes."

Meanwhile, the crisis is so great, and the journeys of some athletes have been so harrowing, that the Refugee Team's march into Maracanã Stadium under the Olympic flag during the opening ceremony, just before Brazil's delegation, figures to be irresistible. There will be swimmer Yusra Mardini, 18, of Syria, where a five-year civil war has killed more than 400,000 people and scattered four million refugees across the Middle East and Europe. In the summer of 2015, Mardini, one of Syria's top freestylers, boarded an inflatable dinghy in Izmir, Turkey, bound for the Greek island of Lesbos. When the boat's motor died, she jumped into the Aegean Sea with her older sister, Sarah, and another refugee and kicked for three hours, pushing and pulling the boat to safety. "I hated the sea after that," Yusra said at a news conference in March.

Land didn't treat her much better. The women trekked and rode trains for 25 days through Greece, Macedonia, Serbia, Hungary (where they were detained in a refugee camp before escaping), and Austria before settling in Berlin. By late autumn Mardini had found a pool and a coach. Her compatriot Rami Anis, 25, a butterflyer, was not far behind.

Shaken by the bombings and kidnappings in his hometown of

Aleppo, Anis had flown to Istanbul in 2011 with two pairs of pants, two T-shirts, and two jackets, expecting to stay there with an older brother for a short time. Four years later, one night in October, Anis paid smugglers to ferry him and his younger brother from Izmir to the Greek island of Samos. It took another nine days for them to travel overland through Macedonia, Serbia, Croatia, Hungary, Austria, and Germany to Belgium, where they decided to stay.

"The part at sea was the worst," Anis says. "As a swimmer, I was worried because we were going to take a raft with children and old people. You have to imagine everything: *What if the boat toppled? Of course, I would not only swim and rescue my life . . . I would try to help as many people as possible*. It was terrible to go through this experience. Thankfully, it passed."

The Syrian war, of course, was the main source of the more than one million refugees who flowed into Europe in 2015, a surge that, paired with fears of terrorism, is challenging (and often transforming) the politics, culture, and self-image of every country from Greece to Great Britain. But long-standing conflict, drought, and instability also scattered 160,000 Ethiopians in that time, including Refugee Team marathoner Yonas Kinde, 36, who has been living, running, and driving taxis in Luxembourg since 2011. "I left because of political problems," Kinde told the IOC, "but I am here and I am lucky."

No Olympic refugees, however, have been flung farther than judokas Popole Misenga, 24, and Yolande Mabika, 28. A five-year civil war in the Democratic Republic of Congo killed some 5.4 million people—including Misenga's mother—before officially ending in 2003, but continued fighting in the east, including the judokas' hometown of Bukavu, has since forced 450,000 people to flee. Misenga and Mabika defected during the 2013 world championships in Rio and never left the city. Mabika, separated from her family as a child, is hoping that her Olympic fame just might be seen by her father, mother, or brother, prompting them to reach out.

Their routes to these Games differ, but all the Olympic refugees share the same mission: to change the conversation. They know that refugees have become easy scapegoats in scared societies, easy applause lines for politicians, and all too easy to caricature as criminal or unclean. In Rio they hope to present an alternative to all the wire photos of crowded camps and dead bodies washed ashore, relieve the basic human fear of the *other*. They want to show that they can march in a parade, wave, smile, run, and compete—just like everyone else.

"It is very challenging when you are chased away from your homeland," says Anjelina Nadai Lohalith, 22, a 1,500-meter runner from South Sudan. "Nobody can feel happy when you are chased or you stay in another country. But right now I feel proud. I'm proud to be a refugee.

"We are representing the millions of refugees all over the world. Maybe, in years to come, I will represent myself. But at this moment we are their light. Wherever they are, at least they will now have some encouragement and know: *We* can *do something*. Wherever they are, they are human beings. They are not animals. That's why we have been given this chance. So they should not be looked down on. Or treated unfairly."

Late on Friday, July 8, word came in that James Nyang Chiengjiek's home was dropping once more into hell. Chiengjiek, 28, a South Sudanese 800-meter runner whose father was killed in 1999 during the Sudanese civil war, had fled his village at 13 to avoid being kidnapped by the soldiers who snatched two of his friends. Now he stood outside the social hall at Loroupe's training center. A teammate walked up, fresh off a phone call from South Sudan's capital. "Fighting has broken out in Juba," he said.

Artillery, machine-gun fire: forces aligned with the president were battling those loyal to the vice president. A tenuous peace in the country's latest, 32-month civil war—with a "unity" government paralyzed by internal distrust—was unraveling fast. Chiengjiek wasn't upset. "No, no, it's good," he said. One side would finally beat the other into submission, he figured, "and after this all the fighting will stop."

In truth, the road to a clear resolution figures to be long and brutal. At least 300 people died and 40,000 fled Juba in the ensuing four days, casting fresh doubt on the viability of the world's youngest nation. A shattered economy had already forced cancellation of festivities marking South Sudan's fifth birthday, and it was just as well; since independence the nation has done little to be proud of. More than half its children don't attend school. In March the United Nations accused the government of war crimes that include the mass murder of civilians and allowing soldiers to rape women in lieu of being paid. South Sudan, the UN report concluded, has created "one of the most horrendous human rights situations in the world."

It seems only right, then, that fully half of the 2016 Refugee Team—Biel, Lohalith, Chiengjiek, 800-meter runner Rose Nathike Lokonyen, and 1,500-meter runner Paulo Amotun Lokoro—call South Sudan home. Aside from age-old disrupters like war and famine, South Sudan features some of the most extreme abuses that drive off today's refugees. Chiengjiek first "ran," as all the runners call it, because the army wanted to brainwash children into being soldiers. Meanwhile, half of South Sudanese girls between 15 and 19—and some as young as 12—are subjected to forced marriage. Lohalith decided, at all of nine years old, to go with an aunt to Kenya because her Didinga community expected her to submit to early marriage.

"But I was planning to go to school by then," she says. "I was wishing to become a doctor."

Political and tribal authorities aren't the only ones creating nightmares. Separating mostly Christian South Sudan from Muslim-dominated Sudan in 2011 seemed a fairly straightforward task compared to reconciling the nation's warring ethnicities. The dominant Dinka and Nuer tribes have forever battled for power, which helps explain the current hostilities: on one side the Dinka, led by president Salva Kiir, and on the other the Nuer, led by vice president Riek Machar. And though some 650,000 South Sudanese have bolted the country since the conflict began in 2013, they didn't leave those tensions behind.

All five South Sudanese runners came through the 25-year-old Kakuma Refugee Camp, a holding area for 185,000 people in northwestern Kenya. "When refugees fight [among] themselves, you face a lot of challenges," says Lokonyen, 23, who lived in Kakuma from the time she was nine until last fall. In 2014 the Dinka and the Nuer battled there for weeks with sticks, guns, and the machetes called pangas. "So many people were dying in that fighting," she says, gesturing to the back of her neck. "I saw: they were cutting one of the young kids, he was Dinka, cut by panga. He passed away. One of my tribe—Didinga—was killed as well."

Preventing tribal divisions from infecting the Ngong training center was a priority when the 30 runners began arriving last October. "It wasn't easy, let me tell you," Loroupe says. She has had more experience with this than most: since 2001 the two-time winner of the New York City Marathon has persuaded rival East African warlords and politicians to run together in well over a dozen "peace races." Aided by Kenya's Olympic committee and coaches, Loroupe put together a roster of refugee Olympic candidates that included runners from Congo, Somalia, Burundi, and Ethiopia, but most were South Sudanese Dinka, Nuer, and Didinga, fresh from Kakuma and from Kenya's even larger refugee camp at Dadaab.

"I did not know that even these people had been fighting," Loroupe says. She split the captaincies between a Nuer and a Didinga and told everyone, "Forget what happened in your camp. We are here as ambassadors. We have been chosen. If I knew we had these kinds of personal issues, I would not waste my time coming all the way to Kakuma. Show a good example. Be a new person that your people in Kakuma will see, so they can also change."

Lohalith, like Lokonyen a Didinga, saw her village burned to the ground by Dinka tribesmen. That act touched off a lonely 16-year journey; Lohalith never spoke to her family again. But she —and her teammates—say that Loroupe's training center never buckled under tribal conflict. Lohalith takes no satisfaction in the fact that no Dinka is included among the five South Sudanese runners eventually chosen. The IOC made the final decision and, Miró says, based it solely on the ability of each refugee to, if not medal, "compete, at least, in the Games."

"In running they don't choose according to tribe, but by performance," Lohalith says. "We were selected as *refugees,* so we should not think about tribe. Let us leave the things of the past and live like one people. Right now we are working for the competition and the Olympics. Let us focus on only one thing, as a team."

Early on July 9, South Sudan's eclipsed Independence Day, two dozen runners at Loroupe's training center gathered on the rutted dirt road outside the barred gate. Fighting continued in Juba, about 700 miles to the north; no one spoke of it. Instead, the human mix of nations, tribes, sexes—some of them Olympians, the rest those who'd once hoped to be—stretched and milled until someone gestured. Then they formed a tight knot, flung arms across each other's shoulders, and pulled. All heads bowed. "Almighty Jehovah father, we thank you for the new day that you've given to us," said a raspy voice from within. "We always pray for you to come upon us and give us protection and also heal us from all injury. In Jesus's name that we pray and we believe. Amen."

The refugees all said "Amen" again, together, and straightened up. Then they ran off, slow at first, into a morning cool and calm.

At first sight Loroupe's training center presents a feast for spoiled Western eyes, teeming as it is with all that isn't there. The name prepares you for one of those state-of-the-art sweat palaces built by D-I colleges to woo blue-chippers, yet the four-building facility couldn't be more basic. The orphanage and former trade school features one bench press, one set of weights, and a pair of cows to supply the athletes' twice-weekly ration of milk. Everyone sleeps four to a room. Breakfast is white bread and a cup of sweet tea.

To say that these runners don't know what they're in for next month is no exaggeration. For some, last fall's flight from Kakuma to Nairobi was their first time on an airplane. None of the final five have ever watched an Olympics, much less competed in an elite meet. "They ask us, 'You guys will be going to Rio?'" says Lokonyen. "I didn't even know what *is* Rio."

But in a sense the refugees have already moved to the cutting edge of modernity, at least by the standards of rural Africa. Growing up in the Pokot tribe, Loroupe heard constantly that because she was a girl, she was "worthless" and shouldn't bother with studies. Her father had four subservient wives. "I was the first girl to do sport in my family and the first to go to school without permission," says Loroupe, 43. "My community, when they realize that you're a very good person, will support you 100 percent, like a man. But you have to work for it."

Inveighing against tribalism is one thing. But the women who arrived at Loroupe's training center last fall were stunned to hear her rule of daily engagement: the women were not to wait on the men. They all were athletes first, and the men would share the responsibility of cleaning and maintaining the center. After Saturday's morning run both sexes scrambled to sweep the courtyard; Chiengjiek mopped a floor. "We have to follow Madame Tegla," he says. "She is peacemaking."

Perhaps no one was happier to hear that message than Lokonyen. Growing up she loved to play soccer, against her father's wishes; he'd beat her, she'd promise not to play again, then run out the next day to find a game. "If I come back, and he do a quarrel with me or beat me, I just say, 'No problem,'" she says. "Because I have passion to play."

In 2002 the 10-year-old Rose began life as a refugee when a gun-toting band of Toposa tribesmen burned her Didinga community in Ngatuba; her family hurried into the bush and within three days made it to Kakuma. If there was anything good about being displaced, it was that unlike back home, she got no grief from elders about playing soccer. In 2007, just about the time the 15-year-old Rose started running in high school, her parents left Kakuma to return to their village and see if any relatives had survived. She hasn't spoken with them since.

"I stayed with my four siblings, and I was the one taking care of them, as the eldest," she says. "I have to come to school and work at the same time for them, fetching water, cleaning the compound, and washing the uniforms. It was very hard for me to concentrate in school. Your parents are away, and you don't know if they're still alive. They were supposed to take care of you, yet you're now the one who is taking care of the younger. You are now the parent, and yet you have nothing."

Not quite. Lokonyen is quick to say that she's grateful for Kakuma. The Kenyan camp—which the government is planning to close, having decided to accept no more refugees—provides residents with food, shelter, medical care, and schooling. But no one wants to be there for long, and its environs can be dangerous. Shortages of firewood send refugee women out into the bush to forage, where they are often set upon by Kenyans from the surrounding community. "They do rape people in the forest," Lokonyen says. "So many of them. One of the women was raped because she . . . didn't know how to run [fast]. I found the woman: she was just crying."

Lokonyen knew how to run fast. Last August, Loroupe, in concert with the UN Refugee Agency, went to Kakuma to quietly hold 10-kilometer qualifying races for men and women; Lokonyen's second-place finish got her an invite to the training center in Ngong. She hesitated for only a moment. Her brother is now 17; she figured it's his time to fetch water and look after the three youngest. She calls once a week. Her siblings go to school hungry sometimes, and she worries about them walking alone.

"This is a great opportunity for me, so I have to go and leave them," Lokonyen says. "God only knows whether they are well, but let them stay. At least they are in their own house, and God will protect them." She pauses. Then she says, "I came out of the family, and I left them alone."

Lokonyen once asked her siblings whether that was the right decision, knowing the answer. It was what any refugee in a camp would say to someone handed a lifeline. Go ahead, they told her. Work hard. Maybe you'll win and make money, enough to come back and change our lives.

When asked her personal best in the 800, Lokonyen says, "2:22," then smiles and adds, "I need to reduce." It's true: the Olympic qualifying time is 2:01.50. But then, all the South Sudanese runners have come up well short of the qualifying times for their events and been waived into the games by the IOC. Of the 10 refugee athletes, in fact, only marathoner Yonas Kinde would have made it to the Olympics strictly on athletic achievement—had he a nation to represent.

The team's current statelessness, of course, makes membership an honor only if it's temporary; the sooner the athletes lose refugee status, the better. That's why perhaps the most successful candidate in the selection process didn't make it. Taekwondo fighter Raheleh Asemani of Iran was atop the short list after winning the women's under-57-kilogram class in European qualifying in January, but in April she was granted citizenship in Belgium. She will compete under its flag in Rio.

The rest will be guaranteed only a walk in the opening ceremony, a bed in the athletes' village, and a place in qualifying. That's plenty, of course, but the refugees point out that they've been training just nine months, while other Olympians have had a lifetime to prepare. Before last October none of the South Sudanese had ever worked out with weights, thought about diet, or endured twice-daily practices, timed and charted. None had ever lived as an athlete or raced so often—much less in a cooler climate and under a new kind of stress. Knees barked. Chests got congested. More than half of the runners at Loroupe's training center, including the lone Dinka woman, got sent back to Kakuma or Dadaab. Lohalith came down with malaria.

"A lot of injuries, diseases that never come up: our bodies were responding," says Lohalith, whose personal best for the 1,500 is 4:52. (Olympic qualifying is 4:07.) "A few managed to bear with it, then the team began a lot of trials. I came up with [a faster] time. Even though we were told, 'You are not *that* qualified,' at least we were better. Now we are getting used to it. I cannot hope to win, but I will go and try my best to compete—no matter how hard it is. I cannot walk off the field. I have to at least try to finish."

It's impossible to miss the Walter Mitty factor here; Hollywood screenwriters should be taking notes. Being on this team is the closest an Everyman will ever come to competing in the world's most prestigious sporting event. Never mind the irony of trying to prove that refugees are "like anybody else" by lining them up against the most uncommon humans alive. Before their luck turned, Lokoro and Biel herded cattle. Misenga loaded trucks. Chiengjiek was studying to be a car mechanic. Concede an accident of fate, of being born in the wrong place at the wrong time, and they've been like anybody else all along.

Still, they don't want to hear that. The five South Sudanese runners intend to return to Loroupe's training center after their longest journey yet (Nairobi to Johannesburg to Rio and back again); they want to see if, with more training, they actually can be elite athletes. And it looks as if Madame Tegla will have them. The IOC's $2 million training fund is all but exhausted, Miró says, but he expects it to be renewed. "We have a lot of, let's say, offers to cooperate in something for these 10 people," he says. "What we'd like is that these offers will continue after the Games for many other people."

All of the South Sudanese runners speak of wanting to follow Loroupe's example: win races around the world, build careers, pass on what they've learned. "If I do something better in my life, I want to help the refugees who have suffered like me," Lokoro, 24, says. "So many refugees have talent but don't have a chance. I want to have a place like this so they can rise up, run, and go somewhere, visit other continents like me now. It is all opening up for me. My life, it's like a new one."

Unwittingly, perhaps, the IOC has given the 10 something they've never had—a bit of control. Refugees, especially young ones, spend most of their lives shunted about by great forces such as war, climate, tribe, and bureaucracy. Even now the refugee Olympians are being directed daily by Loroupe's foundation, coaches, UN refugee officials, media handlers, and the imperatives of the IOC. But for the first time they've been given room to hope, and better: to make a plan.

"I know I have a message to tell the world," Biel says. "First, I feel a lot of pressure because millions of refugees are looking to us to tell what they are living. Secondly, it's about my nation: South Sudan. If I succeed and only go live abroad, there's no legacy that I give to other people. I want to come back and serve the nation, show them the way as a peacemaker, tell the world that we can challenge our leaders. Because the leaders make the problems. Thirdly, it's about my family. The background I come from; it's a terrible history, you see. I must change that. Maybe I can go back to that village now to help the young people. Because I know that it's not only my family that was suffering, and I can go serve them. I am going to rescue my people from that disaster."

No, Yiech Pur Biel didn't die. Because what the refugees say is true, of course: they are not animals. They are like anyone else, capable of great good amid even the worst times. The neighbor lady, Rebecca Nyagony Chuol, did not desert Biel the day after his mother walked away in 2005—though no one would have blamed her if she had. Her husband had just been killed, and she had two boys to raise alone, and the UN people triaging the chaos in Nasir had tabbed Chuol and her children to be rescued first. The truck for Kakuma was filling up. "We are going," Chuol told Biel. "But I don't think your mother is coming back. And we're not going to leave you here."

So she told the UN refugee workers that Biel was part of her family. And he went with her to Kakuma and lived with her like a third son. "I call her Mom because she's caring for me and treats me the same as she did her own children," Biel says. "They saved my life."

He didn't grow up running. He loved soccer; a lanky defender ranging across the grassless pitches of Kakuma, he could go all day if asked. He ran the occasional school relay, to help out, but never more than a lap or two. Then, a year ago, a posting went up in the camp: Tegla Loroupe was coming in August to stage a 10-kilometer race, and the best would earn spots at her training center and

a chance at the Olympics. Biel liked that runners controlled their
own fate. He thought, *Why not me?*

He had one pair of sneakers, barely; holes gaped under the
balls of both feet. "There was no sole," he says. "I was tying them,
and I say, 'God help me now.'"

Biel, running the whole way on his toes, finished third. The
flight from Kakuma to Nairobi was his second, the first having
come when the UN flew Chuol's family into Kakuma a decade before. After news got around that Biel was one of the 30 chosen, he
received a phone call from an uncle in Juba. "Your family is alive,"
the man said. "Your mother, your brother, even your father. They
are all back in Nasir."

Biel has no idea if this is true. He still hasn't spoken to anyone
in his family, can't go back himself, and says that in his culture,
people lie rather than confirm bad news long-distance. "I cannot
believe it," he says, "because when you are far away, they cannot
tell you the truth: they don't want you to be hurt. But sometimes I
think about it and say, okay, maybe they are alive, and it makes me
happy. I say . . . *maybe*. Imagine: for 12 years I never see my father,
and then this guy tells me that he's alive. It's hard."

Still, all the while Biel kept working, improving, surviving cuts:
when 16 of the originals at Loroupe's training center were replaced in February, when the IOC named the 43 final candidates
worldwide in March, when the list of candidates at the training
center was sliced down to 14 later that spring. And with each step
an idea took firmer shape: if he makes something of this chance,
makes any money, he will get Chuol and her sons out of Kakuma.
"That is the way I can thank them," Biel says.

On June 3 the runners gathered inside the social hall at
Loroupe's training center for the IOC's announcement. No hints
had been given. The coaches kept warning them: only one of you
might go to Rio. It's okay. Don't despair if you're not chosen.

A video screen popped to life, relaying the image of Thomas
Bach sitting at a table in Lausanne, Switzerland. Some runners
prayed. Some felt their hands shaking. Then they heard their
names being read from far away, one by one, five of them inside
that room in Kenya. "It felt like a dream," Lokoro says.

The first was Biel's. At the unreal sound of it—*him, his name!*—
coming out of a TV on a wall, his eyes filled. He thought about his
mother and the last time, 11 years ago, he had cried. Now he wept

again, happily. When the cameras and reporters and his team-mates crowded around him, he could barely speak.

"It was too big," Biel says, but if you've never lost everything, you might not understand. That was the bell signaling the last leg of a long, desperate run. A refugee is on the move. Cheer hard. Look at him—look at all of them—go.

JOHN BRANCH

Why Steve Kerr Sees Life Beyond the Court

FROM THE NEW YORK TIMES

THE LAST TIME Steve Kerr was in Beirut, his birthplace, with the bombs pounding the runway and the assassination of his father six months away, he left by car.

The airport was closed. There was talk of taking a cruise ship to Cyprus, or accompanying an ambassador on a helicopter to Tel Aviv, or even crossing into Israel on a bus. A military plane headed to Cairo had an empty seat, but it went to someone else. Finally, a hired driver took Kerr over the Lebanon Mountains and across the Syrian border to Damascus, then on to Amman, Jordan. It felt like an escape.

"I'm fearful that all this uncertainty and inconvenience, not to mention even a sense of physical danger, has not done Steve's image of Beirut much good, and in his present mood he wonders what any of us are doing here," his father, Malcolm H. Kerr, the president of the American University of Beirut, wrote to other family members that day in August 1983.

A few months later, Malcolm Kerr was shot twice in the back of the head outside his university office.

Steve Kerr was 18 then, quiet and sports-obsessed. He was a lightly recruited freshman at the University of Arizona, before it was a basketball power. It took a vivid imagination to see him becoming an NBA champion as a player and a coach, now leading the Golden State Warriors.

But perhaps it should be no surprise that, at 51, Kerr has found his voice in public discourse, talking about much more than basketball: heavy topics like gun control, National Anthem protests, presidential politics, and Middle East policy. With an educated and evenhanded approach, he steps into discussions that most others in his position purposely avoid or know little about, chewing through the gray areas in a world that increasingly paints itself in bold contrasts.

In many ways, he has grown into an echo of his father.

"The truly civilized man is marked by empathy," Malcolm Kerr wrote in a foreword to a collection of essays called *The Arab-Israeli Confrontation of June 1967: An Arab Perspective.* "By his recognition that the thought and understanding of men of other cultures may differ sharply from his own, that what seems natural to him may appear grotesque to others."

In a rare and sometimes emotional interview this fall, Kerr spoke about the death of his father and his family's deep roots in Lebanon and the Middle East. Some of the words sounded familiar.

"Put yourself in someone else's shoes and look at it from a bigger perspective," he said. "We live in this complex world of gray areas. Life is so much easier if it could be black and white, good and evil."

Providing commentary on the state of today's politics and culture is not a prerequisite for Kerr's job. There are sports fans, maybe the majority of them, who wish athletes and coaches would keep their non-sports opinions to themselves—stand for the anthem, be thankful for your good fortune, express only humility, and provide little but smiles and autographs.

Kerr understands that. Sports are a diversion for most who follow them, "only meaningful to us and our fans," he said. In a sports world that takes itself too seriously, that perspective is part of the appeal of Kerr and the Warriors. They won the 2015 NBA championship, were runners-up last season, and remain a top team this season. They seem to be having more fun than anyone else.

But Kerr also knows that sports are an active ingredient of American culture. He knows, as well as anyone, that players are complicated, molded by background, race, religion, and circumstance.

And Kerr is too: a man whose grandparents left the United States to work in the Middle East, whose father was raised there, whose mother adopted it, whose family has a different and broader perspective than most. The Kerrs are a family touched by terrorism in the most personal way. Malcolm Kerr was not a random victim. He was a target.

That gives Steve Kerr a voice. His job gives him a platform. You will excuse him if he has a few things to say.

"It's really simple to demonize Muslims because of our anger over 9/11, but it's obviously so much more complex than that," he said. "The vast majority of Muslims are peace-loving people, just like the vast majority of Christians and Buddhists and Jews and any other religion. People are people."

He delved into modern Middle East history, about World War II and the Holocaust and the 1948 creation of Israel, about the Six-Day War in 1967, about peace accords and the Israel-Palestine conflict and the Iraq War and the United States' scattered chase for whatever shifting self-interest it has at any particular time.

"My dad would have been able to explain it all to me," Kerr said. Instead, he absorbed it as a boy and applies it as an adult. "He at least gave me the understanding that it's complex. And as easy as it is to demonize people, there's a lot of different factors involved in creating this culture that we're in now."

Malcolm Kerr was a professor at UCLA for 20 years, and the sprawling ranch house where the family lived in Pacific Palisades, California, has a flat driveway and a basketball hoop bolted to the roof above the garage. Steve Kerr spent countless hours in the driveway practicing the shot that would give him the NBA record for career three-point percentage that still stands. But not all memories in the driveway are about basketball.

"I remember when the Camp David accords happened," Kerr said, recalling the 1978 peace talks between Menachem Begin of Israel and Anwar el-Sadat of Egypt, shepherded by President Jimmy Carter. Kerr had just entered his teens.

"One of my best friends was a guy named David Zuckerman, a Jewish guy, and his father was an English professor," Kerr said. "Mr. Zuckerman and David drove me home from baseball practice or something, and we pull up in the driveway and my dad sees us and comes running out. Mr. Zuckerman's name was Marvin, and my dad said: 'Marvin, Marvin! Did you see the picture today of Begin and Sadat?' It was the biggest thing. It would have been the equivalent of the Dodgers winning the World Series. He was so excited for that moment because that is what he really hoped for: Middle East peace. That was his dream. That day, I'll never forget it."

Kerr paused.

"And then it was only a short time later that Sadat was killed," he said.

The Sadat assassination was in October 1981, just 27 months before Malcolm Kerr was killed.

"We Were the Good Guys"

Malcolm Kerr's parents, Stanley and Elsa Kerr, were American missionaries who met in the Middle East after World War I. He worked for American Near East Relief in Turkey during the slaughter of countless Armenians (detailed later in his memoir *The Lions of Marash*). She had traveled to Istanbul to study Turkish and to teach. They married in 1921 and moved to Lebanon to run orphanages. They went on to teach at the American University of Beirut for 40 years.

Malcolm was one of their four children. He went to the United States for prep school and graduated from Princeton before he returned to AUB for graduate school. It was there that he met Ann Zwicker, an Occidental College student from California spending a year studying abroad.

Beirut was a cosmopolitan, sun-kissed city on the Mediterranean, a mix of Christians and Muslims seemingly in balance, if not harmony. AUB was founded in 1866 (it celebrated its 150th anniversary on December 3) as a bastion of free thought and diversity, welcoming all races and religions. As wars and crises suffocated the Middle East in recent decades, it has often felt like an island, protected by prestige and open-mindedness.

Malcolm and Ann married and raised four children: Susan, John, Steve, and Andrew. The first three were born in Beirut. Malcolm Kerr took a teaching job at AUB, but the Kerrs settled in California when Steve was a toddler. Malcolm Kerr's tenure at UCLA was sprinkled with sojourns and sabbaticals that persistently pulled the family back to the Middle East.

Steve Kerr spent two separate school years in Cairo. There were summers in Beirut and Tunisia, another year in France, and road trips circling the Mediterranean in a Volkswagen van. Steve "was not always thrilled," he admitted, to leave friends and the comfort of California. He hated to miss sports camps and football and basketball games at UCLA, where the Kerrs had season tickets.

In hindsight, though, his family's long history in the Middle East, beginning nearly 100 years ago, shaped him in ways that he only now realizes.

"It's an American story, something I'm very proud of, the work that my grandparents did," Kerr said. "It just seemed like a time when Americans were really helping around the world, and one of the reasons we were beloved was the amount of help we provided, whether it was after World War I, like my grandparents, or World War II. I'm sort of nostalgic for that sort of perception. We were the good guys. I felt it growing up, when I was living in Egypt, when I was overseas. Americans were revered in much of the Middle East. And it's just so sad what has happened to us the last few decades."

Kerr was in high school when his father was named president of AUB in 1982. It was Malcolm Kerr's dream job. But the appointment came as Lebanon was embroiled in civil war. Yasir Arafat's Palestine Liberation Organization, expelled from Syria, had its headquarters in Beirut. Iranian Shiites, followers of Ayatollah Ruhollah Khomeini, had moved into Lebanon and given voice to the impoverished Shiite minority there. The Christian population was shrinking, and Lebanon was in the middle of a tug of war between Israel and Syria.

"I bet there's a 50-50 chance I'll get bumped off early on," Malcolm Kerr told his daughter, Susan, in March 1982, she recalled in her memoir, *One Family's Response to Terrorism*.

He accepted the job the next morning. The Israeli invasion of Lebanon, and the countermove by the Iranians to send its Iranian Revolutionary Guards there through Syria, began in June 1982, weeks before Malcolm Kerr was to start the new job. In the chaos, Iran-backed militants were organizing and would eventually become Hezbollah.

Malcolm Kerr was kept in New York until things settled, but AUB's acting president, David Dodge, was kidnapped in July, and AUB was in need of leadership. Malcolm Kerr arrived in August, expressing hope that the destruction and death closing in on the campus could be kept outside its walls. (Dodge, who was released by his captors after a year, died in 2009.)

Back in California, Steve began his senior year and starred on the basketball team.

"I wanted him to be at games, but I knew that he was doing what he loved," Kerr said. "And when you're 16 or 17, you're so self-absorbed. You just want to play and do your thing."

Malcolm Kerr wrote letters home almost daily. They detailed tense meetings with political leaders, the latest assaults on Beirut, the assassination in September 1982 of the Lebanese president-elect, Bashir Gemayel, the interviews with foreign journalists. Most were filled with optimism and good humor.

"The thought of being in Pacific Palisades for Christmas is more appealing than I can say, and I wouldn't miss the chance for anything," he wrote in one. "Hopefully I'll get there in time to catch a few of Steve's basketball games and watch Andrew wash the cars."

That December, the Kerrs posed at their California house wearing matching AUB sweatshirts.

Steve Kerr went with his mother and brother Andrew to Beirut in the summer of 1983, before he went to play at Arizona for the first-year coach Lute Olson. A few months before, militants had bombed the United States embassy in Beirut, killing 63, including 17 Americans. But the visit fell during what felt like a lull in the war.

"We went hiking in the mountains above Beirut and swimming in the Mediterranean," Kerr said. "The house where they lived was on campus—the presidential house, the Marquand House. It was beautiful. It was surreal. There was a butler. We didn't have that back home. But now he was living the life of the president. We had a great time during the day, and then we played cards after dinner outside."

The trick was leaving. Ann Kerr went with Steve to the airport in August.

"There was some question about whether flights would be going out because of everything that was happening," Kerr said. "We were in the terminal, and all of a sudden there was a blast. It wasn't in the terminal but on the runways. The whole place just froze.

Everybody just froze. People started gathering, saying, 'We've got to get the hell out of here.' My mom grabbed me, and I remember running out of the terminal and through the parking lot. It was really scary. I remember thinking, 'This is real.'"

The Kerrs pondered options for getting Steve out. They learned that a private plane of diplomats was going to the United States Marine base and there might be an available seat on the flight back out. Steve spent hours waiting, talking to Marines. In the end, there were no seats. The Kerrs eventually made arrangements for a university driver to take Steve over the mountains, through Syria to Jordan. (The driver, a longtime friend of the family, was killed by a sniper in Beirut in 1985.)

On an early morning in October 1983, a truck bomb destroyed the four-story Marine barracks. Among the dead were 220 Marines and 21 other service members.

"I remember looking at all the photos afterward," Kerr said. He started to cry. "I see all these, the nicest people, who I met and they were showing us around the base and just trying to do their jobs and keep the peace. And a truck bomb?"

Kerr said he recognized some of the faces of the dead.

"There is a chaplain who had come over and kind of taken us under his wing," he said. "The nicest guy. And I saw his face . . ."

Kerr wiped his eyes and took a deep breath. "What has it been, 30 years? And it still brings me to tears."

In December, John visited his parents in Beirut. They had a videotape of Steve's first game for Arizona a couple of weeks before. The picture was fuzzy, shot without sound from a camera high in the gym, and they could not always tell which player was Steve. It did not matter.

"I think he scored three baskets, and we must have watched each of them 10 times, rewinding the tape over and over again just to relish every detail," John wrote in an entry for a family scrapbook made on an anniversary of Malcolm Kerr's death. He called it "Dad's and my high point as sports fans."

In the middle of a night in January 1984, Kerr got a call in his dorm room from Vahe Simonian, a family friend and a vice president at AUB who was based in New York. Simonian told Kerr that his father had been killed.

The assassination on January 18, 1984, was international news, including on the front page of the *New York Times*. Malcolm Kerr,

52, had stepped off the elevator toward his office in College Hall and was shot in the back of the head. The two unknown assailants escaped. A group calling itself Islamic Holy War took responsibility later that day.

"Dr. Kerr was a modest and extremely popular figure among his 4,800 students and faculty, according to his colleagues here," *Times* reporter Thomas L. Friedman wrote from Beirut that day. "He was killed, his friends insist, not for being who he was, but because now that the Marines and the American Embassy in Beirut are smothered in security, he was the most vulnerable prominent American in Lebanon and a choice target for militants trying to intimidate Americans into leaving."

Andrew Kerr, who was 15 at the time, heard about his father's death on a radio in a shop near AUB's campus. Ann Kerr learned about it while waiting at a campus guardhouse, out of the rain, for a friend. She ran to College Hall, to the second floor, where she found her husband "lying on the floor, face down, his briefcase and umbrella in front of him," she wrote in her memoir, *Come with Me from Lebanon.*

A memorial service was held a few days later. John came from Cairo and Susan came from Taiwan. Steve was the only one of the children who did not attend. He missed another one at Princeton, but attended a third in Los Angeles.

"It sounds bad," he said. "Obviously, the basketball wasn't more important. But the logistics were really tricky. And it was cathartic for me to just play."

He had a breakout game in a victory over rival Arizona State two nights after his father's death. The Wildcats had been 2-11, but won eight of their final 14 games. The next year, they reached the NCAA tournament on their way to becoming a lasting national power.

Four years later, Kerr was the target of pregame taunts at Arizona State. A group of students shouted, "PLO, PLO," "Your father's history," and "Why don't you join the Marines and go back to Beirut?"

"When I heard it, I just dropped the ball and started shaking," Kerr said at the time. "I sat down for a minute. I'll admit they got to me. I had tears in my eyes. For one thing, it brought back memories of my dad. But, for another thing, it was just sad that people would do something like that."

Where the Vision Comes From

Ann Kerr-Adams is 82, wears Keds, and keeps her hair in a chin-length bob. She is the longtime coordinator of the Fulbright program at UCLA and oversees a class called "Perceptions of the United States Abroad." She is also an emeritus trustee at AUB and usually goes back to Beirut once a year for meetings.

She remarried in 2008. She and Ken Adams share the California house that she and Malcolm bought in 1969.

The stately living room, with a grand piano and views of the Pacific Ocean, is neatly decorated with treasures of a well-traveled life, like etchings of Cairo and Ann's framed watercolors of Tunisia. The mantel has an oval-framed photograph of Steve and Andrew in a field of flowers in Morocco.

"I would say Steve's intellectual interests really blossomed in the last 10 years," she said. "But I don't think of Steve being like Malcolm."

They shared a passion for sports (the children's hour-a-day limit for television did not apply to sports) and an irreverent sense of humor. But Steve is more diplomatic than his father, she said.

A nearby guest room was where the three Kerr boys slept. The bunk beds that Steve and Andrew shared are gone, but there is a painting that Steve did as a boy—a self-portrait of him in a UCLA shirt and a Dodgers cap, his blond hair hanging past his ears. The bathroom has a painting of poinsettias he did when he was nine, and a closet contains his screen prints of boats in Cairo.

"Here's a picture of Steve, the ornery teenager," Kerr-Adams said on a recent Sunday afternoon, stopping in a hallway lined with family photographs. "He was always snarling in pictures. Now he has to smile for photos. The irony of it all."

Across the hall is the room that Malcolm used as an office. His children harbor happy memories of the sound of his typewriter clacking and the smell of the popcorn that he liked as a snack.

The backyard, with wide ocean views that test the flexibility of the human neck—from Los Angeles on the left, to the Santa Monica Mountains on the right—features a broad patio. On Sunday afternoons, it was frequently filled with professors, neighbors, visiting dignitaries, and friends from around the world. It was the family's connection to the Middle East that made his childhood unique.

"It would be totally different without that," Kerr said. "Totally different. I wouldn't be exposed to not only the travel and the interaction with people, but I wouldn't be exposed to the political conversations at the table and at barbecues about what was going on in the world."

But talk around the house was more likely to involve the Dodgers or Bruins. Malcolm was a good athlete, a basketball player growing up and an avid tennis player until the end. He and Steve spent a lot of time at the high school hitting and fielding, and Malcolm sometimes joined Steve in the driveway.

"He was a lefty and had a nice hook shot," Kerr said with a laugh.

Kerr credits his father for his demeanor on the sideline as an NBA coach: calm and quiet, mostly, and never one to berate a player. Kerr was not always that way.

"When I was eight, nine, ten years old, I had a horrible temper," Kerr said. "I couldn't control it. Everything I did, if I missed a shot, if I made an out, I got so angry. It was embarrassing. It really was. Baseball was the worst. If I was pitching and I walked somebody, I would throw my glove on the ground. I was such a brat. He and my mom would be in the stands watching, and he never really said anything until we got home. He had the sense that I needed to learn on my own, and anything he would say would mean more after I calmed down."

His father, Kerr said, was what every Little League parent should be. The talks would come later, casual and nonchalant, conversations instead of lectures.

"He was an observer," he said. "And he let me learn and experience. I try to give our guys a lot of space and speak at the right time. Looking back on it, I think my dad was a huge influence on me, on my coaching."

Kerr played for some of the best basketball coaches in history—Olson at Arizona, Phil Jackson with the Chicago Bulls, and Gregg Popovich with the San Antonio Spurs among them. By the standards of basketball coaches, they were worldly men with interests far beyond the court.

"I remember Phil talking to the team about gun control, and

asking the players: 'How many of you have guns? How many of you know that if you have a gun in your house you're more likely to have a fatality in your house?'" Kerr said. "It was a real discussion, with guys saying that we need to have some level of protection, because we are vulnerable in many ways too.

"And I remember one presidential election, it was probably 2000, I was with the Spurs and we did two teams shooting—the silver team against the black team or whatever," he said, referring to a drill run by Popovich. "Pop was like, 'Okay, Democrats down there, Republicans down here.' I think it was about 12 against two at that point, so he had to even up the teams a little bit. He would just make it interesting."

Kerr—who has three children, all young adults, with his wife, Margot—has never talked about his father in front of the team, and Warriors players have only a vague notion of Kerr's family history. It is context, mostly, an unstated part of his background.

"I really realized from Pop and Phil that I could use my experience as a kid and growing up to my advantage as a coach," Kerr said. "And connect with players and try to keep that healthy perspective. Keep it fun, and don't take it too seriously."

It was during Kerr's tenure with San Antonio that the family, after years of reflection following the 1996 passage of the Antiterrorism and Effective Death Penalty Act, decided to sue Iran. The Kerrs came to believe that Iranian-sponsored Hezbollah had targeted Malcolm.

"I didn't need revenge, I didn't need closure," Steve Kerr said. "So I was indifferent to the lawsuit. But then I recognized that it was important to a couple of members of my family, my sister and my younger brother, in particular."

When it came time to testify in United States District Court in Washington in December 2002, Kerr was with the Spurs, in the last of his 15 seasons in the NBA. He did not want to miss games.

"There's nobody better than Pop to talk about something like this," Kerr said. "I told him, 'I don't really want people knowing what it is.' I didn't want the attention. But I also don't want people thinking I'm injured. So Pop said: 'You missed two games for personal reasons. Big deal. Your reputation precedes you. Nobody is going to question what's going on with you.' And he was right. I told my teammates and nothing ever really came of it."

He testified in a nearly empty courtroom, missing two Spurs

road games on the West Coast. The Kerrs learned two months later that they had won the suit — millions of dollars that they may never see. But money was never the point.

"It provides a structure to enable people to channel their feelings through justice and the rules of law, rather than become vigilantes," his sister, who is now known as Susan van de Ven, said in a phone interview from England, where she is involved in politics as a county councilor. "It gives a very focused approach to people who are rightly and insanely aggrieved. That's the kind of culture we should have. We shouldn't be responding with violence. I'm sure that's why Steve talked about guns. It's all related, isn't it?"

Her book detailed the family's experience with the lawsuit.

The night before the Warriors visited President Obama to celebrate their 2015 NBA championship, Steve had dinner with Andrew, who works for an architectural design and residential builder in Washington. They discussed what Steve might say to the president. Andrew recommended complimenting him on his efforts toward gun control. Kerr did.

In June, at the end of a podcast with Bay Area sports columnist Tim Kawakami, Kerr asked if he could raise one more topic. Our government is "insane," he said, not to adopt stronger background checks on guns that most Americans agree upon.

"As somebody who has had a family member shot and killed, it just devastates me every time I read about this stuff, like what happened in Orlando," Kerr said, referring to the June massacre at a Florida nightclub. "And then it's even more devastating to see the government just cowing to the NRA and going to this totally outdated Bill of Rights right to bear arms. If you want to own a musket, fine. But come on."

Since then, Kerr has become a go-to voice in sports for matters of bigger meaning. It surprises his family in some ways, knowing that he was probably the quietest of the siblings as a child.

"He's carrying around the family business in another discipline," said John Kerr, a professor of community sustainability at Michigan State. "There was no way he would do anything for a living that didn't involve sports. No way. And now that he's at the pro level, he has the opportunity to speak out. He's smart enough to realize he can do it."

NBA training camps began just as debate swirled over the decision by Colin Kaepernick, the San Francisco 49ers quarterback, not to stand for the National Anthem, a protest over the killing of unarmed black men by police officers. Amid the divisiveness, Kerr was a nuanced voice in the middle.

"Doesn't matter what side you're on on the Kaepernick stuff, you better be disgusted with the things that are happening," Kerr said.

He added: "I understand people who are offended by his stance. Maybe they have a military family member or maybe they lost someone in a war and maybe that anthem means a lot more to them than someone else. But then you flip it around, and what about nonviolent protests? That's America. This is what our country is about."

In November, after the presidential election, Kerr was among the NBA coaches, including Popovich, who criticized the state of political discourse in the age of Donald J. Trump.

"People are getting paid millions of dollars to go on TV and scream at each other, whether it's in sports or politics or entertainment, and I guess it was only a matter of time before it spilled into politics," Kerr said. "But then all of a sudden you're faced with the reality that the man who's going to lead you has routinely used racist, misogynist, insulting words."

It is no surprise, then, that Kerr also has opinions on the Middle East. Like his father decades ago, Kerr said he believes that American policies have muddied the region. The heart of the problem, he said, stems from the lack of a two-state solution for Israel and Palestine. The Iraq War made things worse.

"To use Colin Powell's line, 'If you break it, you own it,' and now we own it," Kerr said. "And it's, like, 'Oh, my God, wait, it's so much more complicated than we thought.' Everybody looks back and thinks we would have been way better off not going to war. That was really dumb. But history repeats itself all the time. We didn't need to go into Vietnam, but circumstances, patriotism, anger, fear—all these things lead into war. It's a history of the world. It just so happens that now is probably the scariest time since I've been alive."

In Beirut, AUB still thrives. On its campus overlooking the Mediterranean is a new College Hall, a virtual replica of the one where Malcolm Kerr was killed, the building destroyed by bombs in 1991. There is the dignified Marquand House, where Malcolm

Kerr lived when he was a young professor and returned to when he became president.

In an oval garden between College Hall and the chapel, there is a banyan tree that Malcolm Kerr climbed as a boy and carved with his initials, now high out of sight. Under the tree is a Corinthian column that the family chose in the days after his death to mark the spot where his ashes were buried.

"In memory of Malcolm H. Kerr, 1931–1984," the engraving reads. "He lived life abundantly." Those were the words that Susan wrote on a piece of paper that marked the site until the stone was etched. The paper is still there, on a plaque that also features an excerpt from Kerr-Adams's book. "We are proud that our dad and husband came to AUB," Susan wrote, in words that are now faded with time.

Steve Kerr has never seen it. He has not been back since his father was killed. But, more and more, he hears the echoes.

PATRICK HRUBY

Four Years a Student-Athlete

FROM VICE SPORTS

BEFORE ROBERT and Amy McCormick could see the racial injustice at the heart of big-time college sports, they had to wake up —literally. It was the summer of 2002, and the McCormicks, a married pair of professors at Michigan State University, were living in an East Lansing neighborhood located between a block of student housing and the school's athletic department.

Every morning around 5:30 a.m., Michigan State athletes would ride their bicycles past the McCormicks' house on their way to practice. Among them was Charles Rogers, one of the best college football players in the country, a tall, speedy wide receiver whom professional scouts were likening to National Football League star Randy Moss.

One morning, Robert saw Rogers whizzing by, his six-foot-three frame dwarfing a rickety bike that barely seemed roadworthy. *He's a first-round NFL draft choice,* thought the sports and labor law professor, who had attended Michigan State himself and taught a sports law class at the university since 1984. *Next year, he'll be making millions. But now, he's making nothing.*

The imbalance ate at the McCormicks: college sports were a multibillion-dollar business, and here was a top talent stuck with a dilapidated two-wheel. While standing on the field at the school's Spartan Stadium during a football game, something else struck Robert, an image he couldn't shake. The players were in uniform, covered in Michigan State's green and white colors, but Robert could see their bare lower legs. "Almost all of them," he says, "were black." Just like Rogers. Meanwhile, everyone else—the coaches, the administrators, the faces in the crowd, and Robert himself— was overwhelmingly white.

"I saw a small group of black faces in the stands, and they were [football] recruits," Robert says. "It was incredible. I realized all of the people being paid or getting the pleasure out of the game were white, and the vast majority of the people playing and risking their health were black."

When the championship game of the National Collegiate Athletic Association's men's basketball tournament between the University of North Carolina and Villanova University tips off tonight in Houston, the scene will be similar, a microcosm of major college revenue sports as a whole. Most of the players on the court —whose sweat and sacrifice make the whole show possible—will be African American. Almost everybody else, from Tar Heels coach Roy Williams and Wildcats coach Jay Wright to the corporate glad-handers in the luxury boxes, will not. The game will be the culmination of another successful season for a cash-rich campus athletics industry—and thanks to the NCAA's long-standing amateurism rules, which apply to college athletes and no one else in America, the lion's share of that money will flow from the former group to the latter. From the jerseys to the suits.

From black to white.

"You have two sets of legal rules that treat two different classifications of people differently, and it's unjustified," Amy McCormick says. "I would never say college sports are as bad as a system where people are jailed and killed, but it's an Apartheid system."

In 2010, Amy and Robert coauthored a law journal article titled "Major College Sports: A Modern Apartheid," arguing that revenue-producing campus football and men's basketball hold black athletes in "legal servitude for the profit and entertainment" of whites. "These are sharp words," they wrote, "but the facts are indisputable."

Others agree. Sports agent Don Yee, whose firm represents NFL players including New England Patriots quarterback Tom Brady and retired linebacker Dhani Jones, calls the NCAA's refusal to pay athletes a racial injustice. Nobel Prize–winning economist Gary Becker described campus amateurism as a regressive wealth transfer from mostly poor African American athletes and their families to mostly well-off white managers, nonrevenue sport athletes. and their families. Pulitzer Prize–winning civil rights historian Taylor Branch has written that Division I revenue sports exude "an unmistakable whiff of the plantation," while former NCAA executive director Walter Byers—a man who ran the organization for decades and essentially built modern college sports as we know them—wrote in his *Road to Damascus* memoir that his creation was suffused with a "neo-plantation mentality" in which the economic rewards "belong to the overseers," with "what trickles down after that" going to young men such as Rogers.

It's not hard to see what's happening, the McCormicks say. You just have to look.

"One group is predominantly white, the other is predominantly black, and only one has the power and writes the rules for its benefit," Robert says. "I was a big Michigan State fan for a long time before we wrote our first article, and it's kind of embarrassing it came so late in my life. But once you see it, you can't unsee it."

Understand this: there's nothing inherently racist about amateurism itself. And there's no reason to believe that its defenders and proponents—including current NCAA president Mark Emmert—are motivated by racial animus. When amateurism was fashioned out of whole cloth by Victorian-era English aristocrats, its ethos was strictly classist: snobby upper-class rowers didn't want to compete against unwashed bricklayers and factory workers, and concocting an ersatz Greek athletic ideal of no-pay-for-play provided convenient justification. Likewise, the American colleges that copied their English counterparts at the dawn of the 20th century weren't looking to plunder African American athletic labor—not when their sports and campuses, like society at large, were still segregated.

Today, the economic exploitation within college sports remains race-neutral on its face. The association's strict prohibition on campus athletes receiving any compensation beyond the price-fixed value of their athletic scholarships applies equally to players of every color. White former Texas A&M University quarterback Johnny Manziel couldn't cash in on his market value any more than black former Auburn University quarterback Cam Newton could. When black former Vanderbilt University center Festus

Ezeli was suspended in 2011 for accepting a meal and a hotel room from a school alumnus, it wasn't any different than when white former University of Nebraska quarterback Eric Crouch was suspended eleven years earlier for accepting a plane ride and a ham sandwich from a candidate for the school's board of regents.

And yet, while the NCAA's intent is color-blind, the impact of amateurism is anything but. In American law, there is a concept called *adverse impact,* in which, essentially, some facially neutral rules that have an unjustified adverse impact on a particular group can be challenged as discriminatory. For instance, the Supreme Court ruled in a landmark 1971 case that a North Carolina power company could no longer require prospective employees to have a high school diploma and pass two intelligence tests—a screening process that didn't relate to job performance but did have the effect of excluding high numbers of African American applicants at a workplace that already was highly segregated. Similarly, sociologists speak of *structural racism* when analyzing public policies that have a disproportionately negative impact on minority individuals, families, and communities. State lottery systems that essentially move money from predominantly lower-class African American ticket buyers to predominantly middle- and upper-class white school districts fit the bill; so does a War on Drugs that disproportionately incarcerates young black men; so does a recent decision by officials in Maricopa County, Arizona, to drastically cut the number of presidential primary polling stations in and around Phoenix, which unnecessarily made voting far more difficult for the residents of a nonwhite-majority city.

Big-time college sports fall under the same conceptual umbrella. Amateurism rules restrain campus athletes—and only campus athletes, not campus musicians or campus writers—from earning a free-market income, accepting whatever money, goods, or services someone else wants to give them. And guess what? In the revenue sports of Division I football and men's basketball, where most of the fan interest and television dollars are, the athletes are disproportionately black.

According to the NCAA, 58.3 percent of Division I basketball players and 47.1 percent of Division I football players in 2014–15 were black, making them the largest racial group in both sports. Focus on the Power Five conferences that gobble up most of Divi-

sion I's broadcast revenues, and the picture largely looks the same
—black participation percentages are a bit lower in the Big Ten
and Pac-12, and the same or higher in the others:

Conference	Percentage of Black Football Players in 2014–15	Percentage of Black Men's Basketball Players in 2014–15
SEC	57.6	66.7
Big Ten	41.5	51.2
Pac-12	37.5	49.2
ACC	51.3	57.0
Big 12	50.0	60.2

African Americans also make up a disproportionate share of
the very best, most valuable athletes in college sports—that is, the
prep recruits ranked the highest coming onto campus, and the
departing players most coveted by the NFL and the National Basketball Association. The McCormicks found that 82 percent of the
top 250 high school football seniors and 88 percent of the top
150 high school basketball seniors in 2010 were black. Don Yee,
the sports agent, calculates that in recent NFL drafts, five times as
many black players were taken in the first two rounds as white players. In the last five NBA drafts, 84 percent of the top 10 selections
who played college basketball were black.

According to the U.S. Census, blacks made up 12.3 percent of
the nation's total population in 2012. Meanwhile, a 2016 study by
the University of Pennsylvania's Center for the Study of Race and
Equity in Education found that black men made up only 2.5 percent of the overall student population at the schools in the five
biggest Division I conferences. In other words, African Americans
aren't just overrepresented in big-time college sports; they're *wildly*
overrepresented.

This does not hold true, however, when it comes to positions of
power. The head of the NCAA always has been a white man, and
none of the Power Five conferences has ever had a nonwhite com-

missioner. A 2015 study by the University of Central Florida's Institute for Diversity and Ethics in Sport of the 128 Football Bowl Subdivision schools—most of the major college sports money-makers —and a second UCF study of campus athletics as a whole found that industry decision-makers were overwhelmingly white:

Football Bowl Subdivision School Positions	Percentage White in 2014–15
University president	89.8
Athletic director	86.7
Head football coach	87.5
Assistant football coach	67.2
Conference commissioner	100
Faculty athletic representative	89.9
Full-time faculty	75.2

NCAA Division I Positions	Percentage White in 2013–14
NCAA senior executive	76.5
NCAA director	81.9
NCAA administrator	79.8
Division I associate athletic director	87.2
Division I assistant athletic director	88.1
Division I men's head basketball coach	86.8
Division I athletic administrator	84.6

The white-majority leadership of college sports has a long history of acting in its own economic self-interest when it comes to the rights of black athletes. Consider basic participation: in the 1930s and 1940s, Northern teams typically benched their African

American players in order to participate in profitable Southern bowl games—Boston College twice benched Lou Montgomery to play in the Cotton and Sugar Bowls—while in the 1960s and 1970s, Southern teams integrated their football squads because failing to do so was competitive (and financial) suicide. Does the current amateurism status quo reflect more of the same? It's hard not to wonder.

"You could argue that the system is not failing us, that it is doing exactly what it is intended to do," says Eddie Comeaux, an associate professor of higher education at the University of California–Riverside who has studied race, diversity, and structural inequality in college sports, and once played Division I baseball at the University of California–Berkeley. "Think of the stakeholders. The coaches, presidents, the people in positions of privilege and power—namely, white men—all benefit handsomely from this enterprise."

Now follow the money. The NCAA takes in roughly $700 million annually from CBS, Turner, and ESPN for the broadcast rights to March Madness—a sum that reportedly will jump to nearly $900 million per year from 2019 to 2024. ESPN is paying $7.3 billion over 12 years to televise the College Football Playoff and four other bowl games—about $470 million annually, or roughly $67 million *per contest*. Major football conferences are collecting hundreds of millions more through their own television deals and networks—the SEC [Southeastern Conference] made a NCAA record $455.8 million in 2014–15—and Yee says college sports merchandising and licensing revenue exceeds $4 billion annually.

According to *Institutional Investor*, the 124 schools with major football teams brought in a combined $8.2 billion in athletic revenue in 2014, double what they made a decade earlier. Dan Rascher, a San Francisco–based economist and expert witness for the former athlete plaintiffs in the recent *O'Bannon v. NCAA* federal antitrust trial, estimates that Division I football and men's basketball generate between $10 billion and $12 billion in yearly revenue.

No matter how you measure it, that's a lot of cash. Where does it go? Mostly not to the predominantly black athletes who play the games. NCAA rules restrict player compensation to athletic scholarships, small cost-of-living stipends—worth roughly $2,000 to $5,000 per semester—and association hardship funds for things such as travel for family medical emergencies. (Oh, and athletes are also allowed to keep up to $1,350 worth of bowl game swag bags and gifts, like the Xbox One video game consoles handed out at the Military Bowl.) The result, Rascher says, is that Division I college football and men's basketball players only receive about 10 percent of the total revenue they help generate.

The rest largely ends up in white pockets. Outside of the athletes, compensation levels across major campus sports are astronomical. Williams and Wright, the coaches in tonight's men's basketball championship game, earn $2 million and $2.5 million a year, respectively. NCAA president Emmert was paid $1.8 million in 2013. The five power conference commissioners, all white men, earned between $2.1 million and $3.5 million the same year. University of Alabama football coach Nick Saban, who won the college football championship earlier this year, makes about $7 million annually; his program's *strength coach* (who is also white) reportedly makes over $600,000. Clemson University football coach Dabo Swinney was the lowest-paid College Football Playoff coach at $3.3 million per year, and has a "chief of staff" who makes only $252,000.

According to *USA Today*, nine campus athletic directors in 2013 were paid more than $1 million a year, and the average salary for the position at FBS schools was roughly $515,000. Average base pay for head football coaches at the same universities exceeds $2 million, while 37 of the 68 head coaches in this year's NCAA men's basketball tournament made more than $1 million annually. Yee notes that bowl game directors can make nearly $1 million for administering a single game. There are other job perks too. The *Washington Post* reports that the Pac-12 gave commissioner Larry Scott an interest-free, $1.86 million loan to buy a four-bedroom, four-bathroom, wine bar–equipped 4,600-square-foot home in 2009. Expense report documents viewed by VICE Sports show that former University of Washington football coach Steve Sarkisian, who made about $2 million a year in salary, was also given football and basketball tickets in 2011–12 valued at almost $19,000, all while the school leased his wife a $55,000 sport utility vehicle.

Then there are non-revenue sport athletes: swimmers and rowers, golfers and cross-country runners, tennis and lacrosse players, most of them supported and subsidized by the profits from big-time football and men's basketball. Like the people in charge of college sports, NCAA statistics indicate that this group is primarily white:

Division I Sport	Percentage of White Athletes in 2014–15
Cross-country	72.9
Field hockey	77.4
Golf	65.9
Ice hockey	62.3
Lacrosse	85.6
Rowing	75.4
Soccer	66.1
Softball	71.6
Swimming	77.3
Tennis	43.2
Volleyball	67.6

This matters too. As *Fortune* points out, U.S. Census data indicates that African American households make around $35,000 a year, about 35 percent less than the average white household. Meanwhile, the Aspen Institute's Project Play reports that the poorer the family, the less access their children typically have to the increasingly expensive youth sport feeder system that stocks the rosters of these non-revenue sports. The result? Black athletes paying the freight for white ones, even though the former group is more likely to need the money than the latter. "The idea that you rob the poor to pay the rich is what's happening," says Renae Steiner, a Minneapolis-based antitrust lawyer who worked on the *O'Bannon* case. "The [college] lacrosse team gets no revenue. Well, who plays lacrosse?"

Add it all up, and this is the amateurism-enabled wealth transfer that Nobel Prize–winning economist Becker and others have diagnosed, the one the McCormicks can't unsee. Just how much money is being extracted from black athletes and their families by the major college sports industry? Let's do some back-of-the-envelope math. In the NFL and NBA—where football and basketball players are free to unionize and collectively bargain with their employers—athletes receive about half of total league revenues. In major college sports, it's 10 percent. Bump that up to a pro-level 50 percent, and that's an extra $4 billion annually for all revenue sport athletes.

Since African Americans make up about 53 percent of football and basketball players put together, that means they're losing about *$2.2 billion,* each and every year.

Of course, that's a rough guess, and one that lumps both sports and every Division I conference and school together. In 2011, the National College Players Association, a college athlete advocacy group, and Drexel University professor Ellen Staurowsky published a study estimating that if FBS football and basketball players received the same percentage of industry revenues as their professional counterparts, the average football player would be worth $121,048 per season, and that the average basketball player would be worth $265,027. For the very best athletes at the biggest, most lucrative college programs, those numbers could be even higher: the average University of Texas football player would be worth $514,000 a season, while the average Duke University basketball player would be worth $1 million.

Keep in mind, those numbers were based on college sports revenues in 2010–11; given the subsequent influx of additional television money, those estimates would be even higher today. Moreover, Staurowsky's estimates don't take into account any potential outside athletic income—like athletes signing autographs for cash, or starring in commercials for local car dealers, or getting paid for wearing Nike hightops instead of seeing coaches and administrators pocket money for wearing branded shoes during golf outings with donors, and sticking the company's swoosh logo on equipment trucks. Nevertheless, they help show what amateurism costs the average African American major college football or basketball player: somewhere between $500,000 and $1 million over a four-season campus career, a tidy sum that those same athletes will never, ever get back.

A well-known NCAA television advertising campaign claims that "there are 400,000 NCAA student-athletes, and almost all of them will go pro in something other than sports." This is true. Only 1.2 percent of college basketball players are drafted by the NBA; just 1.6 percent of college football players reach the NFL. So for the vast majority of those revenue-sport athletes, the four years they spend starring on ESPN's *Big Monday* or in the Battlefrog Fiesta Bowl are the prime earning years of their athletic lives, and likely of their lives in general—in 2010, the percentage of American households with adjusted gross incomes of over $500,000 a year was less than 1 percent in 49 of 50 states.

"Several black athletes have told me how even when they get a [cost-of-living] stipend, they have to send it back home to help family out," says Billy Hawkins, a University of Georgia professor who studies the sociology of sports and is the author of *The New Plantation: Black Athletes and College Athletics.* "Whereas the majority of white athletes coming from middle class families don't have those same responsibilities. So even if and when white athletes are experiencing economic exploitation, it can still be a disproportionate impact."

When African American former Northwestern University quarterback Kain Colter led a high-profile push to unionize his school's football team in 2014, he did so for a number of reasons: deep misgivings over the power imbalance between NCAA schools and athletes; a lack of financial support for players, especially ones from poorer families; a pattern of steering athletes away from useful and demanding courses of study, the better to keep them eligible for sports; and a system that didn't seem to do enough to protect football players from brain trauma, nor provide medical coverage for athletes whose campus injuries can afflict them for life.

According to the book *Indentured: The Inside Story of the Rebellion Against the NCAA,* Colter also had a personal motivation for demanding change: the story of his uncle, Cleveland, a former football star at the University of Southern California.

Cleveland Colter was supposed to be one of the athletic one-percenters. As *Indentured* reports, he went from top high school recruit to All-American safety, and was considered the best athlete on a Trojans defense that also featured future NFL stars Junior Seau and Mark Carrier. However, a debilitating knee injury his senior year derailed his professional prospects. Years of investing his time and sweat into a sport, and he wouldn't have a cent to show for it. Today, he runs a school lunch catering business. Imagine what an extra $500,000 would have meant to him, and how it might have changed his life. Imagine what that would mean to any black revenue-sport athlete. That's money to start a business. Buy a home or a rental property. Pay for a child's education. Take care of a sick relative. Stick into a stock market index fund, ignore for 40 years, and then retire with peace of mind. Imagine black athletes building lasting wealth for themselves and their communities—in 2013, the median net worth of white American households was $141,900, while the same figure for African American households was just $11,000—instead of watching powerful white people do the same.

"They've imposed a tax on football and basketball players," says Sonny Vaccaro, the longtime shoe company dealmaker who helped spearhead the *O'Bannon* lawsuit and has become one of the NCAA's most vocal critics. "That's what it is. A tax. Like what the British put on the Americans. They take the money that could be pouring back into those player's lives. The money comes from mostly one segment of society: African Americans.

"It is *Downton Abbey*. We just won't accept it."

Hold up. Aren't African American football and men's basketball players receiving something of immense value from the NCAA system? Aren't they getting a college education—and a debt-free education, to boot?

Isn't that a fair and just exchange?

A few days before the Final Four, Pac-12 commissioner Scott, a white man who made $3.4 million in 2014, and Big East commissioner Val Ackerman, a white woman whose salary is unreported— her predecessors in the job reportedly made around $500,000 annually—copublished an editorial on CNN.com arguing as much. Under a headline reading "College Athletes Are Educated, Not Exploited," they claimed that 67 percent of all Division I athletes will go on to become college graduates—a slightly higher graduation rate than that of non-athletes—and that campus athletes receive something even more important than a degree: namely, "they're taught how to be successful in college and in life."

For black athletes, however, this is too often not the case. Already disproportionately shut out of an economy they power through sweat, blood, and concussions, they disproportionately receive substandard educations as well.

Seventeen years ago, a NCAA report examining Division I athletes who enrolled in school in 1992–93 found that just 42 percent of black football players and 33 percent of black basketball players had graduated after six years—far below a 54 percent graduation rate for male students in general. Today, the situation has improved, but not by much. In 2012, a University of Pennsylvania study reported that the six-year graduation rate for black male college athletes in six major Division I conferences was 50.2 percent, less than comparable graduation rates for all students (72.8 percent), all college athletes (66.9 percent), and all African American male students (55.5 percent). In 2016, an update found that the black male graduation rate had slightly improved to 53.6 percent. Also this year, a University of Central Florida study found that the NCAA's graduation success rate—another six-year measure that accounts for school transfers—for black men's basketball players on this year's 68 NCAA tournament teams was 75 percent, 18 points lower than the rate for white players. (The graduation rate for black football players on 2014–15 bowl teams was 66 percent, 19 percent lower than the rate for white players.)

"Disproportionately, they are not graduating," Comeaux, the UC Riverside professor, says. "It's largely based on a notion that it's not a priority, that classes are just there to maintain eligibility so they can participate in sports."

Indeed, graduation rates don't tell the whole story. In his research, Comeaux has found that engagement with faculty is crucial for academic achievement, yet professors tend to spend much more out-of-class time with white male athletes than black ones. Furthermore, athletes frequently find themselves choosing (or steered into) undemanding majors, which is hardly surprising given that playing big-time college football or basketball is a year-round, high-pressure, physically taxing, 40–60-hour-a-week job with frequent and irregular travel demands. African American former Duke basketball player Shane Battier, an excellent student, majored in religion because it didn't conflict with his basketball schedule. Kain Colter started at Northwestern as a premed student, but switched his major to psychology after football practice forced him to miss too many science classes. In 1991, African American former Ohio State University running back Robert Smith, an aspiring doctor, quit the school's football team for a year and instead ran track after accusing coaches of not taking his academic responsibilities seriously.

This year's Final Four featured two schools, Syracuse and North Carolina, whose basketball programs were recently involved in academic scandals. A NCAA investigation found that Syracuse's athletic staff members accessed the email accounts of several athletes, communicated directly with faculty members while pretending to be those athletes, and also did school work for them; most notably, the Orange's former director of basketball operations helped former Big East Defensive Player of the Year Fab Melo remain eligible by completing one of his papers. Meanwhile, malfeasance at North Carolina was far more widespread: school employees steered 1,500 athletes over 18 years toward no-show "paper classes" in the school's Department of African and Afro-American Studies that never actually met and only required students to hand in a single research paper. African American former Tar Heels basketball player Rashard McCants, a member of the school's 2005 national championship team, told ESPN that he even made the dean's list in the spring of 2005—despite not attending any of the four classes for which he received straight A's. Last year, McCants's sister Rashanda, a former North Carolina basketball player, and African American former UNC football player Devon Ramsay filed a federal class action lawsuit against the school, alleging that athletes were harmed by the paper class scheme—a practice that lead plaintiff's lawyer Michael Hausfeld said "was nothing more than an integral, foreseeable part of the entire enterprise of big-time contemporary college athletics, in which academics is truly the stepchild to athletics, and the meaningful education that the NCAA promises and commits to is nothing more than an illusion."

McCants's case is extreme. But are second-rate athlete educations all that uncommon? Eight years ago, *USA Today* investigated the phenomenon of academic "clustering"—that is, large numbers of athletes taking particular majors at much higher rates than the general student body, possibly (or presumably) because those majors are less demanding and will help them remain eligible—and determined that it was commonplace at big-time sports schools. A 2009 study of clustering in ACC football found that black players were more likely to cluster than their white counterparts, and that at six schools, over 75 percent of the black players were enrolled in one of two majors.

"Graduation doesn't equal education," says Hawkins, the University of Georgia professor. "That's one of the things I've always been critical of. I've been on this campus 20 years. We can graduate athletes. But what's the quality of that education, and does it lead to gainful employment in fields that are comparable to what they've studied? We've studied football players 10 years out and we find that's not the case. Players are working in fields that are sort of beneath their degree. I think that's a pattern."

On the first night of the NCAA tournament's Sweet Sixteen— around the same time Villanova tipped off against the University of Miami, Florida—sociologist and longtime civil rights advocate Harry Edwards stood behind a podium at the National Constitution Center in Philadelphia, addressing a college athletes' rights conference.

"Let's be honest and straight up," he said. "When we talk about football and basketball, we are talking about the black athlete."

In the early 1960s, Edwards had been one of those athletes himself, a basketball player and record-setting discus thrower at San Jose State. Looking around, he saw a campus that was mostly white—students, faculty, administrators, curriculum; everything save its sports stars—and an athletic department that was defined by its "willingness to exploit black athletic talent." He saw white athletes "get [summer] jobs that black starters didn't get," and "tours to places that black athletes didn't even know were being given." After returning to the school as a part-time instructor, Edwards presented a list of civil rights grievances to San Jose State's leadership on behalf of the school's black students and athletes; the group, which included black football players, threatened to sit out the first game of the 1967 season if their demands—including more black students and professors, equal access to student housing, and desegregated fraternities and sororities—weren't met. (Shortly thereafter, Edwards would become famous for attempting to organize an African American athlete boycott of the 1968 Summer Olympics, an effort that inspired John Carlos and Tommie Smith's seminal black power salute on the medal stand in Mexico City.)

"Why should we play where we can't work?" Edwards said, recalling that San Jose State canceled the game. (The cancellation prompted a war of words with then–California governor Ronald Reagan, who called Edwards "a criminal, unfit to teach." Edwards dubbed the future president "a petrified pig, unfit to govern.") "People thought that question was insane at the time," Edwards continued, adding that the school's athletics and campus sports in general could be characterized as "a plantation structure."

"Fifty years later, that statement can still be made," he said. "It has not changed."

Most of the people who currently run college athletics would disagree. Vehemently. The entire enterprise can't possibly be unjust, let alone racially unjust. Not when athletes—including African American athletes—are given so much. Small cash stipends. Four-year scholarships. Unlimited snacks. Access to world-class coaching and palatial training facilities. Athletes get to play exciting games before large crowds of adoring fans; they get academic tutors to help them learn, and to literally walk them to and from class. Exploited? If anything, they should feel grateful—and not like the former players suing the NCAA in federal antitrust court, whom Texas women's athletic director Chris Plonsky, a white woman who makes roughly $500,000 a year, says are entitled malcontents who "sucked a whole lot off the college athletics pipe."

Except: the injustice in college sports isn't just about the terms of the deal. It's about the terms of the dealing. Amateurism deprives athletes—again, predominantly black athletes—of freedoms and rights the rest of us take for granted. The same antitrust laws that prevent schools from colluding to limit assistant basketball coach salaries don't protect campus athletes, even when federal courts rule that the NCAA and its member schools are violating those laws. Sports labor lawyer Jeffrey Kessler, who is currently leading a bellwether case against the association, says athletes "don't have any rights under federal labor laws. They don't get to form a union, strike, collectively bargain, or file unfair labor practice complaints. That's not available to college athletes." Instead, they exist as second-class citizens, separate and unequal, just as the NCAA intended—according to former association director Byers, the term "student-athlete" was a legalistic ruse specifically created in the 1950s to prevent injured football players from collecting workers' compensation.

Throughout American history, exploitation has flowed from in-equality. It flowed after blacks were deemed three-fifths of a person at the original Constitutional Convention, and when they were later denied due process under Jim Crow; it flowed when women were denied the right to vote. Under Apartheid, the McCormicks write, South African laws prevented black workers from striking —sapping whatever bargaining power they otherwise might have flexed—and also mandated specific wages and hours for many blacks. Meanwhile, whites were allowed unfettered access to a free market. Sound familiar?

"I've used the term 'racial injustice' [to describe college sports], but I try to avoid using the term 'racism,'" says Yee, the sports agent. "I can't look into someone's heart and know their intentions. But the facts are in plain view.

"I've never ever had one of my [athlete] clients ever say to me that the current system is equitable. Nobody. In fact I have one caucasian client who grew up with black friends, played at a prominent school, has done very well for himself, came from an upper-class family. And he thinks this is one of the greatest injustices in American society. It really bothers him at his core."

Yee's client is in the minority, at least among whites. In 2014, a *Washington Post*/ABC News poll found that while 66 percent of nonwhites supported college athlete unionization, only 38 percent of whites did. Similarly, 51 percent of nonwhites favored paying college athletes—but just 24 percent of whites agreed. A HBO *Real Sports*/Marist poll last year revealed more of the same: while 59 percent of African Americans felt college athletes should be paid, only 26 percent of whites concurred.

Numbers like those caught the attention of Tatishe Nteta, a University of Massachusetts political science professor whose research focuses on ethnic politics. So did a 2014 soliloquy from then–ESPN radio host Colin Cowherd, who caught flack from civil rights groups after making arguably coded statements about pay-for-play. "I don't think paying all college athletes is great, not every college is loaded and most 19-year-olds [are] gonna spend it—and let's be honest, they're gonna spend it on weed and kicks," Cowherd said on air. "And spare me the 'they're being extorted' thing. Listen, 90 percent of these college guys are gonna spend it on tats, weed, kicks, Xboxes, beer, and swag. They are, get over it!"

Nteta knew from previous studies that underlying racial animus helps shape whites' attitudes toward health care, welfare, and criminal justice—in short, the more resentment a white person feels toward African Americans, the more likely they are to oppose public policies they perceive as benefiting blacks. "Say you ask a question about building a wall between the U.S. and Mexico," Nteta says. "Rather than think about how much that will cost, or how ridiculous the idea is, you just think about your attitudes toward undocumented immigrants and Mexicans, and that influences how you think about building a wall."

Do white attitudes toward amateurism work the same way? In the fall of 2014, Nteta and two academic colleagues attached a set of targeted questions to a larger public opinion poll connected to congressional midterm elections. They found that race isn't the *only* reason whites oppose pay-for-play, but it's a major one. In fact, Nteta says that negative racial views about blacks were the single most important predictor of white opposition to paying college athletes, with higher levels of resentment corresponding with higher levels of opposition. "We tried to look at factors like interest in college sports, your love of the NCAA, if you were a college athlete, if you were a union member," he says. "We found that none of that is important. But race can't be divorced from this story."

Nteta cautions that his research is preliminary, and not quite ready to publish in an academic journal. Additional work is needed. Still, it raises an unsettling possibility: if college sports carries Branch's "whiff of the plantation," then perhaps the rest of us do too.

A few weeks ago, Yee spoke to students and faculty at the University of Virginia's School of Law, his graduate alma mater. When college sports came up, he noted that most NCAA-level women's cross-country teams are made up of white runners. He then asked listeners to participate in a thought exercise. Imagine, he said, if those teams brought in millions of dollars. Then imagine if the money mostly went to well-paid black administrators, and to black athletes competing in non-revenue sports. Would that situation be tolerated, let alone tolerated for decades?

"The reaction was largely silence," Yee says.

BOMANI JONES

Kaepernick Is Asking for Justice, Not Peace

FROM THE UNDEFEATED

FRIDAY NIGHT, in a league whose business is Americana, Colin Kaepernick took a stand rarely seen in pro sports. It wasn't from his seat on the sideline, where he paid no regard for the National Anthem in its favorite game. It was after—when Steve Wyche of the NFL Network asked why he sat while others stood. Kaepernick was strident, unflinching, and unapologetic. When reporters surrounded his locker Sunday for more, he gave it to them.

The attention he's received was ineluctable, but he hadn't courted it. Had he done so, more than one reporter would have noticed that he stayed seated and asked him about it. Or asked after the *previous* game, when—though he didn't play—he did the same thing. But he did not hide when confronted, as New England Patriot Tom Brady did while giving airtime to GOP presidential nominee Donald Trump via conveniently placed campaign paraphernalia in his locker. With more to lose than Brady, he made himself clearer.

There's an undeniable nobility in what was an impactful—but ultimately harmless—display, even if one disagrees. Kaepernick didn't do this in a crowd, surrounded by thousands. He sat alone, wearing a red, white, and blue shield on his jersey. The NFL takes many of its cues from the military and has encouraged the idea that reverence for the military is a citizen's requirement, not choice. The draft is gone, but we've all been conscripted as unquestioning devotees whose gratitude can be demanded by anyone at any time.

Kaepernick wasn't addressing the military, but that was widely and predictably inferred. In spite of this, Kaepernick had the audacity to sit in opposition to what he felt he'd stood for too long.

This wasn't what Carmelo Anthony and Friends did at the ES-PYS, a moment that was important but took great pains to make a statement that offended no one. It wasn't what the belated Michael Jordan did on this website when he announced he was donating money to groups representing the interests of black people and the police. To paraphrase Peter Tosh, they asked for peace while Kaepernick cried out for justice. That distinction is both subtle and significant.

Kaepernick even went beyond the WNBA players who stood in solidarity with the Black Lives Matter movement and asked their league to do the same. He made no plea to both sides, nor did he make a call for unity. He's not concerned with whether his team or his league has his back. When he could have smoothed over any pending reaction to his actions, he focused squarely on racism, the most consistent and overpowering impediment to black success in America, and the thread that connects every era of its history. While the major party candidates for president spent the week pointing at each other with charges of who is or isn't *the real racist,* Kaepernick pointed at the flag and, by extension, every person who takes pride in the American flag. And he did so alone, fully aware that backup might never come.

This is what a stand looks like. For better or worse, stands that demand people come together rarely have that effect. And contrary to popular belief, stands do not create divisions and fissures. They *amplify* them. The whole point of a stand is to put them on *display,* to ask the world to confront and examine their hypocrisies and ask why they're on one side and not the other. Protests that don't offend aren't worth the effort. The ones that do are the ones that can change the world.

Now let's be clear: Kaepernick's stand will not change the world. Neither did Muhammad Ali's, nor have very few individual actions. The dramatic acts of individuals sound good in history books, but rarely seem so in real time. What Kaepernick did won't change America or even the NFL.

That's not his fault, though, and that's no excuse for minimizing what he chose to do and say. America's remarkable stability is the product of a structural resistance to fundamental change and its history is interwoven with racism that was once self-evident but now operates with winks and nods that few in power are willing to fight. To oppose racism is righteous. To deny its existence, no matter the reason, is cowardice. To treat a peaceful protest like an act of war against whiteness or America—notions used interchangeably in this debate, which is problematic—is hypocrisy.

The easy question to ask is whether one agrees with Kaepernick's manner of protest—thus allowing respondents to ignore the substance of his thoughtful, measured critiques. The most disingenuous answers tend to come from those who defend his right to ignore the National Anthem while making sure the world knows there were better ways for him to make his point, while, of course, stopping short of addressing the point itself.

The meat of the issue is his words. Kaepernick declared that this country oppresses black people and its law enforcement officers kill black people with impunity—often receiving pats on the back for doing so. Both history and the newspaper support his belief. We've seen Americans give from their own pockets to police officers known only for killing black teenagers. Even George Zimmerman took in hundreds of thousands of dollars in donations from strangers, and he wasn't even an officer of the law.

To ignore the National Anthem for those reasons is to challenge the very notion of what America is. It's to ask whether what he's fighting against is represented by the flag rather than thriving in spite of it.

It's the flag that flew when slaves were freed, but that took nearly a century. It's the flag blacks fought for all over the world, upholding a notion of freedom they wouldn't experience themselves. And now, in 2016, it's the one cowards wrap themselves in while promoting the decidedly un-American notion of exclusion.

That's why the flag generates conflict in many blacks, while white people have the luxury of saluting it without scrutiny. It's also the banner, in theory, that affords Kaepernick the right to pay it no mind. In line with essayist James Baldwin's assertion that his love for the nation is what drove him to critique her mercilessly, Kaepernick's challenge to America is actually the most American thing he can do.

So many of those who have demanded our nation earn their respect loved it the most. Jackie Robinson loved America and served in the military, but wrote in his autobiography that he would not stand for the National Anthem. Paul Robeson's patriotism was questioned by Joseph McCarthy, but it drove his fierce demand to be treated as a true citizen. There's nothing American about settling for good enough, let alone being satisfied with not-as-bad-as-it-used-to-be.

And there's nothing American about muzzling a dissenting voice, especially one whose life is the sort of story people cite as an example of the American dream. A black child adopted by white parents becomes a rich celebrity, praised for his talents and giving credence to the idea that anyone can make it. But nothing in that heartwarming tale has protected him from racism, nor will any of that make him safer when he's pulled over by the police. His parents may be white, but that didn't matter a bit when cops pulled a gun on him, a story Kaepernick relayed Sunday.

What should protect him is American citizenship, and there's too much evidence to indicate that's not working for him and millions of others. If a man willing to risk his livelihood to say so can't get his country to even *consider* what could bring him to that point, how could anyone *honestly* dismiss his point?

There seems to be no objective argument that makes Kaepernick's refusal to stand for the anthem—which will continue, he says—wrong, even if one doesn't think it was right. Just as one can oppose the war in Afghanistan and respect Pat Tillman's decision to fight there, one can respect Kaepernick's much smaller sacrifice. The only way one can't is if one sees no nobility in his cause. And if someone struggles to see the merit in standing for the black and brown people who have been continually mistreated in this country, perhaps it is that person's patriotism that should be questioned, not the man willing to stand before his country and take whatever comes next.

DAVE ZIRIN

Andrew Cuomo Would Have Blacklisted Muhammad Ali

FROM THE NATION

GOVERNOR ANDREW CUOMO is a thuggish, tin-eared politician. Yet there is a near-poetical deafness about his latest decision: a timing so awful it's beautiful. In a week where the world is mourning the great Muhammad Ali, Governor Cuomo has taken the step to unilaterally criminalize New York State businesses and individuals who exercise their freedom to stand with the people of Palestine. Signing an executive order for a "Boycott Divestment and Sanctions blacklist," Governor Cuomo said, "If you boycott against Israel, New York will boycott you. If you divert revenues from Israel, New York will divert revenues from you. If you sanction Israel, New York will sanction you." He was immediately "saluted" by Israeli Prime Minister Benjamin Netanyahu. Senator Chuck Schumer also followed up immediately to say that said he was excited to make this blacklist federal law.

Muhammad Ali was many things: boxer, humanitarian, draft resister. He was also someone who unapologetically stood for Palestinian liberation. Despite the fact that Ali had already felt the sting of a blacklist, banned by boxing from 1967 to 1970, he did not stop speaking out upon his return to ring. In 1974, Ali visited the Palestinian refugee camps of southern Lebanon and, amid the crushing poverty and disease, said, "In my name and the name of all Muslims in America, I declare support for the Palestinian struggle to liberate their homeland and oust the Zionist invaders."

Unlike some of Muhammad Ali's polarizing politics on questions of racism and U.S. empire, which faded over time as the movements of the 1960s dwindled and Parkinson's disease seized brutal control of his body, the question of Palestinian liberation was something that he did not surrender easily. At a 1988 rally in Chicago amid the First Intifada, a six-year period of mass resistance by Palestinians to Israeli occupation, Ali proudly stood with solidarity activists.

Few U.S. newspapers have openly wrestled with this part of Ali's political history. But the Israeli newspaper *Haaretz* dived right in. The paper ran an ugly obituary of the Champ hours after his passing with the cringe-inducing title "Muhammad Ali's Complicated Relationship with the Jews." It attacked Ali for having dear Jewish friends but being a merciless critic of the Israeli state. In an objective analysis, such a dynamic would only speak to the Champ's beautiful heart. He loved his Jewish friends. He respected the Jewish religion. (Rabbi Michael Lerner, at Ali's request, will be part of his funeral services this Friday in Louisville.) But he opposed the actions of a colonial state in the Middle East, just as he opposed the actions of the colonial state he called home when it entered Vietnam.

What *Haaretz* was doing—conflating criticism of Israel with anti-Semitism—is politically and morally bankrupt. It is also exactly what Andrew Cuomo and Chuck Schumer are doing with this push to criminalize Palestinian-rights activists in the United States. As Senator Schumer said in a speech, "What does it mean that those who are at the core of the BDS movement are so fond of statehood for every other people but not the Jewish people? There's an old word for it, we always have a word for it. It's called anti-Semitism. Not simply just—bad enough anti-Israel, they're anti-Semites."

This is a horrific political calculus by Schumer: raise your voice against the death of any child in Gaza, any home that is bulldozed by the IDF, any prisoner dying while on a hunger strike in an Israeli prison, and you are an anti-Semite even if—like myself—you are proudly Jewish. Even if—like Muhammad Ali—you hold your Jewish friends close to your heart. It makes sense now that, when asked his thoughts on the news of Ali's death, all Schumer could offer was this thin gruel: "What I thought of is, I was playing basketball and our high school coach would tell us, be like Muhammad Ali, float like a butterfly, sting like a bee."

I highly doubt that is all Senator Schumer thought about upon hearing of the Champ's passing. But such wafer-thin statements are what you say when you don't want to expose your own bigotry. It is what you say when you want to bask in the glow of the Champ while denying the actuality of who he was, what he believed, and why his courage inspired so many across the world.

To deny Muhammad Ali's pro-Palestinian politics is erasure. It's whitewashing. It's violence. It's performing the ugliest possible sin: lying about someone's life over their dead body. Upon Ali's passing, Andrew Cuomo tweeted, "RIP Muhammad Ali, you inspired us all and will always be #TheGreatest." Get the Champ's name out of your mouth, Governor, and tell the disturbing truth. If Muhammad Ali was in his prime today, he would be your target: someone denied the right to make a living in the state of New York.

JOHN COLAPINTO

Some Very Dirty Tricks

FROM VANITY FAIR

ON AUGUST 22, 2015, seven days after his loss at the Spingold, an annual week-long bridge championship held last year at the Chicago Hilton, Boye Brogeland posted a teasing comment to the website Bridgewinners.com. "Very soon there will come out mind boggling stuff that would even make a Hollywood movie surreal," wrote Brogeland, a 43-year-old Norwegian bridge player who is ranked 77th in the world. "It will give us a tremendous momentum to clean the game up, from the bottom to the very top." He followed this, two days later, with another comment advising players what to do if they have cheaters on their team, and announced that he and his teammates Richie Schwartz, Allan Graves, and Espen Lindqvist were relinquishing all the titles they had won in the previous two years. He made no mention of the pair with whom the six-man team had won those titles, Lotan Fisher and Ron Schwartz (no relation to Richie) — a deliberate omission, Brogeland says, to spare Bridge Winners any potential legal liability.

But two days later, Brogeland launched his own website, Bridge cheaters.com. The welcome page featured a huge photo of Fisher and Schwartz, a young Israeli duo who, since breaking into the international ranks in 2011, while still in their early twenties, had stunned the bridge world by snapping up the game's top trophies. Grinning, arms around each other's shoulders, they appeared under the tagline "The Greatest Scam in the History of Bridge!" Brogeland described an altercation he'd had with Fisher at the Spingold over a phantom trick (Fisher claimed 11 tricks in one hand when, in fact, he'd held the cards for 10), and posted examples of what he claimed to be suspiciously illogical hands played by the pair. He also included a "Cheating History"—information he had dug up from the Israel Bridge Federation and had translated from the original Hebrew. Brogeland said it laid out a pattern of alleged cheating and bad sportsmanship going back to when Fisher and Schwartz were in their midteens: in 2003, Fisher was suspended for a year for forging results and for unsportsmanlike conduct in the final of the Israeli championships; at the 2004 Tel Aviv International Bridge Festival, he was suspended for a month for calling another player a "faggot"; in July 2004, he and Schwartz were investigated for suspicious hands after winning the three-day Shaufel Cup; a year later, Schwartz was suspended for forging match results.

The site, in its first 24 hours, received more than 100,000 hits. For the game of contract bridge, the technical name for a 91-year-old pastime that also happens to be a multimillion-dollar business, it was an earthquake equal to the jolt that shook international cycling when Lance Armstrong was banned from competition for doping. Before going public with his accusations, Brogeland, aware that he was taking on powerful interests (at the professional level, the game runs on the sponsorships of CEOs and multimillionaires), consulted the Norwegian police, who, Brogeland says, advised, "When you blow the whistle, do not be at your home address." Fisher and Schwartz, denying all wrongdoing, hired lawyers, who dispatched a letter to Brogeland threatening a lawsuit and offering to settle if he paid them $1 million. Last fall Brogeland received a text that had originated with a teammate of Fulvio Fantoni and Claudio Nunes, the Italian pair who, for more than a decade, have reigned as the game's number-one and number-two players. Brogeland had also publicly accused them, along with two other top-ranking bridge pairs, of cheating. The message read, "Tell your friend Boye that whenever he needs a wheelchair we have plenty of those in the south." Fisher posted to his Facebook page a comment that Brogeland took as a message directed at him: "Jealousy made you sick. Get ready for a meeting with the devil." (Fisher denies that this message was intended for Brogeland.)

When I asked Jeff Meckstroth, widely recognized as one of the best bridge players in the world, about Brogeland, he answered me bluntly. "The guy has the biggest balls of anyone I've ever known."

*

Brogeland is a boyish, athletically built man whose blond hair, blue eyes, and easygoing smile mask a ferocious competitiveness. The son of a butcher father and teacher mother, he was born and raised in the tiny, isolated town of Moi (population 1,977), in southern Norway. Today he lives in Flekkefjord, a short drive from where he grew up, in a house he shares with his wife, Tonje, and their two young children. "I come from a place where everybody knows everybody," he says. "Integrity is part of what *makes* you in such a community." Early tragedy also had a decisive effect on his character, he says. He was 11 years old when his mother committed suicide. "When those things happen, I think it makes you think a lot about big questions in life," he says, "fairness and justice."

Having learned bridge at age eight from his grandparents, he fell in love with the game, and turned pro at 28. He has won several international tournaments, runs a successful Norwegian bridge magazine, and in 2013 was recruited by his current sponsor, Richie Schwartz, a Bronx-born bridge addict, mathematician, and program analyst, who made a fortune at the racetrack in the 1970s. When choosing bridge players for his teams, Schwartz often hires undervalued European players who cost less than Americans. "I always fought to get the best deals," says Schwartz—who nevertheless admits that he will pay up to $200,000 to play in three annual U.S. nationals with a given pair. "Some pay $500,000 or more, though," he adds. Brogeland says Schwartz pays him travel expenses and a base yearly salary of $50,000—with big bonuses for strong showings in tournaments.

Not long after Brogeland joined Schwartz's team, he learned that Schwartz was hiring Lotan Fisher and Ron Schwartz. Brogeland had heard the rumors: in 2012, Fisher and Schwartz won the Cavendish, one of bridge's most coveted titles, but under circumstances suspicious enough that other top players refused to play in the tournament the following year if Fisher and Schwartz played. (They did not.) But because Brogeland had never played against them and did not know them personally, he reserved judgment. "I try to base my opinion of people on what I experience myself," he says, adding that he did, however, warn his new teammates. "I told them, 'I've heard the rumors. Whatever you do, play straight.'"

Over the next two years, the team of Brogeland, Lindqvist, Fisher, Schwartz, Graves, and Schwartz won a string of championships: the 2014 Spingold, the 2014 Reisinger, the 2015 Jacoby Swiss. During that time, says Brogeland, he regularly checked Bridge Base Online, a website that archives tournament hands, so he could monitor how his new teammates were behaving when playing at the table adjacent to him. He saw "maybe five or six" suspicious-looking hands, he says, "but nowhere near enough to say, 'You're cheating.'" Nevertheless, he says he was relieved when, in the summer of 2015, the pair was lured away by the deep-pocketed sponsor Jimmy Cayne, former CEO of the defunct investment house Bear Stearns. "When they changed teams," Brogeland says, "I didn't have to be faced with this kind of environment where you're not sure—you feel something is strange but you can't really tell."

Fisher, meanwhile, was enjoying his position at the top of the game, where the lives of many successful young pros more closely resemble those of well-heeled, globe-hopping rock musicians than what might be conjured by the term "bridge player." Convening nightly at a hotel bar in whatever city is holding the competition —Biarritz, Chennai, Chicago—they drink until the small hours, rising late the next day, since tournament organizers mercifully schedule the first matches for one in the afternoon. Fisher, hailed as the "wonder boy of Israeli bridge," was a fixture of the bar scene. Charismatic, and darkly handsome, with a widow's peak and heavy brows, he posted Instagram photos of himself posing in well-cut suits in five-star hotels, behind the wheel of luxury cars, or partying with an array of young people—spoils of his status in a game where, for three years, he had been drawing an almost unbroken string of wins that brought bonuses amounting to six figures. There was only one problem: the persistent rumors that he was a cheater. Many people were whispering about it, according to Steve Weinstein, a top American player who writes for the website Bridgewinners.com. "But it's an unwritten rule that you not publicly accuse anyone—even if you're *sure*," Weinstein says. It was a Catch-22 that Fisher seemed to delight in flaunting, shrugging off questions about his suspicious play as if daring anyone to openly accuse him. "He had the Nietzschean superman personality," says Fred Gitelman, a former champion and cofounder of Bridge Base Online. "He just thought he was in a different league."

Champs and Cheats

Contract bridge is built on the rules of the 18th-century British game whist: a deck of cards is dealt to four people, who play in two-person partnerships, sitting opposite each other at a table. The player to the left of the dealer leads with a card of any suit —heart, diamond, club, or spade—and each player in succession plays a card of the suit led; the highest card wins the trick. It's a deceptively simple game only slightly complicated by the existence of the trump: a card in a suit that overrules all others. In whist, trump is determined randomly, before the start of each hand. In auction bridge, a game popularized in England in 1904, trump is determined in each hand's opening "auction," when the teams, communicating solely by way of spoken bids ("Three spades," "Two hearts," "Three no trump"), establish which (if any) suit will be trump and how many tricks they think they can take. Pairs who take more tricks than contracted for are awarded extra points for those tricks. The pair with the most points, after all 13 tricks are played, wins the hand.

Contract bridge emerged from devilish refinements introduced, in 1925, by the American railroad magnate Harold S. Vanderbilt. While on a cruise through the Panama Canal, he sought to goose up a game of dull auction bridge by awarding escalating bonus points to pairs who took the greatest risk in the opening auction, and imposed steep point deductions on pairs who failed to make the tricks contracted for. Thus did a polite and mannerly British parlor game take on some of the brash, hypercompetitive, sweaty-palmed excitement of the big-money trading Vanderbilt was familiar with from Wall Street.

The game became a craze during the Great Depression, when an evening's entertainment for two couples could be had for the price of a deck of cards. How-to manuals, written by actual bridge celebrities, like the publicity genius and Romanian immigrant Ely Culbertson, sat atop best-seller lists; bridge hands were analyzed on the radio; millions of bridge fans nationwide followed the 1931 murder trial of Kansas City housewife Myrtle Bennett, who gunned down her husband after a spat in which she called him "a bum bridge player." (She was acquitted.) After the Second World War, bridge took on a new sheen of glamour and exclusivity, joining baccarat and casino poker in the array of upper-class pastimes enjoyed by that emblem of postwar suavity, James Bond. In the 1955 novel *Moonraker,* Bond (in one of the most thrilling scenes Ian Fleming ever wrote) faces off, at M's club, in a game of high-stakes bridge against arch-villain Sir Hugo Drax, whom Bond coolly unmasks as a cheater. ("And don't forget that cheating at cards can still smash a man," M tells Bond.)

In the 1960s, international tournament bridge took on some of the swashbuckling heroics associated with downhill skiing and Grand Prix racing, with legends like the powerhouse Italian "Blue Team" winning 16 world titles between 1957 and 1975 and heartthrob Egyptian actor Omar Sharif (a professional player who ranked in the game's top 50) telling an interviewer, "The real question is why I spend so much time making movies when I could be playing bridge." Meanwhile, the game, which draws on innate gifts of logic, problem solving, planning, and risk assessment, became particularly popular among Wall Street traders (who rely on those skills professionally) and, to this day, counts as its most devoted fans many highly successful CEOs and entrepreneurs, including Bill Gates and Warren Buffett.

In the popular imagination, however, bridge has all but vanished. Last year, the *New York Times* dropped its long-running bridge column, and today the American Contract Bridge League (ACBL), the game's governing body in North America, lists only 168,000 members, with a median age, despite the hotel-bar set, of 71. Yet the professional, tournament game has only increased as a serious, moneymaking pursuit, with rich bridge addicts assembling stables of top players, paying them ever-rising retainers and bonuses—all for the privilege of playing hands with the pros in important tournaments. (The first American "dream team," the Dallas Aces, was put together in 1968 by businessman Ira Corn to challenge Italy's Blue Team.) "It's like paying to play a few games of doubles at Wimbledon with Federer or Djokovic," says Christopher Rivera, a game director at Manhattan's Honors Bridge Club.

Except that the top sponsors today also happen to be very strong players. Cayne, now 82, was a bridge professional before joining Bear Stearns in 1969. His obsession with the game has even been cited as a contributing cause of Bear Stearns's demise. As the firm spiraled in 2007 during the subprime mortgage crisis, CEO

Cayne was reportedly at bridge tournaments, distracted and unreachable. Pierre Zimmermann, a Monaco-based real-estate multimillionaire who sponsored the Monaco team on which Fantoni and Nunes played, took up bridge in his thirties and is one of the game's strongest players. Both men reportedly pay up to half a million dollars annually to individual members of their five-man teams—when they win. Gail Greenberg, one of the game's greatest women champions, says that such paydays have fueled cheating by players hoping to be recruited by deep-pocketed sponsors, or to hang on to the one they've got. Chris Willenken, a leading American professional, says, "There is definitely enough money involved that it's easy to understand why not *everybody* might be honest."

And then there's the sheer ease of cheating. Pairs are forbidden to say what high cards they hold or in what suit they might be strong—except by way of the koan-like bids ("Two no trump") they make in a hand's opening auction. Any other communication is outlawed by Rule 73.b.2 of the ACBL's *Laws of Duplicate Bridge:* "The gravest possible offence is for a partnership to exchange information through prearranged methods . . ." In one of the game's biggest scandals, British champion J. Terence Reese and his partner Boris Schapiro, at the 1965 Bermuda Bowl, in Buenos Aires, were discovered using finger signals—clutching their cards variously with two, three, or four fingers, with an array of odd spacings between the digits—to communicate the number of hearts they held. The scandal exploded in newspapers around the world.

Tournament organizers would eventually respond by erecting screens to block partners' view of each other. "It limits the channels of communication under some circumstances," says Bob Hamman, an original member of the Dallas Aces. "But no method of this nature is an adequate defense against a determined adversary." When players were discovered communicating via footsie (two members of the Italian Blue Team were among those accused of engaging in this type of cheating at the 1975 Bermuda Bowl), barriers were installed under tables. In 2013, the "coughing doctors"—German physicians Michael Elinescu and Entscho Wladow —were caught using coded throat clearings at the D'Orsi World Senior Bowl, in Bali, and banned from playing bridge together for life. (They denied the charges, with Wladow blaming the coughing on his asthma.) Pairs can come under suspicion even when no signaling is detected—simply through illogical play. "In bridge at the highest level," says Willenken, "the best players play in a *relent-lessly* logical fashion, so when something illogical happens, other good players notice it. And if that illogical thing is consistently winning, suspicions can be aroused." Even variations in the speed of play, which to professionals has a particular pace and rhythm, can raise alarms.

Getting the game's governing bodies to act quickly on charges of cheating is another matter. Given the potential for lawsuits, the organizing bodies necessarily have to work carefully to collect evidence, which can take time. Jeff Meckstroth was in the finals of the 2014 Vanderbilt—an annual seven-day tournament—in Dallas against Fantoni and Nunes when he says he believed his opponents were placing their discarded tricks on the table in a suspicious manner. Meckstroth was convinced they were signaling. "They turned the trick' the wrong way to say, 'I don't have anything in dummy's weak suit,'" he says. He reported Fantoni and Nunes to the ACBL—then badgered the organization for more than a year to do something. "They just put their head in the sand," he says. (The ACBL says that, in fact, it did begin monitoring the pair.) Fantoni and Nunes continued to compete—even after an incident at the 2015 Italian championships, when Nunes played an ace-of-diamonds lead so wildly illogical (yet successful) that his only defense, when questioned by the Federation of Italian Bridge, was to claim that he "had a mental blackout" in midplay. Even this opera buffa moment was not enough to get them banned from the game. (An investigation by the Italian federation led to an acquittal when the two judges hearing the case couldn't agree.)

By the summer of 2015, the grumbling about cheaters had reached critical mass. "Last June, I was at the European championships, in Norway," Meckstroth says. "I was with a group of top players and they were all complaining: 'What are we going to do? These guys are cheating.' I threw up my hands and said, 'I've been trying for 18 months and met with nothing but frustration.'"

That all changed three months later, when Brogeland—defying the game's governing bodies, ignoring the unwritten rule that players never accuse one another, and risking his own expulsion if unable to prove the charges—went public. "It's a perfect example of civil disobedience," says Willenken. "There's this wall of silence because of the rules about accusing other people. And everybody is seeing that the system—that whole paradigm—is breaking down.

It's not allowing for an honest game. Boye comes along and says, 'I don't care what the rules are. I don't care what they do to me. I'm going to come out and say all this stuff.'"

"I did this because I love the game," Brogeland says. "I asked, 'What would my parents do? My grandparents?' It was clear. I just wanted to focus on what was *right*."

Less than a month after Cayne had lured Fisher and Schwartz away from Richie Schwartz's team, Brogeland met the pair again—this time as opponents, in the quarter-final of the 2015 Spingold, at the Hilton hotel in Chicago. It was a match that would change bridge forever.

Brogeland's team was the clear underdog. Team captain Richie Schwartz and his partner, Allan Graves (a septuagenarian with a friendly, philosophical temperament), faced off against the suspect pair at one table, while Brogeland and his regular partner, fellow Norwegian Espen Lindqvist (a soft-spoken 28-year-old with spiky blond hair and wire-rimmed glasses), played Cayne and Alfredo Versace at a neighboring table. In a more than eight-hour battle, Brogeland's team won, in an upset, by the slimmest margin possible: a single point.

Or seemed to. Fisher immediately contested the result on a technicality. After a nearly two-hour arbitration that stretched until 1:30 a.m., the win was overturned: Brogeland's team had now *lost* by one point and been knocked out of the tournament—a crushing defeat compounded by Brogeland's seeing Lotan Fisher run from the committee room punching the air and screaming in triumph.

"If we had won that match," Brogeland admits, "I would have gone to bed and tried to get as much sleep as I could, to try to win the semifinal the next day. I might have said, 'Maybe they cheat, but I don't want to put my life and career on the line . . .'"

But as things stood, Brogeland could not sleep. After tossing and turning all night, he rose at 7:00 a.m., went to his laptop, and opened Bridge Base Online. "I checked the BBO files to see *how* we lost," Brogeland says. He claims he immediately noticed something odd at the neighboring table. Ron Schwartz had opened a hand by playing a club lead. Yet, as Brogeland now believed, Schwartz's hand indicated that a heart lead was the obvious play. "I wondered, 'How could he not lead a heart?'" Brogeland says. "All top players that I know would have led that suit. But he didn't. If it was *wrong* for him not to do it, then okay. But of course it was *right* for him not to lead it. I think, 'Wow, this is strange.'"

Then, he says, he saw something even stranger.

In one of the final hands, Fisher had claimed 11 tricks—giving his team the winning edge. Except Fisher, as BBO showed, held the cards for just *10* tricks. "I say, 'Fuck, what is *this?*'" Brogeland recalls. Dumbfounded, he gathered with his teammates and asked what had happened on that hand. Graves recounted to Brogeland how Fisher, claiming to have made all 11 tricks he'd contracted for, had briskly stuffed his cards into the slotted board at the center of the table where cards are returned after a hand. Bridge players usually go by an honor system when a player says he has made all of his tricks. But Graves made a point of asking to see Fisher's cards. Fisher yanked them from the board, showed them to his opponents, then shoved them back into the slot. Eleven tricks were duly entered on the scorecard. Brogeland now wondered if Fisher had pulled the oldest scam in bridge: hiding a losing card behind the others. In any event, the miscount could not be corrected: challenges must be raised within a half-hour of a match. The loss would stand.

Brogeland went in search of Fisher. He found him by the hotel elevators. Brogeland says Fisher admitted to miscounting the hand, but claimed it was unintentional. "I made a mistake," he said. "It happens."

"No, Lotan," said Brogeland. "You never make these kinds of mistakes."

Fisher went on the attack. "Do you call me a cheater?"

"No," Brogeland said. "But this does not look good."

A Grand Coup

Brogeland spent the next two days at the tournament scouring BBO and comparing notes with other players. By the time he flew back to Norway (after watching Fisher and Schwartz win the Spingold in a final that carried moments that seemed suspicious to Brogeland and those he was watching with), he was convinced the pair were cheating. And he was determined to expose them.

He knew it wasn't going to be easy. Although he felt certain that they were signaling to each other, Brogeland had no idea *how*. Still, he believed that if he amassed enough illogical hands, he could make a convincing case—however circumstantial—to present to the game's governing bodies.

For the next week, he hunkered over his computer in Flekke-fjord, working all day collecting suspicious hands on BBO and sleeping only three hours a night. "I was going on pure adrenaline," he says. He phoned trusted players around the world—Ishmael Del'Monte in Australia, Per-Ola Cullin in Sweden, Brad Moss in the United States—to canvass for other suspect hands. Thomas Bessis, a French champion who had played as a junior with Fisher, had been keeping a folder of suspicious hands on the pair for years.

Brogeland contacted governing bodies on both sides of the Atlantic, including the European Bridge League and the ACBL. An official at the EBL told Brogeland to submit an official complaint, in writing, so that the organization could consider whether to initiate a formal investigation. "He said, 'No, this is going to take too long a time,'" recalls the EBL official to whom Brogeland spoke. Brogeland also pressed the ACBL for immediate action. When he gave suspect hands to ACBL officials, he was told to supply more hands. Brogeland grew frustrated. "They had plenty of hands," he says. "Fifty, 60 hands. I said, 'How many do you need? One hundred? Two hundred? Please, do something!'"

ACBL CEO Robert Hartman—a tall, dark-haired man who had previously worked as general manager of a Thoroughbred racetrack in the Bay Area—declines to discuss specifics of ongoing investigations, but admits that the process for reviewing cheating is lengthy, and is frustrating for players who can feel, he says, as if their complaints "have gone into space." The process ordinarily begins when a player, directly after a match, files a memo detailing specific claims against an opponent. "The memo is sent to ACBL headquarters, in Horn Lake, Mississippi, where it is submitted to a five-step process of review and appeals," says Hartman. The process can take a year or longer to play out.

Brogeland had no intention of waiting that long. He wanted the pair out of the game before the upcoming Bermuda Bowl—a month away. He would have to bypass official channels and go public. He weighed the risks to his career and reputation—which included possible charges of unseemly self-interest in pursuing a

pair whom he played alongside, for two years, and accused only
after an infuriating loss at the Spingold. He dismissed the worry.
"Does anyone really think I would risk my career and livelihood
because of a single match?" he says. "I publish a bridge magazine,
I play professional bridge—this is what I *do*. This is my life. If I was
wrong here, I would just have been more or less out of bridge."

And so, on August 24, he dropped his hint about Fisher and
Schwartz on Bridge Winners, then went live two days later with
Bridge Cheaters, where he pulled no punches, calling Fisher a
"Con Man" and laying out his evidence.

Incriminating as Brogeland's claims might have seemed to non-
experts, experienced cheating investigators were underwhelmed.
Kit Woolsey—an owlish 72-year-old with a master's in mathematics
—is a top American bridge and backgammon professional, and
the investigator who had conducted, for the ACBL, the statistical
analysis that implicated the "coughing doctors." On Bridge Winners, Woolsey voiced doubts about Brogeland's evidence. "His example hands are certainly interesting, and an indication of possible wrongdoing," Woolsey wrote. "But I do not believe that by
themselves they are any kind of proof of anything, or even any real
reason to believe that there were signals being given." Woolsey,
a statistician, thought the sample size wasn't complete and thus
skewed the evidence against the pair. Barry Goren, a U.S. professional (and no relation to the revered Charles Goren, who, in the
1950s, inherited Ely Culbertson's title of "Mr. Bridge"), slammed
Brogeland for conducting a "mad crusade" against Fisher and
Schwartz over the Spingold loss and excoriated him for publicly
accusing the pair without due process. "Personally," Goren wrote
on Bridge Winners, "I think Boye should be thrown out of Bridge
for the way this was handled."

As if in tacit acknowledgment of how his failure to uncover actual signaling by Fisher and Schwartz weakened his case, Brogeland had included links to three YouTube videos of the pair in
match play. (The videotaping of full bridge tournaments and their
posting online had occurred for the first time only a year earlier, at
the 2014 European championship, in Croatia.) Brogeland and his
wife had spent hours squinting at the videos, scrutinizing Fisher
and Schwartz's every twitch and cough, but had been unable to de-
tect any definitive signaling. Brogeland resorted to asking viewers,

in a caption to one of the videos, "What do you think was Fisher's reason to lead a heart?" Seventy-two hours after the site went up, no one had any good theories.

Then, on August 30, Brogeland's friend and fellow bridge professional Per-Ola Cullin, at home in Stockholm, watched one of the posted videos—the one with Fisher's suspicious heart lead. Cullin noticed that at the start of the hand Schwartz—a plodding player with a round, prematurely balding head pasted with tendrils of sweaty-looking hair who seemed, to many, the perfect patsy co-conspirator—placed on the table the small slotted board that holds the cards. This was normal. But he didn't place the board in the *center* of the table, its usual position. Instead he slid it a few inches to the right, to one side of the opening in the trapdoor of the anti-cheating screen. "It really struck me as weird," Cullin says. He decided to watch the previous hand. The board had been placed in the same peculiar spot—but this time by *Fisher*. As with the succeeding hand, the team led hearts. "My adrenaline started pumping," Cullin says. "I started watching all the matches from the European championships."

After several hours, Cullin was convinced he had cracked the code. The board's placement seemed to signal what suit the partner should lead with: if put in the center, play a diamond; if pushed through the trapdoor to the partner's side of the table, a spade; if to one side of the trapdoor, a heart; if to the other, a club. Cullin tested the hypothesis on his girlfriend, who doesn't play cards. According to him, she was able to guess the pair's actions every time. "It was ridiculous," says Cullin, a former criminal judge. "I've sent people to jail on much less convincing evidence."

At a little after three in the morning, he texted Brogeland: "Boye. I broke the lead signal code. 100%. Do you allready [*sic*] know it?" An hour later, Brogeland texted back: "Awake?" The two men got on the phone. The next day, Brogeland forwarded the information to analyst Kit Woolsey.

Three days later, Woolsey posted to Bridge Winners an essay, "The Videos Speak," confirming Cullin's hypothesis and urging readers to continue scouring videos of the pair pending an official investigation by the game's governing bodies. "We must build an airtight case here," Woolsey wrote, and added, "Boye has gotten the ball rolling, and it is our job to complete his work." Shortly after that, Jimmy Cayne released a statement saying ("with heavy heart") that Fisher and Schwartz were off his team, unless ultimately cleared of all charges, and he offered to forfeit the 2015 Spingold trophy that he had won with the pair. Fisher and Schwartz were suspended by the Israel Bridge Federation and the ACBL and placed under investigation by those bodies and the EBL.

It was an extraordinary exoneration for Brogeland. But he wasn't done yet.

Maaijke Mevius, a 44-year-old mother of two living in Groningen, in the Netherlands, is a physicist specializing in astronomy, and an avid recreational bridge player. Galvanized by news of the allegations against Fisher and Schwartz, she idly wondered if *she* could spot any illegal signaling in YouTube videos of top players. She recalled an item she'd seen on the website NewInBridge about the game's reigning pair, Fantoni and Nunes—the bizarre incident in which Nunes claimed to have had his "mental blackout" when playing a highly suspicious lead. "I thought, 'Okay, this is possibly an interesting pair to look at,'" Mevius says.

Searching for illegal signaling in bridge videos is difficult even for top professional players, but Mevius, although an amateur player, was nevertheless well suited to the task. "From my work as a scientific investigator I know how to distinguish very well between noise and signal," she says. Five minutes into watching her first video, she saw something. "I said, 'Hey, these guys are placing the cards in a non-natural way.'" When laying their lead card face up on the table, they sometimes placed it vertically, sometimes horizontally. Did it mean something? Mevius spent the next eight hours watching videos of the pair, hand after hand. She took careful notes. She was convinced that Fantoni and Nunes were using the way they placed the card to signal to their partner whether they held any high honor-cards (ace, king, or queen). Placed vertically, they had at least one high honor; horizontally, they didn't. Mevius emailed the information to Brogeland, whom she had never met. "I think this may be a code," she wrote. Brogeland forwarded the email to his friend Del'Monte, an expert cheating analyst and a top bridge teacher who has given lessons to Bill Gates. Del'Monte quickly agreed with Mevius's suspicions.

Brogeland says that he had never suspected Fantoni and Nunes. Furthermore, he considered them friends. He liked Nunes's shy, self-effacing manner, but was particularly close to Fantoni, a bear of a man with a friendly disposition—indeed, to some, too friendly. Meckstroth, acerbic and blunt-spoken, says he detected in Fantoni a calculated friendliness. "He was obsequious away from the table," Meckstroth says. "I mean, nobody is this nice, going out of his way to show people pictures on his iPad. 'Fantoni the Phony,' I always called him." But Brogeland found him genuinely warm; he and his wife, Tonje, had visited with Fantoni and his wife, Iolanda, in Rome. Fantoni and Nunes once secured a spot for Brogeland on a team sponsored by the Italian businessman Francesco Angelini. "These were good friends," Brogeland says, "people I went to dinner with, I respected, I traveled with. But to me, you don't cross that line."

Brogeland wanted to expose the pair without delay, but Brad Moss, the American player who had helped gather evidence against Fisher and Schwartz, urged caution. "Their sponsor is Pierre Zimmermann," Moss says, "the most powerful person in bridge. There have been several examples in the past where the rules were—let's just say—*interpreted favorably* for Mr. Zimmermann. He's not a person you took on lightly." (Zimmermann, in an email, claims the opposite: "I tend to lose bridge appeals in surrealistic rulings.") Moss and others warned Brogeland that if Zimmermann chose to litigate Brogeland could be ruined. "We begged him, 'Why don't we take some time, gather up as much evidence, build up a dossier, and *then* go after them?'" Moss says. "And Boye was like, 'No. I don't care. What can they do to me? If I live in a tent, I live in a tent. It's now or never—look at the momentum.'"

Before publicly accusing the pair, Brogeland says, he phoned Fantoni and offered an ultimatum. They could confess, and thus hope to gain some sympathy from the governing bodies—who might let them back into the game in a few years—or Brogeland would out them. They had 24 hours to decide. "I said, 'Fulvio, we have the evidence. Please go out and admit to something. Don't do like Fisher and Schwartz and deny everything; this is just hopeless.'" Fantoni seemed to consider the offer. "He said, 'I don't like to fight,'" Brogeland recalls. But no announcement came.

On September 13, Bridge Winners published "The Videos Speak: Fantoni-Nunes." Using the signaling code Mevius had suggested, Woolsey submitted for analysis some 85 hands played by Fantoni and Nunes. On all but three, Mevius's code predicted the vertical or horizontal orientation of the opening lead—a statistical impossibility, Woolsey says, unless the players were colluding with a prearranged signal. "If you flip a coin 85 times, what are the chances it's going to come up heads 82 times?" Woolsey says. "I mean, it's one over you-don't-want-to-know-how-many zeros." The pair, who were suspended by the ACBL and placed under investigation by the body and the EBL, withdrew from competition. In a statement last November, the pair said, "We will not comment on allegations at this time, reserving our right to reply in a more appropriate setting."

Disbelief greeted the news. On Bridge Winners, readers posted more than 1,100 comments (where 50 constitutes a robust reaction), the first of which said it all: "Is this the end? Speechless now . . ."

It wasn't quite the end. Brogeland soon received an anonymous email tip from someone identifying himself as "No Matter." The tipster advised taking a look at videos of Germany's top-ranking pair, Alex Smirnov and Josef Piekarek, and Polish pair Cezary Balicki and Adam Żmudziński. No Matter even pointed out what to look for: illegal signaling based on where the pair placed the special bidding cards in the bidding tray that is passed between the players during the auction part of each hand.

Astonishingly, when Brogeland checked the videos, he thought the tip seemed valid. Smirnov and Piekarek, told of Brogeland's discovery, admitted to the violation in a statement: "We regret that in the past as a partnership we committed some ethical violations," Smirnov wrote. "Josef and I have voluntarily agreed never again to play competitive bridge together and to take two years off . . . We hope that after such a time has elapsed, that we might be welcomed back . . ." Balicki and Żmudziński, who denied the charges, had their credentials for the Bermuda Bowl withdrawn by the World Bridge Federation, and the pair is now under investigation by the EBL.

Still more astonishing, however, was the person behind the mask of No Matter. It appeared to be the disgraced Lotan Fisher.

Jack to a King

Brogeland cannot explain why the man who had issued threats against him was now, anonymously, helping in the quest to root out cheaters—unless Fisher, by helping to expose others, hoped to take the focus off himself and his partner. Fisher, in an email to me, claims that he only helped No Matter and that his motivation was the same as Brogeland's—to clean up the game. "I love [bridge] more than Boye, Ish or anyone else," he wrote, adding, "My next step is to prove that me and Ron Schwartz didn't cheat. NEVER." Fisher declined to say how he broke the other pairs' cheating codes, but Brogeland says it's no mystery. "It takes one to know one," he says. (Having voluntarily withdrawn from play pending rulings by the European, American, and Israeli federations, Fisher and Schwartz last fall submitted a defense claiming that they did not engage in any collusive cheating.)

Rulings on the fate of all four pairs, by the game's governing bodies, are expected this month. Generally, players believe that anyone found to have cheated will face lifetime bans. In the meantime, Brogeland's actions have already had a permanent effect on the game. Last December, the ACBL held one of bridge's biggest annual tournaments, the American nationals, at the Sheraton hotel in Denver, which drew 4,372 players from countries around the world. For the first time, the ACBL had installed small video cameras and microphones at the tables to record all quarter-final through final matches—since no one imagines that every dishonest pair has been rooted out. "I don't know how deep this goes," says ACBL president Hartman. "Four pairs have been suspended. But are there 20 more behind that? And 20 more behind that? Who really knows? So we're doing everything we can to see if it does go deeper." At the end of the tournament, Hartman convened the first meeting of a new anti-cheating task force made up of eight top players, who discussed means for streamlining the process of submitting complaints and investigating them. Fred Gitelman, of Bridge Base Online, unveiled a proposed anti-cheating device, an iPad-like tablet on which players manipulate virtual cards—an innovation that the game's top players have so far resisted, since card feel is a critical part of their experience at the table. The adoption of such a device, however, seems inevitable in a game where the ease of cheating, and the financial inducements to do so, have dogged the professional game since its inception.

Players say that all of this has introduced a level of paranoia heretofore absent from tournament play. Steve Weinstein, of Bridge Winners, says that when he competed in the Bermuda Bowl last October, a month after the cheating scandal broke, he was unusually conscious of how he handled the cards. "I was noticing how I was leading," he says. "Eventually I had to go: 'I don't cheat! Stop thinking about this!'" Cullin, whose sharp-eyed viewing of YouTube videos helped lead to the suspension of Fisher and Schwartz, says, "I actually went through my *own* videos at the Europeans to see how I played the cards. It was in all directions—and I was like, 'Oh, I hope there is no pattern here, because I'm going to be fucked!'"

But for all the watchful unease that now hangs over the game, Brogeland has become its hero, named Bridge Personality of the Year last fall by the International Bridge Press Association. The fears of a reprisal from the game's powerful sponsors proved unfounded. (Pierre Zimmermann says that he has no plans to sue Brogeland.) He's been hailed, by Dallas Ace Bob Hamman, as the "sheriff" who cleaned up Dodge. Brogeland prefers to say that he ran a "Bridge Interpol," since it reflects the collaborative, international effort critical to cleaning up the game.

In any case, Brogeland has become bridge's reigning luminary. When he arrived for his first match at the Denver nationals, he had to fight his way through the crowd of hundreds of players and fans who had collected outside the tournament room. "Thank you for your service," said a bearded man who had stopped Brogeland at the door of the game room.

"Well, I had to do it," Brogeland said, shaking the man's hand and trying to move off.

"You really put yourself on the line," the man persisted.

Brogeland shrugged, smiled. "Bridge deserves it," he said, and then headed for his table.

Welcome to the Big Time

FROM ESPN: THE MAGAZINE

THERE'S A GAME within the game that requires a different set of skills," actor Edward Norton says in the voice-over as quick-cut video images show young men and women bathing a dog, jogging on the street, sweating in a sauna—all while staring, hyperfocused, into their smartphones. "There's no off-season. This is a play-as-much-as-you-want, whenever-you-want fantasy league. And we don't just play—we are players. We train. And we *win* . . ." Now those men and women are jumping, cheering, fist-pumping—each celebrating mammoth, seven-figure jackpots. "This isn't fantasy as usual. This is DraftKings. Welcome to the big time."

At its peak last summer, a daily fantasy get-rich-now commercial aired every 90 seconds on television. Combined, industry leaders FanDuel and DraftKings plunged more than $750 million into TV commercials, radio spots, digital ads, and other promotions. In the weeks leading up to the 2015 NFL season, the two start-up companies spent more on advertising than the entire American beer industry.

Daily fantasy's meteoric rise—breathtaking for its breakneck speed, avalanche of investors' cash, and ever-spiraling valuations —spurred the two companies' endlessly annoying, record-shattering arms race for new customers and industry dominance. In only three years, DraftKings zoomed from an idea hatched by three buddies in a Boston barroom into a nearly $2 billion company, replete with comparisons to overnight Silicon Valley unicorns like Uber and Snapchat. FanDuel was right there too. The two companies processed a combined $3 billion in player-entry fees in 2015.

The companies were everywhere: logos emblazoned in ballparks, on NBA floors and NHL boards, and in ESPN studios. They became the darlings of the major American sports leagues, media companies, dozens of professional teams, and a deep bench of investors—from Comcast and Google to private equity firms and a pair of the NFL's most influential owners, Jerry Jones and Robert Kraft.

But as quickly as it boomed, the industry bottomed. One year after their headiest moments, FanDuel and DraftKings are still not profitable. Both privately held companies' valuations have been sliced—by more than half, according to some estimates. The companies have hemorrhaged tens of millions of dollars in legal and lobbying expenses. (DraftKings' attorneys' fees once ran as high as $1 million per week.) And the fog bank of the industry's uncertain future has made it nearly impossible for either company to raise new money. (FanDuel's auditors have raised "significant doubts" about the company's future if more states do not declare daily fantasy sports legal.) Three federal grand juries—in Boston, New York, and Tampa, Florida—have alerted one or both companies that they are under criminal investigation. A merger—once unthinkable to many—is on the table.

It has been, by any measure, a spectacular fall.

The industry's implosion began with a series of tactical mistakes made by a pair of bitterly hostile start-up companies that all but dared federal and state authorities to shut down the sites over concerns the games constituted illegal gambling. *Outside the Lines* interviewed more than 50 company executives, current and former players, legislators, lobbyists, lawyers, investigators, and industry consultants and found that the companies' troubles were triggered, in part, by a toxic combination of young executives' hubris and ignorance, reckless risk-taking, and raw political naïveté. Infused with a false sense of security from FanDuel's and DraftKings' surging valuations and soaring revenues, the companies' cofounders and CEOs—Nigel Eccles, 41, of FanDuel and Jason Robins, 35, of DraftKings—waged a self-destructive, kill-or-be-killed race toward industry supremacy and a life-changing payday that they now acknowledge was crazy for all of the cash it torched, the wrong messages it sent, and the legal and media tsunami it unleashed.

For years, the two companies' leaders had been warned by investors, lobbyists, consultants, and even some players about a coming day of reckoning. Yet they relentlessly promoted their games as a means to get rich quick when they knew only a tiny percentage of their customers were winning more often than losing. They failed to aggressively move against big-bankrolled players who dominated newer players, sometimes with predatory behavior or technological advantages. And they allowed their own employees to play—and win millions—on their rivals' sites, despite their having access to odds-improving proprietary data.

"This industry blew up so quickly—no one adequately planned or prepared for it," says Gabriel Harber, 29, a former high-volume player at DraftKings and FanDuel. "[The executives] didn't make the substantial investment on self-regulation and the regulatory side that was obviously needed . . . Every PR person and lawyer should be fired. How could you let your client engage in this kind of crazy advertising if every legal loophole wasn't closed? How stupid can you be?"

The daily fantasy industry has an unwitting—and unlikely—founding father: George W. Bush.

On October 13, 2006, President Bush signed the Unlawful Internet Gambling Enforcement Act. UIGEA was intended to reverse the momentum of America's Internet gambling boom by prohibiting banks from processing bettors' credit card deposits with illegal betting operations. With the blessing of the major sports leagues, a carve-out in the law was made for the wildly popular season-long fantasy leagues that an estimated 57 million Americans now play. But the drafters of UIGEA were silent about daily fantasy contests because no such thing existed. By 2007, however, a handful of lightly played daily fantasy websites had opened in the United States, but overseas, things were moving much faster.

A group of sharp entrepreneurs from the United Kingdom, some of whom had worked as online poker executives, started considering the possibilities. An entrepreneur named Nigel Eccles had concluded, correctly, that season-long fantasy leagues were far too slow for action-junkie millennials, who thrived on instant gratification and who'd soon routinely watch sports on TV while glued to a second screen, usually their smartphone.

So in July 2009, Eccles and his colleagues launched FanDuel

in Edinburgh, Scotland. It was a spin-off of Hubdub, their failed prediction site on which users bet virtual money. Unlike Hubdub, FanDuel would accept real-money wagers.

A soft-spoken, lanky Brit, Eccles had printed out a copy of UI-GEA and studied its fine print. From day one, he concluded that the law would provide "safe harbor" for daily fantasy games. In early meetings with potential investors, Eccles was a passionate evangelist for daily fantasy sports as a game of skill, similar, he liked to say, to a golf tournament, a 5K race, a chess championship, or a spelling bee. His initial pitches steered clear of gambling parlance: "bets" were not wagers but "entry fees," and competitors were not vying for "jackpots" but preset "cash prizes." "We can show with FanDuel that the high-skill players will win predominantly," Eccles would tell investors, the media, anyone who'd listen.

The chase for financing was slow going at first; the initial investors were Ian Ritchie, a Scottish software millionaire, and Kevin Dorren, a Brit who founded a meals-on-wheels diet service. Eccles nearly gave up when investors' cash dried up. But he and his co-founders pressed on, and by the end of 2011, FanDuel had combined smart product design and savvy marketing to establish itself as the industry leader. The company's later financial backers, like Mike LaSalle of Shamrock Capital Investors in Los Angeles, were hooked by Eccles's vision for explosive growth, with a target of 20 million to 30 million active users within several years.

During their first meeting in Manhattan in April 2014, LaSalle says, he was particularly impressed that Eccles wasn't a daily fantasy player but a disciplined businessman committed to developing new products. Five months later, LaSalle's firm made a major investment in FanDuel as part of the company's financing round that raised $70 million.

"We thought the regulatory issues were going to have to be flushed out at some point," he says. "But no one anticipated the fervor of what happened and the way [the authorities] directed their energies" against the industry.

As FanDuel grew, the three young men who would launch its principal competitor were still working near Boston for Vistaprint, the printing and business cards company. The trio were Jason Robins, a Duke graduate with degrees in economics and computer science who minored in math; Matt Kalish, a Columbia grad and fantasy baseball addict; and Paul Liberman, an electrical engineering and computer science graduate of Worcester Polytechnic Institute in Massachusetts. On a Tuesday in January 2011, Kalish pitched an idea to Robins: an online sports venture that would jam all the excitement of a season-long fantasy league into a single day—even a few hours. Robins was in. They recruited Liberman. They would become discouraged after discovering that FanDuel and other companies already had a strong foothold. But Robins told his pals the crowded field proved there was a marketplace for daily fantasy. They'd just have to find a way to beat FanDuel.

By that weekend, the trio were holed up developing their idea inside the spare bedroom of Liberman's town house in Watertown, Massachusetts, and, on occasion, over draft beers at Boston Beer Works.

Robins is a quick-thinking, fast-talking entrepreneur, a natural-born salesman who is articulate, supremely confident, and a little brash. Some investors call him "the closer." In the beginning, however, he didn't close anything. He pitched DraftKings to nearly 50 potential investors, none of whom bit. But after meeting Robins in November 2011, an investor named Ryan Moore says it didn't take long to hand him a $1 million check. "I'd say within an hour, maybe 90 minutes," recalls Moore of Atlas Venture.

Three months later, Robins, Kalish, and Liberman were still at Vistaprint while moonlighting on DraftKings inside Liberman's spare bedroom. That's when Moore challenged them with a difficult question: if they don't believe in the company enough to quit their day jobs, why would any other investor—or any customer—believe they are serious? It was the push Robins, Kalish, and Liberman needed.

They quit, and on April 27, 2012, the trio hosted their first daily fantasy baseball contest at DraftKings. A few dozen family members and friends paid $20 per lineup and competed for a pot worth nearly $400. The three cofounders' cut was $40.

From the beginning, DraftKings built a reputation for being hyper-aggressive, racing to build a user-friendly mobile product and the first to recognize the importance of signing credibility-boosting major league sponsorships. The company also would eventually offer fantasy contests on sporting events that FanDuel wouldn't touch, like PGA golf tournaments, mixed martial arts, esports, and

NASCAR. FanDuel had avoided those sports over its interpreta-
tion of federal law: that fantasy games must involve multiple contests, such as an evening's worth of NBA games rather than a single
NASCAR race.

But the wider smorgasbord of games proved popular. Draft-
Kings always "shot for the moon—pushed the envelope in every
way to make up ground on FanDuel," says a consultant for both
companies.

FanDuel had a three-year head start, but DraftKings broke from
the scrum of dozens of start-ups to establish itself as the Boston-
based rival that FanDuel, in New York, would need to reckon with.

The early, relatively low-stakes games being offered were intended to cater to friends playing for fun rather than money. Two
months after going live, DraftKings offered its first guaranteed
jackpot contest, for $5,000. But on the lightly trafficked site, many
contests wouldn't fill up with enough players to cover the large
guaranteed payouts. This meant DraftKings had to defray the difference, a figure that ran into tens of thousands of dollars that
executives would come to view as a marketing expense. Gamblers
loved the "overlay" because the guaranteed jackpots, with fewer
players, improved their odds, and they viewed the cash difference
as free money. For the sites, it turned out to be cash well spent:
word of the overlay opportunity in DraftKings' bigger-money contests ricocheted among frequent daily fantasy players, attracting
waves of new customers and helping DraftKings emerge from the
pack and close the gap with FanDuel.

Before long, both companies' executives discovered that the
easiest way to lure customers was to offer the long-odds promise of
lucrative jackpots. On December 8, 2013, in the FanDuel Fantasy
Football Championship, a Sioux City, Iowa, sales manager named
Travis Spieth turned $10 into daily fantasy's first one-day million-
aire prize. A year later, in the same contest, a Pasadena, California,
personal trainer named Scott Hanson was minted as the first daily
fantasy multimillionaire by winning the $2 million grand prize.

By 2014, DraftKings had become the second-largest daily fantasy site, buoyed by its purchase that summer of the third-largest
site, DraftStreet. The industry was consolidating in multiple ways.
FanDuel and DraftKings had developed similar platforms and offered many of the same products. They also shared a cross-section
of players.

And investors, businesses, media companies, and America's major sports leagues noticed the two companies' mind-boggling growth. Even more important, they loved how daily fantasy turbocharged TV ratings and fans' engagement with all sports, even for something as mundane as a midseason Monday night slate of NHL games. Entry fees in the United States had jumped from $20 million in 2011 to $1 billion in 2014. In a confidential pitch memo to investors, DraftKings projected an astonishing $15 billion to $20 billion in industrywide entry fees in 2017.

Most investors, including the pro sports leagues, weren't blind to the danger that the gravy train could be derailed by legal challenges. Among the early skeptics were Major League Baseball executives, who conducted a two-year study of the legality of daily fantasy sports. But an outside law firm hired by MLB concluded that DraftKings "overwhelmingly" offered games of skill, not chance.

After that assurance, MLB became the first league to partner with the industry, accepting a small equity stake in DraftKings before eventually naming DraftKings its official daily fantasy game. MLS, the NHL, NASCAR, and the UFC followed. FanDuel, meanwhile, became the exclusive partner of the NBA, in exchange for an equity stake.

At the same time, DraftKings and FanDuel did their own diligence on whether their games would survive a legal challenge. To investigate the issue, DraftKings hired a Las Vegas lawyer named Anthony Cabot, who had cowritten an article touting the legalization of online poker for the *UNLV Gaming Research and Review Journal.* Cabot concluded that the company's "pay-to-play fantasy sports service" was legal in 45 states as long as each contest's outcome was "within the control of the users."

"The key to the distinction between fantasy sports and sports wagering is that fantasy sports require the consistent and recognizable involvement of the contestants to achieve success," Cabot told DraftKings executives in the letter obtained by *Outside the Lines.* FanDuel was given a green light by a law firm that conducted a similar exhaustive study, documents show. Executives say these assurances led the sites to flatly state on their websites that daily fantasy was legal in most states and to pass those assurances on to investors and would-be partners.

*

The skill set needed to win at daily fantasy most closely resembles the skills needed to win at the racetrack. Like the horseplayer handicapping a Pick Six by scouring the *Daily Racing Form*'s miniaturized type, a daily fantasy player chooses a combination of pro players who he or she believes will perform the best based on their past performances and an array of other factors. When the thoroughbreds bolt from the gate, the horseplayer becomes a deeply invested though passive observer, in the same way the daily fantasy player can only watch and root for players to run up the points after the kickoffs of Sunday's early NFL games.

That parallel wasn't lost on some industry insiders and even a few leaders of the Fantasy Sports Trade Association, the 18-year-old volunteer trade group representing about 250 member fantasy sports companies. At the FSTA's winter conference, held at the Mirage in Las Vegas in January 2013, FSTA president Paul Charchian warned the daily fantasy executives assembled not to emphasize the monetary aspect of their contests or they'd risk a legal or regulatory pushback. In particular, he urged the executives to keep all gambling lingo from their websites and to refrain from emphasizing winning and winning big in marketing campaigns.

"Don't f— this up," Charchian told the industry leaders, including the CEOs and top executives of DraftKings and FanDuel.

Charchian and other FSTA leaders also worried that as the industry grew, it would seize the attention of casino and thoroughbred racing executives, who would lobby elected officials to try to stop daily fantasy from cutting in on their action. In April 2014, Eccles himself wrote a better-business charter of consumer protection, warning companies to "avoid the use of gambling terms in the promotion and marketing of their games." The FSTA adopted the guidelines but did not enforce them.

Trade association officials and other insiders also urged FanDuel and DraftKings to adopt a best-defense-is-offense strategy. Yet prior to 2015, FanDuel and DraftKings executives had balked at numerous proposals to invest in an expensive state-by-state campaign seeking regulatory and legal clarity on the gambling issue. They also considered but rejected numerous attempts to form a self-regulatory, industrywide board that would field customers' complaints and aggressively police the companies' integrity, fairness, and transparency.

"The industry moved too slowly," says Rick Wolf, a founding

board member of the FSTA, whose annual lobbying budget in 2014 was $75,000, barely enough to mount a battle in a single state. "We began looking at regulation two years ago, but the attempt kept getting punted. No one wanted to take it on."

One reason that some industry leaders resisted: their marketing had been successfully targeting poker players and sports bettors to become their customers. DraftKings embedded gambling phrases into its website to help gamblers find it using Google searches like "fantasy golf betting" and "weekly fantasy basketball betting," documents show. That occurred despite its leaders' assurances that it offered legal skill games and, in the fine print of its ads, that DraftKings is "not a gambling website."

Confidential investor pitches obtained by *Outside the Lines* were rife with comparisons to online sports wagering and casino gambling. "Sports Wagering Vertical is a large addressable market," DraftKings told potential investors, suggesting that its contests would appeal to American customers illegally wagering billions of dollars at offshore sportsbooks and online poker sites.

FanDuel was also blunt about its products' appeal to gamblers in materials provided to investors, documents show. FanDuel executives told one investor their target market was male sports fans who "cannot gamble online legally" and that their customers have "a higher preponderance to gambling." FanDuel also compared its performance with that of Bwin.Party, a sports bookie that is one of the world's largest online gambling companies. In a pitch to investors, FanDuel noted that nearly 20 percent of its users, in a survey, said they bet or gamble and that their friends would describe them as "a bit of an addict."

"We always knew there was no law on the books," a longtime lobbyist says, "and if you make it about gambling and winning big checks, you can blow it all."

Like any poker website or online bookmaker, DFS companies need two vastly different types of players to keep depositing money. Small-stakes players were needed to join—and continue playing—but the high-volume players, some of whom entered thousands of lineups in hundreds of contests a night, had become the sites' most reliable cash machines. The companies, whose total revenue last year was $280 million, make their money in the same way horse tracks and poker rooms do—by taking a 6 percent to 15 percent cut, or "rake," of players' wagers. The higher the betting volume, the more the sites get to keep.

By some estimates, 60 percent of the daily fantasy industry's revenue comes from the roughly 15,000 high-volume players wagering at least $10,000 a year. Nearly 50 players, most of whom are savvy, analytics-driven professionals, each wager at least $1 million a year. And some go even higher: two sharks played hundreds of high-stakes heads-up NBA contests during the homestretch of the NBA's 2014–15 season. After 20 consecutive nights, one of the players had lost nearly $2 million.

The winner of that binge was "maxdalury," who is really Saahil Sud, a late-twenties former data scientist who lives a few blocks from DraftKings' Boston headquarters. A 2011 graduate of Amherst College with degrees in math and economics, Sud is a daily fantasy pro notorious for entering hundreds of different lineups in every big-money contest—and some modest-sized ones. For the deep-pocketed player, this strategy is expensive, of course, and so is the exposure. But your chances of winning improve exponentially with 900 lineups in a field of 35,000 when most players have one or two. Sud was also a prolific user of computerized scripts. In one NBA DraftKings contest in which he entered 400 lineups, Sud's last-minute, scripted swap of veteran Magic big man Channing Frye for late-scratched center Nikola Vučević helped him win an estimated $500,000.

"It's only a skill game if you have the biggest bankroll and the best technology," says John Sullivan, 50, a former FanDuel consultant who quit playing high stakes after becoming disenchanted with the lopsided ecosystem. "That's the dirty little secret."

One of the more extreme examples of this phenomenon happened in DraftKings' $1 Million Mega Payoff Pitch contest on May 26, 2015. Sud posted 888 baseball lineups at $27 per lineup. He destroyed the field, scooping up the first-place prize of $100,000. His lineups finished in five of the top 10 spots. Twenty-nine of his lineups placed in the top 100, and 454 of his 888 lineups made money. With a $23,976 investment, Sud won more than $221,000.

An analysis of that contest's results shows the futility of entering a handful of lineups—even as many as 90—in any big-jackpot contest. Nearly all players who entered fewer than 100 lineups finished with a negative return on investment, most in the double digits. Even those who entered more than 25 lineups (costing at least $700) but fewer than 100 lineups had ROIs of minus-22 percent to minus-27 percent. Of the 21 players who posted more than 100 lineups, Sud and two others had a profitable night.

Regular, smaller-stakes players weren't blind to the winning methods of sharks like Sud, and they weren't shy about complaining.

DraftKings and FanDuel responded slowly to the demands by some of their customers for greater transparency and to limit or prohibit the high-volume players' favorite tools, like the sharks' multiple entries, scripting, and other predatory practices.

Adam Krejcik, the managing director of Eilers & Krejcik Gaming, observed that the sharks-versus-fish dynamic threatened daily fantasy's very existence. "The biggest risk for the DFS industry is *not* regulation but whether it can attract mass market appeal and avoid becoming too 'hardcore,'" Krejcik wrote in a January 2014 presentation. There's a "very delicate balance that needs to be maintained between 'grinders' and 'casual' players."

But the two sites lavished perks only on their high-volume grinders and contest winners. FanDuel gave its big winners NFL luxury box tickets and autographed jerseys, but DraftKings did even more—a party attended by VIPs inside a Gillette Stadium luxury box; the Las Vegas "Tiger Jam VIP Experience," in which winning players rubbed shoulders with Tiger Woods in the MGM Grand's poker room and at Shadow Creek Golf Course; a private party for grinders and other VIPs at the LIV nightclub in Miami Beach. And the list goes on.

"Here's the thing—taking high-liquidity players on junkets is really stupid," says Joe Brennan Jr., the CEO of rival FastFantasy. com. "Steve Wynn wouldn't do it—he'd be giving the treats to the high-liquidity *losers.* The sites should be treating the high-liquidity losers, the guys who are losing all that money that goes right to their bottom line."

Another way to look at how the companies were allowing their haves to prey on their have-nots: "DraftKings reminds me of the college kids having a kegger and the cops say, 'Turn the music down,' and they say, 'We're sorry,' and the cops go away and they turn the music back up," Sullivan says. "They have bravado—for lack of a better term, it's balls."

Some critics now say the companies' CEOs even had the balls to publicly preach the benefits of hooking large schools of novice fish for their sophisticated, big-bankrolled players to devour.

On RotoGrinders—daily fantasy's most popular online community where players vent and kvetch—Robins, the DraftKings CEO, told users that his company was spending large sums on advertising to attract new players who would presumably make the site more attractive to the tiny clique of high-volume, consistently winning players. "The goal in how we are set up and the tremendous amount of money we spend on marketing are meant to attract and retain casual players, which in turn should make it an attractive environment for those who profit," Robins wrote on the message board.

Eccles, the FanDuel CEO, said something similar on RotoGrinders, arguing that the best way for high-volume grinders to enhance their return on investment would be for the site to recruit thousands of new players, presumably with less experience and expertise, rather than have the site reduce its rake percentage. "To be honest," Eccles wrote, "at the moment, we've focused more on bringing in new players, which by our calculations is a lot more important to grinder win rates than cutting rake."

Robins and Eccles might have found a consensus on that strategy, but they disagreed about many other ways to grow their businesses. Their hostility toward each other was often out in the open.

More than once, Eccles dismissed DraftKings as a "clone" that didn't pose much of a threat to FanDuel's dominance. The way Eccles saw it, he and his cofounders had created the industry, and DraftKings' reckless, risky corporate ethos that pushed the envelope legally would be its undoing. FanDuel also believed that DraftKings overpaid software engineers and analytics employees, raising the cost of doing business for everyone. Robins deeply resented the disrespect, using Eccles's barbs to motivate his young staff to write better code, develop better products, and beat FanDuel for customer experience. The competition and clashing corporate philosophies turned into bad blood between some of the two companies' senior executives, and the bitterness ran deepest between Eccles and Robins, consultants and employees told *Outside the Lines*. Neither Eccles nor Robins denies the bad blood.

For the executives, it was easy to ignore signs of trouble because fresh investors' money kept flowing, and waves of new customers kept flocking to both sites. It was also easy to ignore the biggest threat to the industry's best shot for long-term success: nearly all daily fantasy players lose.

On a late autumn weekday afternoon, I sign up for DraftKings and deposit $100. With nearly 250,000 lineups and a top-heavy payout structure, "The Millionaire Maker" seizes the boldest headlines. But the sites also offer countless opportunities to play against small fields for modest stakes. (Contest entry fees range from 25 cents to $10,600, but the most popular entry fee is $3, the sites say.) There are head-to-head matchups, small tournaments of five or nine players, "50-50" games in which players finishing in the top 50 percent win (usually only a few bucks), double-up games in which you can turn $5 into $10, and "invite-only" contests in which you can compete against your friends and colleagues.

So I cobble together a team of players competing in that night's seven NBA games and post my lineup in a head-to-head contest for a $50 entry fee. Almost instantly—it took six seconds—my team is scooped up by a player named "condia." I don't know who condia is, or even what that word means, though a check of RotoGrinders breaks the bad news that condia is the number-one-ranked NBA fantasy player in America. Somewhat despondently, I watch the games on NBA League Pass as my players are annihilated by condia's lineup by 80-plus points.

The next day, I tell Harber, the former high-volume player, how quickly and effortlessly condia had torched me.

"You got bum-hunted," he says with a laugh.

Excuse me?

"Bum-hunted. He had a crawler on the page, and it ate up your game," Harber says. Other players call the condias "lobby hawks," perched and waiting to pounce on rookies like me who show up in the lobby shopping for a head-to-head game.

Harber is still chuckling. "All these high-volume guys are archiving all the data to find out who is a good player or a bad player —or a complete novice like you," he says. High-volume players are so sophisticated that their computerized scripts and other automated systems are often invisible to the sites, Harber and other high-volume players say, though the sites deny that. Some scripts are ones of convenience: allowing high-volume players to change hundreds of lineups to make a late substitution when a player is a last-minute scratch. Others are more predatory, scraping live data from the sites to target the worst of the losing players, the same trick mastered by professional online poker players.

For years, FanDuel had given quiet permission to customers who asked to use certain scripts, a request almost always made by their most valued high-volume customers. DraftKings says it forbade the use of all automated tools before July 2015, but high-volume users say they routinely used such tools—or knew others who did—before then on the site. There was little or no transparency; sites refused to divulge the identities of players who were warned, suspended, or banned for using predatory scripts or violating any of the sites' other ever-evolving terms and conditions. FanDuel says it has suspended thousands of customers. Says a DraftKings spokeswoman, "We do not reveal specifics about our user activity."

I soon discover that condia isn't just a famous, prolific, and high-stakes player, he's also pretty widely disliked by the regulars. As far as I can tell, he's disliked not because he plays so much but because he wins so much. He is renowned for trolling the sites' lobbies for every kind of action, including games for as little as $3, despite having a prodigious bankroll in the high six figures.

Condia's real name is Charles Chon, and he is a self-deprecating 30-year-old who lives in Denver and majored in accounting at Colorado State. A few months after I join DraftKings, I tell Chon about our instant head-to-head matchup and how effortlessly he hoovered my $50.

"I'm sorry, man," he says, squeaking out a laugh. "It was just me finding you in the lobby. I like playing the smaller players because it's easy money—it's like free money for me. I mean, why wouldn't you take it? There have been times when I tried to get action against anyone I could, including newer players. I probably got you for that reason."

Chon denies the persistent accusations on the RotoGrinders message boards that he has cheated by using scripts and other technological edges to find and bankrupt lousy players. "I always try to play by the rules," he says. "I know some other guys don't."

Despite all of their ongoing hostilities, Robins and Eccles met for dinner at the Bellagio in Las Vegas during the FSTA's winter conference in January 2015. The unthinkable between the two rivals was broached: a merger. Robins pitched the idea at the urging of Jonathan Kraft, president of the New England Patriots and an early DraftKings investor through the Kraft Group. From a long-term financial perspective, a pair of daily fantasy companies trying to outspend each other into oblivion didn't make sense. Satellite radio rivals Sirius and XM avoided a mutual assured death by merging. Why couldn't DraftKings and FanDuel?

One proposal had FanDuel and its investors getting 60 percent of a new tied-in company. Although those terms were more favorable to FanDuel, Eccles rejected them, sources say. Eccles "wants to be the Mark Zuckerberg of the industry, to be seen as the godfather of daily fantasy sports," a consultant with firsthand knowledge of the negotiations told *Outside the Lines*. Eccles and Robins "really do hate each other. And their egos got in the way." Says another industry insider privy to the talks, "Guys with cooler heads would have likely gotten it done—a merger made all the sense in the world."

A month after the dinner, FanDuel hired Christian Genetski to be its chief legal officer, a job that hadn't previously existed, to build a new legal team. He knew one of his biggest missions would be to try to clarify the gray zone on the legality of DFS in states nationwide, a challenge he viewed as somewhat defensive. "If we were a beach house, we needed to winterize," says Genetski, 45, who had done legal work at Yahoo before working for several years in the video game industry. "The *Farmers' Almanac* didn't call for the Category 5 hurricane that hit us."

Genetski reached out to Tim Dent, the chief financial officer of DraftKings, and both sites soon agreed to work together on a modest, defense-only lobbying effort and share the costs of an attorney general consultant.

On May 7, 2015, Genetski, Dent, and a throng of lobbyists and lawyers met to discuss legislative and regulatory opportunities at a midtown Manhattan lobbying office. Again, they discussed FanDuel and DraftKings taking the lead to create an industrywide board that would aggressively self-regulate, similar to the movie ratings board created by the Motion Picture Association of America, while also fielding consumer complaints. When the meeting broke up, there was fresh momentum for the rivals to pursue the proposal, with the tentative name the "Fantasy Sports Control Agency."

A week later, DraftKings struck a sponsorship deal with NASCAR and introduced contests on its races. FanDuel had also discussed the sponsorship, but after DraftKings landed it, Eccles and his colleagues were furious, telling investors they were convinced that their rival's new contests violated federal law. "How were they going to self-regulate when one company didn't agree with what the other company was doing?" a senior industry consultant says. "It really was the end of any hope for cooperation."

Besides the CEOs' mutual mistrust and simmering resentments, there were a variety of other reasons the industry never established the board. It was expensive, for one thing. It also required the political skills to cobble together a coalition of dozens of companies with conflicting agendas. "We had a lot of discussions about it," Robins says, "and we were in the process of collaborating on it. And everything just kind of moved too quickly."

"We had thought through things like self-regulation, how that would look," Eccles says. "But we hadn't invested nearly as much as we should have, if we had known what was coming."

It was a costly missed opportunity. When investigators and prosecutors began scrutinizing the industry, a self-policing Fantasy Sports Control Agency might have bought some goodwill.

Instead, FanDuel and DraftKings marched toward an expensive war for market share, in part at the urging of impatient investors who wanted the sites to grab a larger chunk of the 57 million Americans who play season-long fantasy sports. The rivals seemed unable to extract themselves from a vicious cycle: The more their executives could show investors the exponential growth rates of new customers and entry fees, the more investor money they could attract. The more investor money the executives could attract, the closer they would come to an IPO and life-changing paydays for everyone.

The summer of 2015 began with soaring financial promise. Everyone wanted in.

In June, ESPN's parent, the Walt Disney Company, was finalizing a $250 million equity stake in DraftKings. In return, DraftKings pledged to spend a whopping $500 million in advertising on ESPN properties over several years. The deal had been discussed for months and seemed a certainty as industry leaders gathered in midtown Manhattan for the start of the FSTA's summer conference on June 22. But by the end of that day, word began circulating that the deal had blown up after a top Disney attorney warned executives that he was uncomfortable with the legal uncertainty surrounding DraftKings' contests.

Undeterred by that setback, and with much fanfare, the industry leaders closed a record-shattering funding round in July—$275 million for FanDuel and $300 million for DraftKings—that pushed both companies' valuations considerably higher than $1 billion. And then DraftKings raised even more, in another funding round that wasn't made public.

But trouble loomed.

In late July 2015, an ominous-sounding letter arrived at both companies' headquarters. It was from a U.S. attorney in Tampa, alerting executives that their companies were the subjects of a criminal tax investigation, sources told *Outside the Lines*. Despite receiving those notices, the executives moved forward with their marketing plans to try to become number one.

"In hindsight," an influential consultant close to both companies says, "those commercials were even more insane because they knew they were under federal criminal investigation."

There was more bad news, but this time it hit publicly. McKinsey & Company released an alarming study showing that a tiny percentage of daily fantasy players win consistently—only 1.3 percent playing baseball. Analyzing three months of results scraped from FanDuel, McKinsey's study raised major questions about the long-term viability of fantasy sports' "ecosystem."

"Investors are overlooking a fundamental operating challenge: the risk that the skill element of daily fantasy is so high that DFS pros will wipe out recreational players in short order," wrote the report's coauthors, Dan Singer and Ed Miller. The "whales," who Singer and Miller say lose thousands a year on baseball contests, bolster the sites' revenues. "If those whales get discouraged—and they have a negative-31 percent return of investment, so it's easy to see why they'll get discouraged—the industry will die," Singer says.

Neither company was discouraged, and they pressed forward. DraftKings had always intended to invest a big chunk of its new money on a bid to firmly establish itself as the leading daily fantasy site. During the 2014 NFL season, FanDuel boosted its market share by spending more on ads than DraftKings, whose executives vowed they'd never be outspent again. Initially, FanDuel wasn't planning to spend nearly as much in 2015 as its rival, but executives had watched as DraftKings significantly closed the gap on total market share before surpassing FanDuel in July with nearly 60 percent of the market. FanDuel concluded that the only way to reverse its bleeding market share was to try to match DraftKings' enormous ad buys that autumn during football season.

Fortified with their overstuffed war chests, the two companies were prepared to spend as much money as it would take to destroy the other guys.

During the NFL's opening week, DraftKings advertised that $10 million in winnings was up for grabs, including a $2 million grand prize, in its Millionaire Maker contest, the largest daily fantasy contest ever. Not to be outdone, FanDuel boasted: "Paying out $75 million a week!"

On October 5, the *New York Times* reported that a young Draft-Kings employee named Ethan Haskell had won $350,000 in a Fan-Duel NFL contest by finishing second overall and beating 229,883 entrants. The *Times* story alleged that Haskell used inside information—the percentage of ownership of various players by contestants that was unavailable to the public—to help win on the site of his company's rival. The online headline dubbed it "insider trading," and though the newspaper quickly changed it after Draft-Kings complained, the damage was done.

The sites' employees had competed for years on each other's platforms, despite the practice being long frowned upon by some lobbyists and industry consultants. Even the companies' engineering and customer service employees had access to proprietary data that could give them an unfair advantage playing elsewhere. The numbers are alarming: DraftKings employees won an estimated $6 million playing on FanDuel, though executives at both sites insist most of their employees ended up losing more money than they won.

The optics only worsened when it became public that FanDuel, in a 2012 internal memo, had warned its employees playing on DraftKings to "do no harm" or raise suspicions by winning too often: "Never be among the top five players by volume on any one site (based on site leaderboards). Never be among the top 10 overall on the RotoGrinders leaderboard. Top players frequently become targets for accusations by other users."

"This was destructive—and done because the sites felt they were untouchable," says a longtime industry lobbyist. "It's obvious that condoning this practice could easily backfire."

Robins and Eccles now acknowledge that the practice angered customers and raised stubborn doubts about the games' integrity. However, they both insist that their own investigations showed no employees had used proprietary information to win a single contest, though employees' winning streaks attracted derision on message boards. A law firm hired by DraftKings later determined that Haskell, who declined to comment, did not consult inside information before posting his winning lineup on FanDuel.

But by then the finding didn't really matter, because New York Attorney General Eric Schneiderman was a *New York Times* reader and a TV viewer who, like nearly everyone else in America, had become annoyed and exasperated by the onslaught of daily fantasy ads.

At 61, Schneiderman, a graduate of Amherst and Harvard Law School, had established himself as a hard-charging attorney general, pursuing a variety of attention-seizing targets, including the Airbnb industry, corruption-rife state contracts, and Medicaid fraud. Allies of the daily fantasy industry later grumbled that he had received more than $150,000 in campaign contributions from state gambling interests during his run for attorney general.

The morning after the *Times* story, lawyers and investigators from Schneiderman's various divisions—consumer fraud, investor protection, the Internet bureau, taxpayer protection—huddled for a two-hour meeting in a large conference room at the office's lower Manhattan headquarters. "We had no idea what we were looking at—we didn't know what we didn't know," says Kathleen McGee, the Internet bureau chief. They were concerned about the insider trading allegations, but in interviews with *Outside the Lines*, they said they quickly became far more concerned with FanDuel's and DraftKings' promises of instant wealth that they kept seeing on television. "Everyone in the office was saying, 'Their ads are everywhere,'" McGee says. "You couldn't escape them."

Within hours of their first meeting, several lawyers and investigators from Schneiderman's office opened DraftKings and FanDuel accounts and began playing their contests. The sites' lobbies "felt like online poker sites—or an online casino," a senior investigator told *Outside the Lines*. And the investigators and lawyers would soon discover that the sites didn't just offer daily fantasy contests on a single day's full slate of games. The sites offered hourly fantasy contests, with an evening's slate of NBA and NHL games carved into smaller and smaller slices with fewer and fewer players to draft—"turbo" contests for three NBA games tipping off at 8:00 p.m. ET, for example, or a fantasy contest based on two West Coast NHL games in which fantasy players would assemble lineups from only four teams.

Schneiderman's lawyers and investigators initially focused on the insider trading allegations, sketching investigative avenues on a chalkboard-sized whiteboard as they wondered whether the companies were defrauding and deceiving customers. Early on, they say, they didn't ponder the question of whether daily fantasy sports were legal under New York law.

Schneiderman's top deputies asked FanDuel and DraftKings to provide information about their customers, consumer protection safeguards, and the names of employees with access to proprietary information, such as player data, roster values, and the contestants' ownership percentages for pending and historical contests.

At separate meetings at the attorney general's office on October 8, Robins of DraftKings and FanDuel's outside counsel, Marc Zwillinger, fielded questions about their business practices while pledging their full cooperation. Still, executives and their lawyers were alarmed by the investigation. After all, the two companies had operated openly in New York State—and with no interference —for years. The company executives and their lawyers left Schneiderman's office confident that, at most, they'd be forced to pay a hefty fine and then would have to seek a daily fantasy bill in the New York State Assembly, a recollection disputed by lawyers in Schneiderman's office.

A senior AG lawyer recalls the DFS executives "running into our door and begging us, more or less, to regulate them and not shut them down."

"Denial is a powerful drug," says Eric Soufer, the AG's senior counsel for policy. "Even beyond the illegal gambling claims, the evidence of false and deceptive advertising was massive, and it was clear to all sides that those claims would be moving forward."

The move by Schneiderman had an immediate impact on both companies. ESPN, which had agreed in June to a two-year, $250 million exclusive branding and promotions deal across multiple platforms, decided on October 6 to remove all DraftKings-sponsored elements from its shows.

Ten days later, the Nevada attorney general released an opinion concluding that daily fantasy is sports wagering and that DraftKings and FanDuel needed gambling licenses to operate in the state. At the same time, the sites were preparing to enter the U.K. market, where they were seeking gambling licenses to be regulated as bookmakers. Both decisions reinforced the impression that daily fantasy is a game of skill in some places but considered a game of chance in others.

Meanwhile, during the daily strategy meetings before the whiteboard, the attorney general's lawyers and investigators began discussing whether, in fact, daily fantasy constituted illegal gambling under New York law. "It quickly became apparent this was so much bigger than a consumer fraud issue," McGee says. "This looks like gambling—and we kept asking, 'How does this happen right under our noses? These guys are huge.'"

On November 10, Schneiderman sent cease-and-desist letters to FanDuel and DraftKings, declaring that their games constituted illegal gambling under state law and ordering the companies to stop accepting "bets" from New York residents. "It is clear that DraftKings and FanDuel are the leaders of a massive, multibillion-dollar scheme intended to evade the law and fleece sports fans across the country," Schneiderman declared.

Inside FanDuel's Manhattan offices and DraftKings' Boston headquarters, executives were asked, by an ESPN reporter, about the letters before they had been delivered. Robins was in Sacramento at the statehouse; he got word of Schneiderman's move 10 minutes before meeting with an influential California legislator about a daily fantasy bill. Eccles was in Edinburgh, visiting his mother, when a colleague called him with the bad news. At no point had anyone from Schneiderman's office told them they were facing the prospect of being shut down.

"I was shocked," Eccles says.

Recalls a top DraftKings executive, "We never saw it coming."

Welcome to the big time.

On November 13, three days after Schneiderman's cease-and-desist letters were delivered, FanDuel's and DraftKings' top executives, lawyers, and lobbyists gathered for a summit meeting at the midtown Manhattan offices of Orrick, Herrington & Sutcliffe, a San Francisco–based global law firm. The session was attended by Robins and Eccles and nearly two dozen attorneys, lobbyists, government affairs specialists, and crisis communications consultants. Before the meeting began, "the only thing the two companies could agree on was us," says Jeremy Kudon, a 45-year-old lawyer and lobbyist who is the founder of Orrick's public policy group.

After three hours, the two rivals agreed on a uniform strategy to push for legislation clarifying daily fantasy's legality in dozens of statehouses around the country. FanDuel and DraftKings executives agreed to share the exorbitant costs of going on offense to seek DFS legislation that would regulate, and tax, their industry in any state where there was legal uncertainty or even the slightest chance that an attorney general might move against the industry. It was a marriage of necessity.

But the sites continued fighting other, separate legal battles. An investor recommended that DraftKings hire David Boies, the 75-year-old lawyer who became famous representing Al Gore before the U.S. Supreme Court in the deadlocked presidential election in 2000.

Boies was kept busy. Seemingly every day, a new civil lawsuit was filed against the companies and their executives; the companies now face more than 40. The biggest lawsuit alleges that DraftKings and FanDuel granted scores of advantages to an elite group of high-volume players. "The vast majority of bettors who are small guys, playing one or two contests a day for $20 at most, are over-matched by an elite few who have the algorithms, the technological advantages, all the advantages to win the biggest money," New York attorney Hunter J. Shkolnik says. "No one tells you that in the commercials."

Now consolidated in a Boston courtroom, the sprawling 266-page class-action lawsuit—alleging conspiracy, fraud, negligence, and RICO violations, among other claims—represents losing DFS players from 25 states and the District of Columbia. Shkolnik alleges that FanDuel revealed to its investors that only the top one-tenth of a percent of its customers actually win money. "The top 10,000 users had a negative-9.5 percent return on investment," the lawsuit alleges. In another lawsuit, one of the plaintiffs, Brandon Peck, a 42-year-old losing player from California, says that "DFS sites knowingly and intentionally pulled the wool over the eyes of many Americans when quoting the UIGEA. We deserve our money back."

DraftKings and FanDuel deny the accusations. Robins and Eccles declined a request by *Outside the Lines* to discuss any of the legal proceedings and criminal inquiries.

Throughout the autumn, Schneiderman's lawyers kept investigating. They became even more offended by the companies' grandiose advertising claims and the promises to customers that both companies made—and, the lawyers say, had repeatedly broken—in their bonus programs.

Schneiderman's action had a dramatic ripple effect across the country. In nearly two dozen states, including Illinois, Texas, and Alabama, offices of the attorney general quickly opened investigations. In some states, AGs released reports declaring that daily fantasy was illegal, while legislators began considering bills that would legalize the games and regulate the industry.

"I've never seen attorney general opinions weaponized like this before," Kudon says.

Says Boies: "I think DraftKings, and the industry in general, did not do as much as it could have . . . to regulate itself, to impose rules and regulations. It was a new industry. It was a growing industry. And I think that [DraftKings] focused much more on their product and their service than explaining it."

The parade of negative headlines also appeared to erode customers' trust. In the second half of the NFL season, DraftKings and FanDuel experienced week-by-week reductions in entry fees and major tournament payouts, according to data compiled by SuperLobby.com. By week 14, for example, DraftKings' large tourney entry fees were down 32 percent from a week 5 high of $25 million. And FanDuel's tourney entry fees had dropped 53 percent from a week 6 high of $40 million, SuperLobby.com found. (FanDuel and DraftKings dispute these statistics, saying there was only a slight drop-off in large contests but that their ads attracted hundreds of thousands of new customers, many of whom have become loyal players.)

On December 11, a New York Supreme Court granted Schneiderman a temporary injunction against the two companies, but they quickly appealed and won, allowing them to continue accepting wagers in New York. The pushback infuriated Schneiderman's lawyers, who filed an amended complaint on New Year's Eve seeking enormous financial penalties against DraftKings and FanDuel for allegedly violating New York's false advertising and consumer fraud laws. Schneiderman accused the sites of misrepresenting the ease and simplicity with which the average user could win big payouts and the amount of skill needed to win their contests, among other accusations.

Inside both companies, morale plummeted. They had been the hottest thing going; job applications had flooded into their headquarters. No more. And for the CEOs and executives, the stress level was relentless and the realities ever-present.

"People asked me, 'Where do you work?' And I'd say, 'I work at FanDuel—I'm sorry about the commercials,'" says Andrew Giancamilli, FanDuel's 37-year-old vice president of revenue and customer retention marketing.

By the end of last winter, 38 states were weighing daily fantasy legislation. Armed with a team of 105 lobbyists, Kudon and his colleagues discovered that despite their skill-game arguments that daily fantasy is not illegal gambling, influential gambling interests saw them as a threat and blocked them in states where they were entrenched, just as Charchian and others had predicted. Rivers Casino, located in Des Plaines, Illinois, helped kill the state's daily fantasy bill, and the Illinois attorney general issued an opinion that daily fantasy is illegal under state law. In California, Florida, Connecticut, Oklahoma, and Arizona, Native American tribes with casinos managed to kill or thwart daily fantasy bills. The companies now don't accept wagers from players in 11 states, up from five a year ago.

In early March, Virginia was the first state to pass DFS legislation, a bill critics dismissed as "industry-friendly." Five other states followed: Indiana, Tennessee, Mississippi, Colorado, and Missouri. The Massachusetts attorney general introduced extensive regulations aimed at increasing transparency and fairness, which the state adopted in August.

But the fight's epicenter was the New York Capitol in Albany. No state was more important to daily fantasy's future than New York, where each company had the highest number of customers, who spent a total of $268.3 million in fees in 2015, second only to California. In February and March at DraftKings and FanDuel, executives debated whether they should settle the Schneiderman complaint by agreeing to stop operating paid contests in New York. "It was tough," says Genetski, the FanDuel executive. "Shutting down seems counterintuitive, and we'd be second-guessed if it failed, but in my view it was clearly the right decision."

When the settlement was announced on March 21, Schneiderman waved the victory flag. "As I've said from the start, my job is to enforce the law," he said, "and starting today, DraftKings and FanDuel will abide by it."

For the companies, it was a worthy trade: they'd stop accepting wagers from New York residents for their less active NBA, NHL, and MLB contests in exchange for clearing a major hurdle with state legislators to get a DFS bill passed. "If we didn't get a settlement," Kudon says, "I don't think we'd have gotten the bill introduced in the Assembly."

Without New York, Eccles and Robins worried legislatures in other important states with entrenched gambling interests would be more likely to reject daily fantasy bills—and, the thinking went, failure in New York might embolden prosecutors pursuing the trio of federal investigations.

"The reality is, neither company was in a position to continue to operate without New York," Kudon says. "They both needed for this to happen. When I had spoken to investors, everyone agreed on its importance—it was less a financial thing and almost a psychological thing. They'd say, 'We won't believe this industry will survive unless New York happens.' How's that for pressure?"

But getting the bill passed was far from a certainty, and FanDuel and DraftKings had to play a political game now.

One of the bill's staunchest opponents was Batavia Downs, a harness racetrack and casino in western New York owned by the quasi-public Western Regional Off-Track Betting Corporation. Over a frantic weekend in early June, FanDuel struck a $300,000 marketing agreement with Batavia Downs, a sum that caused the track's owners to flip and throw their support behind the DFS bill.

FanDuel and DraftKings enlisted retired quarterbacks Jim Kelly and Vinny Testaverde to meet legislators. An email campaign produced a windfall of more than 100,000 emails from New York residents, urging their legislators to vote for the bill. Lobbyists from every corporation with a financial stake in DraftKings or FanDuel, including Verizon and Comcast, pushed the bill. Even still, in the final 48 hours before the Assembly recessed, the bill appeared on the brink of being defeated. "It felt as if they might just kill our bill for the sport of it," Kudon says.

Just after 2:00 a.m. on Saturday, June 18, the DFS bill passed by a wide margin. And on August 3, Governor Andrew Cuomo signed it into law.

"Monumental," Eccles calls it. "The most important victory in daily fantasy history."

Despite their rousing victory in New York, both companies' executives continue to spend millions of dollars on multiple legal and regulatory fights. DraftKings has tried to cut costs by renegotiating contracts with vendors while reducing affiliates' bonuses. Merger talks were renewed this summer, with some investors insisting that a merger would be the best way for the cash-strapped companies to survive (and, not incidentally, the best way for investors to protect their stakes). Several industry insiders say a merger is inevitable—after the upcoming NFL season, if not sooner—because the sites are duplicating so many exorbitant costs.

"I think DraftKings will survive financially," says Boies, its lawyer. "I do think that the distraction and the expenses have been harmful to the company. I think it's very unfortunate the way some of this stuff has mushroomed and, in many respects, is unfair."

Meanwhile, inside their corporate offices, the two companies' top executives spent the summer devising ways to make the skill games' ecosystem less challenging and more fun despite the inevitable outcomes.

"How do you make the games less hard? There are ways to do it—share information more broadly to take away edges that some players may have, limit the number of entries, have beginner areas," says Giancamilli, the FanDuel vice president. "If you want to play $100,000, I'm okay with it if you are doing it in just one part of my playground. There should be places in the playground for players of all skill levels—safe spaces, safe harbors, with single-entry limits, things that make the beginner player feel comfortable and welcome."

Besides beginners' games, the sites have introduced a multitude of other safeguards against predatory play. By February, both sites banned all third-party scripting. DraftKings allows players to block others. Both sites' employees are forbidden from competing on rival sites. Both sites have limited the number of entries to 150. They have created tiered levels in their lobbies so players can avoid tangling with savvier, higher-bankrolled competitors. And they have moved even more aggressively against users' predatory behavior. (Giancamilli made a point of saying that FanDuel had slapped a one-month suspension on a high-volume, predatory player who failed to heed multiple warnings.)

"Integrity is the issue," says Peter Jennings, a champion daily fantasy player and former ESPN expert. "How do you balance the ecosystem of these top players, who are really important to the site because it gives them the volume they need, and still make it fair and fun for the other guys?" Another way is to improve transparency: FanDuel introduced "Experienced Player Indicators," and DraftKings has "Experienced Player Badges," which are affixed to the more seasoned players.

Robins says the industry is evolving, in the same way any young industry confronts, and tries to solve, its customers' most pressing concerns. Didn't Facebook manage to overcome a host of problems, from privacy issues to advertisers spamming users? "To paint all this as an Armageddon for the industry is silly," Robins says. "It's common in any emerging technology for there to be a very healthy cycle for product makers to get feedback from their customers."

Still, executives have had to tamp down the expectations of their restless investors. Some states passing DFS bills will tax the companies' revenues from their residents. (New York is the highest, at 15 percent.) Boies says the new taxes will probably be passed on to players, meaning the sites' rakes will likely be increased. While Robins and Eccles insist that they remain optimistic about their companies' futures and chances for profitability, the sky-high growth projections of a year ago have been shelved.

The gigantic jackpots have not been retired. For the NFL's opening week, DraftKings is hosting a $5 million guaranteed contest, with the winner getting $1 million. The entry fee is $3. But the messaging is being recast. No longer will the companies emphasize oversized checks and overnight fortunes. This fall there won't be another endless run of dueling TV ads with backward baseball cap–wearing bros fist-pumping over a sudden $1 million payday.

Robins says his biggest regret is selling daily fantasy mainly as a fast way to win big money. "We've done a lot of research, and winning money is maybe, like, reason 4 or 5 why people play," he says. "The main reasons they play are they enjoy the thrill of competition, they like doing things with their friends." The first impressions created by all those ads will take patience and money to erase. "I think we did ourselves and did the industry a disservice," Robins says. "That was a mistake . . . It made us come across more like used-car salesmen and less like we have a great luxury automobile here that you're really going to enjoy."

For his part, and perhaps not surprisingly, Eccles isn't fully signed on to Robins's mea culpa. "Unfortunately, there have always been negative consequences from it," he says of the ads, "but I don't really regret our decision . . . I feel the mistakes we've made were errors of overenthusiasm, of feeling we can get further faster . . . Maybe we tried to be too aggressive, but I feel those are . . . the right mistakes to make."

In a way, fantasy sports have come full circle from the rotisserie baseball league co-invented in late 1979 by editor and author Dan Okrent. That was a season-long league, a chance to pretend to be a big league general manager and win bragging rights among a circle of pals. The money didn't matter. "Daily fantasy bears no relationship, really, to what those of us who played in our living rooms with our friends were doing 30 years ago," says Okrent, 68, who lives in the same Upper West Side apartment building as New York's attorney general. (Okrent says he nods at Schneiderman, his downstairs neighbor, in the elevator, but he insists they've never discussed the DFS legal battle.) "It's become a kind of malignant mutant version of something that began as simple and pure."

By preaching that daily fantasy, like Okrent's inaugural league, is an affordable way to have some fun, FanDuel and DraftKings are betting their futures on attracting and keeping players who will buy in to the argument that there's more than one way to measure a return on investment.

In August, FanDuel redesigned its website, game platform, and marketing strategy. Its new one-word slogan is "SportsRich," a trademarked term it defines as "the experience of having all the great stuff sports has to offer."

In block letters in promotional materials, FanDuel says its customers should now expect "excitement, thrills, camaraderie and fantasy. These are all examples of what it is to be SportsRich. NOTE: None of them have anything to do with money."

GEORGE DOHRMANN

Hooked for Life

FROM THE HUFFINGTON POST

IN EARLY 2007, Brandissimo was a fledgling youth marketing agency with a corporate frat house vibe. Its 20 employees worked out of a cramped three-room office in Southern California's San Fernando Valley; some desks were packed together so tightly that you couldn't back out of one chair without bumping into another. It was the kind of prank-heavy place where you might walk in one morning to find your computer surrounded by 10 empty water cooler bottles, or where you might be talked into joining a zombie unicorn drawing competition, no matter how busy you were.

And then the National Football League called. For decades, the NFL had funneled most of its advertising dollars to large, New York-based legacy firms. Everyone knew what to expect from that arrangement: commonsense product tie-ins, 30-second ad spots. By tapping Brandissimo, the league made it clear that it wanted a different kind of partner for a different kind of project.

Brandissimo's founders had previously worked for Disney and had helped produce well-known kids' television shows like *Doug* and *Thomas the Tank Engine and Friends*. But they didn't bill themselves as just TV guys or mobile guys or video game guys—they sold a more complete vision. They were the experts in grabbing a child's attention and then holding on to it across the most popular platforms. One of Brandissimo's mottos was: "Because kids who play with your brand, stay with your brand."

Shortly after landing the multimillion-dollar NFL account, Brandissimo hired a quiet 29-year-old named Allison Guiliotis. Even though Guiliotis grew up in the football-obsessed Southeast, she knew almost nothing about the sport and cared even less. She got her bachelor's degree in ceramics from the Kansas City Art Institute and moved to L.A. so that she could work at a gallery. She only joined Brandissimo because she got tired of being broke.

The NFL was a demanding client—before long, she was working 60-hour weeks—but unlike many others, it made its objectives clear. It wanted to "get to kids as early as possible," Guiliotis says. "They talked about creating lifelong customers." To that end, the league had Brandissimo create a website and a virtual world meant to entice kids.

The league was also aware that nothing had boosted people's investment in the sport quite like fantasy football, which incentivizes fans to pay attention to several games every week. "It is an incredible mechanism if you are trying to create an addiction to football at a young age," says Gregg Witt, the executive vice president of youth marketing at Motivate Inc., another Southern California agency. So the NFL asked Brandissimo to help connect kids with NFL Rush Fantasy, the first such game created by a pro league aimed exclusively at young children.

Kids as young as six years old were encouraged to pick a team of NFL players each week and compete for the most fantasy points with other kids across the country. And the prizes were extraordinary. Between 2008 and 2015, weekly winners of NFL Rush Fantasy could receive an Xbox One or a $1,000 scholarship. For several years, the season-long grand prize was a $10,000 scholarship. But, tellingly, the word "scholarship" was surrounded by quotation marks in the fine print of the game's rules. Kids just got checks in the mail and were free to do with the money as they wished.

In June, I called Kyle Turley, a former NFL player who has become an outspoken critic of the league, particularly its treatment of former players. He isn't easily shocked by the NFL's methods, but when I told him about the fantasy game, which he'd never heard of, he let out an exasperated growl. "The NFL is desperate," he said. "This is the kind of thing you do when you don't care about anything but making sure the money keeps rolling in."

From the outside, the NFL looks like one of the jewels of American capitalism. It remains the most profitable sports enterprise in the world, with $12 billion in revenue in 2015. (The NBA generated about $5 billion last year.) The league also has hundred-million-dollar deals with corporate sponsors like Microsoft, Gatorade, and Anheuser-Busch as well as close relationships with several federal agencies, including the military, which uses the sport's popularity to bring in new recruits. Going into this season, a throwaway matchup between two teams with losing records would often draw more eyeballs than a World Series game, putting to rest any questions about what the national pastime really is.

But a closer look at the trend lines reveals that the NFL's financial and cultural dominance may be at risk. The damage the sport does to young men's bodies and brains has simply become too obvious to ignore. A growing number of public figures, from President Obama to LeBron James to Brett Favre, have said that they wouldn't let their children play the game—and polling shows that 40 to 50 percent of parents agree with them. Between 2009 and 2014, youth participation in the game dipped markedly. What's more, the number of men between 18 and 24 watching NFL games dropped by 5.3 percent from 2010 to 2013, according to Nielsen data. And one of the main story lines of the first half of this season was the precipitous collapse in ratings. The game is losing athletes *and* fewer young people seem to be in love with the league, two bright red flags.

In response, the NFL has initiated a campaign to secure the next generation of fans that is unprecedented in the history of professional athletics. And the fantasy game is just a sliver of it. Brandissimo is just a sliver of it. The NFL has infiltrated the school system, it has produced a football-themed animated television show that aired on NickToons, and it is currently executing a multidimensional plan to convince concerned moms to let their kids play. There's a team of people working out of NFL headquarters in Manhattan whose professional lives revolve around getting kids interested in the game.

And this is all happening at a time when almost no one who is knowledgeable about the sport, including me—a former high school player who's in two fantasy leagues and still watches NFL games every Sunday (and Monday and Thursday)—feels comfortable with football's impact on children. How it can alter their brain chemistry, how a handful of young players die each year, how we're only beginning to understand the extent of the damage that's being done. That's why so many of the people I interviewed for this article made a point of saying that the NFL's youth efforts, while brilliant, are absolutely devious. Over and over, I heard comparisons between the league's marketing work and that done by the coal industry or Big Tobacco, conjuring images of Joe Camel in a helmet and shoulder pads.

The league believes its efforts are more benign. "We are always looking for new ways to engage the next generation of NFL fans and connect with kids in unique and authentic ways," a spokesperson told me.

Being a part of the NFL's apparatus eventually began to eat away at Guiliotis. She dreaded going to work. When she participated in calls with members of the NFL's Department of Fan Development & Marketing, she said they applied constant pressure on Brandissimo to find new ways to hook kids. "It was a weekly, almost daily thing: how do we increase kids' time on site," she said. And she hated that around Brandissimo's offices, "there was no self-reflection. No pause," she said. "It was, 'What can we get kids to do that makes the NFL happy?'" (Andy Babb, Brandissimo's president, declined to comment and referred all questions to the NFL.)

After three years at Brandissimo, and almost as soon as her husband got a job that enabled her to work less, she quit. She teaches ceramics to kids now and says she's happier than she's been in years. But every so often, the old anxiety creeps back in.

"I see a game on TV and I just get mad," she says. "I have seen the NFL's motivation and what a big corporation like that is willing to do, and it's scary. I parent differently now because of what I know. But I can only shield my child from it. What about other kids?"

In August 2012, Amanda Rodriguez was unsure if she should let her young son play football. Will, the second of her three children, had a strong interest in the game, but he was only six. Too young, she thought, too fragile, especially considering all that she had heard and read in recent years about head trauma. But Will *really* wanted to play and "I guess I just got tired of fighting about it," she told me. Almost as soon as she enrolled Will in a local league in a Maryland suburb of Washington, D.C., she started thinking about ways to take him out.

At around the same time, the NFL was doing some soul-searching of its own. League officials, beset by an endless stream of reports about concussions and player safety, were developing new strategies meant to combat the idea that football was dangerous for kids. They wanted to try out their pitch on some moms. So they contacted managers at two female-centric websites—iVillage and Babble. Both were owned by broadcasting partners of the league (iVillage by NBCUniversal; Babble by Disney/ESPN), so the officials knew they would be presenting to a friendly audience.

That's how Rodriguez, who contributed videos and blog posts about her parenting adventures to iVillage, found herself in a conference room at NFL headquarters, along with about a dozen other moms. Roger Goodell, the league's commissioner and a smiling, broad-shouldered charmer when he needs to be, started the event by assuring the moms that the league was implementing programs that would "change the culture" of the game. He then took some photos with everybody before turning the presentation over to a series of speakers who made it clear that they wanted "to learn what our fears were about football," Rodriguez says.

According to her and Sharon Rowley, another parent who was there, the officials spent a good part of the day telling the moms about a player-safety initiative they were developing called Heads Up Football. The program would require coaches of kids' teams to receive a certificate for teaching tackling techniques that reduce helmet-to-helmet contact. Rodriguez and others in the room loved the simplicity of that approach. Heads Up Football would also call for more parental involvement in youth leagues, the officials said. For instance, parents would be encouraged to monitor the tackling drills that coaches used. The moms responded well to this too —they liked feeling as if they had agency over the safety of their children.

The NFL's messaging in other areas still needed tinkering. When the presenters were asked how concussion concerns in soccer and other sports compared to those in football, they didn't have a good answer. So at a later gathering with Rodriguez and some of the same moms, they came prepared. They brought speakers from other sports who said that football was not alone in dealing with this issue. The basic argument was: if soccer and lacrosse were just as risky, what justification did moms have for blacklisting football? And it worked. Today, when other moms tell Rodriguez that they can't believe she lets Will play football, she responds, "I can't believe you let your child ride a skateboard."

Its message sufficiently honed, the league started putting together "Moms Football Safety Clinics"—larger, more polished versions of the Manhattan meetings—all across the country. The early clinics, held during the 2013 season, were heavily promoted by the league and covered extensively by the press, but I wanted to know what happened when no one from the league knew the media was present. So I asked Carolina Gazzara, a 22-year-old graduate student in journalism at the University of Alabama, to go to the May 17 clinic in Birmingham. She preregistered online (at no cost) and gathered with about 120 other women—predominantly black, many with kids already playing in local leagues—at 6:00 p.m. in the cafeteria at Spain Park High School.

The first order of business was the buttering up. Moms were given Atlanta Falcons T-shirts and a bag with the team's logo on it. They were treated to a dinner catered by Outback Steakhouse and given coupons for the restaurant. As they ate, Freddie Falcon, the Atlanta mascot, buzzed around on a hoverboard posing for pictures.

After that, a group of speakers, including a couple of former players, explained the theory behind Heads Up Football and claimed the sport is now much safer because of it. The presenters offered just enough general health and safety information to be able to argue that the clinics provide a broader service, and just enough talk about concussions so that no one could say the issue was ignored. Former Alabama quarterback John Parker Wilson acknowledged that he had suffered a few head injuries over the years, but he and former Falcons linebacker Buddy Curry told the women that they'd play football over again if they could.

At the end of the clinic, the moms were led outside and put through some Heads Up Football drills. One exercise required them to get into an alert tackling position, knees bent, butt out. "Ohhh, I *like* it," one of the coaches said to the group. "Let me see that boom-boom." Gazzara said that none of the moms seemed to mind; a few even flirted back.

All the parents she spoke with at the clinic said that they left feeling comforted. The event had affirmed their choice to let their kids play football, and they liked all the free gear they could bring home. "They were mostly just excited to be involved with an event put on by an NFL team," Gazzara said.

It's clear that these events work brilliantly as promotional devices for the league. But if you judge them by the depth and validity of the information provided to parents, they are shameful. As

Anne Osborne, a professor at Syracuse University who cowrote the book *Female Fans of the NFL,* told me, "The goal of the Moms Clinics isn't really education. It is indoctrination."

For one, the league seriously downplays the risk of head injuries. NFL surrogates have become experts in deflecting questions and muddying what we know about brain trauma. Amanda Dinkel, the Falcons' community relations coordinator, admitted to the group of moms in Birmingham that "concussions are on the rise." Then she waited a beat: "At least in the media." (A spokesperson for the Falcons said he spoke to Dinkel and reviewed her notes for the Moms Clinic. "We feel confident that is not exactly what she said," he told me.) At other Moms Clinics, it's been said that children are more likely to get a concussion riding a bike than playing football. But that's only true if you include girls in the data set or limit it to boys under 10. In boys over the age of 10, football is clearly the greater danger.

"Like all contact sports," a league spokesperson said, "there are risks, and we are committed to ensuring parents and players have the facts and information to make the best decisions for their families."

The Birmingham clinic also passed without anyone addressing chronic traumatic encephalopathy, or CTE, a degenerative brain disease found in 90 of 94 NFL players whose brains have been studied after their deaths. "That omission is intentional," says Chris Nowinski, CEO of the Concussion Legacy Foundation. "The NFL focuses on concussions because that seems like a problem that can be solved through initiatives," like Heads Up Football (which was actually found to have a minimal effect in reducing concussions). "The concern for parents," Nowinski continued, "should be preventing the numbers of hits to the head their children are taking overall, not just whether or not they get a concussion. You can get CTE without suffering a concussion."

Nowinski believes that if kids didn't play tackle football until high school, their chances of developing CTE would be greatly diminished. But that is a damaging proposition from the NFL's perspective. League research shared with the *Wall Street Journal* showed that 60 percent of die-hard fans begin following the sport in elementary school, whereas a majority of casual fans find the sport later. "Nothing attaches a young person to a sport more than playing," says Doug Allen, an original board member of USA Football, the nonprofit the NFL founded in 2002 to promote the sport. If parents took Nowinski's advice, it would devastate football's pipeline of players and fans.

Only in March, after years of denial, did the league acknowledge that CTE was linked to football. This new stance, however, hasn't cracked the messaging at the Moms Clinics. During a break in Birmingham, Gazzara asked Curry about the risks of CTE. "He tried to avoid the question before finally telling me it wasn't as prevalent as it's made out to be," she said. (Curry, when asked for comment, said, "I don't recall answering the question that way." He added, "I never answer that question. It's a science question.")

At a different clinic in Chicago I attended, a mom asked Nick Greisen, a trainer with USA Football who also played in the NFL, when parents should let their children play tackle football. "A good indicator they might be ready," he said, is if a child's neck is strong enough to hold up a helmet.

When I told that story to Nowinski, he remarked that it was a perfect encapsulation of the league's overall approach. The NFL and the people who profit from it will do whatever it takes to get kids to play football, he said, "science be damned."

About 40 years ago, a Nobel laureate named Herbert Simon forever altered the study of how people make decisions by popularizing the concept of "bounded rationality." He argued that since we have limited information, time, and ability to process complex matters, we often default to the option that feels acceptable in the moment over the one that is ideal. "In order to have anything like a complete theory of human rationality," he wrote, "we have to understand what role emotion plays in it."

Though that may sound intuitive now, it was a groundbreaking insight at the time. Previously, researchers on decision-making had ignored emotion, treating it as either irrelevant or too unwieldy to take seriously. They were wrong. Emotion is "the dominant driver of most meaningful decisions in life," according to a 2014 paper, "Emotion and Decision Making," written by Harvard professor Jennifer S. Lerner and three colleagues.

With that in mind, I joined about 75 parents and their children this April in Chicago's Grant Park for something called the NFL Draft Family Football Clinic. (Why the league insists on such clunky names for its initiatives should be the subject of another article.) While the rain started to pick up and kids were put through football drills on a nearby field, the parents sat on aluminum bleachers arranged in a half-circle under a strand of leafless trees. They politely listened to a doctor, a trainer, a nutritionist, and a former Chicago Bear run through an agenda similar to the one at Moms Clinics. But they perked up for the real stars of the show: the husband-and-wife team of Mike and Christine Golic.

Mike Golic is an aggressively good-natured former NFL defensive lineman who cohosts ESPN's *Mike & Mike* and is one of the network's most influential voices on radio and television. In Chicago, he assumed the role of celebrity jokester, feigning shock when the nutritionist suggested Doritos were not a good snack. Christine Golic, who goes by Chris, is known mostly for being the embodiment of the football mom fantasy. She has a wealthy and famous husband who played the game and two sons who earned football scholarships to Notre Dame. As a speaker, she isn't Tony Robbins–style slick, but she has an unassuming, Middle American air, one that easily inspires confidence. She stood in front of the group wearing jeans and a sweatshirt, her brown hair tucked under a white NFL Draft hat. Everyone loved her.

When one mother wanted to know if there was a right age for a child to begin playing tackle football, Chris didn't get into thorny matters of brain science or youth development. She spoke about what she knew. "As a parent," she said, "you have to take into consideration what your child's friends are doing, the social aspect. They want to play with their friends."

I've studied Chris's presentations and interviews from the past few years, and in all of them, she prefaces much of what she says with "as a parent" or "as a mom" and often references her own family to drive a point home. In Chicago, it created a contrast between her and the other speakers. The trainer, the doctor, the nutritionist—they were professionals offering an opinion. She was a mom, sharing her experiences and feelings.

Near the end of the panel discussion, one mother asked what she should say to people who refuse to let their kids play football. Chris Golic answered first. She talked about how so much of what happens to children in the world is out of their parents' control. Then she paused meaningfully and said: "I never wanted my kids to not chase their dreams because I was afraid of something."

Many of the parents in the stands cheered when they heard

that. Roger Goodell, who was also in attendance, nodded along. With one sentence she had reframed the choice facing parents. It was no longer: is football safe for kids? It was: are you going to stand in the way of your child achieving his dreams? After the panel ended, some moms greeted Chris Golic with a hug.

In its effort to convince mothers to let their kids play football, the league seems to realize that it's not enough to manufacture programs and spin narratives that make the sport seem safer. The league has also injected what psychologists call "incidental emotions"—ones you wouldn't necessarily feel unless prompted—into the calculation. "Parents may already be worried about their child getting a concussion or getting hurt playing football. Those are emotions they are naturally facing with this choice," says Piercarlo Valdesolo, a psychology professor at Claremont McKenna College and one of the authors of "Emotion and Decision Making." "But making parents feel guilty for denying a child an opportunity to play football is framing the choice using an incidental emotion."

This tactic, most prevalent in politics, aims to reduce a choice down to a gut-level decision. Why? Because "everyone's gut can be manipulated," Valdesolo says.

That helps explain the NFL's recent focus on emotional branding,* particularly to women. Since 2014, the league has executed a "Football Is Family" ad campaign that leans hard on melodrama. Some commercials feature current or former players talking about their childhood and parents. One had a wide receiver sharing what lessons he hopes to teach his son ("The most important thing is not always about what he can do for himself but how he can help other people"); another featured competing grandparents sending Packers and Bears onesies to a newborn.†

There's also the "Together We Make Football" contest, framed

---

* The concept of emotional branding goes way back. In 1929, the American Tobacco Company gave cigarettes they called "Torches of Freedom" to women before New York City's Easter Sunday Parade. The stunt promoted female empowerment —women's rights activists supported it—and the number of female smokers more than tripled over the next 12 years.

† Bob Costas, who hosts the pregame show for NBC's *Football Night in America,* ripped these commercials in an interview with the *New York Daily News,* saying: "Yeah, that's right, the first thing I think of when I hear about 25 percent to 30 percent, by the NFL's own admission, of its players will have cognitive difficulties is 'Football Is Family.'"

as "an invitation to anyone who has been touched by the game of football" to tell a story of why they love it. The winning entries are turned into polished, sentimental works by NFL Films and are then aired on *The Today Show,* with its notoriously mom-heavy viewership. One video centers on Felicia Correa-Garcia, a no-nonsense mother of two from Virginia. It shows her teaching the sport to her children and horsing around with them in the backyard before building to the big reveal that she has multiple sclerosis. "Being I'm a single mother of five, and maintaining two jobs, coach sports year-round, it is hard, but, I mean, you only live once," she says near the end of the short. You'd have to be emotionally vacant not to love Felicia (and football) by the end of it.

Anne Osborne, the Syracuse professor who studied the NFL's marketing to women, told me that the league enlists its corporate partners to advance similar football-and-family messages. Just think about Kia's "Built for Football Families" commercials, or Campbell's Chunky Soup's "This One's for Mom" campaign. "That is not coincidental," she told me. "They work in concert."

The NFL's gut strategy is so resonant that even non-affiliated organizations, from the foundation that runs the College Football Hall of Fame to innumerable high school teams and youth leagues, have picked up on it. One of those leagues, St. Raphael Football, based in the Chicago suburb of Naperville, has operated tackle football programs for elementary and middle school kids since 1963. Naperville is the kind of football stronghold that the NFL cannot lose if it wants to survive. In 2007, St. Raphael had 2,500 kids. In 2015, it was 1,500.

After reading about the Moms Clinics, officials at St. Raphael organized their own event at the local VFW hall last year. They served food and wine and handed out hats. The highlight, according to Paul O'Toole, St. Raphael's president, came when the mother of an alumnus who now plays quarterback for Illinois State stood in front of everyone to talk about how much football had meant to her family—how it brought them closer and instilled values like nothing else in their lives had.

"At one point she unfolded this beautiful quilt, and it had her kid's high school jersey on it," O'Toole said. "She was crying up there, and all the moms, 100 moms in the crowd, they were crying too."

Chris Golic surely understands. When her youngest child went off to Notre Dame in 2012, she found herself with too much free time and in search of something that would "speak to me." Then the NFL asked her if she'd contribute to the league's efforts to reshape the game and its image. She now believes that this is her calling in life.

"I felt like I could be this voice to say that, yes, things need to be addressed, absolutely, but also be the person to say that isn't happening to everybody," she told me. "There are plenty of people who are playing football, enjoying a football career, and while they are walking away with bumps and bruises and aches and pains like my husband has, they are not suicidal and that kind of thing."

Osborne says that companies facing scientific proof that a product is dangerous regularly use people like Chris Golic to shift the message. "They focus on the anecdotal," she told me. "It is like people justifying smoking by saying: 'My grandpa Joe smoked and he lived to be 92.'"

"The NFL puts a family up there that has made it to the pinnacle and says, 'See, this is what you can be with football,'" says Nate Jackson, a former Denver Bronco and the author of *Slow Getting Up*, a memoir of his playing days. "They hit you with the message that if you want a happy family, you need football."

What makes Chris Golic so effective is that she doesn't come across like a salesperson. She truly does not believe that she is doing the league's bidding. "I'm a mom and your kids are everything to you and I would never want to sell parents something for a company to make money," she says. She isn't going to argue with people who say football is unsafe, or who would prefer their children to play other sports. But she will speak—at length and with passion—about her family and her choice to let her kids play.

"If I ever thought there was information out there that was going to change my opinion on what I am talking to moms about, I would for sure reevaluate my position," she told me.

But that's not going to happen. We talked all about how harmful football can be. She knows the risks. Chris Golic made her choice and, coincidentally, she made it based on emotion. When I asked her if she understood the criticism that the Moms Clinics were selling a dangerous game to parents, she said people could "spin it that way." She then added that she knows it's not true because the people involved in the program have good intentions. How does she know that?

"I call myself the kind of person who follows her gut."

"The propagandist is knocking at the school door," the National Education Association warned. The year was 1929, and the group had discovered, to its alarm, that soap manufacturers, banks, insurers, and "electric light companies" were sneaking marketing materials into classrooms. The NEA issued a damning report, but over the next several decades, major corporations continued to barge into America's schools by creating lesson plans and sponsoring essay contests. As Chevron, the American Coal Foundation, and many others found, few tools inspired lifelong product loyalty quite so effectively.

Today, some of that old propaganda is known by a softer term — "sponsored education materials" or SEMs. With school budgets thin and classrooms overcrowded, SEMs give teachers readymade and vaguely educational lesson plans that just so happen to reinforce how thick Prego spaghetti sauce is or suggest that global warming may be a sham.

The NFL got heavy into SEMs around 2005, partnering with Young Minds Inspired, one of the largest companies in the field, whose other clients include everyone from UNICEF to McDonald's, Pfizer to Newman's Own. YMI claims to reach 8 million preschoolers and 28 million elementary school kids each year. And its sales deck promises that its educational materials "break through the clutter of traditional media" and "deliver the message that your company values learning and cares about family."

The league first worked with YMI on a program designed for fourth- and fifth-graders, called "NFL School Smarts." Each student was given 28 trading cards, and teachers were sent a list of activities that incorporated them. Some of the exercises had apparent educational value, such as plotting a player's height and weight on a graph. Others seemed more at home in a casino sports book. For the final activity in the 2006 version of School Smarts, entitled "Game-Day Experiment," students were required to "come up with individual hypotheses about who will win" an NFL game. Teachers were then told to "have students watch the game at home, with their families, to see if their hypotheses were right!" In other words, the assignment was to pick a winner, and the homework was to sit through three hours of television—not exactly a triumph of the scientific method.

The most recent lesson of School Smarts gave kids some tips for safely browsing the web, such as not giving out their home addresses on unfamiliar websites. At the end of the activity, students were directed to a screen that congratulated them on a job well done, with a cross-promotional cherry on top: "Good call! You know the rules for having fun on the Internet. Now check out the rules for having fun at the NFL RushZone. (We call it NFLRZ for short!)"

Faith Boninger, a research associate at the University of Colorado who coauthors an annual report on schoolhouse commercialization trends for the National Education Policy Center, told me that lesson plans like this essentially turn teachers into salespeople. They have to explain football and its rules to every student —not just the ones who like the sport. "I have seen all of the different ways corporations try to get in front of kids," she said, "but these sort of SEMs may be the worst."

The frustrating part is that SEMs don't have to be this bad. Educators have long debated the value of using sports to teach complex subjects. In 2010, the National Science Foundation, NBC Learn, and the NFL partnered to produce a series of video lessons on math and science. They used football to explain Newton's Second Law of Motion (using field goal kicks) and projectile motion (using a punted ball).

Compare that to a School Smarts assignment, which urged parents to become more engaged in their child's educational experience by hosting a "kitchen table tailgate party." Before kickoff, parents were encouraged to ask their child the following questions:

1. How many teams are there in the NFL?
2. Which two states have the most NFL teams?
3. Which NFL team's home stadium is farthest West? farthest East? farthest North? farthest South?
4. There are 16 NFL teams with animal mascots—how many can you name?

A few years ago, Josh Golin, the executive director of the Campaign for a Commercial Free Childhood, was sitting in his office near South Station in Boston when he got a call from a friend of his, a public health attorney. "Have you seen what is going on with the NFL?" she asked him. He didn't know what she was talking about, so he started to poke around and came across the league's use of SEMs. "You hope teachers would see these for what they are and toss them in the recycling bin," he told me. As Golin and his team of four dug deeper into what the league was doing, "the more we were like, 'Oh my God, the NFL is using every trick in the book to market to kids.' Junk food promotion, fantasy football, promoting sedentary screen time. They were using mobile, a TV property, live events, online, getting into schools. It was a 360-degree marketing approach to children."

NFL Rush Zone, the league's animated television show that aired on NickToons from 2011 to 2014, was an especially cynical ploy. The show revolved around a heroic young boy and his friends as they try to guard the NFL from various aliens and robots bent on its destruction. The kids take orders from a blue-skinned general who works out of the NFL's Hall of Fame and says things like: "Without one of their star running backs* *and* their mega-core, the Bills are particularly vulnerable!" Then, every so often, and with only the slightest nod toward plot, real-life NFL footage is spliced in while a monotonal narrator offers league history. ("The Bills have 17 playoff appearances and are 10-time divisional champions.") There are also random appearances by "Rusherz," Oompa Loompa–like creatures that wear NFL apparel and have giant heads, presumably for maximum exposure of the team logo on their helmets.

Kids' television is littered with shows that are camouflaged commercials for a product. How "toyetic" a program is—how easily its characters can be turned into merchandise—is a major factor in whether it gets made. But even in a world where the line between art and marketing has faded, *NFL Rush Zone* stood out. One person who worked on the show surmised that the reason it didn't air on Nickelodeon (sort of the HBO of kids' programming) and instead ran on NickToons (more of a Cinemax) might have been because "the inception of the idea was a little dirty . . . It was pretty NFL in your face. I'm sure some parents saw it and thought, 'God, this is a just a big commercial for the league.'"

---

* They were talking about C. J. Spiller, a perpetual disappointment for fantasy football owners who has already played for three different teams this year. The aliens can have him.

One of those parents was Kyle Turley, the former player who now advocates for NFL alumni. Several years back, he sat down with his son, Dean, who is now seven, to watch the show. "I was gritting my teeth," Turley says. "Not only was it about trying to get kids connected to football, but it also created this perception that there were people out there trying to hurt football and little kids were enlisted to put their lives at risk to protect the game. I couldn't believe they were spreading that propaganda."

The TV show spawned a trading card game, a comic book series, toys, T-shirts, and hats. In 2013, the NFL partnered with McDonald's and produced *NFL Rush Zone* Happy Meals that featured 32 collectible toys and *NFL Rush Zone* trading cards. "Think about what kind of statement that makes," Golin says. "We want to reach kids so badly we are not going to worry about luring them in to eat the worst crap there is."

Until it unexpectedly pulled the plug this summer, the NFL also hosted "RushZone," an online role-playing game that Brandissimo modeled after Club Penguin, one of Disney's online worlds. Within Rush Zone, kids were able to visit various "lands" of NFL teams to collect virtual gear, chat with friends, interact with the same big-headed "Rusherz" from the TV show, or track the real-life happenings of football players and teams. Occasionally, NFL players would visit the RushZone for chats, which Guiliotis moderated. "We were told not to forward any questions about injuries or concussions," she said.

According to Guiliotis, the league was particularly focused on getting kids to buy virtual apparel—whether it was an Inuit suit to stay warm in the chillier parts of the online world, wingtip shoes in NFL colors, Halloween costumes, or NFL team "masks" like a Mexican wrestler might wear. The hope was that children would see an avatar with the premium stuff and then buy it for themselves by plugging in their parents' credit card. "There were internal discussions about how to get the kids to want what other kids have," says Guiliotis, who also said that the NFL used software to track the time kids spent in each world and tweaked its strategy to keep them engaged longer.

NFLRush.com, the league's main website for kids, features a bunch of other tools meant to keep them captivated. The site houses more than 80 mini-games, almost all of them football-related, along with polls and trivia challenges. Children can also participate in a "pick 'em" game, where they guess the winners of NFL contests and pit their prognosticating skills against others.

The league's efforts to engage children online have worked. In 2009, the Rush Zone had 1.5 million registered users. In 2010 it was 2 million, and by 2013 the NFL had signed up 3 million kids. The NFL now knows the names, emails, genders, birthdays, and favorite teams for all these kids—a marketer's treasure trove. Golin is afraid of all the power that this new information gives the league as it figures out its next moves. "It's hard to find anything equivalent to what the NFL has been doing," he said.

And then there is this: after several years of decline, the number of American children playing tackle football rose 2 percent in 2015, according to an analysis by USA Football. It's hard to say how much of that can be attributed to the league's marketing initiatives, but that's more than 40,000 kids between the ages of six and 14 who have been persuaded to strap on a helmet in the middle of a health crisis we still don't fully understand.

In all my research of all the tactics the league has used to secure a long, prosperous future for itself, I found only one that was easy to get behind. Over the last few years, the NFL and USA Football have emphasized a youth program called NFL Flag. NFL Flag is similar to normal football, except safer: there's no tackling. It also gives local leagues replica NFL jerseys at a heavy discount and provides them with a football for every five children they register, a boon for the underfunded. "We've got footballs coming out of our ears," Richard Rosenthal, the assistant director of recreation for the Medford Parks Department in Oregon, told me.

Thanks in part to those moves, the number of kids playing flag jumped to 1.7 million in 2015, an increase of nearly 10 percent over the previous year. Chris Nowinski, CEO of the Concussion Legacy Foundation, loves this trend. He told me that it would be "so much safer" if more of the roughly 2.1 million kids between six and 14 years old who play tackle only participated in flag football before high school. And while that wouldn't be ideal from the NFL's perspective, it's far from catastrophic. "It's still getting football as a brand into a kid's psyche," says Michael Cihon, the founder of the United States Flag & Touch Football League in Ohio. "I have kids in my leagues so young that when they run, their flags are dragging on the ground. Where do you think those kids are going to be at 33? They are going to be in the Dawg Pound cheering on the [Cleveland] Browns."

On the face of it, another tactic the NFL relies upon also seems noble. For the past few years, Goodell, Mike Golic, and others have railed against the dangers of specialization, the practice of kids playing a single sport year-round. They talk about how it can lead to overuse injuries and psychological stress. Goodell has mentioned it in speeches and pivoted to it under questioning about concussions and CTE. Dr. Neeru Jayanthi of Emory University, recognized as a leading expert in specialization, told me he appreciates that the NFL is drawing attention to the issue. But he hopes that it isn't being used to draw attention away from football's own health concerns.

In the crisis management business, there is a term for what the NFL seems to be doing with specialization, says Gene Grabowski, a partner at kglobal. It is called "switching the witch." If people have a negative opinion of you or your company that can't be dismissed, give them something they can label as a bigger concern.

In a better, alternate universe, the NFL might realize that these sorts of deflections are dangerous. But we don't live in that universe. Where we live the leverage the league has over the advertising and media industries almost perfectly ensures that nobody will call the NFL out. "If you pay attention, you'll notice everyone sticking to the same script," Nate Jackson told me. That's why plenty of people were outraged but few were surprised when ESPN pulled out of a concussion-related documentary with *Frontline* in 2013 — a decision made after league officials reportedly expressed their displeasure to network executives during a tense lunch in midtown Manhattan.

Consider the league's rap sheet over just the last half-decade. There's been a major concussion crisis (accompanied by congressional hearings); the mishandling of several domestic assault cases (accompanied by congressional hearings); as well as a gruesome assortment of other alleged offenses, including child abuse, sexual assault, and murder. Yet none of the league's major corporate partners has pulled its support. NFL sponsorship revenue actually grew in 2015, up 4.4 percent to $1.5 billion.

And the possibility that anyone from within the NFL would blab about the league's moral failings seems unlikely. There's a cultlike creed around headquarters: "Protect the Shield." It means that an employee's first priority is, and must always be, the survival of the league. The concept breeds loyalty. People who work for the NFL rarely leave, and those who do often end up at a corporate partner, like Nike or ESPN. Which means that everybody loses money if somebody talks. It's a closed loop.

Earlier this year, the league made big news by hiring Joe Lockhart—who founded the Glover Park Group, one of Washington, D.C.'s most effective crisis shops—to be its executive vice president of communications. (Before that, Lockhart served as Bill Clinton's press secretary during the Monica Lewinsky scandal.) The move made sense: the NFL has benefited from its long relationship with the Glover Park Group, seeking its advice after the Ray Rice domestic battery video came out and using it to lobby Congress over broadcasting rights. Lockhart's arrival was interpreted as a high-profile, chest-thumping signal that the league was going to pursue its detractors more aggressively than ever. But less attention was focused on Paul Hicks, the man Lockhart replaced at the NFL. He went straight to work at the Glover Park Group. (He's also the father of Hope Hicks, Donald Trump's spokesperson.)

Josh Golin has spent a lot of time over the last two years fighting against this monolith. In February 2015, he helped release a scathing report on the league's "intense campaign to target children" in the hopes that it would spark outrage. It didn't. So he narrowed his focus just to NFL Rush Fantasy and teamed with the National Coalition on Problem Gambling. After a series of meetings, the league tacitly admitted this summer that it had gone too far by changing the rules of the game. Prizes are now awarded via a drawing involving all participants rather than to the highest scorer. "No longer will a child make money off Eli Manning throwing for 300 yards," Golin says. The NFL also agreed to stop distributing SEMs that promoted the fantasy game.

But none of this signaled a shift in policy. The kids' fantasy football game is still easy to find on the NFL's digital properties. Moms are still being told that the game is safe for their children. And there are still plenty of boneheaded NFL SEMs swimming around American classrooms. When I asked Golin if he was disappointed, or if he felt there was more he could've done to save kids from the NFL's marketing tactics, he just shrugged. "Sometimes you have to try and get a win where you can," he said.

GRAYSON SCHAFFER

The Most Successful Female Everest Climber of All Time Is a Housekeeper in Hartford, Connecticut

FROM OUTSIDE

LHAKPA SHERPA AWOKE before dawn on a cold Connecticut morning in January 2015 and shuffled into the kitchen of her two-bedroom apartment in West Hartford. The walls were covered in drawings and coloring-book pages of Disney princesses shaded in crayon and pencil by her two daughters, ages 8 and 13. She brewed up a small pot of coffee rather than the milk tea she grew up on in Balakharka, a village in the Makalu region of the Nepalese Himalayas. The apartment was clean, the girls' toys packed away against the walls, and the building, though older, was more or less in good repair. It seemed secure.

"I'm very sad inside, but I never show people sad," she said. "I'm all the time happy." I asked whether she was sure she wanted her story told. She was.

Lhakpa made breakfast sandwiches for the girls as her 18-year-old son, Nima Sherpa, left for community college in nearby Hartford. Each time she stepped out into the hallway of her building, one of her daughters would jump up and dead-bolt the door behind her. When she walked them to their respective schools—she doesn't drive or read or write, though she's learning—Lhakpa kept her cell phone charged and remembered to stay alert, just as the women who took her in at Interval House, a local shelter for victims of domestic violence, had told her to do.

All of this—her whereabouts, her basic routine—was known to her husband. "Ex-husband," she caught herself, saying it twice, trying out the prefix for the first time. She had just finalized her divorce, after 12 years of marriage, from a Romanian American named George Dijmarescu, 55, a nine-time Everest summiter and home renovation contractor. Following a civil trial in Connecticut Superior Court during which, according to Judge Jorge Simon's memo of decision, Dijmarescu had to be "verbally restrained by the court repeatedly to cease his continued personal assault," Lhakpa—a permanent resident of the United States on the path to citizenship—was awarded sole legal custody of the girls, both of whom are U.S. citizens. At the time, Connecticut still had a criminal trial pending against Dijmarescu for breach of peace and second-degree assault against Lhakpa. He's since been convicted of the first charge, found not guilty of the second, and given a six-month suspended sentence and a year of probation.

On the witness stand at their divorce hearing, Lhakpa said through an interpreter that Dijmarescu had told her the same thing on multiple occasions—that if she took his girls away, "First I will kill you, and then the girls, and then myself."

All along, Dijmarescu has maintained, as he testified in his deposition, that Lhakpa "clearly cannot distinguish her lies from the truth," that she orchestrated the abuse narrative as a way to rob him of his daughters, though he was the plaintiff in their divorce case. Now she'd won the girls in court. And so she was watching her back. Once they were at school, she'd go to one of her two jobs —housekeeping for an in-home health care service and working as a cashier at a 7-Eleven. Combined they earned her $400 per week. She was embarrassed by both of these occupations.

Lhakpa, whose Nepalese passport says she's 43, but who's probably closer to 40, is also a climber. A good one. She has summited Everest six times, more than any other woman in the world. Five of those trips were organized by Dijmarescu. In 2000, she became the first Nepalese woman to summit Everest and make it back down alive. In 2010, she made it to Camp 3 on K2 and spent two days there before the weather forced her to descend.

Yet few people are aware of her mountaineering exploits. The

Wikipedia page that catalogs Everest records contains listings as specific as "first twins to climb Mount Everest together," but there's no mention of Lhakpa. A 2013 ESPN.com article on five-time Everest summiter Melissa Arnot mentioned Lhakpa as an aside, calling Arnot "either the most accomplished female Everest climber ever, or the most accomplished non-Sherpa woman. (A Nepali named Lhakpa Sherpa is said to have from four to six Everest summits.)"

"I'm not sure why no one knows about her," Arnot, who is climbing Everest again this year, recently wrote in an email. "When I ask around to Nepalis, not many have heard of her. The first time I heard about her was in 2011, when I met her father when I was going to climb Makalu."

Lhakpa's obscurity owes partly to the fact that Sherpa climbers are still perceived as a homogenous workforce so gifted at getting to the summit that their accomplishments are often referred to in the collective. But in Lhakpa's case there's something more. Since 2004, she has been too frightened to speak to reporters. That's the year she says she was punched in the head by Dijmarescu in Everest's north-side base camp, in Chinese-controlled Tibet, in full view of expedition teammates from Connecticut—a charge that Dijmarescu insists was self-defense. Photographs published in the *Hartford Courant* (which Dijmarescu claimed in court were doctored) showed her being carried limp and bloody to the kitchen tent for treatment. After that incident, Lhakpa became very quiet about her achievements. Her six diploma-like summit certificates —five from the Chinese government and one from Nepal—are stored in a closet.

Now she's going for seven. Last spring, newly liberated, after a 10-year hiatus from Everest, she planned to make another attempt on the summit. But as she waited in base camp, again on Everest's north side, the April 25 earthquake hit, prompting both the Nepalese and Chinese governments to suspend climbing for the season. A year later, she's back on Everest to try again.

When you look at court records, medical records, and news reports, there is little question that Lhakpa Sherpa has had a rough go of things. But to view her solely as a victim would be to underestimate her.

"A queen among the Sherpa people" is how Oregon climber

Dave Watson describes her. Watson was with Lhakpa and Dijmarescu on the 2004 expedition that ended with the public altercation. In 2005, a *Times of London* reporter who was in Everest's
north-side base camp described her as somebody very much in
control: "Lhakpa, who received me on her collapsible chair as if
on a throne, had sought me out specifically to write about her next
great adventure."

Lhakpa's parents, both still alive, own several teahouses in
Makalu. Her brother Mingma Gelu Sherpa, who has summited
Everest eight times, is a director at Seven Summits Club, a success-
ful expedition outfitter based in Kathmandu.

Growing up in Makalu, a middle child among 11 siblings,
Lhakpa was something of a tomboy. "I am very different kind of
girl," she told me. "I have seven sisters, but my mama say I mostly
look like a boy. 'Whatever boy doing, you doing. You never doing
girl things. Mostly you're doing boy things.'" Like many Sherpa
women in the late seventies and early eighties, she received no
schooling.

In her family, that meant going into the trekking and climbing
business. Like the boys, she started carrying loads for an outfit-
ting company at age 15. Her uncle hired her as a kitchen boy for
expeditions attempting 27,838-foot Makalu. (The title still applies
to the small number of girls who help the cooks peel potatoes and
do dishes.) But Lhakpa quickly moved to carrying loads, ferrying
tents and sleeping bags up the trails leading to base camp. She carried between 25 and 50 pounds, often walking on ice.

Early on, she got her foot stuck between two rocks. "I fall over,
broke femur," she says, hiking up her sweatpants to show three
large scars on her upper left thigh where doctors had cut into
her wounds to let them drain. Lhakpa was working for an Indian
army expedition at the time, and it took her two weeks to make it
back to Kathmandu. "Two, three days walking," says Lhakpa, "and
my three friends help me. I come by bus. So painful." The basic
medical care was covered by the state, but the drugs were not. She
couldn't afford antibiotics, never mind pain meds, so she sold her
two gold earrings for a little more than $10.

The next year, she again worked as a porter but also gave climbing a try, first on Mera and Yala, two 6,000-meter peaks that are
popular stepping-stones to the 8,000-meter giants like Everest. As a
Sherpa, Lhakpa doesn't need to purchase a climbing permit, and

she was able to borrow gear from family members in the climbing and portering industries.

Lhakpa's son, Nima, came from a short relationship she had in the late 1990s, when she was living in Kathmandu. (Now in the U.S. as a permanent resident, Nima is exceedingly intelligent, motivated, and good at science and engineering.) Around the same time, she had a friend help her dictate a letter to the prime minister's office. She wanted to climb Everest. It had been several years since Pasang Lhamu, a 32-year-old Sherpa, had become the first Nepali woman to summit Everest, only to perish during her descent. Lhakpa appealed to the government and to dozens of corporate sponsors to fund an all-Sherpa women's expedition.

"They were scared," Lhakpa said. "And me, I say, I wanna go to the summit. Really this is my dream."

The Nepali Women Millennium Everest Expedition set up their base camp on the south side of Everest in the spring of 2000. "Lhakpa had taken a lot of training around Langtang and Manang regions for ice climbing," says her brother Mingma Gelu. "The other women also took the training, but they saw that my sister knew things and she had leadership potential."

As sometimes happens, the expedition was beset with undercurrents of dissent against its lead organizer. Lhakpa was the only one from the Makalu region, and she didn't mesh with the other climbers, who were from the Khumbu. The way Lhakpa tells it, the five women and the largely Khumbu team of male Sherpas wanted a Khumbu woman to make it to the summit. Lhakpa was the outsider.

"She was definitely the odd man out," Ramyata Limbu, one of the producers of *Daughters of Everest,* a documentary about the climb, confirmed recently in an email. "Not in a victimized way, though. She was aloof, above base camp politics and gossip. It was a do-or-die mission for her."

In climbing parlance, Lhakpa might be called a sandbagger, somebody who understates her abilities in order to beat expectations. Lower on the mountain, in the Khumbu Icefall, the rest of the team labored up the trail at top speed, jockeying to see who was stronger. (The icefall is the dangerous and unpredictable section below Camp I that was the site of a deadly avalanche in 2014, during which 16 workers died.) There, Lhakpa received valuable advice from one of the so-called Icefall Doctors, Sherpas who maintain the fragile network of aluminum ladders and safety ropes over the route's crevasses.

"This Icefall Doctor say, 'Why you running there, girl?'" Lhakpa recalled. "You not summit now. Four thousand meters up the top of the mountain. Up there you run. Not here."

So she slowed down. The other women asked if she was sick, if she had a headache. She said yes.

"I wouldn't say she was manipulative," recalls Limbu. "But I think she was prepared to go to lengths to ensure that she made the ascent."

When Lhakpa reached Camp IV, at the South Col, at 26,000 feet, the clouds formed a sea below her, thick and full of lightning flashes. But the skies above were clear. Her companions were in their tents melting water, or so she thought, until she looked out and saw three headlamps heading toward the summit.

She started to cry. "Tears of ice," she told me. "And I said, 'Ah! I'm losing!'"

Lhakpa pulled on her boots and convinced her male Sherpa climbing partner to get out of his tent and head up. Within a couple of hours, they'd caught and passed the lead party, which soon turned around.

At 6:00 a.m.—dawn on May 18, 2000—she and her climbing partner reached the summit, which, she says, was beneath a rainbow. They were the only two members of the expedition to make it. She was received by a crowd in Lukla and flown by helicopter to her home in Makalu to celebrate.

At a party held shortly after the climb at the Rum Doodle, a popular bar in Kathmandu's touristy Thamel neighborhood that serves free food for life to all Everest summiters, she met her future husband. George Dijmarescu was standing against the wall. Then a handsome 39, he stood six-foot-two and weighed over 200 pounds.

"He hanging around the Khumbu Sherpas," recalls Lhakpa. "You know, coming, teasing me, saying, 'Oh, Lhakpa!' And he's looking nice. Long hair. You know, strong man. Sherpas say, 'Oh, he summit without oxygen.'"

Lhakpa spoke little English then—only what Dijmarescu would later refer to in court transcripts as "gibberish." But other Sherpas helped the two communicate. Lhakpa went to visit her sister

Cheng at her adopted home in Daytona Beach, Florida. (She has a sister in New York City and a brother in Hartford as well, part of Nepal's thriving U.S. expatriate community.) When Dijmarescu called from Hartford, Cheng helped relay his messages to her sister.

Dijmarescu bought Lhakpa a plane ticket to Connecticut. Along with several other Sherpas, she worked doing demolition for the home renovation company that Dijmarescu and his brother, Claudio, owned. In 2001, Lhakpa and Dijmarescu climbed Everest together, her second ascent, from the Tibetan side. In the fall of 2002, they were married in a civil ceremony at Hartford's city hall.

When I visited her last winter, Lhakpa was walking the girls home from school, taking the bus to the supermarket, and visiting with her English tutor, Elizabeth Hanlon, who'd been helping her write — mostly essays about her time in Nepal, like the time she says she was stalked by a snow leopard. She was starting to make more friends, but it was still difficult.

"I cannot talk to anybody," Lhakpa said over coffee. I'd been told that she could seem guarded and quiet, but the woman I met was gregarious and funny, laughing often and smiling constantly while her girls played *Minecraft* and entertained friends. "I love to talk," she said. "I stay in house and I . . . God, I'm still thinking about the mountain. You know, my God, I need to go to Nepal."

Lhakpa's attorney from the nonprofit Greater Hartford Legal Aid clinic, Ramona Mercado-Espinoza, came over to read a copy of the judge's ruling that gave her sole legal custody of the girls. Dijmarescu had tried to argue in court that because Lhakpa can't read or write in any language, she was unfit to parent. "What George didn't know," said Mercado-Espinoza, "is that Judge Jorge Simon's parents came here also from another country" — he's of Cuban descent — "and that they didn't speak English. Everybody is afraid of George, but I'm not afraid: I'm Puerto Rican."

For a time, the Dijmarescus' marriage was peaceful. Lhakpa testified that it didn't start to deteriorate until 2003, when their first daughter was born. "The relationship was good before I had children, but once I had children, he started hitting me," she said on the witness stand last year.

The couple climbed together from the Tibetan side of Everest in 2003, 2004, 2005, and 2006 — Lhakpa's third through sixth ascents. In 2003, her younger sister Ming Kipa joined the team.

She was 15, making her, at that time, the youngest person to climb Everest.

The 2004 expedition was documented by reporter Michael Kodas in a series of stories for the *Hartford Courant,* work he later incorporated into the 2008 book *High Crimes: The Fate of Everest in the Age of Greed.*

The single incident that horrified the climbing world came on that trip. The expedition, called Connecticut Everest, was made up mostly of climbers from New England; it was organized by Dijmarescu and co-led by Lhakpa and Trinity College field hockey and lacrosse coach Anne Parmenter. The team, including Kodas and his wife, Carolyn, ascended Everest's north side.

"Success here was a triumph of physiology rather than mountaineering skill," Kodas wrote in the *Hartford Courant.* "And in this world, George and Lhakpa's strength was obvious. They stayed so far in front of the pack that I wasn't sure which figures on the landscape were theirs." The higher the team climbed, he wrote, the "more remote" Lhakpa seemed. She rarely carried a pack, he alleged, and "coaxed those whose packs seemed light to carry some of her gear."

The altercation took place after Lhakpa had just summited for the fourth time, and Dijmarescu, after failing to summit, had helped rescue a Mexican climber who'd had trouble descending. "He is all frostbit on his fingers and toes, and Lhakpa starts to become jealous and starts accusing George of being gay," climber Dave Watson, who helped with the rescue, told me by phone. "We're about to leave base camp and start driving back to Kathmandu. This is the last day. And it finally fucking boils over, you know? George is in a tent with the Mexican climber and a couple other guys, and Lhakpa comes in and starts throwing huge rocks at George."

In his deposition for the divorce case, Dijmarescu said that Lhakpa had attacked him and the other climber. "She charge at him and she grab him by the throat," he said. "He was all bandaged, he had severe frostbite, we just rescued him. And calling him 'fag,' that he had just had an affair with me." Dijmarescu testified that, as Lhakpa pelted them with rocks, "I opened the tent door, and I pushed her out."

The version Lhakpa presented in court was that Dijmarescu had become angry when she protested that "he was not treating the people that we walked with nicely."

According to testimony from Anne Parmenter, who was present at the altercation, Dijmarescu lashed out at his wife, hitting her. In his cross-examination of Parmenter, Dijmarescu—who acted as his own counsel throughout the trial—disputed her testimony. "Ms. Parmenter has not witnessed any hitting," he said.

Lhakpa told me at her kitchen table last January that she remembered being knocked out. "I'm flying, and I'm at my mama's house. And I hear people singing, yelling. I heard some birds," she said. "I opened my eye, and I look at Everest. And half is red and half is white." She thought that blood vessels had ruptured inside her eye.

Dijmarescu declined to comment for this story, but his brother and former business partner, Claudio, speculates that so much time at altitude may have affected his brother. "He isn't the same person he was before he started climbing," he wrote me in an email.

In a Facebook message to me, Dave Watson called Dijmarescu "very tough, very misunderstood, and very kind. He taught me how to play the extreme-altitude game, and I feel very fortunate to have had him as a mentor . . . I know I can count on him and have trusted my life to him. We've been through mountain combat together, and now I consider him a brother."

Some of Dijmarescu's toughness no doubt grew out of his own difficult immigration story. A soldier in the Romanian army, he escaped from the Communist country in 1986 or 1987, at age 25, a few years before the overthrow and execution of dictator Nicolae Ceaușescu in 1989.

"My departure took two years of training in an Olympic swimming pool. I trained myself to cross the largest river in Europe, called the Danube," Dijmarescu said in his deposition. "It took me two years to prepare myself for this journey, took me two years learning where the border patrol was." He then walked across the former Yugoslavia and into Italy, where he lived for a time at a refugee camp. Because he'd served in an Eastern Bloc army, which meant he might have useful intelligence, he was able to defect to the United States and become a citizen.

*

When *High Crimes* was released in 2008, says Lhakpa, she retreated deeper into the shadows. According to her, Dijmarescu was furious. "Here is your Michael Kodas book!" she told me he shouted as he hit her with the book.

The Dijmarescus bought a house in 2009, a four-bedroom craftsman in Hartford with a trampoline out back. The girls each had their own room. Dijmarescu's ailing father, Valeriu, 80, who the girls call Nunu, lived upstairs. According to court documents, he'd had a liver transplant and was on dialysis, and Lhakpa looked after him.

By this time, Lhakpa had been out of the spotlight for four years, having claimed her six summits and retreated to home life in Connecticut. But despite having been able to fund nearly a dozen trips to Everest, Dijmarescu was in financial trouble, hit by the recession and hospital bills from a diagnosis of sarcoma.

It was during his battle with cancer, in May 2011, that Dijmarescu wrote Lhakpa a letter—which Lhakpa's attorney introduced as evidence during the court proceedings—promising that things would get better. "I know, Lhakpa, I hurt you many times," the note read. "I'm sorry. I said it to you before. If God grants me another chance, I'll make you my queen and I will devote my life to your happiness. I was wrong, and I did not know the meaning of happiness, the meaning of true life and prosperity. I know I found it now and am ready to use this knowledge."

But by the summer of 2012, the stress had gotten worse. The family was on food stamps. Nima had received a green card and moved from Kathmandu to Hartford, but it quickly became clear that he'd need to live with his uncle, Lhakpa's brother, rather than with her and Dijmarescu. According to court records, things blew up that summer, resulting in the incident for which Dijmarescu was later convicted of breach of peace. July 1 was their older daughter's birthday, and Dijmarescu wanted to throw her a party. Lhakpa rode the bus to Stop & Shop to buy food for the party, only to find there was no credit on the state-issued benefits card.

On the witness stand, Lhakpa testified, "I came back and told him that it does not work. He accused me of not making food that day."

"He started hitting me for that," she said. "He also tells me to buy alcohol with the card, but you actually cannot purchase alcohol with the food stamp."

Lhakpa told the judge that their older daughter ran to her grandfather Valeriu's room and turned up the television. But, she testified, the younger daughter stayed, crying and shouting, "Don't hit mama, don't hit mama." According to Lhakpa, Valeriu tried to intervene and shield her from the blows. Afterward, she said, Dijmarescu drove off in his pickup truck and she called a neighbor who she often confided in. Her friend called the police.

At Hartford Hospital that night, Lhakpa met with a social worker. The medical records from the case, which Mercado-Espinoza provided to me in Lhakpa's presence, summarized her claims like so: "States she has been abused by her husband for 11 years."

From the hospital, Lhakpa and the girls were transported directly to a women's shelter, where they effectively disappeared. When they reemerged a month later, Dijmarescu filed for divorce.

After two years of legal wrangling and a trial, Judge Simon issued his ruling on January 5, 2015, dissolving the marriage. While he said that he did not find all of Lhakpa's claims credible, his written opinion was pointed. "It was clear to the court that the husband treated the wife more like chattel than a human being; someone more suitable for the rigors of carrying loads than raising children," Simon wrote. "Ms. Sherpa embodies all the qualities of first-generation immigrants to the United States seeking a better life for themselves and their children."

Lhakpa didn't train for Everest. She was born and raised above 13,000 feet and believes her strong will and genetics will get her to the top of the mountain, just as they have in the past. She has summited in fierce winds, in whiteouts, and eight months after the birth of her first daughter. She went back up Everest when she was two months pregnant with her second child, a fact the younger daughter holds firmly over her big sister's head. "I walk every day," Lhakpa said, describing what passes for her conditioning strategy. "I go to my work walking, pick up my children walking."

According to Mercado-Espinoza, it's been a calm year in relation to Dijmarescu, who is allowed to visit with his daughters as long as his mother or another designated supervisor is present. Last month, Lhakpa left the girls with Claudio Dijmarescu and his wife and returned home to Nepal, where she'll climb Everest on a trip run by her brother's outfit, Seven Summits Club. Mingma Gelu will provide her with everything she needs. "We will climb together," he says. "We have a great climbing family. She doesn't need a Sherpa. She is so strong."

By early May, the Sherpa fixing team had set ropes to 27,000 feet, well ahead of schedule for Everest's north side. Lhakpa had been doing her acclimatization rotations to the North Col and beyond. Everest, she had told me before she left, isn't a physical challenge so much as a mental one. It requires the strength to endure and to keep getting up, putting icy boots on, and stepping out of your tent even when you're cold and tired, no matter how bad you feel. That much Lhakpa knows she can do.

Even if she succeeds in nabbing her seventh summit, she'll almost certainly return to housekeeping in a world that is slow to validate her accomplishments. It's not that she wouldn't welcome a little recognition. She wants to have a movie made about her, and she desperately wants to meet Oprah Winfrey; she's carried copies of *O: The Oprah Magazine* to the summit on multiple occasions. For now, though, Lhakpa is happy to have her freedom, and she has no plans to move. "I like my friends," she says. "I don't want to have to find new ones." And the girls have their friends and their school and a place in the world."

But that doesn't mean Lhakpa is at peace. Last winter, I asked her for the fifth time whether she was sure that she wanted me to tell the details of her story. She said that she did. Then she added, "You tell me when this story is public. I must watch which way I walk."

JON BILLMAN

(Long) Gone Girl

FROM RUNNER'S WORLD

The car chugs around switchback after switchback, crunching gravel beneath its tires as it ascends the Loop Road through Sinks Canyon in mid-central Wyoming. Its headlamps cast twin beams of light that pierce the midnight blackness. Todd Skinner and Amy Whisler scan the edges of visibility for something—anything —that would hint at their neighbor Amy Wroe Bechtel's whereabouts. To their right lies the inky Frye Lake, which was to be the terminus of a 10K hill climb Amy was planning for the fall. They pass the lake, drive a few miles, round a bend—and then they see it. Directly ahead, a flash of white where the road forks.

Amy's white Toyota Tercel wagon is parked by the side of the road where the Loop Road splinters out to the smaller, pine-shrouded Burnt Gulch turnoff. There are puddles below the driver's door and behind the vehicle, but no footprints, no tire tracks in the mud. If she parked before it had stormed that afternoon, did she get caught in the rain? Where did she go?

There is no sign of Amy, though, so Todd pulls out his cell phone to call her husband, Steve.

From here, the calendar will hurtle forward days, months, years at a time. Meanwhile, Steve, authorities, Amy's family and friends—America—will re-wind the clock on that single day, patching together hazy eyewitness accounts and scarce facts in hopes of uncovering what happened to the runner who never came home.

AMY WROE BECHTEL, 24 at the time of her disappearance, has been missing for 19 years. Nineteen years, with nary a shred of evidence, other than what was found in her car in those early morning hours on the Burnt Gulch turnoff. There were her sunglasses, her car keys left on the driver's seat, and a to-do list—a small scratch of paper written in Amy's light, busy hand. Her last words to the world. She'd already contacted phone and electric companies to have services turned on at her and her husband's newly purchased home (*check*), dropped off the recyclables from the gym where she worked at the recycling center (*check*), been to the photo store (*check*). There were other things she hadn't yet done, or at least hadn't yet checked off the list. At the bottom: run.

It's heartbreakingly ironic that what would become such a disorganized investigation began with this tidy little window into Amy's plans for the day.

True crime mysteries have always captivated America, in the same macabre way a car accident attracts rubberneckers, but they've struck a cultural nerve lately. In late 2014, NPR released *Serial*, a podcast that unraveled the mystery of a murdered high-schooler and the conviction of her boyfriend, week by agonizing week. A month and a half after the season aired, the boyfriend, Adnan Syed, was allowed to challenge a previously denied appeal on the grounds that he'd been provided ineffective counsel. Early last year, HBO aired *The Jinx*, a documentary series that detailed how New York real estate scion Robert Durst evaded convictions in the deaths of three people despite a preponderance of circumstantial evidence that seemed to incriminate him and only him. Stunningly, Durst appeared to confess to the killings over a hot mic during the show's finale, and the night before its airing he was arrested by the FBI for one of them.

Perhaps, in this age of ubiquitous information, people have grown increasingly intrigued by the questions that remain unanswered. The cable television network Investigation Discovery took a crack at answering Amy's case in a 2013 episode of its *Disappeared* series; a flurry of local news stories followed suit. Behind the renewed interest in Amy's case: a new lead detective taking a fresh look at decades-old clues.

Wyomingites are fond of describing their state as America's biggest small town, and like nearly every other resident in 1997, my soon-to-be wife, Hilary, and I followed Amy's disappearance in the *Casper Star-Tribune*—the paper of record in the state—and on KUWR, Wyoming Public Radio, day-to-day as it transitioned from a local to a national story that made Amy Wroe Bechtel a household name. The story was featured on *Unsolved Mysteries*, the *New York Times* covered it, and *Runner's World* went so far as to put Amy's photo on its cover in January 1998 for a story by John Brant. (The story generated more reader mail than any other in the magazine's history.) Most media accounts, driven by the hunches of the lead investigators, named but one suspect: Amy's husband, Steve Bechtel.

Nearly two decades later, however, it appears that there were hardly enough facts to merit such an intense focus on Steve. In the absence of hard evidence, what happened in the immediate aftermath of Amy's disappearance more closely resembled a work of fiction than the stories documented in *Serial* or *The Jinx*. In HBO's award-winning 2014 crime drama *True Detective*, Marty Hart, played by Woody Harrelson, tells his partner, "You attach an assumption to a piece of evidence, you start to bend the narrative to support it, prejudice yourself."

The "evidence" investigators had was Steve's journals. They contained poetry that sometimes erred on the violent side and included troubling philosophies about male-gender dominance. Steve, in conversation as on the page, was a cocky, wisecracking, superfit slam-dunk. It's almost always the husband, right?

A week and a half after Amy vanished, Steve sealed his public fate as the villain when he lawyered up and refused to take a polygraph test.

The narrative bent toward Steve. *Chauvinist. Coward. Wife killer.*

Meanwhile, potentially crucial evidence was rendered useless by shoddy crime-scene management. Meanwhile, a critical lead was ignored.

Meanwhile, a monster roamed free.

July 24, 1997, 10:30 p.m. *"Uh, yeah, hey, I've got a person missing here, I think, and I wondered if you had a spare around anyplace?"*—Steve Bechtel, in a phone call to Lander (Wyoming) authorities to report his missing wife.

Amy and Steve had been married for a year and a month. After they'd graduated from the University of Wyoming in Laramie with degrees in exercise physiology, the couple moved to Lander, population around 7,000, and lived at Number 9 Lucky Lane, a small white house in a group of 12 utilitarian miners' houses the locals call Climbers' Row. The Bechtels were tenants of the neighbors who would eventually find Amy's abandoned car, Todd Skinner and Amy Whisler. Skinner, who died in a tragic fall at Yosemite in 2006, was a world-renowned climber and Steve's frequent climbing partner.

In 1997, Lander was on the cusp of becoming an elite climbing town and, in that world, Skinner—and to a lesser extent, Steve —were stars. Today, it has evolved into an outdoor enthusiast's mecca, hosting the colossal climbers' playground of Sinks Canyon in its backyard, the National Outdoor Leadership School (NOLS), and an emergent road-racing and ultrarunning scene. Now, just as then, cowhands sit on stools next to "rock rats" at the historic Lander Bar, the prominent watering hole that happens to be owned by a climber. But in 1997, to some, the climbers who now in many ways give the town its identity were aliens, transients who didn't appear to have real jobs. They were fraternal and secretive, almost cultish.

Amy was a runner within this climbing clique. She had been a standout distance runner at Wyoming—she ranked first in school history in the indoor 3,000 meters (9:48) and second in the indoor 5,000 (18:07) in 1995—and, with a marathon PR of 3:01, had aspirations of qualifying for the 2000 Olympic Marathon Trials. She and Steve both worked part-time at Wild Iris, the local climbing shop, and Amy also waited tables at the Sweetwater Grill and taught a youth weight-lifting class at Wind River Fitness Center. The two had the appearance of happy young newlyweds. They had recently bought a house in the residential heart of Lander and were preparing to take the leap out of their "no-need-to-knock-door's-never-locked" climbing-bum shanty on Lucky Lane.

When Amy vanished, Lander divided. The climbers and NOLS crowd rallied around Steve, insulating him when it was clear the authorities suspected him. That raised suspicions with many of the townies, fueled by frustrated questions in the newspapers posed by law enforcement and Amy's family. As Bryan Di Salvatore, a Montana-based writer who reported on the case for *Outside* magazine in 1998, puts it, "That town was freaked out. Scared and angry."

The fact that there was no body, no real sign of violence even, made Steve the go-to target in the fog of mystery. After all, he was familiar with many of the remote mountain areas in Wyoming. In the first few days after Amy vanished, however, Steve was hardly a suspect—he was helping lead the search. In fact, for the first few days, foul play wasn't even considered by investigators.

"Here's the whole problem," says Fremont County Patrol Sergeant John Zerga, who was assigned Amy's cold-case file in 2010 and remains the lead detective today. "Nowadays, everything is viewed as a homicide. Back then it wasn't viewed that way. She was just a missing runner. For three days."

A stuffed wild turkey keeps watch from the corner of Zerga's small office in the Fremont County Sheriff's Office facility in Lander. A stout 48-year-old with a close-cropped haircut and a cowboy's Fu Manchu mustache, Zerga is essentially the Lone Ranger on Amy's case, and has the nigh impossible task of cleaning up a 19-year-old mess made by the first lead investigator on Amy's case, Dave King.

"We didn't close off any routes out of here," Zerga continues. "We didn't close off any vehicles. All we had was a bunch of people up here looking for a missing runner. We actually ruined it with the vehicle, because we allowed the Skinners to drive it home. [The investigation] was not good for at least the first three days. There was a lot of stuff that was lost."

"King rolled in a week late," says John Gookin, PhD, a search-and-rescue expert who helped coordinate the mountain search for Amy. "He was off in the mountains on a horsepacking trip—so this guy who had just been promoted to detective from jailer was in charge of the search. The promoted jailer asked me, 'Well, what do I do?' The detective asking the volunteer running the search teams, 'What do I do?'"

The search began with just Steve and two dozen of his friends, but later that day there were ATVs, dogs, dirt bikes, and over 100 volunteers on the ground. The next day horses and helicopters joined in, and by the third day, the search area had been expanded to a 30-mile radius—a big wheel of rough country. But it would take a full week after Amy's car was found for the area around it to be declared a crime scene.

On August 5, an FBI agent named Rick McCullough accused Steve of murdering Amy. Steve then retained the counsel of Kent Spence. By then, Steve had already been interviewed four times by investigators, and Spence advised him to refuse the FBI's request to take a polygraph test. Spence thought the situation had taken a turn to harassment.

Then, two months after Amy vanished, King relinquished the case to Detective Sergeant Roger Rizor and turned his focus on campaigning for Fremont County sheriff, a position he would be elected to in 1998. The campaign didn't stop King from discussing the case alongside Amy's sisters on *The Geraldo Rivera Show* in

February 1998. Spence would later say that he believed King used Amy's case as a grandstand to help him get elected sheriff. King wouldn't hold that title long, though: on November 3, 2000, he resigned amid allegations of impropriety, and was later convicted of stealing cocaine from a law enforcement storage locker.

"Everybody that investigated this was focused on Steve," Zerga says. "And they had good reason. But there again, there was information coming in pointing in different directions."

One tip came from a man named Richard Eaton, who told investigators that his itinerant stumblebum of a brother, Dale Wayne Eaton, may have been involved. Rizor's team, dead-set on nailing Steve, was unconvinced, and may have missed its chance to close not just Amy's case, but at least nine cold-case murders. By not pursuing the lead, they may have allowed the notorious Great Basin Serial Killer to get away.

JULY 24, 1997, 4:30 p.m. *Steve arrives home after a day of scouting climbs with Sam Lightner Jr., a travel writer. Amy's not home, but he knows she had had a busy day planned.*

Earlier in the day, he had rendezvoused with Lightner in Dubois—a town roughly equidistant from Steve's home in Lander and Lightner's in Jackson, 80 miles or so. The climbing partners had a history. They'd climbed throughout the West and in Asia, but just a year earlier, on a trip with Amy to Australia, the men were not getting along, and Lightner flew home early. But they always trusted each other on the rocks. From Dubois, the two climbers, accompanied by the Bechtels' yellow Lab, Jonz, had ridden north together into the Cartridge Creek area of Shoshone National Forest. They'd both carried guns, Lightner and Steve will later tell authorities, because "that's where they dump all the bad bears from Yellowstone." But the scout had been a letdown. The rock wasn't that great for climbing, had been a slog to get to, and wouldn't have been worth the effort. Thunderstorms had lurked nearby and had driven Steve and his friend back to Dubois, where they'd gone their separate ways.

A few hours pass. Amy's not home for dinner. Steve makes a few calls. Nobody's seen Amy, so he drives around town and rallies friends to help him find her. A few more hours pass.

Steve begins to panic.

"I actually got along with Amy better than I did with Steve in Australia," Lightner will say years later, reflecting on the constant skepticism he received from investigators. "I'm not gonna cover for somebody who might have murdered a friend of mine."

Lightner, and the trip to Dubois, will be Steve's alibi.

*

A trip to Dubois was the beginning of the end for Dale Wayne Eaton.

It's a wonder Eaton was a free man at all when police found him just outside the mountain town on July 30, 1998, nearly a year to the day after Amy's disappearance and, more specifically, just 10 and a half months after he attempted to kidnap the Breeden family.

The botched kidnapping took place in an area called Patrick Draw, less than a three-hour drive from Lander. Shannon Breeden, her husband, Scott, and their five-month-old baby, Cody, were traveling the country when their van broke down at a pullout along Interstate 80. An overweight, disheveled 52-year-old stopped his off-green '85 Dodge van and offered them assistance. The man —Dale Eaton—asked Shannon to drive. Eaton then pulled a rifle from the back of the van, kidnapped the family at gunpoint, and directed them south of the highway into the desert.

In a scene straight out of a B-grade '70s chase movie, Shannon stepped on the gas and turned in a tight circle instead, which enabled Scott to jump out of the van with the baby and Shannon to get out the other side. Eaton grabbed her and would have plunged a knife into her ribs had Scott not grabbed Eaton's arm and gun and hit him over the head with the rifle butt. A struggle ensued in the dirt, and ended with Eaton stabbed with his own knife, beaten with his own rifle, and left in the dirt while the family sped for help in the van.

It wasn't long before Eaton was arrested, and he quickly confessed to the attempted kidnapping.

The incident got Eaton's brother, Richard, thinking. He knew that Dale had been camping in the Burnt Gulch area at the time of Amy Bechtel's disappearance. Burnt Gulch, average elevation 7,860 feet, is not far from where Amy was marking her 10K route, and was a favorite elk-hunting and trout-fishing spot of the Eaton brothers. But after Richard called Rizor with his suspicions, the detective dismissed the tip, choosing to believe instead the word of Eaton's niece, who said Dale was visiting her in Greeley, Colorado, on July 24. A $100,000 reward out for information leading to a resolution of Amy's case was enough to cast suspicion on Richard's motives.

Astonishingly, a plea deal for the attempted kidnapping meant Eaton would serve just 99 days in jail, where samples of his DNA were taken, before being paroled to a halfway house in Casper due to prison overcrowding. He remained on strict probation—which included a curfew—but was allowed his Dodge van so that he could work welding and construction jobs.

Eaton, however, failed to report to work on June 16, 1998, and a warrant was put out for his arrest. Police finally spotted his van more than a month later on a short dead-end spur road near Dubois in the Bridger-Teton National Forest. He was arrested at gunpoint, and told police he was about to commit suicide. A shotgun was found in his van, leading to his imprisonment on federal weapons charges.

Four years later, those DNA samples taken while Eaton was incarcerated would be linked to unspeakable horrors.

JULY 24, 1997, 2:30 p.m. *She walks into the portrait studio on the second floor of the Camera Connection in downtown Lander, dressed for running.*

No, not like she's already gone for a run, Lonnie Slack, who worked part-time at the studio back then, remembers in his mind's eye. She's not sweating. She looks like she's about to go for a run.

She drops off some pictures to get matted and framed. She's excited, talking about her forthcoming entries in the Sinks Canyon Photo Contest.

She's there 15 minutes, maybe. Then she leaves out the back door.

Well, it was after lunch. Maybe it was two o'clock.

Would Amy have approved of the photo?

I can remember the race T-shirt for the Amy Bechtel Hill Climb vividly. A large color photograph of smiling, blond-haired Amy had been hastily screen-printed on the front, along with the words HAVE YOU SEEN AMY? and a phone number: 1-800-867-5AMY. I remember that Amy's photograph started to mute with the first wash, and that it wasn't long until she faded to the white of the shirt, like a ghost.

My wife and I were living in Kemmerer at the time, two and a half hours southwest of Lander, and when the race was announced, we put it on our calendar: September 28, 1997.

Race morning was a sunny autumn day on the eastern shoulder of the Wind River Range, and 150 or so runners gathered for a bittersweet attempt to actualize the 10K course that Amy had been working on when she'd gone missing. The run was to be a steep, steady, warm, and dusty climb up the gravel switchbacks of the

Loop Road that ended at Frye Lake, where divers had searched for a body. Most of the field had been involved in the search or were close to Amy through running or to Steve. There were NOLS employees and a posse of hard-core climbers who run to stay in shape but don't consider themselves runners. Amy's sister Jenny was there. As was Steve, who by this time had come under intense scrutiny from investigators and a sizable segment of the Wyoming public as the number-one suspect in the case.

Steve was remarkably composed during a prerace talk. *Amy had wanted to do this race for a couple of years,* he said. *She was told the only people who would show would be eight of her former track teammates.* This brought cheers from the field. *We're in this together. We know Amy is alive.*

I remember trying to size up Steve Bechtel—is this a man who was capable of killing his wife and hiding the body? He didn't carry himself like my idea of a sociopath. He had been, after all, the one manning the phones and computers at the recovery center in his and Amy's garage and kitchen, responding to leads that poured in from all over the country, none fruitful. But then how are you supposed to act when your wife disappears? A 10K seemed like the best thing for exorcising anxiety, in part for lack of knowing what else to do—and because it was what she had wanted to do—and it got a little media coverage that kept the search alive.

But after the local search fizzled out, Amy's mom, dad, brother, and two sisters returned to their respective homes and tried to carry on with lives that would never be the same again. Their concerns about Steve grew a few weeks later when they were presented with previously undisclosed information about the search findings and Steve's journal entries. Although each family member responded differently, their frustrations with Steve's lack of overall cooperation and engagement with the investigators lingered. Amy's father, Duane, told a news source years later, "I still feel angry, because if he's not guilty of anything, the son-of-a-bitch should take the lie-detector test and give us some peace." Her brother, Nels, was especially angry at Steve's reluctance to take the test and cooperate fully with investigators. When her sisters, Casey Lee and Jenny Newton, appeared on *The Geraldo Rivera Show* with detective King, the host made a plea for Steve to be more cooperative with authorities.

A year passed, then two, then four. Steve followed a new girl-

friend to Salt Lake City, but found he missed Lander, so he moved
—with the girl—back to town two years later. He still refused to
take the polygraph, and many people in town continued to believe
he was responsible for Amy's disappearance. Steve's girlfriend
ended up leaving. More years slipped by. Eventually, Steve had
Amy declared legally dead, and in 2004 he married Ellen Sissman,
with whom he now has two children.

All these years later, Nels Wroe has accepted that the family may
never find closure, but remains frustrated with Steve's refusal to
take the polygraph. "I will not shy away from that," Nels said to me
when I visited him at a coffee shop near his home in Longmont,
Colorado. "The one person who can help the most in possibly re-
solving what happened to Amy is the guy who for whatever reason
—cowardice, selfishness, I don't know—refuses to engage.

"This stressed the family out. My father passed away a number
of years ago. The whole situation with Steve not being cooperative,
that really caused frustration for the family."

JULY 24, 1997, 10:30 a.m. *"Boy, if it were me, I'd be running* down *the
mountain," Erle Osborne jokes out his window as he drives past the woman
running up the Loop Road. The mechanic for the county slows down so as not to
dust her, as he makes his way uphill to change the carburetor on an old fire truck
that sat idle at a youth camp.*

*The woman, blond, blue-eyed, and wearing a light-colored singlet, black
shorts, and a fanny pack, smiles and waves at Osborne.*

*Odd, he thinks, a runner on the third switchback of the Loop Road. It would
be years before this would become a common sight. And yet authorities will later
confirm that another witness, a road surveyor, independently described seeing the
same woman on the Loop Road at around the same time of day.*

*Osborne arrives at the fire truck and works with haste—he can feel a storm
closing in. He gets back in his truck and rolls up the windows just in time for
the rain and lightning to come down. A goose drowner. Raining so hard he can
hardly see the road.*

*He remembers the woman running uphill. If he sees her on his way down,
he'll offer a ride.*

*But Osborne doesn't see the runner again. He does, however, have to inch
around an old blue-green vehicle—he'll later strain to recall that it may have
been a van—stopped in the road.*

It's possible, if highly unlikely, that the surveyor and Osborne saw a
different runner who just happened to look like Amy. Petite, pretty

—Amy looked like a lot of women, like a lot of women who also vanished without a trace from the Great Basin region of Nevada, Utah, Idaho, and Wyoming.

Amy's isn't even the most famous case. A series of other murders between 1983 and 1997 have been suspected to have come at the hands of one Great Basin Serial Killer, but the case of only one of them has been resolved: Lil Miss.

On March 25, 1988, 18-year-old Lisa Marie Kimmell was driving alone from Denver to visit a friend in Billings, Montana, in her black 1988 Honda CRX Si, which had a Montana vanity plate that read LIL MISS. She'd first planned to stop to see her boyfriend in Cody, Wyoming, but she never made it. Eight days later, two fishermen found her body tangled in the weeds along the North Platte River near Casper, and an autopsy showed that she had been repeatedly raped, bludgeoned, and methodically stabbed. After her family buried her, a strange note signed "Stringfellow Hawke" was found on Kimmell's grave.

Few answers emerged for the next 14 years, until July 2002, when investigators researching cold cases examined the seminal DNA from her rape kit and found a match for an inmate incarcerated on weapons charges since 1998: Dale Wayne Eaton. Eaton was due to stand trial that fall on a manslaughter charge after killing his cellmate with a lethal punch to the man's vertebral artery—but he was never convicted. He wouldn't be so lucky this time.

A handwriting analysis from the note left on Kimmell's grave also matched Eaton. Then, following a tip from neighbors who recalled seeing Eaton digging in his desert-scrub yard, authorities found her car buried on his property in Moneta, just an hour-and-45-minute drive east from Lander. The sewer line from his decrepit trailer house had been run into it—he'd been using his victim's car as a septic tank. A portion of the Montana vanity plate LIL MISS was found nearby. Inside his trailer, authorities also found women's clothing and purses, and newspaper reports about other murdered women.

In the ensuing investigation and trial, it was determined that Eaton had kidnapped Kimmell at a remote rest area in Waltman, then held her captive in a filthy converted school bus and repeatedly raped her before murdering her and tossing her body off a bridge. An FBI profiler who examined the case would note that this public display, the trophy-keeping of Kimmell's car, and the known kidnapping attempt of the Breedens all fit the profile of a serial killer.

In the Kimmell trial, Eaton was charged and found guilty of all counts, including first-degree murder, and sentenced to death by lethal injection in March 2004. Eaton's lawyers won him a stay of execution in December 2009, arguing among other things that he was mentally unfit to stand trial and that he'd previously been given ineffective counsel by the Wyoming Public Defender's Office. He remained Wyoming's lone death row inmate until November 2014, when a U.S. district judge overturned his death sentence on similar grounds—though Eaton will never be released from prison, where he is serving a life sentence, plus 50 years. (My repeated attempts to reach Eaton and his brother were all rebuffed.)

No one believes Kimmell is Eaton's only kidnapping and murder victim. Sheila Kimmell, Lisa's mother, mentions Amy's case in her 2005 book *The Murder of Lil Miss,* and is very well versed in other disappearances and homicides connected with the Great Basin Murders. "The Utah Criminal Tracking Analysis Project suggested that the Great Basin murders stopped around 1997. That's about the same time Dale Eaton went to prison," Kimmell writes.

That's why, beyond closure for the Wroes and Bechtels, Amy's case still matters, why Richard Eaton's tip, delivered years before his brother was known to be a killer, still matters. A confession by Eaton may resolve not just Amy's case but numerous other cold-case mysteries swirling in the abyss of the Great Basin.

And yet, even after Eaton's conviction, Steve Bechtel remained the prime "person of interest" in Amy's disappearance. In July 2007, the 10-year anniversary of her disappearance, Roger Rizor, the detective who succeeded Dave King on the case, commented on the cold case to the *Billings Gazette.* "In my mind there is only one person that I want to talk to, only one person who has refused to talk to law enforcement," he said, "and that's her husband."

That thinking didn't begin to change until 2010, when Detective Sergeant Zerga's supervisor dropped Amy's cold-case file on his desk, asking him to see if something would jump out at him. That something was a note about Richard Eaton's tip. It was enough for Zerga to put other cases on hold in order to travel with an FBI agent to Colorado to try to interview a madman's brother, and to Wyoming's death row to interview the madman himself.

"Dale's brother and sister-in-law are absolutely convinced he was in the area at the time," Zerga says about his summer 2012 meeting with them. "I told his brother that's not a place to camp. The area is, like the name has it, a gulch—there are more picturesque camping spots close by." But Richard Eaton described in detail the beaver ponds and a fire wheel and other specific geographical details of the area. "To me, once Richard said Dale was there when she went missing—and he has those capabilities—immediately that went up on top."

But Dale refused to speak with Zerga. And with the death penalty no longer hanging over Eaton's head, Zerga doesn't have any bargaining leverage.

When I met with Nels Wroe, he brought up the subject before I could ask. "Are you familiar with Dale Eaton?" he asked me. "There are some things like that that have bubbled up. If it was to be a random occurrence, or some high-probability random occurrence that may have happened, Dale Eaton is one. But even though there's no real compelling evidence at all that he may have anything to do with it, the circumstances that surround him, where he was, the way he operated, it certainly raises him as a high level of interest, maybe. What hasn't changed, which drives me crazy, is Steve's lack of involvement, and lack of cooperation."

I asked JoAnne Wroe, Amy's mother, in an email, if the new focus on Eaton has affected her life. "Though I am constantly aware that he may be responsible for Amy's disappearance," she writes, "it's very difficult to allow my mind to dwell on this, knowing what he has done to his victims. Not knowing what has happened to Amy or who is responsible is constantly in my thoughts, which makes me very frustrated and angry. It has taken me a long time to learn to live with this and there are days when it overwhelms me."

Periodically, cadaver dogs have been brought in from as far away as Montana. The dogs are so deft they will run straight across wildlife carcasses; they're looking for human carcasses and know the difference. This happened a couple of years ago when they followed a scent down Burnt Gulch and stopped at a depression. "We were pretty stoked when we found that sunken bog," Zerga says. "We thought it was what we'd been looking for for a long time." They sifted through every ounce of dirt in the hole and found only a single bread tie.

Zerga hasn't officially ruled out Steve as a suspect. But he talks about Steve, who now runs a gym just a couple of blocks from Zerga's office, in tones that imply respect, as if he were talking about a friend. Still, there are elements in the case that puzzle the detective. The fact that they had no log showing that Steve phoned the hospital when he said he did. A youth camp minister's account of seeing a vehicle that matches the description of Steve's truck being parked by itself on July 24 in the spot where Amy's car was found.

"The thing with Steve, and the shape he was in," Zerga says, "is he could run a marathon in three and a half hours. He had that type of capability. He coulda *run* back to Lander." Though it has to be in a list of scenarios, Zerga doesn't buy it. "To me, why would he wait until she was running? It would be so much easier in the house.

"I would really like to rule Steve out," Zerga says. "My only way is to sit down with Steve. *You know what, let's do the polygraph. You'll be able to choose who's gonna do the polygraph. You'll know the questions before they're asked. And they're not gonna be questions like, 'Did you kill your wife?' They'll be questions like, 'Is it true the last time you saw your wife, alive, was the morning you woke up and went to Dubois?'"*

I point out there's not an attorney in the West who would advise a client to take the test, and Zerga agrees. "That's exactly what attorneys do—the first thing they do is say, 'Don't take the polygraph.' To me, I can understand it in a sense. But the way polygraphs are, if you really wanted to rule yourself out, you'd take one."

"This is a whole different generation," Steve, now 46, says. I meet him at Elemental Performance and Fitness, his Lander gym, where he jokes with clients and checks in with his wife, Ellen. Steve—rarely seen without a baseball cap—has short gray blond hair and the modesty and forearms of Peter Parker. Now he's taking me for a tour of his world in '97. We drive to Lucky Lane—Climbers' Row—in his 2006 Toyota Tundra pickup; there are kids' car seats in the back. He shows me the garage, where he and friends ran the recovery effort. "After the initial search shut down," he says, "as we started realizing we weren't just looking out in the woods for her, we moved to a nationwide search the best we could."

According to Detective Zerga, authorities had been to Lucky Lane with a search warrant within the last five years. "We've actually done luminol searches with the FBI in that building," Zerga told me. "We brought in cadaver dogs. And luminol picks up any type of blood splatter, whether they paint over it or whatever." The dogs found nothing and the luminol tests came out negative. Zerga even followed up on a rumor that Steve had buried Amy below the driveway of their would-be new home at 965 McDougal Drive before the concrete had set; he found nothing there either.

"I'm impressed with him," Steve says of Zerga, "because he's taking, for all intents and purposes, this cold case and he's really working on it. He got handed this really badly put-together case. Looking back on King now, he had drug problems, problems telling the truth. So what's really fascinating and really sad was they were so cycloptically focused on '*Let's see if we can nail the husband,*' that they missed a lot."

Steve estimates he hasn't talked to his attorney, Kent Spence, in 10 years. Spence is the son of the buckskin-wearing Wyoming native Gerry Spence, 87, who gained fame defending high-profile clients like whistleblower Karen Silkwood, Randy Weaver of Ruby Ridge standoff fame, and Earth First! eco-radical Dave Foreman. Many thought Kent Spence was suspiciously high-powered. "He pro-bonoed I don't even know how many hours to us," says Steve. "Just hiring those guys was controversial. But imagine having heart surgery and saying, '*Well, I'll just get a crappy doctor.*'"

Steve drives at a contemplative mosey. "Living is so fascinating. I have these two little kids and more than anything in my life, those two are what I was born for, to raise those kids. It means everything to you. And the thing that's a really profound challenge emotionally for me is knowing that those two kids never would have existed if I would have been able to keep hold of Amy. You look through history and these tragedies happened in order for wonderful things to happen."

There's a tendency to talk about Amy-the-victim rather than Amy-the-person, especially when you're badgered by law enforcement and writers, but it's clear Steve thinks about Amy often. "It breaks your heart," Steve says. "She was so cool, Jon. Her greatest fault was that she was so friendly she was always taken advantage of. '*I'll take your shift.*' '*I'll watch your dog.*' It just makes you so sad."

We drive up the canyon on the now-paved Loop Road. I haven't been here since the awareness race.

"You could take the strongest woman—a Division I athlete— and the average guy is gonna be able to overpower her," Steve continues. "And a man will be able to sprint faster and he's gonna have this capability of overpowering this woman. There's a fantasy of knowing self-defense moves or that an athletic woman, a runner especially, is going to be able to outrun a guy. In practice that doesn't occur, I don't think." This gender philosophy may fit with some of the poetry and lyrics that raised eyebrows with investigators and members of the Wroe family in the early weeks of the investigation. (Due to the ongoing investigation, Zerga wouldn't let me see Steve's journals.) Steve tells me he still regrets bringing Jonz to Dubois with him the day Amy disappeared, since she most likely would have taken the dog on her run.

I ask him about Nels Wroe, his former brother-in-law. "He and I haven't talked in more than 15 years." Steve talks about being interviewed by the FBI. "What happened with these guys was that they decided what they wanted the answer to be and then tried to build the story around it."

In 2002 Steve and his father, Tom, went to the sheriff's department in neighboring Natrona County when the Eaton theory wasn't taken seriously in Fremont County after news of the Lil Miss murder broke. They wanted to see if any evidence taken from Eaton's property belonged to Amy. "Maybe there's a watch or a shoe or something we might recognize," Steve says. But the Natrona officials wouldn't let them see anything, claiming that the Fremont County sheriff had already looked everything over.

"It was funny," Steve says. "I got home from climbing, it's just a normal day, get unpacked, feed the dog or whatever, then I start wondering, *Where is she?* Make some calls, drive around a little bit. It gets to be like 8:00 p.m., 9:00 p.m., 10:00 p.m., that incredible anxiety builds up. You're just worried. I hope she didn't break her ankle, I hope she didn't run out of gas, those normal things where you're like, *This sucks.* But you're not going, *I hope my wife wasn't grabbed by some psychopathic serial killer.*"

The pavement ends and we hit a mixture of frozen mud and snow. We soon come to a branch in the road. "Right here," he says. "Her car was parked right in there." Steve narrates the night she disappeared.

"It's one or so in the morning, find the car, get here. I brought sleeping bags and a cookstove and food—first-aid kit—we gotta find her. Todd and Amy had been driving and found the car. They called. We raced up here. You get here—this was a big error—we're looking for a missing runner. Everybody was crawling through that car. Knowing what we know now we should have cordoned the thing off—fingerprints. It's like the classic cluster of stupid crap."

I ask him if he'll take the polygraph to relieve Zerga of all doubt. "The polygraph is like one of those monkey traps," he says. "Anybody who needs me to take that test—I don't need them in my life." He holds the relaxed confidence of an athlete, even while talking about a painful past. "I don't need people to be looking at Eaton," he says. "I don't mind being a suspect, but to me everyone else is a suspect."

Lizard Head, the mountain, looms in the east as we head back toward Lander. "Running is this beautiful thing for people—it's the thing they *get* to do," Steve says. "You have all these things you *have* to do, then once a day you *get* to go running. You don't want that to be compromised." He seems to understand that people want answers because they can't accept that something as simple and pure as running could end in terrible tragedy. "I think that's the thing: you don't want to be afraid."

We pass underneath the massive dolomite that lines Sinks Canyon. "My wife will go running alone," Steve says. "*My wife.* She knows as well as anybody the story of Amy."

JULY 24, 1997, MORNING *The day is filled with possibility. Steve is off from his part-time job at Wild Iris, and Amy has her shift at the fitness center before she is off too. The morning sunshine tugs at both of them to get outdoors.*

Steve's plan is to go scout some dolomite bands with Sam Lightner in the mountains above Dubois. It's grizzly country, so he's taking guns, bear spray —and Jonz.

Amy is going to take care of some errands, including scouting the course for her 10K in September. Wow, is it only two months away? And she still needs to design the fliers, plan for the road closure, measure the course . . .

She sits down to make her list. The last thing she writes is run. *Amy would never check it off.*

Why not?

If detective Zerga finds out, by way of an Eaton confession, we may also learn why Naomi Lee Kidder never came home. Why Belynda Mae Grantham never came home. Why Janelle Johnson never came home. Why perhaps at least nine other young women never came home. The question persists, obscured in a Great Basin haze.

Why didn't the runner come home?

WRIGHT THOMPSON

The Secret History of Tiger Woods

FROM ESPN: THE MAGAZINE

Act I

TEN YEARS AGO, Tiger Woods sat in his boyhood home across
from his father's body, waiting on the men from the funeral home
to arrive and carry Earl away. It was around three in the morning. Outside this bedroom in Cypress, California, the mechanism
of burial and good-bye sputtered into action, while inside, Tiger
and his half-sister, Royce, floated in those gauzy first hours after a
death, when a loved one isn't there but doesn't quite seem gone
either. About an hour earlier, Earl had taken two or three final
breaths that sounded different from the ones that came before. Tiger got the call and came straight to Cypress, passing the Navy golf
course where he learned to play, turning finally onto Teakwood
Street. His dad never sold the house because he liked the easily
accessible nostalgia. If Earl wanted, he could go see the Obi-Wan
Kenobi poster still hanging on Tiger's closet door, or find an old
Nintendo or Lego Star Destroyer. Earl died three steps from his
son's old room.

Royce says she sat with her father on the bed, rubbing his back,
like she'd done the last few hours as he faded.

"You're waiting for him to wake up?" Tiger asked.

"Yes," Royce said.

"I am too."

Three days later, on May 6, 2006, the family gathered at a private
air terminal in Anaheim to take Earl's remains back to Manhattan,
Kansas, where he grew up. Tiger's mom, Tida, and his wife, Elin,

sat together in the Gulfstream IV, facing each other, according to Royce. Elin did college homework, which she often did during any free moment, in airplanes or even on fishing trips, working toward her degree in psychology. Tiger's half-siblings came along; Royce and Earl Jr. sat at a table, and Kevin sat across from them on a couch. There were six passengers total, and Tiger plopped down in his usual seat, in the front left of the plane. He put the urn holding his father's remains directly across from him—Royce made a joke about "strapping Dad in"—and when the pilot pushed the throttles forward to lift off, Royce said, Tiger stretched out his legs to hold the urn in place with his feet.

The flight took two hours and 20 minutes. His siblings tried to talk about the old days. Kevin retold a favorite about a camping trip with a 10- or 11-year-old Tiger, in a forest of tall trees: While walking to use the bathroom, Tiger had stopped and peered high into the branches.

"What are you looking at?" Kevin had asked him.

"Ewoks," Tiger said.

Sitting in the plane, Tiger didn't say much. He and his siblings landed and drove to the Sunset Cemetery, a mile southwest of K-State's campus, past the zoo and a high school and a cannon dedicated to the memory of dead Union soldiers. Earl, a former Green Beret and Vietnam combat veteran, would have liked that. The graveyard was cool in the shade, the hills rolling from the street toward a gully. Woodpeckers hammered away in the trees. The family gathered around a hole in the ground, between Earl's parents, Miles and Maude Woods. Two cedars and five pines rose into the air. Tiger stayed strong, comforting his mother, and Earl Jr. watched him, impressed. They buried the ashes and left.

After a brief stop at the house where Earl grew up—strangers owned it, so the Woods family stood in the front yard and told a few stories, and this being rural Kansas, the neighbors didn't interrupt or ask for autographs—everyone headed back to the airport. Seventy-seven minutes after touching down in Kansas, Tiger took off again for Orange County.

Consider him in that moment, 30 years old, the greatest golfer in the world, winner of 10 major championships and counting, confident that the dreams he and his father conceived on Teakwood Street would eventually all come true. His pilot climbed above the clouds. The return trip took 40 minutes longer, exactly three hours, and nobody said much, feeling heavy, processing the idea that they'd left Earl behind in the Kansas dirt. Tiger Woods sat in his usual place, facing forward, the seat across from him empty now.

Almost 10 years later, on the far western end of an island in the Bahamas, Tiger Woods is where he feels most comfortable: hidden behind multiple layers of security and exclusivity, standing with two or three friends in the dark of a marina. It's early December, 28 days before his 40th birthday. His annual tournament begins at a nearby course soon. Both his boats float a few dozen yards away, in two of the first three slips: the 155-foot yacht named *Privacy*, alongside the smaller, sleeker diving boat he named *Solitude*. On the main deck of the big boat, there's a basket of sunscreen, a pile of rolled towels, and a white orchid. The marina around them couldn't be more private, without a coffee shop or store, not even showing up on the navigational charts in some maritime GPS systems. (Woods's camp declined to comment for this story.)

Docking in a luxury marina is about the only place to catch a random glimpse of Tiger, who moves through the world in a cocoon of his own creation. When he bought his plane, he blocked the tail number from tracking websites: it ends in QS, the standard code for Net-Jets. Many athletes, by contrast, have some sort of vanity registration, and some even have custom paint jobs; Michael Jordan's plane is detailed in North Carolina blue, and his tail number is N236MJ—the "6" is for his titles. Jack Nicklaus flies around in N1JN nicknamed Air Bear. Sitting on a tarmac, Tiger's plane looks like it belongs to an anonymous business traveler, nothing giving away its famous owner. He comes and goes quietly.

Tonight the running lights glowing just offshore belong to Steven Spielberg's *The Seven Seas*. Marina staff members come across a lot of celebrities, and when they gather away from work, they tell stories, about how Johnny Depp is down-to-earth or how Tiger isn't a diva but is just, well, he's just really weird. Once, when his dog left a tennis ball in the harbormaster's office, Tiger called down and asked someone to "secure" the ball until a crew member could retrieve it, and the staff still laugh and roll their eyes about it. They don't know that he often uses military lingo, a small window into how deep he's gotten into that world, words like "secure" and "downrange" and even, in text messages to his friend Michael Jordan, "roger that."

Standing at the southwest corner of the marina, Tiger and his group make plans for later, and then he walks off down the road. There's no entourage or Team Tiger, no agent or handlers or managers, just a middle-aged man alone, coming to terms with himself and his future, which will hold far more quiet marinas in the years ahead than packed fairways. Not long ago, he asked Jordan a simple yet heavy question: *How did you know when it was time to walk away?*

Tiger hasn't hit a golf ball in about two months. He can't really run; not long ago, he told *Time* magazine, he fell down in his backyard without a cell phone and had to just lie there until his daughter happened to find him. Tiger sent her to get help. He's had two back operations in the past three months. Yesterday at a news conference, he said for the first time in public that his golf career might be over.

A reporter asked what he did for exercise.

"I walk," he said.

And?

He smiled.

"I walk and I walk some more."

He paused, and asked himself a question. "Where is the light at the end of the tunnel?"

"I don't know. I think pretty much everything beyond this will be gravy."

His friends started hearing these admissions about a month ago. His college roommate Notah Begay texted him around Halloween. Tiger loves Halloween. He's a big kid in many ways. When he lived in Orlando, a former neighbor said, he liked to ride on a skateboard behind a golf cart in the gated country club he called home. He loves the Transformers and comic-book heroes; in the past, he's checked into hotels under the name Logan Howlett, which is Wolverine's human name in *X-Men*. When he booked his free-diving lessons in Grand Cayman, instructor Kirk Krack recalled, he reserved his spot under the name Eric Cartman. So of course he loves Halloween, and when Notah asked about his costume, Tiger wrote back.

"I'm going as a golfer known as Tiger Woods."

Sitting at a steakhouse in the Bahamas one night, Begay is quiet for a moment. He's here for the Golf Channel, forced years ago by his own bad back to make the same admissions that Tiger is making now: the dreams he dreamed as a boy are ending. They met as children—Tiger was nine and Notah was 12—playing youth golf in California. They saw each other, perhaps the only nonwhite, nonwealthy people around, and Notah walked up to Tiger and told him, "You'll never be alone again." They've been friends ever since, passing together through each stage of life. A few weeks ago, he and Tiger were hanging out at the house in Jupiter when Woods realized they needed to make a carpool run and get his kids at school. They drove over and parked in line with the other parents, about 30 minutes early, and to kill the time, they laughed and talked about Stanford. "Tiger and I do a lot of looking back," Begay says. "He loves to talk about college."

Tiger told stories about how his daughter likes soccer and is already a prankster, and Begay said how his girl loves gymnastics and drawing, and then they looked at each other and just started laughing: *Can you believe we are sitting in a carpool line?* Tiger is facing the reckoning that all young and powerful men face, the end of that youth and power, and a future spent figuring out how those things might be mourned and possibly replaced. This final comeback, if he ever gets healthy, will be his last.

"He knows," Begay says.

The decade separating the cemetery in Kansas and the marina in the Bahamas has seen Tiger lose many of the things most important to him, and the more time passes, the more it's clear he left some essential part of himself there in the ground between Miles and Maude Woods. How did all he'd built come undone so quickly and so completely? That's the question that will shadow him for the rest of his life. The answer is complicated and layered. He fell victim to many things, some well known and others deeply private: grief, loneliness, desire, freedom, and his fixation with his father's profession, the military. These forces started working in Tiger's life almost as soon as his G-IV landed back in Orange County after he buried his father's ashes. The forces kept working until finally his wife found text messages from Rachel Uchitel on his phone and he ran his Cadillac Escalade into a fire hydrant. (That car, incidentally, is owned by a man in rural Arkansas who bought it used from a local dealer, neither of whom knew its secret history.)

After Thanksgiving in 2009, his life split open in the most public and embarrassing way—can you imagine having to talk about your sex life in a news conference with your mom in the front row? —but that car crash wasn't the beginning of his unraveling. In an odd way, it was the end. Everything he's endured these past seven years, including admitting that his golf career might be finished, is a consequence of decisions he made in the three years after he lost Earl. He'd been hurtling toward that fire hydrant for a long time. On some level, he even understood what was happening to him, or at least was invested in understanding. There was a book in his car the night of the wreck, and it ended up on the floorboard, covered in shards of glass. Its title was *Get a Grip on Physics*.

The topic fascinated Woods. He'd long struggled to sleep, and when he wasn't texting or playing video games, he'd read, often military books about lone men facing impossible odds, such as *Roberts Ridge* or *Lone Survivor,* or books about theoretical physics and cosmology. The intro to *Get a Grip* laid out the basic rules of early science, from Newton and Galileo, focused on the concepts of friction and gravity. These had long interested him. Five-year-old Tiger once made a drawing that showed stickmen swinging different clubs, with the clubface sketched, as well as the flight path of the ball, including distance and apex.

That drawing is a window into something Woods himself perhaps still can't articulate; even at that age, he was curious enough to be thinking about physics. From the beginning, his golf talent has seemed to be an expression of his genius, not the genius itself. He is a remarkable person, and not because he once won 14 important golf tournaments, but because he thinks about how he came to occupy his particular space in the world. "He certainly had his mind open to big questions, such as who he was, or who anyone was," says a close friend who requested anonymity, "and had his mind open to the idea that sometimes the question is the answer." Six pages into *Get a Grip*, author John Gribbin sums up a truth governing both the world and the relationship between Earl and Tiger Woods: "There was a fundamental law of nature which said that, left to their own devices, things move in circles."

*

There's always a layer of mystery between fathers and sons, even those as close as Tiger and Earl Woods. They lived such different lives. Earl joined the Green Berets because he saw them as the only place a black man could be treated fairly, and when he retired, he played golf day after day. (Before his son, Earl had the lowest handicap at the Navy golf course near their home, despite not picking up a club until he was 42.) There were things Tiger could never know about combat, just as Earl could never really understand the cost of his son's fame.

"I know exactly how you feel," Earl said once.

"No, Dad, you don't," Tiger replied.

He grew up without siblings or many friends. Tiger and Earl did everything together, hitting balls into a net out in the garage, or spending hours at the golf course, and when they'd finish, Earl would order a rum and Diet Coke, and Tiger would get a Coke with cherries, and they'd sit and nurse their drinks like two old men. The golf pro at the Navy course, Joe Grohman, worried that Tiger didn't have friends his own age until high school. His friends were Earl and Earl's old military buddies. That's who he played golf with, retired old soldiers and sailors and marines, with the occasional active-duty guy stationed near Los Angeles. Fighter jets took off and landed at the airstrip parallel to the 17th and 18th fairways. Tiger heard the stories and saw the deep love even strangers felt for each other. His entire childhood revolved around these men and their code.

Tiger and Earl held strong opinions about how things should work and nursed deep stubborn streaks, so they often butted heads. The most serious rift between them, which festered for years, centered on Earl's love for women. Tiger hated that his dad cheated on his mom and cried to his high school girlfriend about it. His parents never divorced but moved into their own houses, and the only reason they still needed to communicate at all was their son's rising golf career; like many overachieving kids in a broken home, Tiger found early on that his talent could help create the family he wanted. He could mend the broken places inside all of them. It's also clear that Tiger grew up first emulating his dad and then trying to be better than Earl. All sons, whether they love or hate their fathers, or some combination of both, want to cleanse themselves of any inherited weakness, shaking free from the past. This is certainly true for Tiger, whose father seems to evoke conflicting emotions: the best and worst things that have happened in his life happened because of Earl.

As Tiger got famous, Earl traveled the world with him. The definitive book about Tiger and Earl, Tom Callahan's *His Father's Son*, details the women in Earl's orbit. There was a "cook" at the 2001 Open Championship, and when Callahan said she must be a good cook, Earl grinned and said, "She sure knows how to keep that potato chip bowl filled up." At another event in South Africa, a stream of escorts made their way to Earl's room. Callahan reports that near the end of Earl's life, Tiger and Earl stopped talking for a while. "Tiger's mad at me," he told the author, and implied that he'd gotten into some sort of woman trouble that his son paid to make go away. Ultimately, Callahan wrote, Tida is the one who persuaded Tiger to make peace, telling her son that he'd regret it if Earl died before he made things right.

"He's going to be gone and you're going to be sorry," she told him.

They fixed the rift, perhaps because as Tiger's circle of trust tightened to include virtually no one, he still knew he could talk to his dad about anything, even if he didn't particularly like Earl at the time. Earl never judged. They were father and son, and teacher and student, best friends and running buddies and together, one complete person.

Just after the 2004 Masters, Tiger and his dad took a trip together to Fort Bragg, where Earl had been stationed with the Green Berets. A group of Earl's old military buddies came along, while Tiger got the VIP tour, running with the 82nd Airborne and tandem-jumping with the Golden Knights, the Army's parachute team. The man assigned to take Tiger out of the plane was a soldier named Billy Van Soelen, who explained the difference between broad daylight at Fort Bragg and pitch-black combat situations. "Your dad was doing tactical jumps," he said, nodding around at the controlled environment. "This is Hollywood."

Van Soelen strapped Tiger to himself and then the two flung themselves out into space, smooth with no bobble. Tiger grinned the whole way down.

Earl was waiting in the drop zone, Van Soelen says, and he gave Tiger a big hug.

"Now you understand my world," he told his son.

Earl needed an oxygen tank during that trip. He'd been dying slowly for years and regretted that he wouldn't live to see the end of Tiger's journey. His second heart attack happened in Tulsa, Oklahoma, during Tiger's initial year on tour, and by the winter of 2005, a year and a half after Fort Bragg, it was clear to everyone that Earl didn't have much time. Now consider Tiger Woods again, in this moment the best golfer in the world, taking his first break ever—24 days without touching a club, the most since he was a boy—watching his father die. He spent a lot of that break on Teakwood Street, struggling to sleep, three days passing before he finally drifted off on the floor. On December 25, his dad woke up and threw a shoe at a sleeping Tiger.

When Tiger groggily looked up, Earl said, "Merry Christmas."

That vacation ended—they both knew Earl was dying and Tiger made his peace with it—and Woods planned to open his season at the 2006 Buick Invitational near San Diego. But three days before his first competitive round of the year, Tiger arranged for a VIP tour of the Coronado BUD/S compound (Basic Underwater Demolition/SEAL training), where recruits are turned into SEALs. Most classes start with about 200 students, and if 30 graduate, that's a great percentage. It's the most difficult military training in the world.

When he arrived, Tiger spoke to Class 259, there waiting for First Phase to begin, and told them something he'd never said in public: he wanted to be a SEAL when he was young. The class loved Tiger's advice about mental preparation and focus, while the instructors rolled their eyes when Tiger said he would have been one of them were it not for golf. They've seen Olympic medalists and Division I football players quit, unable to stand the pain. A top-ranked triathlete washed out.

The tour visited Special Boat Team-12 and SEAL Team 7. During one stop, a SEAL named Thom Shea helped conduct a weapons demonstration, with seven or eight guns spread out in front of him, from the Sig Sauer pistol through the entire sniper suite of weapons. Three years later, Shea would earn a Silver Star leading a team into battle in Afghanistan. Tiger stood on one side of the table, his arms crossed, a pair of Oakley sunglasses resting on the back of his knit cap. Shea says Tiger remained very quiet, taking in as much as he could, only turning on his famous smile when someone asked for a picture or an autograph. After the table show, Shea walked Tiger to another building for the next part of this tour.

The two men talked on the way, and even a decade later, Shea remembers the conversation, because of everything that would happen later. Tiger wanted to know how SEALs kept their home life together despite the strain of constant travel and long separations. Shea told him that balance was the only thing that worked. He says Tiger asked how they kept this up, year after year of stress, the long slog always outlasting the romance of a job title. "It's a life," Shea remembers saying. "You just do it. You keep practicing."

The following Sunday, Tiger Woods won the Buick Invitational in a playoff.

Three months later, Earl died and everything started to fall apart.

Act II

Twenty-five days after he buried his father and 15 before the 2006 U.S. Open, Tiger went back to visit the Navy SEALs, this time to a hidden mountain training facility east of San Diego. The place is known as La Posta, and it's located on a barren stretch of winding road near the Mexican border. Everything is a shade of muted tan and green, like Afghanistan, with boulders the size of cars along the highway.

This time, Tiger came to do more than watch.

He tried the SR-25 sniper rifle and the SEALs' pistol of choice, the Sig Sauer P226. One of the instructors was Petty Officer 1st Class John Brown, whose father also served as a Green Beret in Vietnam. Brown pulled Tiger aside. The sun was shining, a nice day, and the two men talked, standing on the northeast corner of a shooting facility.

"Why are you here?" Brown remembers asking.

"My dad," Tiger said, explaining that Earl had told him he'd either end up being a golfer or a special operations soldier. "My dad told me I had two paths to choose from."

Brown says Tiger seemed to genuinely want to know about their way of life. Tiger asked questions about Brown's family and they figured out that Brown's wife and Tiger shared the same birthday. Tiger told him not to ever try to match Michael Jordan drink for drink. They talked about Earl, and Brown felt like Tiger wanted "safe harbor" from his grief, a way to purge some of it even, to prove something to himself, or maybe prove something to the spirit of Earl, whose special ops career never approached the daring of a SEAL team.

"I definitely think he was searching for something," Brown says. "Most people have to live with their regrets. But he got to experience a taste of what might have been."

The instructors gave Tiger camo pants and a brown T-shirt. He carried an M4 assault rifle and strapped a pistol to his right leg. On a strip of white tape above his right hip pocket, someone wrote "TIGER." SEAL Ben Marshall (his name has been changed for this story because he remains on active duty) took Tiger to the Kill House, the high-stress combat simulator where SEALs practice clearing rooms and rescuing hostages. Marshall is a veteran of many combat deployments and was with Tiger making sure he didn't get too hurt. The instructors ran the golfer through the house over and over, lighting him up with Simunition, high-powered paint rounds that leave big, painful bruises. "It was so much fun to hit him," Marshall says. "He looked like a deer in the headlights. I was spraying him up like it was nothing."

The instructors set up targets, some of terrorists holding weapons and others of innocent civilians. Under fire and stress, Tiger needed to decide who should die and who should live. During one trip through the Kill House, the guys switched out a target of someone with a gun for one of a photographer, and when Tiger came through the door, he killed the person with the camera, according to two witnesses. The SEALs asked why he'd shot a civilian.

First Tiger apologized for his mistake.

Then he made a joke about hating photographers.

Eventually, Woods learned how to clear a room, working corners and figuring out lanes of fire, doing something only a handful of civilians are ever allowed to do: run through mock gun battles with actual Navy SEALs. "He can move through the house," says Ed Hiner, a retired SEAL who helped oversee training during the time and wrote a book called *First, Fast, Fearless*. "He's not freaking out. You escalate it. You start shooting and then you start blowing s— up. A lot of people freak out. It's too loud, it's too crazy. He did well."

At one point, Marshall put him through a combat stress shooting course, making him carry a 30-pound ammunition box, do overhead presses with it, do push-ups and run up a hill, with shooting mixed in. Tiger struggled with slowing his heart rate down enough to hit the targets, but he attacked the course.

"He went all out," Marshall said. "He just f—ing went all out."

Marshall got his golf clubs at one point and asked Tiger to sign his TaylorMade bag. Tiger refused, sheepishly, saying he couldn't sign a competing brand. So Marshall challenged him to a driving contest for the signature. Both Marshall and Brown confirmed what happened next: Tiger grinned and agreed. Some other guys gathered around a raised area overlooking the shooting range. Marshall went first and hit a solid drive, around 260 or 270 yards. Tiger looked at him and teed up a ball, gripping the TaylorMade driver.

Then he got down on his knees.

He swung the club like a baseball bat and crushed one out past Marshall's drive. Tiger started laughing, and then all the SEALs started laughing, and eventually Marshall was laughing too.

"Well, I can just shoot you now and you can die," Marshall joked, "or you can run and die tired."

The military men and their bravado sent Tiger back in time to the Navy golf course with Earl and those salty retired soldiers and sailors. He missed his dad, of course, but he also missed the idea of Earl, which was as important as the man himself. Sometimes his dad traveled to tournaments and never visited the course, staying put at a hotel or rented house in case Tiger needed him. They could talk about anything, from the big questions of life, like Tiger's completely earnest belief in ghosts, to simple things a man should know, like how to order spacers of water between beers to keep from getting so drunk. (That last bit came about after a bad night at a Stanford fraternity party.) Without Earl, Tiger felt adrift and lonely. He threw himself back into his circus of a life, moving from place to place. And in the months after the funeral, the extramarital affairs either began or intensified. That summer of 2006, he met at least two of the mistresses who'd eventually hit the tabloids.

To be clear, he'd always talked a good game about women, long before he married Elin Nordegren in 2004. In 1999, in the quiet Oregon woods near the Deschutes River with Mark O'Meara and one of the best steelhead guides in the world, Tiger held court about the perks of being a professional athlete. "I'm walking down

the trail with him and he's bragging about his sexual conquests,"
says guide Amy Hazel. "And this is when everybody thought he was
the golden boy."

He told just filthy stories that Hazel wouldn't repeat, but even
with the boasts and dirty jokes, she saw him as more of a big kid
than a playboy. "Nerdy and socially awkward" are her words, and
he seemed happiest standing in the river riffing lines from the
Dalai Lama scene in *Caddyshack.*

The sexual bravado hid his awkwardness around women. One
night he went to a club in New York with Derek Jeter and Michael
Jordan. Jeter and Jordan circulated, talking with ease to one beautiful woman after another. (Both declined to comment about the
episode.) At one point, Tiger walked up to them and asked the
question that lives in the heart of every junior high boy and nearly
every grown man too.

"What do you do to talk to girls?"

Jeter and Jordan looked at each other, then back at Tiger, sort
of stunned.

Go tell 'em you're Tiger Woods, they said.

If Tiger was looking for something, it was seemingly lots of different things, finding pieces in a rotating cast of people. He and
Rachel Uchitel bonded over their mutual grief. His fresh wounds
from losing Earl helped him understand her scars from her father's cocaine overdose when she was 15, and her fiancé's death
in the World Trade Center on September 11. The broken parts of
themselves fit together, according to her best friend, Tim Bitici.
Sometimes Rachel stayed with Tiger for days, Bitici says. Nobody
ever seemed to ask Tiger where he was or what he was doing. Bitici
went with Rachel down to Orlando to visit Tiger, who put them up
in a condo near his house. When he came over, he walked in and
closed all the blinds. Then he sat between Tim and Rachel on the
couch and they all watched *Chelsea Lately.*

"This makes me so happy," Tiger said, according to Bitici.

Many of these relationships had that odd domestic quality,
which got mostly ignored in favor of the tabloid splash of three-
somes. Tiger once met Jaimee Grubbs in a hotel room, she told
a magazine, and instead of getting right down to business, they
watched a Tom Hanks movie and cuddled. Cori Rist remembered
breakfast in bed. "It was very normal and traditional in a sense,"

she says. "He was trying to push that whole image and lifestyle away just to have something real. Even if it's just for a night."

Many times, he couldn't sleep.

Insomnia plagued him, and he'd end up awake for days. Bitici says that Tiger asked Rachel to meet him when he'd gone too long without sleep. Only after she arrived could he nod off. Bitici thinks Tiger just wanted a witness to his life. Not the famous life people saw from outside but the real one, where he kept the few things that belonged only to him. This wasn't a series of one-night stands but something more complex and strange. He called women constantly, war-dialing until they picked up, sometimes just to narrate simple everyday activities. When they didn't answer, he called their friends. Sometimes he talked to them about Earl and his childhood.

We never see the past coming up behind because shaping the future takes so much effort. That's one of those lessons everyone must learn for themselves, including Tiger Woods. He juggled a harem of women at once, looking for something he couldn't find, while he made more and more time for his obsession with the military, and he either ignored or did not notice the repeating patterns from Earl's life. "Mirror, mirror on the wall, we grow up like our daddy after all," says Paul Fregia, first director of the Tiger Woods Foundation. "In some respects, he became what he loathed about his father."

The military trips continued through 2006 into 2007, kept almost completely a secret. At home, Tiger read books on SEALs and watched the documentary about BUD/S Class 234 over and over. He played *Call of Duty* for hours straight, so into the fantasy that his friends joked that after Tiger got shot in the game they might find him dead on the couch. When he could, he spent time with real-life operators. Tiger shot guns, learned combat tactics and did free-fall skydiving with active-duty SEALs. During one trip to La Posta, he remembered things they'd told him about their families, asking about wives, things he didn't do in the golf world; Mark O'Meara said Tiger never asks about his kids.

"If Tiger was around other professional athletes, storytelling would always have a nature of one-upmanship," a friend says. "If Tiger was around some sort of active or retired military personnel, he was all ears. He was genuinely interested in what they had to say. Anytime he told a military-related story that he had heard or talked about a tactic he had learned, he had a smile on his face. I can't say that about anything else."

One evening, Brown and two other guys put Tiger in the backseat of a king-cab pickup truck and drove him an hour and a half out into the desert to a training base named Niland, where a SEAL team was doing its final predeployment workup, staging a raid on a mock Afghan village that had been built down in a valley. They stood on a hill looking into the darkness. The SEAL platoon charged toward the position. Flares popped off, trailing into the darkness, and the valley rocked with the deep boom of artillery simulation and the chatter of small-arms fire. In the glow, Tiger looked transfixed. "It was f—ing awesome," Brown says, laughing. "I don't know if we just got a glimpse of him in a different light, but he just seemed incredibly humble, grateful."

His golfing team, particularly swing coach Hank Haney, understood the risk, sending a long email scolding Tiger for putting his career at risk: *You need to get that whole SEALs thing out of your system.* Haney does a lot of benefit work, including some for the special operations community, so stories would later trickle back to him about injuries suffered during training. Caddie Steve Williams thought the 2006 U.S. Open, where Tiger missed his first major cut as a pro, was the first time he'd ever seen Woods not mentally prepared. Tiger talked openly about the grief and loss he felt when he practiced, since that activity was so closely wound together with his memories of his dad.

The moments with the military added some joy to what he has repeatedly called the worst year of his life, and he chose to spend December 30, 2006—his 31st birthday—in San Diego skydiving with SEALs. This was his second skydiving trip; a month earlier, in the middle of a seven-tournament win streak, he'd gotten his free-fall USPA A-license, now able to jump without a tandem. Across the country, in Florida, his reps put a news release on his website, revealing for the first time that Elin was pregnant. Tiger Woods was going to be a father.

Elin came with him to San Diego on his birthday, and they rode south and east of the city, near a land preserve a few miles from Mexico, halfway between Chula Vista and Tecate. The road curved at banked angles, and up ahead a small airport came into view.

Nichols Field is a collection of maybe two dozen buildings. To the east of the property, a cluster of metal huts sat behind red stop signs warning, RESTRICTED AREA. This was Tactical Air Operations, one of the places where the SEALs practice jumps. The main building felt like an inner sanctum: a SEAL flag on the wall and parachute riggings hung from the ceiling. They wore blue-and-white jumpsuits, Tiger and the three or four SEALs. He learned advanced air maneuvers. After each jump, the guys would tell Tiger what to do differently and he'd go off by himself for a bit to visualize the next jump and then go back up in the plane and dive into the air, doing everything they'd said. "The dude's amazing," says Billy Helmers, a SEAL who jumped with him that day. "He can literally think himself through the skydives."

The SEALs put a birthday cake on a table in one of the Tac Air buildings. It had a skydiver decorated on it in icing and read "HAPPY BIRTHDAY, TIGER!" The team guys and their families gathered around and sang "Happy Birthday," and then Tiger leaned in and blew out his candles. Everyone took pictures, and in them Tiger is smiling, and it's not the grin that people know from commercials and news conferences. He looks unwatched and calm.

While he made friends with some of the SEALs, many of their fellow operators didn't know why Tiger wanted to play soldier. It rubbed them the wrong way. Guys saw him doing the fun stuff, shooting guns and jumping out of airplanes, but never the brutal, awful parts of being a SEAL, soaking for hours in hypothermic waters, so covered in sand and grit that the skin simply grinds away. One year during hell week, a BUD/S candidate collapsed, his body temperature below 90 degrees; the man, a former wrestler, would rather have frozen to death than quit.

Was Tiger willing to do that?

"Tiger Woods never got wet and sandy," says former SEAL and current Montana congressman Ryan Zinke, who ran the training facility during the years Tiger came around. The BUD/S instructors didn't like the way Tiger talked about how he'd have been a SEAL if he didn't choose golf. "I just reached out to the guys I know who jumped with him and interacted with him," says a retired SEAL. "Not a single one wants to have any involvement, or have their name mentioned in the press anywhere near his. His interactions with the guys were not always the most stellar, and most were very underwhelmed with him as a man."

Then there's the story of the lunch, which spread throughout the Naval Special Warfare community. Guys still tell it, almost a decade later. Tiger and a group of five or six went to a diner in La Posta. The waitress brought the check and the table went silent, according to two people there that day. Nobody said anything and neither did Tiger, and the other guys sort of looked at one another.

Finally one of the SEALs said, "Separate checks, please."

The waitress walked away.

"We are all baffled," says one SEAL, a veteran of numerous combat deployments. "We are sitting there with Tiger f—ing Woods, who probably makes more than all of us combined in a day. He's shooting our ammo, taking our time. He's a weird f—ing guy. That's weird s—. Something's wrong with you."

They're not wrong, not exactly, but the SEALs are also viewing Tiger through their own preexisting idea of how a superstar should act, so his behavior processes as arrogant and selfish. That reaction has colored Tiger's relationships his entire life: people who meet him for 30 seconds love him, and people who spend several hours with him think he's aloof and weird, while people who hang around long enough to know him end up both loving him and being oddly protective. His truest self is shy, awkward, and basically well intentioned, as unsuited for life in public as he is suited for hitting a ball.

"Frankly, the real Tiger Woods isn't that marketable," a friend says. "There isn't a lot of money to be made off a guy who just wants to be left alone to read a book. Or left alone to play fetch with his dog. Or left alone to play with his kids. Or left alone to lift weights. Or left alone to play a video game. Do you see a trend? Tiger was a natural introvert, and the financial interest for him to be extroverted really drove a wedge in his personality. Being a celebrity changed him and he struggled with that—and he struggled with the fact that he struggled with that."

Tiger uses well-rehearsed set pieces as standard icebreakers—things that get trotted out again and again. Famously, in front of a *GQ* reporter in 1997, he told a joke that ended on a punch line about a black guy taking off a condom. He told the same joke in

2006 to a SEAL at a Navy shooting range and to a woman at Butter, a New York nightclub. Talk to enough people who've met him and it starts to seem like he's doing an impersonation of what he thinks a superstar athlete is supposed to be. Once he bought a Porsche Carrera GT, similar to the one driven by many celebrities, but one of the first times he got behind the wheel, the powerful car got away from him, spinning off into the grass near his house. He took it back to the dealership.

Tiger bought a pair of combat boots. They were black, made by the tactical outfitter Blackhawk, popular with ex–special ops guys who become contractors and mercenaries. The boots were inevitable, in hindsight. You can't insert something as intense as the SEAL culture into the mind of someone like Tiger Woods and not have him chase it down a deep, dark hole. He started doing the timed four-mile run in combat boots, required by everyone who wants to graduate from BUD/S. A friend named Corey Carroll, who refused to comment and whose parents lived near Tiger, did the workouts with him. They'd leave from Carroll's parents' home, heading north, out onto the golf course. The rare sighting was almost too strange to process: Tiger Woods in combat boots, wearing Nike workout pants or long combat-style trousers, depending on the weather, pounding out eight-and-a-half-minute miles, within striking distance of the time needed for BUD/S.

Tiger knew the SEAL physical requirements by heart, easily knocking out the push-ups, pull-ups, and sit-ups. When he couldn't sleep, he'd end up at a nearby Gold's Gym at 3:00 a.m., grinding. One of his favorite workouts was the ladder, or PT pyramid, a popular Navy SEAL exercise: one pull-up, two push-ups, three sit-ups, then two, four, six, up to 10, 20, 30, and back down again.

Soon, the training at La Posta didn't cut it. He found something more intense with Duane Dieter, a man allowed by the Navy to train SEALs in a specialized form of martial arts that he invented. Dieter is a divisive figure in the special operations world, working out of his own training compound on the Maryland shore. His method is called Close Quarters Defense, or CQD, and some students look at him as an almost spiritual guide, like a modern samurai. Others think he's overrated. For Dieter, few things were more important than ancient warrior principles like light and dark energy.

Tiger got introduced by the Navy and learned CQD in Coronado. Hooked, he wanted to go further and ended up making trips to Dieter's compound in Maryland. He'd fly in and stay either at the facility or at the nearby fancy resort, Inn at Perry Cabin by Belmond, according to a source who saw Tiger with Dieter. He'd park outside a nearby Target, sending someone else inside for cheap throwaway clothes that they could ruin with the Simunition. The practice rounds left huge bruises. He did all sorts of weapons training and fighting there, including this drill invented by Dieter: He would stand in a room, hands by his side, wearing a helmet with a protective face shield. A hood would be lowered over the helmet and loud white noise would play. It sounded like an approaching train, the speakers turning on and off at random intervals, lasting 30 seconds, or maybe just five. Then the hood would fly up and there would be a scenario. Maybe two people were talking. Or maybe one was a hostile and the other a hostage. If the people posed no threat, the correct response was to check corners and not draw your weapon. Then the hood would go back down, and there'd be more music, and when it came up, the scenario had changed. Sometimes a guy threw punches, to the body and head, and Tiger would need to free himself and draw his weapon. At first, the instructors went easy, not hitting him as hard as they'd hit a SEAL. Tiger put a stop to that and soon they jumped him as aggressively as everyone else. When the drill finally ended, the room smelled like gunpowder.

An idea began to take hold, a dream, really, one that could destroy the disconnect Tiger felt in his life, completely killing off the character he played in public. Maybe he could just disappear into the shadow world of special operations. He mentioned his plans to people around him, one by one. He pulled over a car at a tournament once and told Steve Williams he wanted to join the Navy. He told Haney he thought it would be cool to go through training. Once, Carroll had to talk him down via text message, according to someone present for the exchange, because Tiger wanted to quit golf and join the Navy. There's only one reason to run four miles in pants and combat boots. This wasn't some proto-training to develop a new gear of mental toughness. "The goal was to make it through BUD/S," says a former friend who knew about the training. "It had nothing to do with golf."

To many people inside Tiger's circle, Jack Nicklaus's record of 18 majors wasn't as important to Tiger as it was to the golfing media and fans. He never mentioned it. Multiple people who've spent significant amounts of time with him say that. When Tiger did talk about it, someone else usually brought it up and he merely responded. The record instead became something to break so he could chase something that truly mattered. He loved the anonymity of wearing a uniform and being part of a team. "It was very, very serious," the friend says. "If he had had a hot two years and broken the record, he would have hung up his clubs and enlisted. No doubt."

Tiger talked about some of these military trips with his friends, including describing skydiving to Michael Jordan, who saw a pattern repeating from his own past. Years before, he'd lost his father, and in his grief, he sought solace doing something his dad loved, quitting the Bulls and riding minor league buses for the Birmingham Barons. "It could be his way of playing baseball," Jordan would say years later. "Soothing his father's interest."

Jordan looked sad as he said this, perhaps feeling the heaviness of it all or even the luck involved. He somehow got through his grief and reclaimed his greatness, while Tiger has tried and failed over and over again.

"Ah, boy," Jordan sighed.

The point of no return came on July 31, 2007, a date that means nothing to the millions of fans who follow Tiger Woods but was the last real shot he had to avoid the coming storm. From the outside, he was closing in, inevitably, on Nicklaus. But inside his world, a year after his dad died, things were falling apart.

On June 18, Tiger became a father. In July, he flew a porn star to Washington, D.C., according to a tabloid, to meet him during his tournament, the AT&T National. He'd already met many of the mistresses who would come forward two years later. According to the *Wall Street Journal,* the summer of 2007 is when the *National Enquirer* contacted his camp to say it had caught him in an affair with a Perkins waitress. Negotiations allegedly began that would kill the tabloid story if Tiger agreed to sit for an interview and cover shoot with *Men's Fitness,* owned by the same parent company as the *Enquirer.* He did. The magazine hit newsstands on June 29.

On July 22, he finished tied for 12th at the Open Championship, and then came home. In the weeks afterward, he'd announce that he'd ruptured his left ACL while jogging in Isleworth. His news release did not mention whether he'd been running in sneakers or combat boots. At the time, he chose to skip surgery and keep playing. Tiger's account might be true, as might the scenario laid out in Haney's book: that he tore the ACL in the Kill House with SEALs. Most likely, they're both right. The knee suffered repeated stresses and injuries, from military drills and elite-level sports training and high-weight, low-rep lifting. A man who saw him doing CQD training says, "It's kind of funny, when you have an injury it almost seems like a magnet for trauma. He almost never had something hit his right knee. It was always his left knee that got kicked, or hit, or shot, or landed on. Always the left knee."

Whatever happened, he didn't take a break. Two days before the tournament in Akron, he was in Ohio. That night, July 31, his agent, Mark Steinberg, had people over to his home near Cleveland, including Tiger. According to both Haney's and Williams's books, Steinberg said the time had come for an intervention over Tiger's military adventures. While Steinberg has a reputation as a bully in the golf world, he cares a great deal about his client and friend. This all must have seemed insane to someone who just wanted to manage a great athlete: secret trips to military facilities, running around a golf course in combat boots, shooting guns, taking punches.

That night after dinner, Steinberg took Tiger into his downstairs office, a room in his finished basement. What they talked about remains private. But this was the moment when Tiger could have connected the dots and seen how out of control things had become. Everyone felt good about the talk. Afterward, Haney wrote, Tiger was different and the military trips became less of a distraction.

That's what they thought.

Consider Tiger Woods once more, tabloids snapping grainy long-distance photos, his marriage suddenly in danger and with it the normalcy he lacked everywhere else, his body taking a terrible beating from SEAL training and aggressive weightlifting, a year after losing his father, adrift and yet *still* dominating all the other golfers in the world. They never were his greatest opponent, which was and always will be a combination of himself and all those expectations he never could control. Tiger won Akron, then won his

13th career major the following week at the PGA Championship in Tulsa, and then, 15 hours after getting home from the tournament, he packed up and flew off again to do CQD training with Dieter. Steinberg's warning was just 13 days old.

Everything else might as well have been chiseled in stone on the day he was born. The two knee surgeries in Park City, Utah, a year later. The three back surgeries. The Thanksgiving night he took an Ambien and forgot to erase his text messages, and how that enormous storm started small, with Elin calling numbers in his phone, confronting the people on the other end, including Uchitel's friend Tim Bitici, who was in Vermont with his family when his phone rang. The horrors big and small that followed. The butcher paper taped up over the windows to block the paparazzi. The sheet his crew hung over the name of his yacht. The Internet comments he read while driving to Augusta National before the 2010 Masters, obsessed over what people thought. The questions from his kids about why Mommy and Daddy don't live together, and the things he won't be able to protect them from when their classmates discover the Internet. The tournament where he shot a 42 on the front nine and withdrew, blaming knee and Achilles injuries.

That day, Steve Williams saw a friend in the parking lot.

"What happened?" his friend asked, incredulous.

"I think he's got the yips, mate," Williams replied.

In the 1,303 days between his father's death and the fire hydrant, Tiger set in motion all those things, and when he can finally go back and make a full accounting of his life, he'll realize that winning the 2008 U.S. Open a year before the scandal, with a broken leg and torn ACL, was the closest he ever got to BUD/S. He could barely walk and he still beat everyone in the world. He won and has never been the same. The loneliness and pain tore apart his family, and the injuries destroyed his chance to beat Nicklaus and to leave fame behind and join the Navy. He lost his dad, and then his focus, and then his way, and everything else came falling down too.

But first, he got one final major.

"I'm winning this tournament," he told his team.

"Is it really worth it, Tiger?" Steve Williams asked.

"F— you," Tiger said.

Act III

He's been stuck ever since, in limbo, somewhere between a professional golfer and a retired celebrity. Right now, in early December,
he hangs out on the edge of a putting green in the Bahamas, unable to play but still handling his duties as host. That means posing with a motorcycle and the CEO of the company that made
it. While the camera crews get ready, Tiger walks onto the green.
Zach Johnson and Justin Rose, both friends, knock around some
balls and shoot the breeze. The guys talk about putters, about finishes and how that impacts the roll. Tiger knows the questions to
ask, having developed a deep reservoir of knowledge that serves
no purpose to someone whose body won't cooperate.

As he starts to pose with the motorcycle, Tiger glances back at
his friends.

On his wrist, he wears a thin red string, a Buddhist reminder to
show compassion and to mind the tongue. Like many things, Tiger
keeps his faith to himself—though he has said he was raised a Buddhist—so it's hard to know how much he practices or if he ever
goes to temple. It's interesting to consider. Buddhists don't believe
in heaven or hell, or at least not in the same way as Christians. According to *Essential Buddhism,* by Diane Morgan, either place can
exist on earth, and there are 11 ways for believers to feel pain: lust,
hatred, illusion, sickness, decay, death, worry, lamentation, physical and mental anguish, melancholy, and grief. Since losing his
father, Woods has burned with every single one of these, and in
the years since he rammed his car into a fire hydrant, he's suffered
nearly all of them all the time. He says he'll be back, and if he is
lying to himself, maybe he can be forgiven that delusion, because
according to the basic tenets of his religion, he has literally been
living through hell.

While the media take photographs of the motorcycle, someone
asks him about a golf course in California where Tiger played a
tournament many years ago.

"First trophy," Tiger says.

"How old were you?"

"Four."

*

He talks a lot about the past now, which is new for someone who moved so fast through his first 40 years that he left people and places behind once they'd served their purpose in his life. Earl often spoke with friends about the strangeness and suddenness of Tiger's exit from their lives, and how when Tiger left Teakwood Street for college, he abandoned his computer and Nintendo, his toys and posters on the wall, and even stray cash. This amazed Earl and made him strangely proud and also melancholy. Tiger had become something like a butterfly; Earl believed that his son had flown away unencumbered. When his tax lawyers advised Tiger to leave California after turning pro and set up his life near Orlando, he just vanished, not even stopping by the old Navy course to say good-bye. "He didn't tell me he was moving to Florida," says the pro, Joe Grohman, "and it broke my heart. I thought I was really close to the family. I didn't get to tell him good-bye. It was just over."

Tiger has cut off coaches and caddies and friends, rarely with a confrontation, just vanishing from their lives. It's not out of spite really; he's focused on where he's supposed to be going. The Western High class of 1994 held its 20-year reunion and made sure Tiger got an invitation in the mail, but he didn't show. Grohman understands. "He's still trying to be Tiger Woods," he says. "There's a time and place for things. There will be a day when he wants to come back to where it all began."

Even 10 years later, the loss of his father still exerts force and pull on his inner life. The anniversary of Earl's death is a time when he can't sleep, staying up all night with his memories. The wounds seem fresh. Tiger spent just 77 minutes on the ground in Kansas saying good-bye to Earl, before hurtling back into a destiny previously in progress. It's nearly certain he hasn't been back since. The sexton who runs the place says he's never seen Woods visit, and staff at the small airport nearby say they haven't seen him either. A book by a *People* magazine writer said Tiger visited once in 2007, around Mark Steinberg's military intervention, but that report could not be confirmed. Maybe he sneaked in and out, but if not, one day perhaps he'll walk across the field to the place where they left Earl's ashes, between Maude and Miles, in the shade of a bush and near a big red rock. He'll have to find the spot from memory because there is no headstone, even a decade after the funeral. Maybe he wants it private, or is simply unable to take such a final step, but whatever the reason, Tiger Woods never had one placed.

He buried his father in an unmarked grave.

The real work of his life—how to deal with having been Tiger Woods—will begin only once he accepts that his golfing career is finished. All driven people experience a reckoning at the end of their life's work, but when that work feels incomplete, or somehow tainted, the regrets can fester with time. This reckoning is coming for Tiger, which worries his friend Michael Jordan, who knows more about the next 10 years of Tiger's life than nearly anyone alive. It's jarring to be dominant and then have it suddenly end. "I don't know if he's happy about that or sad about that," Jordan says. "I think he's tired. I think he really wishes he could retire, but he doesn't know how to do it yet, and I don't think he wants to leave it where it is right now. If he could win a major and walk away, he would, I think."

A few months ago, sitting in his office in Charlotte, Jordan picked up his phone and dialed Tiger's number. It rang a few times and went to voicemail: *I'm sorry, but the person you called has a voicemail box that has not been set up yet.* He tried twice more, the phone rang five or six times, and then he smiled.

"Playing video games," he said.

They texted in November, the day after a big group went out to dinner at Tiger's restaurant. Tiger got drunk and they all laughed and told stories, and Michael thought Tiger seemed relaxed, which made him hopeful. Tiger talked about his injuries a lot but not much about the future. "The thing is," Jordan says, "I love him so much that I can't tell him, 'You're not gonna be great again.'"

The day after that, Tiger wrote him and both men sounded like the stay-at-home dads they've become.

TW: Thank you and your beautiful wife for coming. Need to do that more often. Thank the good lord for ice packs. I'm in heaven now. Bring babies next time.

MJ: Haha. Any time my brother. Get some rest. We'll bring the kids next time.

TW: I'm in. After school next week one day when the kids don't have soccer practice.

Jordan talks carefully, with no bravado or swagger, trying to say something important and true and empathetic—maybe hoping his friend will read it?—without crowding Tiger or saying too much. Jordan struggled and flailed in the years after he quit basketball, feeling like he'd hardwired himself with all of these urges that now worked against any hope of future happiness. For years, he just tried to pretend like he wasn't lost. Time stretched out in front of him endlessly, and this same emptiness awaits Tiger.

"What does he do every day?" Jordan asks.

He's quiet and serious.

"I don't know," he says, answering his own question. "I haven't the slightest idea. I do not know."

He worries that Tiger is so haunted by his public shaming that he obsesses over it, perhaps sitting up in the middle of the night reading all the things people write and say about him.

"Rabbit Ears," Michael calls him sometimes.

He hears everything. For Tiger, this dwelling on old mistakes is a path to madness. Nothing can take him back to 2006 and give him a second chance. "That bothers him more than anything," Jordan says. "It looms. It's in his mind. It's a ship he can't right and he's never going to. What can you do? The thing is about T-Dub, he cannot erase. That's what he really wants. He wants to erase the things that happened."

Slowly, year by year, Tiger's name will not be spoken in the same way and with the same frequency. Without a new passion, Tiger just might sit down there in his enormous, empty mansion and slowly go insane. Jordan's post-retirement salvation came because he and his longtime girlfriend, Yvette Prieto, got married. Now they have twins, and he's created a life for himself, something to occupy his time and his thoughts. They are happy together, and more than once Jordan has told Tiger he needs to allow someone new into his circle, to build a new life with a new person and, along the way, find some new perspective about the journey that brought him here.

"He has . . ." Jordan says, and he pauses, searching for the right word, ". . . no companion. He has to find that happiness within his life, that's the thing that worries me. I don't know if he can find that type of happiness. He's gonna have to trust somebody."

*

Tiger is not totally alone, kept company by memories of the life he once knew and those moments when he is happiest: the time he spends with his daughter, Sam, eight, and his son, Charlie, seven. The best of Earl lives in the actions of his son; in fatherhood, Tiger has equaled and even surpassed his own dad. He is utterly devoted to his children. Every single person interviewed for this story says so. Sam and Charlie never met their grandfather and they don't remember Tiger as a dominant golfer, but they will grow up knowing that their father cares more about them than anything he does on the course.

In the Bahamas, *USA Today* golf writer Steve DiMeglio saw them riding in a golf cart with Tiger and asked if they'd rather be their dad or soccer star Leo Messi.

"Messi!" Sam said without missing a beat.

"He's playing," Charlie explained.

Tiger laughed and dramatically dropped his head.

Then he joked, "Well, he's right."

He and Elin have a better relationship now, and Tiger wishes he'd have worked to create this bond while they were still together. His friends talk of how much he regrets losing his marriage, especially in those moments when he and Elin are with the kids and he glimpses little flashes of the life he threw away. Now he shares custody, and when the children go back to their mom's place and his big house falls quiet, he's surrounded by people who work for him and trophies he won as a younger, more powerful man.

There's a clear view out the windows past the two swimming pools and hot tub, toward the four greens he had built, a practice facility for a game he's almost finished playing. He's got endless stretches of time now to stare and think. His old house near Orlando, the last place they all lived, stood in a cluster of trees across from the Isleworth driving range. He loved sunsets there, all of them together, his golf having finally created the family he craved as a boy. Elin and Charlie would sit in a cart and watch. Yogi, a labradoodle, would roll in the grass, sniffing around. Sam would hand him golf balls, and he'd hit punch shots for his border collie, Taz, to chase.

The sun would set and they'd all walk together in the shadows toward home.

TERRENCE MCCOY

Today, Her Whole Life
Is a Free Skate

FROM THE WASHINGTON POST

RICHLANDS, VA. — Debi Thomas, the best African American figure skater in the history of the sport, couldn't find her figure skates. She looked around the darkened trailer, perched along a river in a town so broke even the bars have closed, and sighed. The mobile home where she lives with her fiancé and his two young boys was cluttered with dishes, stacks of documents, a Christmas tree still standing weeks past the holiday.

"They're around here somewhere," she murmured three times. "I know I have a pair," she continued, before trailing off. "Because —what did I skate in?—something. They're really tight, though, because your feet grow after you don't wear them for a long time." Her medals—from the World Figure Skating Championships, from the Olympics—were equally elusive: "They're in some bag somewhere."

Uncertainty is not a feeling Debi Thomas has often experienced in her 48 years. She was once so confident in her abilities that she simultaneously studied at Stanford University and trained for the Olympics, against the advice of her coach. She was once so lauded for the lithe beauty she expressed on the ice that *Time* magazine put her on its cover and ABC's *Wide World of Sports* named her Athlete of the Year in 1986. She wasn't just the nation's best figure skater. She was smart—able to win a competition, stay up all night cramming, then ace a test the next morning.

She wanted it all. And for a time, she had it. After Stanford came medical school at Northwestern University, then marriage to a handsome lawyer who gave her a son—who in turn became one of the country's best high school football players. Higher and higher she went.

Now, she's here. Thomas, a former orthopedic surgeon who doesn't have health insurance, declared bankruptcy in 2014 and hasn't brought in a steady paycheck in years. She's twice divorced, and her medical license, which she was in danger of losing anyhow, expired around the time she went broke. She hasn't seen her family in years. She instead inveighs against shadowy authorities in the nomenclature of conspiracy theorists—"the powers that be"; "corporate media"; "brainwashing"—and composes opinion pieces for the local newspaper that carry headlines such as "Pain, No Gain" and "Driven to Insanity." She thinks that hoarding gold will insulate us from a looming financial meltdown, and recruits people to sell bits of gold bullion called "Karatbars."

There's a conventional narrative of how Thomas went from where she was to where she is—that of a talented figure undone by internal struggles and left penniless. That was how reality TV told it, when the Oprah Winfrey Network's *Fix My Life* and *Inside Edition* did pieces on her.

But nothing is ever that simple with Thomas. She has always bucked convention. She was a black athlete who entered a sport that had exceedingly few. She was the first champion in a generation to combine college and figure skating. She proclaimed unimaginable ambitions—such as becoming an astronaut after securing her medical degree—and dared you to doubt her.

"She's got all these degrees," fiancé Jamie Looney said as he watched television with Thomas inside the trailer. "She's a doctor. She's a surgeon. And she's here. I've got one year of community college. I know why I'm here. I look at her, wondering, 'Why are you not working somewhere else?'"

Such comments upset Thomas. "People are all like, 'Get a job,'" she said. "And I'm like, 'You people are fools.' I'm trying to change the world."

Richlands, populated by coal miners with few mines to plunder, would seem to be an odd place to launch such an effort. The per-capita income is less than $20,000, and the few industries left booming in the wake of mining layoffs include cash-express shops and pain-management clinics. Thomas, riding shotgun as Looney steers a silver SUV on a recent afternoon, passes several such establishments before arriving at a country market.

She greets the store's owners—"I just signed them up for Karatbars, which will help them a lot," she later says—and settles into a booth. Her hair is frazzled. She wears a big, poofy red coat. On her wrists are two bracelets. One is inscribed with BELIEVE. The other, REIMAGINE.

It quickly becomes apparent that Thomas, for all of her talents, is not a good storyteller.

When explaining what brought her to Richlands, she communicates in a rush of thoughts, linked neither by chronology nor association, and exudes frustration when listeners can't keep up. "I'm a visionary and have an ability to put very complex things together," Thomas says. "And most people don't get that."

She says she wants to help a community she frequently describes' as having "socioeconomic struggles." In 2014, she launched a Go-FundMe.com campaign to finance a YouTube.com "show about reality"—not to be confused with a "reality TV show"—that would expose life's hardships and star Thomas. She says she also wants to enlist Richlands' neediest as affiliates of Karatbar—which would pay her a recruitment commission—so they could earn "passive income" if they recruit others to sell the tiny bullion.

Her fiancé, a gregarious unemployed coal miner, sits at her side. He hasn't said much, but looks exasperated. "I want a normal relationship," Looney says.

"I don't want to be normal," she replies. "Normal is not quite right. Normal is not excelling. That's why they call it normal."

She pauses. "I'm very misunderstood because I look at the world differently," she continues. "You can call it the Olympian mentality."

Excelling has always been very important in Thomas's family. Her grandfather, Daniel Skelton, received a doctorate in veterinary medicine at Cornell University in 1939, the only African American in his class. Her mom, who split from Thomas's dad when Thomas was nine, was a computer engineer when the field had few women and fewer blacks. Her brother, Richard Taylor, earned a bachelor's degree in physics from the University of California at Berkeley, then a master's in business at Stanford University.

"I guess I'm somewhat underachieving," Taylor said.

Anyone would be when compared with Debi Thomas. Growing up in San Jose, Taylor said his sister always talked about becoming a doctor and loved mechanics. "One Halloween, she made herself into a calculator," Taylor said. "You would push the buttons . . . and she would give the answer. Even as a kid, she had an engineer's mind."

But she also had the body of an athlete. And after her mom took her to an ice show, Thomas thought she would give it a try. When that lark transformed into something much more serious, when her coach realized he had a prodigy on his hands, when she got deeper into the byzantine and fiercely political world of figure skating, there came a choice. Skating—or school?

"Eighth grade came along, and she comes in second in the nation and her coach wanted her to quit school," her mother, Janice Thomas, said. Instead, she enrolled in high school near an ice rink in Redwood City, California, and for four years her mom drove 150 miles per day—school, then practice, then home. When she dispatched her college application to Stanford, the word she used to describe herself: "invincible."

"Some people are told, 'You can't do that,' and it crushes them," her mother said. "Other people say, 'I'll show you.'"

Other pressures saddled Thomas, though her family isn't sure she noticed. Taylor said he sees his sister whenever commentators remark on professional tennis player Serena Williams's muscles. Figure skating was—and remains—an intensely white and affluent sport, he said, and judges recommended that Thomas "play down certain aspects of her looks," he said. "It was couched in language that the person making the comments wouldn't interpret it racially, but I did."

Thomas ultimately got three nose jobs, brought in a ballet instructor to feminize her aesthetic, and, between the ages of 18 and 21, was considered the only one capable of taking down the worldwide juggernaut of women's figure skating, East Germany's Katarina Witt.

"She was the only one who could really beat me," Witt recalls.

And though she once did—batting Witt down to second place in the 1986 World Figure Skating Championships—it often appeared to be a joyless pursuit. She fretted about the Olympics. "I really want it over with," Thomas told *Rolling Stone* magazine before the 1988 Winter Games. "Last week," she added, "I thought I was going to throw myself through the glass windows at the rink."

Then came the moment. Thomas had skated with precision and confidence in the first Olympic event and would take gold if she stuck the longer performance.

She and her coach had planned two triple-revolution jumps in quick succession at the segment's beginning—something no other top female skater had done—worrying ballet instructor George de la Peña, who had helped Thomas with her routine. "Why not give her some space before the big risky stuff?" he recalled saying. But Thomas thought she could land it.

The first, she did. The second, she flubbed.

Thomas knew it was over seconds into the routine. "I'm sorry," she mouthed to her coach after she finished, eventually taking the bronze medal. She looked disappointed. But her expression conveyed something else: relief.

"Well," she told her coach. "Back to school."

Thomas talks a lot about what she calls the "Olympian mentality." It's a frame of mind among elite athletes that they can will themselves to excellence. Self-doubt and vulnerability are banished. Confidence is everything. Triumph is within reach.

William T. Long, once an academic at the Los Angeles university where Thomas did her residency, saw this psychology at work. Everyone knew Thomas could do the procedures. Patients loved her. But her grades weren't outstanding. There was concern that she wouldn't pass the boards. "And she did it," he said, "against the critics and against many odds."

But that victory also betrayed what would become her signature weakness. Long never saw her appear to be insecure and came to recognize her confidence as a "two-edged sword." It drove her to take greater risks than others would. It made her difficult to coach. Some disliked her because of it.

"She wanted and expected to be treated like a star," said Lawrence Dorr, who offered her a prestigious orthopedic fellowship at the Dorr Arthritis Institute in Los Angeles, but quickly realized he couldn't work with her. "But in orthopedics, she knew she wasn't a star," Dorr said. He added: "She would argue back. It was almost like she was contrarian, like she was trying to argue with everything I do."

Difficulties with other medical professionals would come to define Thomas's career as she left one institution after another after short periods of time. Her first stop was in Champaign, Illinois. Then another in Terre Haute, Indiana. "I've never lasted anywhere more than a year," she said. What she viewed as commitment to perfection, others perceived as recalcitrance. "Olympian mentality is rough because you just get frustrated with how everybody does everything," Thomas explained in a YouTube video. "Everything needs to be done with excellence. I'm a fixer."

If she could be her own boss, she thought things would improve. So in 2010, she left her husband and 13-year-old son—whose school year she said she didn't want to disrupt—and moved to Richlands, where she opened a private orthopedic practice at the Clinch Valley Medical Center. But Thomas—a specialist in a sparsely populated area, with no business experience—was soon falling behind on bills, burning through savings, and clashing with other doctors.

Around this time, she treated a boy's broken wrist, and his dad asked her out. The charming man lived in a gray trailer by the river. She and Looney began an affectionate, but combustible, relationship. She realized that Looney, who had spent years in the coal mines, had an addiction to prescription narcotics. And though she was dating him, according to Virginia Board of Medicine records, she said she prescribed him drugs to "wean him off the narcotics."

As Thomas's troubles mounted, Long said he received lengthy, 10-page emails from his former student. They were "rambling," he said, laced with suspicion that the medical system was conspiring against her. Whatever was troubling Thomas, he said, was "progressive" and worse every time he heard from her.

On April 22, 2012, Thomas and Looney had a disagreement at the trailer, says a psychological evaluation Thomas shared with the *Washington Post*. Thomas got hold of his gun. "She thought, 'If I act crazier than him, he will straighten up,'" the report says. "She then went outside and shot the gun into the ground to scare him," it also states.

Later that day, according to Virginia Department of Health Professionals records, she approached a police officer and told him she had a gun and wanted to hurt herself. He detained her and, on a temporary detention order, brought her to a hospital for treatment. Medical board records show she was diagnosed with bipolar disorder. Clinch Valley officials told Thomas to enter a distressed-physician program. But she couldn't afford it. And a year later, Thomas's staff membership and clinical privileges were revoked. Medical board records say there were "concerns of an ongoing pattern of disciplinary and behavior issues and poor judgement."

Unable to practice—or afford $800 in monthly rent—Thomas moved into Looney's trailer, declared bankruptcy, and let her medical license expire. Last July, the Virginia Board of Medicine ordered a hearing to investigate whether she might have broken any medical laws when she prescribed narcotics to Looney and declined help for a diagnosed mental illness.

In September, Thomas contested the bipolar diagnosis at a board hearing, records show. The diagnosis was made too quickly, she said, proffering a separate evaluation conducted by a psychologist whom she had paid. The doctor, who diagnosed Thomas with depression in "complete remission," said in the evaluation that the Olympian's erratic behavior was not a symptom of bipolar disorder, but "naivete, overconfidence, and her expectation that if she works hard enough, she can overcome any obstacle . . . Her experience as a world-class figure skater reinforced this expectation and confidence."

In October, the board, citing her expired license, took no action.

It's 9:00 a.m. inside the trailer, but Looney has been up for hours, worrying. The only money they have coming in is from some Social Security checks on account of the death of his children's mother. He looks around the mobile home. He says he wants to get out of here, but doesn't know how.

Just then, Thomas arrives from the bedroom and nestles next to him on the couch. He hands her a cup of coffee. She has just finished talking to a prospective Karatbars recruit. "I just had a really interesting conversation with a lady," she says. "This lady completely gets me."

"She sounded to me like she was jacked up," Looney says of the woman, whom he had overheard speaking with Thomas.

The pair so rarely agree that spending time with them can feel like sitting in on a couple's therapy session. He wanted to get a job in the mines; she said he shouldn't. She wanted him to do the *Fix My Life* show; he thought he would be embarrassed on national television. He hates their mobile home; she loves it, expressing disdain for "superficial" things.

In fact, Thomas says she loves almost everything about their life in Richlands. And there's reason to believe her. "I didn't know we even had this beauty in this country," she said. "No one ever treated me badly" in Richlands, she added. "And I was like, 'I like it here.'"

These days, she doesn't have to shoulder the pressure of being the first black anything. She doesn't have to worry about medical exams, whether a patient will recover, or if her practice will succeed—because it already failed. And she and Looney, who has been clean since 2012, say they've calmed their relationship with a 12-step recovery program.

"I expected to be one of the leaders in joint-replacement therapy," said Thomas, now writing a book about her life. "That was what my image was. Then I had an experience that totally changed my mind."

On a recent afternoon, a light snow sprinkled the trailer with white. Looney and his two boys barreled outside to play. Thomas pulled on her red, poofy coat. She walked off by herself, toward the river. She tilted her head back and, with arms held out wide, was quiet as the snow pattered on her face.

Looney asked what she was doing. She said she was re-creating the iconic scene from *The Shawshank Redemption,* when character Andy Dufresne escaped prison following decades of false imprisonment and assumed the same posture in the rain.

"I'm free," Thomas called out to him. "Don't you get it?"

SEAN FLYNN

The Shooter and the Saint

FROM GQ

THERE'S A DEAD MAN spilling out of a Mercedes on Sophie
Wright Place, his feet limp on the pavement, the rest of him
slumped over the seat. His name is Will Smith and he is a Saint,
or used to be a Saint, which is as much an appellation as a job description in New Orleans. Smith played nine seasons in the NFL,
had a Super Bowl ring, retired to the city where he was rich and
famous because he was a big man with an extraordinary gift. He
was an adopted son and a favorite son, out on a springtime Saturday night with his wife and a few friends.

Then he got shot to death in the street.

There's another football player on the street, a native son, New
Orleans born and raised. Bigger than Smith and nearly as gifted,
but he never got famous and he never got rich. Almost 30 years
old and he's humping it in a development league even the local
press doesn't bother covering. He's a workingman, drives a tow
truck, and breeds puppies and pours concrete to pay the bills and
raise his boy.

His name is Cardell Hayes, but his friends call him Bear because
that is his approximate size, 6'6", 305. He shot Smith, shot him
eight times, one in the side and seven in the back. He might've
shot Smith's wife too, once in each leg. Didn't mean to, though, if
that matters at all.

Cardell is scared. He's not running away. He's waiting for the
police to come. His gun, a .45 semiautomatic pistol, is on the hood
of his Hummer, which is pushed up against the back of Smith's

Mercedes SUV. Cardell's already taken out the magazine, set it next to the gun.

He's on his phone, calling his ex-girlfriend, an English teacher he'd been with from the eighth grade until a few months ago. They're still close, raise their son together. His voice is panicky, cracking, like he's gulping for air. He's talking in fragments, not making sense, not to Tiffany, anyway.

I shot someone, he tells her.

I don't know what happened, he says.

And both of those things, right then in the echoing wail of the approaching sirens, are absolutely true.

A lot of people get shot in New Orleans. The city consistently has one of the ten highest murder rates in the country, and most victims die as anonymous statistics, significant only in the aggregate.

Except when they are famous. Unlike Will Smith, none of the 30 people murdered in New Orleans before April 9 this year were retired NFL defensive ends with Super Bowl rings. Famous people die famous deaths, and those need to be publicly explained. If Cardell Hayes didn't know what happened, it was appallingly obvious to everyone else.

Shortly before 11:30 that night, Cardell's Hummer ran into the back of Smith's Mercedes. There was an argument, loud and incoherent, and then *pop pop pop pop pop pop pop pop.* Road rage, apparently. Someone had to be the bad guy, and common sense suggested it was more likely to be the guy with the gun who wasn't dead than the football star with the charitable foundation whose name was going into the Saints Hall of Fame. Cardell certainly *looked* like he could shoot a man over a dented fender: In his mug shot, which went up on the news sites and sports sites and gossip sites within hours, dreadlocks tumble off his head and his neck beard is like a sling holding up his head, hard and round as a cannonball. There was another photo too: Cardell strobed in police light and standing next to a normal-size officer, his arms safely cuffed behind his back, like a giant subdued.

By sunrise, the basic narrative had already been written, perhaps indelibly, and spread globally. "Cardell Hayes," his attorney groused to reporters a few days later, "was tried and convicted before I got out of church Sunday morning."

It only got worse as the day wore on. Reporters—and there were many, because a dead Super Bowl winner, especially one who can be called a Saint without irony, draws a lot of press—quickly pulled up Cardell's criminal record. It was not extensive, but it could be shorthanded, unfairly though not inaccurately, to a drug-and-gun conviction. In 2010 he was pulled over for not signaling a turn. He told the officers about the legal handgun in the car. The police also found six Tylenol 3 caplets, the kind with codeine. Those are not recreational drugs, but they do require a prescription, which Cardell did not have because they were prescribed to his aunt. Thus, he was carrying a weapon while in possession of illegal narcotics. He eventually pleaded to misdemeanors.

Cardell's athletic history was also a matter of relevant curiosity. In 2004, a scouting outfit ranked him as one of the top 50 high school prospects in Louisiana, which sends more men per capita to the NFL than any state except Alabama. But Cardell never even played college ball. Furthest he got was being an extra on a fake team in *22 Jump Street* and a defensive lineman for the Crescent City Kings in the Gridiron Developmental Football League.

There was one more thing, about Cardell's father. The day after Christmas 2005, Anthony Hayes had a card declined at Walgreens. He argued, punched a clerk, and left. The police found Anthony walking down St. Charles Avenue, holding a four-inch knife. He did not want to stop, and he did not want to be arrested. Anthony also had a history of mental illness. More police came. They pepper-sprayed him. Anthony lunged—it's always a *lunge*—at Lieutenant William Ceravolo. Three other officers fired. Anthony was hit nine times, crumpled awkwardly to the pavement, and died.

As of April, Ceravolo was retired from regular duty, a captain in the New Orleans Police reserve. He also happened to be a friend of Will Smith's. Had, in fact, been out with Smith at a place called Sake Cafe not 20 minutes earlier and ten blocks west.

Stray details about Cardell were feathered into the coverage, almost as if to make him bigger and thuggier: how he sometimes did security for the Saints—which isn't true—or how he bred expensive and funny little dogs called bullies, a cross between French bulldogs and pit bulls. (Those dogs, *USA Today* ominously added, "are considered loyal, protective and potentially dangerous—characteristics that apparently Hayes shares.")

But those were just texture. What were the odds that an aspiring professional football player with a criminal record would run into a superstar who just happened to have had dinner with one of the cops who'd been involved in the killing of his father?

In New Orleans, actually, those odds aren't too bad.

An hour before it happened, at about 10:30, Cardell was in Treme, in a storefront barbershop called Lance's. There are bars on the door and a mirror along the back wall, in front of the barber chairs, two worn couches, and a rack of snacks. The only real decorations are Saints posters and Saints pennants and a list of rules— "Number One: No Disrespecting the New Orleans Saints"—taped and tacked to the walls.

Cardell was a regular at Lance's, had been ever since Anthony Williams started cutting his lines, keeping his hair knife-sharp at the edges. He would come just to hang out too, and usually call ahead to have someone order him a large pizza, make sure he had a snack waiting. Late on a Saturday night, people are still working at Lance's, and a few guys are hanging out, looking for something to do.

A little past 10:30, Cardell's phone pinged. He smiled. "House party Uptown," he said.

Everyone wanted Cardell to check it out first, see if it was worth dragging across town. The only one who'd go was Kevin O'Neal. He'd ride shotgun in the Hummer.

Kevin was one of Cardell's best friends, played football with him at Warren Easton High School. "The nerd school," Kevin calls it, because you had to test in. But it had a good football team, and Kevin and Cardell were two of its best players. In 2004, a scouting website called Tiger Blitz ranked Cardell, a six-foot-three, 260-pound defensive tackle who could run the 40 in 4.8 seconds, number 48 on its list of Louisiana high school prospects. Kevin, six-four and 200 pounds, was an outside linebacker who benched 250 and squatted 450. "Very rarely," a site called Rivals wrote about him, "does it happen that a player plays one year of football and is instantly on the minds of over a dozen college programs."

They graduated in May 2005. "But man, you gotta keep in account everything that happened in 2005," Kevin told me. "We had some real serious talent coming out—and then Katrina hit. Football and trying to pursue the NFL? It's like, *My home is gone.* College? *My fucking home is gone.* A lot of people never rebounded from that."

Football would wait. Cardell looked after his mother and his sister and enrolled in Southeastern Louisiana University, an hour's drive north, on the far side of Lake Pontchartrain. Kevin was at Southern University and A&M College, then went to play ball at Compton Community College. Cardell's girlfriend, Tiffany, was at Southeastern too. When she got pregnant in her last year, Cardell left school to pour cement, earn a living.

He never did get his degree, but Tiffany graduated and got a job teaching high school English, and between them, they made a good middle-class life. They bought a house in the city, and Cardell worked for himself so he could take their son to preschool in the mornings and pick him up in the afternoons and be at all the teacher conferences and assemblies. He bought and sold cars and he ran a couple of tow trucks, and, as much for passion as profit, he bred dogs. Cardell was diligent and deliberate with the bullies: mothers artificially inseminated, litters delivered by C-section, a misting system to keep the kennels cool in the summer.

They drove uptown, Cardell and Kevin, both in a good mood. They were playing ball again, defense for the Crescent City Kings, thinking maybe they could get sharp enough for the paying leagues. They'd had practice that afternoon, which always put Kevin in a good mood. Got the blood going, washed out the stress. Kevin was a welder and a boilermaker, had a union card and a college education, but even at 30 years old it felt good to get out on the field.

April 9 had been a near-perfect day, glorious in the Louisiana spring, before the humidity settles in like a compress. After practice, Kevin had gone down to the French Quarter Festival, then watched the sun set over the Mississippi. The house party was a bust, though. Cardell and Kevin left after a half-hour or so, didn't even have a drink, and started driving downtown. They were going to Tipitina's, the famous music club in an old warehouse on the river.

Cardell drove east on Magazine Street. He braked for a red light at St. Andrew. He felt a vibration shudder through the Hummer.

He looked in the mirror at a Mercedes SUV on his bumper, then at Kevin.

"We get hit, big brother?"

"Yeah, soul," Kevin said, low and slow, the way he always talks. "We got bumped."

At the end of every day at Warren Easton High, the principal, Philmon Edwards, would get on the PA and read whatever news or events had to be announced to the student body. Then he finished with the same simple directive: "Govern yourselves accordingly."

Kevin hadn't been sure exactly what that meant back then, before he and Cardell graduated in 2005. But it stuck with him, as any phrase repeated so many times will, and eventually he figured out it was a reasonable guide worth following at any given time.

Cardell remembered it too. So when his Hummer got tapped on Magazine Street, he did the proper thing, which was to pull to the curb. It was probably nothing—"Bear's so big," Kevin told me, "and the car's so big, he wasn't even sure we got hit"—but a person governing himself accordingly will stop when he's been involved in a minor traffic mishap. "I thought we'd get out and look at it and there wouldn't be any damage, and we'd just say, 'All right, forget it, go have a good night,'" Kevin told me a few weeks after the fact. There was no need to get the authorities involved. "Black people," he said, "don't want any encounters with the police."

But the Mercedes didn't stop. It maneuvered around the Hummer, then accelerated across St. Andrew and onto a short street called Sophie Wright Place.

Cardell had been dinged once already in a hit-and-run. His Hummer had been broken into, too, and his insurance kept ticking up.

He wheeled away from the curb and followed the Mercedes. He figured he'd at least get the plate number. Kevin pulled out his phone to call 911.

There are a few reasons Will Smith might not have wanted to pull in behind Cardell's Hummer, the main one being he didn't think he'd hit him, thought he'd braked soon enough and hard enough to stop short. Another was that he was driving a $140,000 vehicle and if some asshole wanted to carjack him, coaxing him to the curb would be a fairly common way to start. A third might be that he'd drunk himself three times over the limit and didn't need to make any unnecessary stops. Or, finally, it may just have been that he was Will Smith: Queens born, Utica raised, first-round pick out of Ohio State in 2004, at one point among the highest-paid defensive players in the NFL, a reported $70 million with all the options.

He'd spent the day at the French Quarter Festival with his wife, Racquel, and a couple they knew from Kenner, where they lived. Pierre Thomas, another former Saint, and Billy Ceravolo, the retired cop, joined them later at Sake Cafe. At some point, their friend from Kenner called her brother, and he drove over in his Chevy Impala.

Thomas and Ceravolo left first, for the bar at the Windsor Court Hotel, a boutique place downtown. The other five left together at about 11:20: Smith, Racquel, and the couple from Kenner in the Mercedes, the brother alone in his Chevy, a car or two ahead.

After Smith got around the Hummer, he caught up to the Chevy at the corner of Sophie Wright and Felicity Street.

Cardell was right behind him. Taillights flashed, Cardell stomped heavy on the brakes. The Hummer's front end dipped, slid into the back of Smith's SUV, not hard enough to pop the air bags but with enough force to shatter the Mercedes's rear window, spiderwebbed glass held together by the tinting film. The Mercedes, in turn, bumped into the rear of the Impala.

Kevin caught his balance. Already, two white guys were charging toward the Hummer.

Govern yourself accordingly.

Kevin left his revolver when he got out.

Cardell opened the driver's door, stepped onto the pavement. He had his .45 in his right hand, held at his side, pointed at the ground.

In New Orleans, that is a perfectly legal thing to do.

"What kind of person," Kevin asks one day, "sees a guy like Bear, someone that big, standing there with a gun, and keeps coming at him?"

He was at a sidewalk coffee shop in Treme, Kevin and three of Cardell's other friends, about a month after the shooting. The question was rhetorical. It is agreed by acclamation that the proper response in such a situation is to abruptly stop, back up, and speak as calmly as possible.

The other question, though, is why Cardell was standing in the street with a .45 in the first place. The reflexive answer to that too is agreed by acclamation: Would you ask a white man that question? "He was a legal gun owner in an open-carry state," Kevin says. He lets that hang there for a moment. "Where the fuck is the NRA?"

An armed society, it has been said, is a polite society.

In any case, it also is agreed that Cardell did not intend to threaten anyone—only to indicate he was capable of protecting himself. He was not a violent man but rather, at that moment, the proverbial good guy with a gun. If anything, Cardell was aware of how much damage a man his size could inflict, how much conflict he could attract from any meathead with something to prove. He was gentle by nature, but even gentler to compensate for his size. "He was the only person I knew who was logical about everything," Tiffany told me. "He always thought everything through." Dwight Harris knew Bear wasn't a tough guy. He was at Lance's before it all happened, and he had his Can-Am, one of those three-wheeled motorcycles, parked behind the chain link around the lot next door. Cardell always wanted to ride it, but he never would. He'd climb on and Harris would start it and Cardell would sit there, pondering. Then he'd shake his head, switch it off. "I ain't about to kill myself today," he'd always say. "I'm gonna run into something."

Harris is at the coffee shop, listening to the gun debate, which keeps coming back to the same question because everything that happened after seems to depend on the answer: why did Cardell have a gun, and why was he holding it? Harris finally lets out a heavy, definitive sigh. "Man, the same reason nuns walk around with guns," he says. "It's New Orleans."

Four days after it happened, at the hospital where Racquel Smith was still being treated, a lawyer for her and the rest of the Smith family, Peter Thomson, explained their version of how it came to be that Racquel's femur was fractured and her husband was dead.

Will Smith did not believe he'd bumped Cardell's Hummer, Thomson said, and therefore didn't see any reason to stop. Everything after, in Thomson's accounting, happened because Cardell is a rageful lunatic. He chased Smith, rammed his Mercedes, leapt out "enraged, yelling and cursing," he said. Racquel, who'd been in the backseat, got out and pleaded with him. "Leave us alone," she said, according to Thomson. "Go back to your car. We have children. This is not worth this."

Right about then, in this version, Cardell kneecapped her, put one round in each thigh. "We have evidence," Thomson continued, "that the killer showed no remorse whatsoever, that he actually stood over Will Smith's dead body, as his wife had crawled away because she couldn't walk and is cowering." And then some especially gangsta shit: "The killer is yelling over the body of Will Smith after he killed him."

(A few hours later, Cardell's attorney held a press conference in front of his office. "The rules of professional conduct prohibit lawyers from speaking ill about other lawyers," John Fuller said, with an edge that made it clear he was, in fact, speaking ill of another lawyer. "But I'll say this: There are some things that I heard that I question." He did not go into great detail, though broadly speaking, it could fairly be summarized as: all of it, except the fact that Will Smith got shot.)

Cardell was in jail, charged with second-degree murder and attempted murder—he's pleaded not guilty—and would remain there for the foreseeable future, a $1.75 million bond being priced beyond his means. As he should be, Thomson seemed to suggest. The attack was completely unprovoked, a man is dead, a woman is maimed, and three children lost their father. "I'm aware of nothing," Thomson said, "that Will Smith did that would cause this killer to be afraid for his life."

That is very carefully worded. He wasn't there. And, in any case, fear is almost wholly a matter of perspective.

Kevin didn't have the door open yet, and already two white men were stomping toward the Hummer. They were not big men, but they were in a fury. One was stripping off his shirt. *I feel played,* Kevin heard one of them say. *I want to fight.*

Kevin found that mildly amusing. Who says that?

The white guys apparently saw the gun in Cardell's hand, because they converged on Kevin. They were throwing punches but not connecting because Kevin is tall and rangy and has a brown belt in Kenpo and squats 350 just to warm up. Mostly, he was worried about avoiding an assault charge. He had his eye on Cardell, though.

Racquel was between Smith and Cardell, keeping distance between two big men. Cardell, Kevin swears, was being careful to keep his right hand at his side. Smith swung once, twice, a third time, three sloppy rights that made glancing contact.

Please don't do that, Cardell said.

He was scared.

Racquel appeared to persuade Smith to let it go, to get back in the car and sort it out later. Smith turned, took a step away. Then, Kevin says, Smith pushed his wife aside. That would not be the first time, allegedly. Smith was known to have a temper and had a history of allegedly striking his wife, having been charged with domestic-abuse battery in Lafayette in 2010 after reportedly dragging her down a sidewalk by the hair. (Racquel later tweeted that the episode was "all bs," adding, "I feel bad for my husband who is innocent in all of this." The charge was ultimately dismissed.)

Smith came back toward Cardell: *You got a gun, motherfucker? I got a gun too.*

Kevin, still holding off the two white guys, reached for Smith's left arm. *Homie, chill the fuck out,* he said. *You're trippin'.*

Smith spun away, then leaned in through the open door of the Mercedes. He kept a licensed 9-millimeter handgun in the center console.

The white guys were still messing with Kevin. Kevin slipped.

He heard *pop pop pop pop pop pop pop pop.*

When Chase Dixon heard that Will Smith had been killed, he shook his head in disgust and thought the obvious thought: more New Orleans bullshit.

Why wouldn't he? There were 164 murders in New Orleans in 2015, an average of more than three every week; 2016 wasn't quite as bad, but Will Smith was the 31st person murdered in 100 days. Old shell casings can at times be a nuisance at fresh crime scenes, and it's not always simple to sort out whether a bullet hole in a clapboard is from a recent stray or has weathered for a while. Eventually, a celebrity was going to be among the statistics.

But then he found out who pulled the trigger.

Dixon knows Cardell and Kevin. They work out at his gym a couple of times a week. Kevin started going there with his martial-arts coach, Steven "Spyder" Hemphill, and Cardell started going with Kevin. Spyder lost his elder brother and his eldest son to the streets, and he's got one boy now, Sean, a light-heavyweight amateur boxer and a damn good one, nationally ranked.

"It was always Kevin, Cardell, and Sean, and Sean doesn't surround himself with bad people," Dixon said one afternoon.

"I don't allow riffraff around my son I have left," Spyder said.

"These dudes," Dixon said, "they're not monsters. They're young black kids growing up in a tough-ass city to grow up in."

There was a preliminary hearing for Cardell scheduled for April 28, not quite three weeks after he shot Will Smith to death. Generally speaking, a preliminary hearing would be good for Cardell: the prosecution would be required to convince a judge they had enough evidence to continue holding him, which meant they would have to present witnesses, whom Cardell's attorney, John Fuller, could cross-examine. Fuller, in turn, would get to present his own witnesses.

As a practical matter, Cardell would have remained in jail— probable cause is not a stringent standard to meet, especially when the evidence includes a celebrity shot eight times—but it would have been a narrative coup, a chance for Fuller to get on the public record a more sympathetic accounting of April 9.

He has argued that Cardell "was not the aggressor" and that he "is legally not guilty," which seems to depend on a debatable reading of Louisiana's stand-your-ground law. He has also hinted, unsubtly, at a cover-up, suggesting there was "possible untoward activity by a former NOPD officer." The implication, for which there is no evidence, is that Ceravolo ditched a gun that Smith might have grabbed and replaced it with a clean one. Ceravolo, through his attorney, denies doing anything improper.

The other way for the prosecution to keep Cardell in jail before trial was to have a grand jury indict him. A secret proceeding, no cross-examining witnesses, no public record of the proceedings except for the end result.

The Orleans Parish grand jury, as it happened, met on Thursday, April 28. Fuller managed to get one witness on the stand before a clerk rushed in with the indictment and canceled the preliminary hearing.

Cardell Hayes may not have reached the level some expected he might, but he still believed he had a chance. Which is why he worked his ass off playing starting noseguard for the Crescent City Kings. A huge man, but fast. "He could run like a deer," head coach Frederick Washington told me one sweltering evening on the sideline. Probably not quick enough to play defense in the money leagues, but offensive guard in the NFL? "For sure," Washington said. He considered that for a moment. "No less than the CFL."

The Kings are a good team too, went 9-2 last season, hosted the championship at Joe W. Brown Memorial Park. You know what the difference is, though? More than 153 million people watched Will Smith win a Super Bowl. How many saw the Kings lose the title game to the Nashville Storm? Anyone?

But Cardell went to practice and he worked out and he paid his bills and he raised his boy. He governed himself accordingly. That night, when he shot that man, he did not run away. He asked other people, witnesses, not to leave. He removed the magazine from his gun and put them both on the hood of his Hummer. He waited for the police, and he called Tiffany. "These white guys kept coming at us," he told her in a raspy panic. "He was going to get a gun . . . I don't know what happened."

And he didn't, not all of it, not the most important part, which would make him famous for all the wrong reasons. Cardell did not know whom he had shot. No one told him until he was taken to jail. He already was crying, just for having killed another human being. But Will Smith? Cardell heard that and sobbed, his big body heaving, tears dripping into his lap because his wrists were still cuffed and he couldn't wipe them away. Will Smith was the kind of player Cardell always wanted to be.

Sucker Punch

FROM THE MIAMI NEW TIMES

SOME BOXERS ENTER the ring scowling dead-eyed at their opponents. But Stan Stanisclasse could never pull it off. His smile came too easily—it'd just creep unbidden across his face. So he began most bouts with a little dance instead, stomping and sliding his feet back and forth in a half-moonwalk, half–Muhammad Ali shuffle, with one glove held high above his head.

For Stan, boxing was joy.

For Darrell Telisme, the sport was vicious, personal, and violent. From the moment Telisme had walked into Elite Boxing, Stan's home gym in a blue-collar corner of West Palm Beach, he hadn't stopped jawing. Never mind that Stan was the best fighter in the city or that he was on his way to a 40-6-3 amateur record, a Golden Gloves belt, and a legitimate shot at the Olympics.

As they circled inside the bright-yellow ring behind a sliding garage door that leaked humid air, the two looked like mirror images: a couple of Haitian American teenagers with diamond-cut biceps. But closer investigation showed Darrell's features were stony and Stan's were open. Stan's face was baby smooth, while Darrell's was marred by a black star inked across his right cheekbone.

Once the punches began flying, the difference was even starker. Stan was a blur. Jab left, duck right. Shoulder roll. Thunderous hook to the head. Jab step. Another full-bodied blow to the gut. Darrell was a tree trunk, a slab of meat hanging from a hook. He was underwater.

Dave Lewter, the crewcut ex-pro who owned the gym, watched

his star fighter pummel the shit-talking newcomer. That day in early 2010, he let the pair spar for two rounds—at least one too many, in hindsight. "I can't even call it a fight," Lewter says today. "It was head shots, body shots . . . Stan just took it to him."

Darrell limped off, bloody, sullen, and silent. Stan did his little shuffle step, a smile creasing his features while his friends hooted and hollered. He'd forget the fight soon enough. Darrell Telisme was just another wannabe brawler steamrolled by the "Iron Man."

But that fight was something else entirely to Darrell, according to police, prosecutors, and friends. His humiliation sowed the seeds of an obsession that ended five years later, when Stan lay dead in his beachside apartment after a bullet pierced his right temple.

The untold story of that crime is a case study in obsession and jealousy, where a sport predicated on violent domination bled from the ring onto the street and culminated in murder.

"I wish I would have known—I could have talked to Stan and warned him," says Frank Gedeon, his longtime sparring partner. "I would have said, 'Stan, just let him beat you up once so you can say, "Look, you win, man. The beef is over, and you can live your life."'"

Gedeon smiles sadly and shakes his head. "But Stan was too competitive. He'd never do it."

If Stan was nervous during his first amateur fight, the 17-year-old gave no hint. Fifty spectators, including his parents, crammed into folding chairs around the ring. "C'mon, Stan!" someone shouted as he calmly climbed over the ropes.

For the fight's first 20 seconds, Stan circled his opponent, a quick, lanky guy clad in black. They both jabbed at the air, sliding their feet, probing.

Then, for the next 10 seconds, the opponent attacked. He landed a soft right hook on Stan's headgear. A weak follow-up caught Stan in the stomach.

Ten seconds later, the fight was over. Stan had backed the skinny guy toward a corner and let go two left jabs as a setup. Then Stan let the hammer down: a right fist whistled through the air, blue leather landing square on a pliant jaw.

The opponent staggered. He tumbled. The crowd roared. The legend of Stan Stanisclasse was born.

"He won his first fight in 40 seconds, knocked the guy right out," Gedeon says. "That's crazy."

Adds boxer Brandon "Mighty Mouse" Desrosier: "That motherfucker hit like he was throwing rocks."

Until that moment, Stan Stanisclasse had led a life strikingly similar to Darrell Telisme's. Both grew up middle-class in Palm Beach County as the sons of fathers who had fled a violent dictatorship in Haiti. And both dreamed of boxing stardom from a young age.

Only their temperaments diverged: Stan was renowned for his wit and kindness, while the withdrawn Darrell flashed a blinding temper that hinted at the violence to come.

Stan's father, Stan Stanisclasse Sr., escaped the waning days of Jean-Claude "Baby Doc" Duvalier's dictatorship in 1984 in Port-de-Paix, his hometown of 250,000 on Haiti's northwestern tip. He found work in Florida as a nurse and seven years later brought his wife Canita to the States. After Stan Jr. was born in July 1992, they settled in Boynton Beach. Three siblings followed: sisters Ashley and Justina and a brother, Ben.

There were early signs the boy was unusual. For one thing, he was huge, weighing nearly 10 pounds at birth. "The third day in the hospital, he grabbed a doctor so hard he hurt his hand," the elder Stan recalls with a deep laugh. "He was always strong."

Stan was a restless kid, but also athletic and bright. One day, he came home with a bright crayon drawing of red boxing gloves, which his family has saved to this day. "Since he was little, he wanted to become a boxer," Canita says. "It was always on his mind."

His parents resisted. They pushed him into football and basketball, but he didn't enjoy team sports. The family's move to rural Palm Beach finally landed him in the ring. In 2007, when Stan was a ninth-grader, his dad finished building a sprawling house on three acres along a gravel road in horse country outside West Palm. He designed it himself. Stan Jr. had to transfer to massive Palm Beach Central High School, where he struggled.

"Kids would pick on him for how he talked," his father remembers. "In private school, it's very proper. In public school, they would say he sounded white."

Driving home one day, the 16-year-old spotted Dave Lewter's boxing gym. It was his chance to finally pull on the gloves he'd long imagined.

Lewter is an unusual ringside guru. Though he moved to Palm Beach before high school, a honeyed Deep South accent still betrays his Kentucky birth. His dad is a preacher and college professor, and his mother is a teacher. He had the gift of quick hands and iron stamina, which led to a 22-4 record as a pro before he hung up his gloves in 2004. "I was a good fighter," Lewter says, "but I'm probably a better teacher."

Soon after Stan showed up the first time, Lewter left for six weeks to work with heavyweights in Europe. When he returned, his staff excitedly grabbed him. "They said, 'Dave, Dave, you gotta see this kid Stan,'" he remembers. "He's good!"

The way Lewter tells it, a kid either has boxing in his genes or he doesn't. And Stan had it. "He was that one-in-a-million kid," Lewter says.

Just a few miles away, Darrell Telisme followed a strikingly similar path to the ring. Telisme's father Daniel escaped his hometown of Gonaïves in 1981 for South Florida. He worked odd jobs —cleaning houses and temping at offices—and eventually settled down with Angela Aird, a Jamaican immigrant. Darrell was born in July 1991, almost exactly a year before Stan. His mother worked as a nurse's aide, while his dad found a steady job at a DoubleTree hotel. His parents split up when he was five, but Daniel says, "He had a good childhood. We were both very involved in his life, always."

His mother lived in suburban West Palm Beach next to a lake on the western fringes of town. Darrell was a moody kid but never a problem. He graduated from Forest Hill Community High School and "was never in any real trouble," his father says.

"He never would strike me as a negative individual, even as a kid," adds Omar Brown, a Jamaican-born barber who cut Darrell's hair most of his life and later sparred with him in boxing gyms. "He was quiet."

But there were clues that a simmering rage lay beneath the surface. One came in October 2009, when Darrell was 18 years old. His sister called the police to their mother's house, where two cops found Darrell in the living room viciously choking his older brother. "Help! I can't breathe!" Christopher yelled, according to a police report. When police wrestled Christopher free, Darrell jumped to his feet in a "fighting stance." The cops had to Taser him to subdue him.

The fight, the cops later learned, had begun when Darrell demanded some leftovers his brother was eating. When Christopher refused, an enraged Darrell called him a "pussy ass nigga," began punching him, and then choked his brother until he feared "he was going to black out or die."

Darrell was charged with felony assault, but prosecutors dropped the case when he agreed to stay away from his brother.

Like Stan's parents, Daniel Telisme tried to dissuade his son from boxing. Daniel had grown up around the sport in Haiti.

"I'd ask him, 'Why don't you go to college and learn things?' But he wants to make money," Daniel says. "I understand that, but I don't want you to make money that way even if you're good at it. I don't want my son fighting."

All Darrell ever wanted to do, though, was prove himself in the ring. When he inked that black tattoo on his cheek, it was a constant reminder: someday he'd be a star.

It was only a matter of time before he decided knocking out the best fighter in town was his only route to get there.

In February 1964, Miami Beach burst onto the international boxing scene with the sudden fury of an uppercut to the jaw. When reigning champ Sonny Liston shockingly conceded defeat to a brash 22-year-old who'd soon change his name to Muhammad Ali, the world's fighting elite turned its attention to South Beach. The grimy Fifth Street Gym where Ali trained became a hotbed for rising young punchers and global stars alike.

South Florida's boxing scene has waxed and waned in the 60 years since, but it has never lost its status as an American boxing mecca, fed lately by a Caribbean wellspring. These days, the best are Cuban purebreds like Guillermo Rigondeaux—currently one of the top-ranked featherweights on earth—and former IBF and WBC champion Yuriorkis Gamboa.

Relatively few of those elite boxers are Haitian, though. And as Stan and Darrell struggled to make their mark on Palm Beach's diverse hothouse scene, they each carried an extra chip on their shoulders thanks to their shared heritage. In a world where flag-draped fighters proudly carry their backgrounds into the ring, both felt the added weight of their immigrant histories.

"As a promoter, you pit the fighters' countries against one another, and fans get behind their homelands too," says Benjamin

Willard, who started Island Boxing in Palm Beach to organize fights for Haitians and Jamaicans there. "The fighters really feel that too in a really personal way."

That added pressure had a very different effect on the two young fighters, though. As Stan scored upset after upset, Darrell unraveled. As his defeats piled up and his rival's star kept rising, Darrell's personal life crumbled—and the beef with Stan spiraled into something darker.

It's tough to pin down what made Stan such a terrifying boxer. He was fast, but not the fastest. He packed every punch with bruising power, but he wasn't the strongest guy in Florida. His best weapon, in truth, was his brain.

"He just dissected guys. He had answers for everything," Lewter says. "It was like playing chess to Stan, and he knew where you were going before you went there."

That ability rapidly led him from walloping opponents in amateur bouts to winning belts. First came a local Police Athletic League title in 2011 and then, in 2012, a statewide victory: the Golden Gloves championship in the 178-pound class. The win gave Stan the chance to fight for a national belt in Las Vegas, but he had already set his sights on a bigger honor: an Olympic bid.

As Stan pulled a Rocky Balboa, Darrell's dreams sputtered. Darrell's fighting career had begun inside one of the biggest gyms in town, Palm Beach Boxing, where any night of the week dozens of the area's best boxers banged fists into bags in a back room perfumed with chemical disinfectant. They were overseen by Lou Martinez, a soft-spoken, 50-year-old ex-pro with a thorny rose tattoo around his still-firm bicep and a golden glove dangling from a chain around his neck.

Darrell, though, never caught Martinez's seasoned eye. "I don't pay that much attention to the guys who just show up here and there, and he was one of those guys," the coach says. "I never really trained him."

That's not to say Darrell wasn't serious. By the time he was out of high school, he was practicing every day. "He worked very hard, and at times he was very focused," says Desrosier, a five-foot-two dynamo who sports two gold grills and earned his "Mighty Mouse" nickname thanks to his powerful punch and diminutive stature. "He was so intent on being a pro boxer."

And he wasn't without skill. "Darrell had a hell of a jab. That was his strongest move," Desrosier says. "He was quick too."

But he had a problem. On the mental level, where Stan excelled, Darrell struggled. No matter how many practice rounds he went with more seasoned fighters, his strategy didn't improve. "He was just a stiff fighter," Desrosier says. "You could freeze him real easy."

A toxic stew—created from the lethal gap between Darrell's lofty dreams and his actual ability—began brewing inside him. He became a nonstop trash-talker. Even worse, Darrell seemed unable to separate the sport from the personal. Between the ropes, boxing is a brutal contest. But it's also a brotherhood, where vicious beatdowns generally breed respect. To Darrell, though, every fight was a beef. When the bell rang, he couldn't just tap gloves and move on.

"Look, it's a competitive sport, people get hot, but with Darrell, he'd think you were the enemy," Desrosier says. "He was quiet a lot of the time, but he was emotional as fuck. You could tell with his body language. He couldn't let stuff go."

By 2012, Stan had set his sights on the Olympics. There was no chance the young fighter could make the U.S. team, but Haiti invited him to battle for a slot. "I want to be that face of boxing," Stan told WPTV News in Palm Beach. "It's not only for me now; it's for my parents' homeland."

Then his chance dissolved in a fluke series of events. Haiti flew him to Mexico to train, but his sparring partner there—after getting pummeled in their first bout—refused to fight him anymore, Lewter says. When Stan arrived in Brazil the next month for the trials, a more seasoned Haitian fighter showed up too heavy, weighing in at Stan's preferred 178 pounds. Stan agreed to lose 10 pounds in a week so he could fight in a lower weight class. "Between the lack of practice and the weight loss, he was weak," Lewter says. "It just didn't work out."

After crashing out of the trials, Stan was crushed. But it didn't stall his career. His parents marveled at his steely dedication. "In the morning, we'd wake up and think he was still sleeping," his father recalls. "But it's 5:00 a.m. and he's already out in the garage training on the bag or running." He continued fighting amateur bouts—by 2013, he'd taken on 49 opponents. He'd lost only six times and won scores of times with straight knockouts.

Stan never fought Darrell in one of those officially sanctioned rounds, but the two sparred regularly at Elite Boxing. Every few months, Darrell would show up and promise to take Stan's belts. Each time, Stan would send Darrell home with a pounding.

"Darrell would get his butt kicked, go back to his other gym, and then come back talking big again," Lewter says.

Lewter even tried to work with Darrell. "I have a system, and he just didn't get the system," Lewter says. "He wasn't a great fighter. He was okay, but he was really just a scrapper."

Every loss irked Darrell. His amateur career was going nowhere. He won a couple of bouts but lost many more. Meanwhile, Stan couldn't stop winning.

"Darrell never beat Stan," Brown, the barber, says. "Let me put it this way: Stan was boxing; Darrell was just trying. You know what I mean?"

Mighty Mouse Desrosier leaped out of bed and grabbed his .40-caliber Glock when the pounding rattled his door. He glanced at the clock: 4:00 a.m. "Help me!" a frantic voice cried. "Darrell shot Stan!"

"I'm thinking it's a big fucking joke," Desrosier recalls today. "But I bust open the door, and it's Stan's roommate. I see his eyes are terrified."

Desrosier lived only a few blocks from Stan on Singer Island, a Palm Beach enclave of white-sand beaches, exclusive condo towers, and more affordable midcentury bungalows. Wearing just his boxers, his gun at his side for protection, the diminutive fighter sprinted to Stan's place, a neat blue building a block from the ocean. He ran through the back door and saw Stan sprawled face-down in the living room.

"I turned his head, and that's when I saw it. The shot hit him right in the temple," Desrosier says. "I'm like, 'Oh, man, no!' Then I see his brain coming out of his head."

Word spread like wildfire through South Florida's tight-knit boxing community: a fighter had killed his rival. The details of that deadly night were told and retold, rebroadcast in TV reports and daily news pieces. But friends and witnesses say there was much more about the lead-up to Stan's murder the night before Thanksgiving than what was portrayed in the media.

"Stan was living the dream everyone else was trying to get to,"

Desrosier says. "And Darrell had the wrong mind-set. He felt like it was someone else's fault he couldn't get there."

The ironic truth, though, was that by the time Darrell put a bullet in his rival's head, Stan's boxing career had stalled as well. In 2013, in the wake of his Olympic disappointment, Stan had gone pro. He also decided to step away from Lewter, his mentor, in favor of Pahokee-based manager Nelson Lopez.

Stan moved to the small town on the edge of Lake Okeechobee, where he lived in a spartan room with no hot water. He was trying to change his narrative before hitting the national stage. "Stan told us people wouldn't buy his story. He wanted to make it tougher," his mother recalls. "People wouldn't respect him coming from suburban Palm Beach, but Pahokee was a tough place."

By 2014, Stan had fought nine bouts in the Dominican Republic, Ecuador, and Miami, and won every time. But he wasn't making real money and struggled to get on a big-name bill. He bristled at his impoverished lifestyle.

In the middle of that year, for the first time in almost a decade, Stan took a break. To his parents' delight, he went back to school for a computer coding certificate, found work with DirecTV, and moved into his place on Singer Island. "Stan was very happy," his father says.

Something else curious happened: Stan began hanging out with Darrell. The two weren't exactly friends, but they ran in the same circle of young boxers. Both enjoyed dancing and nightlife, and now that Stan wasn't in full-on training mode, he had more time for the social scene.

"Darrell could be cool as hell," Desrosier says. "And Stan wasn't going to hold grudges."

Stan hadn't given up on his boxing dreams altogether. A week before he died, he ran into his old sparring partner, Gedeon. Stan promised he'd soon return to Lewter's gym. "I told him: 'How do you go 9-0 as a pro and then quit? You gotta keep going!'" Gedeon remembers.

Darrell's own amateur fighting career was still basting in mediocrity, and he'd found work at Home Depot between training. By late last year, his personal life was imploding. First, he had a baby with a woman he'd met at Palm Beach Boxing; the stress of trying to provide for a kid while stoking the dying embers of his boxing dreams was intense.

"You have to be focused as a fighter. If you bring all that into the gym with you, you're going to fail," Desrosier says. "Darrell and his baby mama wasn't agreeing on shit. His mind wasn't clear."

Darrell's fragile mental state shattered when his girlfriend left him. Just after midnight on a Monday in September, a Palm Beach Gardens police officer found Darrell lingering in the shadows behind a gym. When the cop stopped him, the boxer took a "defensive stance" and refused to answer. The officer had to point a Taser and call for backup before Darrell handed over his driver's license; he was charged with loitering and resisting arrest, though the case was soon dropped.

About a month later, Stan finally realized how unstable his rival had become. "Darrell was stepping to Stan again at some bar, saying, 'I'm better than you; I'm better than you.' But Stan would not fight him," Lewter says.

Soon after, Stan called Desrosier with a startling request: he wanted to borrow his gun. "He said, 'Darrell threatened to kill me,'" Desrosier says. "I told him: 'Stan, you are not a street man. We need to settle this in the boxing ring.' Eventually, everyone was laughing about it. We thought it was settled."

Then, the night before Thanksgiving, Stan agreed to head out to Clematis Street with Darrell and several other friends. Desrosier was invited but decided to stay home. He'd had his own falling-out with Darrell and wanted to steer clear of the temperamental boxer.

There's still disagreement about exactly what happened that evening. Here's what Darrell later told police: The group hopped into Stan's red Saturn and headed to a pizza place, where he claimed Stan began relentlessly boasting. "I'm a championship fighter," Darrell claimed Stan yelled. "I will kick your ass!"

When Darrell didn't back down, he told cops, Stan beat him up. He even provided an excuse for why he'd lost: "[Stan] had training in mixed martial arts and wrestling in addition to traditional boxing," an officer wrote.

Stan's friends say that tale is nonsense. Stan was notoriously humble and had no interest in fighting Darrell, they say. "Darrell wanted to go bare-knuckle right there on Clematis. Stan said no," Gedeon says. "But he was throwing jabs. So Stan body-slammed him. He just picked him up and dropped him, because he didn't want to hit him."

But the party didn't dissolve after that first confrontation. Instead, the group moved on to a rooftop lounge. Darrell told police that Stan "continued to make off-hand remarks . . . about who was the better fighter."

Desrosier doubts that claim. But he says Stan did fan the flames, perhaps by accident. Darrell was already steaming over his split from his girlfriend, and that night, Stan—the better fighter, the better-loved friend, the local boxing hero—also bested him on the dance floor.

"Darrell can't get shit, but Stan got a girl," Desrosier says. "Darrell comes in, interfering with the girl, and now it's an ego thing. A couple words got said, Darrell had a foul mouth, and it got to the best of them. Then hands got thrown."

When the dust cleared, Darrell limped away, beaten and in pain.

Hours after returning home, Stan heard a knock. He peered out and saw Darrell—and wanted nothing to do with him. "Stan wouldn't come out," Lewter says. "He's yelling out the door: 'It's squashed, it's over, it's done.'"

But Darrell insisted he simply wanted to talk it over. "Stan said, 'Let me see your waist.' Darrell showed him his waist—no gun," Desrosier says.

What Stan couldn't see was the silver Colt .45 Darrell was holding in his other hand, just out of view. As soon as Stan opened the door and stuck his head out, Darrell fired a single shot through his temple.

Barely 20 minutes later, a stunned Desrosier stood staring at his friend's bloody corpse. He pulled out his cell phone and texted Darrell.

"Damn u killed Stan," he wrote.

Darrell later texted back: "Call me."

When Desrosier dialed his number, a raspy-voiced, weeping Darrell picked up. Desrosier says, "He was saying over and over, 'I'm sorry, dog. I'm sorry. I'm sorry.'"

Desrosier pressed him: *Why did he do it? Why did he have to shoot Stan?* But Darrell wouldn't answer. "He just kept saying, 'I'm sorry.'"

The elder Stan Stanisclasse carefully maintains a shrine to his son on a table next to the front door. The wooden surface is covered with polished trophies, gaudy championship belts, and framed photos of the sweaty young fighter. But Stan Sr.'s most prized relic is in a dark corner of the garage.

A black punching bag riddled with shallow dents—a permanent reminder of his son's daily practice—silently hangs from a chain, gently swaying in the cool winter breeze.

"This was the third one, actually," Stan's father says, caressing the leather. "He wore through two more of them in this garage."

Stan's parents have spent the past three months asking the same question Desrosier repeated into the phone that horrible night before Thanksgiving: would another boxer really kill their son just because he couldn't beat him in the ring?

"Even the guy's family, some of them have come up to ask me why. They don't know either," Canita Stanisclasse says of Darrell.

Still, the question lingers, debated ad nauseam in boxing gyms from Palm Beach to Miami. In Stan's circle, there's little dispute about what drove Darrell to the crime.

"The entire problem here was Darrell's ego. He wanted to be better than Stan so badly," Lewter says. "That's why he was stepping up to Stan over and over, always saying, 'I'm better than you.' The only person on earth who thought he was better than Stan was Darrell."

There's a strange balance in sports. Athletes have to believe they're the best—often irrationally and against all evidence—to find the mental strength to win. It's a feat of delusion we all celebrate in our heroes. Rocky Balboa was insane to think he could beat the best fighters in the world, but that's what made his story so compelling.

Darrell was the deranged side of that coin, Stan's friends say. His self-belief was so strong that squaring it with his mediocre skills and Stan's dominance became impossible. He had to find a way to top his rival.

"I think it started as more of a friendly rivalry, but Darrell took it to another level," says Willard, the fight promoter. "Stan would win and win, and it's no big deal to him. But Darrell took it more personally because he couldn't beat Stan. It gnawed at him for years."

Police made the same case in charging documents. The morning after the shooting, they found Darrell in his apartment. He soon confessed to killing Stan, they say, and pointed them toward a box under his bed, where they found a Colt .45 and the clothes he wore during the shooting. The motive?

"Mr. Stanisclasse held several championship titles but refused to accept a challenge from Mr. Telisme," police wrote. "Mr. Telisme felt he was missing his opportunity to advance in the boxing community."

The killing was premeditated, prosecutors say. They've charged Darrell with first-degree murder and carrying a concealed firearm without a license.

Despite confessing to police, Darrell pleaded not guilty December 21. His attorney, Scott Skier, says prosecutors have taken the death penalty off the table and he plans to "aggressively defend" Telisme. And both Darrell's father and Desrosier say they doubt he planned to kill Stan that night. "I can't believe that," Daniel Telisme says. "I think it must have been some kind of accident."

Adds Desrosier: "He didn't mean to do this shit. You could tell he didn't. It all just got the best of him. He ain't no evil guy. And I think he has fucking suffered every day since then."

But Stan's family says there's too much evidence Darrell had plotted violence for years.

"It was his jealousy of Stan," Canita says. "He didn't realize that this is something Stan worked for . . . He deserved to be where he is. [Darrell] didn't see how much time Stan spent and how hard he trained. He thinks Stan just walked into it, and [Darrell] wasn't willing to do all that work."

Darrell is scheduled for trial August 22. Beyond the motive, there's one other unanswered question. Witnesses spotted a black SUV driving Darrell to and from the murder scene. Someone enabled him to kill Stan, his family believes, but no other arrests have been made.

Stan's family and friends try to remember the rising star they loved. More than 400 showed up to a wake in December at Iglesia Familiar Family Church to share memories: how a sweat-drenched Stan, with a shit-eating grin on his face, would run up to hug people in the gym; the way he'd teach young boxers to duck a punch; all the times he outfought more seasoned boxers; how he worked the crowd with that little shuffling dance move.

"This kid was going to be Floyd Mayweather in five years," says Charlie Remy, a friend from Elite Boxing. "I really believe that."

Stan's parents have left his memorabilia and punching bag untouched. They're working to start a scholarship in Stan's name to fund schools back in Haiti. "Nobody can answer why Darrell did this," Canita says. "All I can say is Stan is gone. Nothing you can tell me is gonna replace him."

JEFF MAYSH

Why One Woman Pretended to Be a High-School Cheerleader

FROM THE ATLANTIC

ON SEPTEMBER 2, 2008, a shy, blond transfer student strolled into Ashwaubenon High School in Green Bay, Wisconsin. The petite sophomore wore a pink hoodie and carried a new school bag decorated with hearts, eager to start the new term. But just 16 days later, she was standing in court wearing an orange prison jumpsuit and shackles, charged with identity theft. There, prosecutors revealed that Wendy Brown was not really 15, but a 33-year-old mother of two—who had stolen her teenage daughter's identity in an attempt to relive her own high school days. In her weeks as a student, Brown had taken classes with students half her age. She had tried out for the Ashwaubenon High School cheerleading squad and even attended a pool party thrown by the cheer coach.

Television crews surrounded the courthouse and besieged Brown's family at their home in Nevada. "It was bad," recalls her father, Joe. "Every show that's on in the morning called . . . Oprah didn't call. She was the only one that didn't call."

A bespectacled Brown spoke like a teenager as she addressed the court: "I just wanted to say that I'm sorry for what I've done," she said softly. "I feel bad about it. And I regret it. Um, I always have . . . I am not a bad person. I just made a mistake."

Brown's antics baffled the court. Searching for guidance, the judge rifled through his law books, as prosecutors unpacked her troubled past. Brown had served prison time in 2002 for burglary and again in 2004 for obstructing justice; she was also accused of writing a Dairy Queen a bad check for $13. "I can only guess if history repeats itself her motive has something to do with money," Lieutenant Jody Crocker, Ashwaubenon's captain of investigations, told reporters. If the allegations of identity theft were true, Brown would face up to six years in prison and a $10,000 fine. Yet her only crime while posing as a teenager was to bounce a $134.10 check for her cheerleader uniform.

Back in her home state of Illinois, Cass County state's attorney John Dahlem recognized Brown on television and asked the question on everyone's minds: "My first thought was, 'Why would you want to go through high school again?'" he told a local newspaper.

Ben Michaelis, a clinical psychologist, says: "Many people focus on choices they made—or chances they didn't take—as a way of grappling with understanding their current circumstances." For example, in 1986, a failed athlete named James Arthur Hogue, 26, posed as a 16-year-old boy and enrolled at Palo Alto High School, where he won one of the most prestigious high school cross-country races in the country. In 2009, Anthony Avalos, 22, faked a birth certificate on his computer so he could play basketball for Yuma Union High School, and aim for a college scholarship.

In January, Brown agreed to meet me in a noisy coffee shop just five miles from the school, in East Green Bay. In a quiet corner, she removed her chewing gum and rolled it in the plastic wrapping from her banana muffin. She is 41 now, though she looks much younger. She is mouselike, her eyes magnified by thick lenses, her face hidden behind an unruly mop of blond hair. When she speaks, it is from behind a hand that muffles her tiny voice.

This is the first time she has spoken publicly about her motivations. Brown says it wasn't money that drove her to step back in time: "What was I gonna steal?" she asks. "Kids' lunch boxes?" Instead, she says, it was to fulfill a dream that was crushed many years ago.

The only part of high school that Wendy Brown enjoyed, except for the final bell, was long-distance running. It was the summer of 1990. The Berlin Wall was being demolished, and New Kids on the Block topped the Hot 100. In southwest Chicago, Brown would dash through the leafy suburbia of Oak Lawn. For the 16-year-old track star, running was a means of escape.

Wendy had a speech impediment—she pronounced rabbit like

"wabbit"—which led to bullying, and fights. Speech therapists un-covered deeper issues at home. "Brown has a long-standing his-tory of significant emotional problems," a judge later concluded, after reviewing evidence. "They stem primarily from her relation-ship with her mother, which is very abusive." Brown explains: "We fought all the time . . . She put me down, said things about me, I got hit a lot."

She says running helped to put valuable miles between her and home, and the bullies at Harold L. Richards High School. But one day as she was darting across the village, a wave of nausea washed over her. She stopped and threw up. That had been happening a lot recently.

She guessed it might have been the stress of being so unpopu-lar. Though her brother was on the school's football team, the Bulldogs, an invisible barrier seemed to separate her from the cool girls, the cheerleaders who waved black and gold pom-poms on game days. "I was always jealous of them," Brown says. "It just seemed that they had a great life." When Brown's mother found out about her vomiting, she asked her straight up: "Are you preg-nant?"

It was impossible, Brown thought. She was whippet-thin. And anyway, she thought the way she and her boyfriend did it was safe. "I didn't know what made you pregnant," she told me. "My mother never talked to me about things like that." A home pregnancy test registered negative, but her mom and a doctor insisted on an ul-trasound. "You're pregnant," he confirmed. "Four months."

Brown's boyfriend abandoned her instantly, but not before tell-ing everyone at school. The kids threw paper at her, pushed her around. She could take the bullying no longer. "I wanted to get my high school diploma," Brown says, "but there was just too much going on." She quit, and on her 17th birthday, she gave birth to baby Joey, named after her father. Three months later she became pregnant again with a baby girl, Jaimi, this time by another boy.

In the meantime, she watched her younger sister, Jennifer, ef-fortlessly rise through the school's social ecosystem. "I hated her," Brown says. "She got everything that I wanted. I was extremely jealous of her." Seeing Jennifer wear the Bulldogs black-and-gold cheerleader's uniform, she says, was enough to break her heart.

Drifting into her twenties, Brown held a series of short-term jobs at Kmart and Wal-Mart; she poured bad coffee at fast-food restaurants. Her longest period of employment, the court later heard, "was as a stripper." It was a life spent on the move, transporting the kids from Texas, to Michigan, to Nevada, and back to Illinois, where she married a man in June of 2006.

Six months after their wedding day, she says, the violence started. They moved to Cass County, Illinois, where the police chief, Tom Osmer, told the local paper that the police were frequently called to the couple's home. A neighbor told the *Galesburg Register-Mail* in 2008, "[He] knocked all the windows out when he got mad at her."

The couple moved to Green Bay in August of 2008 looking for a fresh start. Brown had an old friend there, and it was far enough from Illinois to leave their pasts behind. They rented a small apartment on Willard Drive, so close to the football fields of Ashwaubenon High School that you can hear the coach's whistle at practice. Due to the violence and instability at home, Wendy says her two kids, by then teenagers, moved to Nevada to live with her parents, Joe and Judith. "I had a breakdown," she admits. It was the lowest moment of her life.

And when she looked out her window she saw a high school, the place where it all went wrong.

When Brown posted photographs on Facebook, she says, friends would comment on her youthful looks, writing, "You look like a junior in high school!" Alone in her apartment one evening, Brown pulled off her baseball cap, and carefully snipped bangs into her hair. She flicked a little curl at the ends, the way the local girls did. And when she looked in the mirror, she thought, it was like looking at her daughter, Jaimi, then a sophomore in high school. (Jaimi was not available to comment on this story before publication.)

Brown says her husband took her to the mall to buy school clothes. (She says he was in on it, even encouraging her plan, but the judge later said that her husband had "no idea.") She selected a fashionable Esprit shoulder bag. Then she flicked through racks of jeans and Levi's clothing in the junior section. She weighed 103 pounds and wore a petite size. Brown tried on a pair of Nike shoes, the brand she always bought her own children. But the real trick was the voice. "I just did that little valley girl thing, the California thing," Wendy says. In the coffee shop, she transforms her voice into an up-speaking teen's. It is disquieting.

With that voice, she simply strolled into the school that August, and introduced herself to the school counselor, Kim Demeny, using her daughter's first name and her own maiden name. She said she was a transfer student from Pahrump High School, Nevada —the same high school that her daughter was currently attending. Demeny declined to comment for this story, but told police that on Brown's registration document, the student wrote that her mother was "difficult to reach at work," and the school should "let her go home on her own if she felt sick." Demeny said Brown "appeared older," but that her demeanor was "consistent with that of a high-school girl." Before their meeting ended, Brown asked Demeny when cheerleading tryouts were happening.

Ashwaubenon High School is a hamlet of red brick buildings with a brutalist concrete gym on its southern edge. More than 1,000 children study under its fluttering American flag, mainly from the surrounding suburban neighborhoods. Brown arrived feeling nervous and excited. Nearly 20 years ago at her high school in Illinois, cheerleading tryouts lasted three grueling weeks. Some schools require a tumbling certification, proving that aspiring cheerleaders can perform such maneuvers as the "standing back handspring" and "round-off back tuck." Hazing is not uncommon for cheerleaders at other schools. New recruits can get smothered with food or drenched by a water hose.

In the last weeks of summer before the new semester began, the cheerleading team held tryouts at the Jaguars' football stadium. It was the first season also for award-winning coach Mary Lee Boyd Johnson. Johnson (who did not respond to interview requests) has 21 years of cheer experience. She coached at rival De Pere High School from 1987 to 1992, taking the cheer team to first-place honors at both the Universal Cheerleading Association and the National Cheerleading Association camps. "I set my goals high," Johnson told the *Green Bay Press Gazette* in 2012, "to make Ashwaubenon cheer a competitive program." Her daughter, Bailee Wautlet, was captain.

Brown arrived at tryouts in a pair of workout shorts and a T-shirt. "I was talking to the girls, they said the tryouts were easy," Brown says. But first, there were rules. The girls sat on the floor and waited for the coach to speak. "She said . . . we were supposed to represent the school, have respect for people, for each other, and for everybody else. We had to be nice, you know, watch our

mouths, no chewing gum during practice because you'd get de-
merits for that." Brown says the coach explained that the team also
had an "honest system," requiring the cheerleaders to be honest
with one another.

At Ashwaubenon High, there was both a dance team and a cheer
squad, and they were fierce rivals. The dance team required gym-
nastic maneuvers and strict dance training. Though both teams
waved pom-poms, the cheer squad was much less challenging. The
established cheerleaders taught the new girls the official cheer of
the Jaguars. The routines at tryouts were simple, which was a relief
to Brown. "I couldn't do cartwheels," she says, "I couldn't do flips.
I couldn't do any of that."

It didn't matter. There were no football players, and the bleachers were empty, but their chants filled the stadium. Brown fell into
the hypnotic routine, with the hand claps and chanting. There
was just one nagging feeling. Unlike the other girls, afterwards she
would return home to her miserable apartment. "I was living two
different lives," she says, "two different people." But for now, she
had a new, intoxicating mantra: "Go! Go! Go! Fight! Fight! Fight!
Win! Win! Win! Go! Fight! Win!"

On August 8, 2008, Johnson invited the cheerleaders to a pool
party at her home. Brown was a ball of nerves. It had been 19
years since she was first a sophomore. Katy Perry now dominated
the Hot 100. When she arrived, the cheerleaders were catching
rays in tiny two-piece suits, enjoying the fading Wisconsin summer. Brown, anxious about the stretch marks from her pregnan-
cies, wore a one-piece underneath a T-shirt, an outfit that she says
puzzled the other girls.

"I told [them] the reason I had the T-shirt on, you know, was
that I used to be really fat. I lost all the weight," she says.

"She's just shy, leave her alone," Brown recalls a cheerleader
saying.

Then she jumped in the pool. Brown tried her best to fit in,
playing volleyball, and copying how the other girls nibbled at the
cheese, pepperoni, and sausage pizzas.

"I just remember eating it how my daughter would eat it," Brown
says, "little bites." Music thumped from a stereo. The games seg-
ued into cheer routines, and Brown began to enjoy herself. "We
had the first home game to practice for," says Brown, still hoping

to be chosen for the squad. From the stereo the sound of fiddling violins soared across the backyard. The girls lined up and waited for the song to kick in:

> If it hadn't been for Cotton-Eye Joe,
> I'd been married a long time ago.

Brown danced to "Cotton-Eye Joe"—the 1995 record by the novelty country band Rednex—more times than any 33-year-old woman should ever have to. The routine was a series of hops and twirls. "It wasn't rocket science," Brown says. But spinning around in circles for an hour made the girls dizzy. They collapsed with laughter. The way she tells it, Brown hadn't been that happy in years.

Just days after the pool party, Brown was at home when her cell phone jingled. It was a local number. She answered: "Who is this?"

It was the coach, she says, asking for Jaimi.

"Yes, hold on a second," Brown said.

She held the phone away from her mouth for a moment.

"Hello!" she said, adopting her teenaged-girl voice.

Brown listened for a minute, then let out a scream.

"Oh my God!" she squealed. "That's amazing!"

Even today, Wendy Brown's face lights up when she talks of making the cheer team. When she walked into her first day at Ashwaubenon High on September 2, she had a spring in her step. She was thrilled when she received her locker, number 19.

In homeroom, Brown remembers, the teacher had to call "Jaimi" three times before she remembered to say she was present.

"You're daydreaming, huh?" Brown recalls the teacher saying. "That's okay. It's your first day? And you're new here?"

Brown nodded. One of the cheerleaders from the pool party was in the same homeroom and greeted her enthusiastically. "She said, 'Oh my God, we have the same schedule! Oh my God, we're in the same classes!'"

During choir, Brown says she did not try to conceal her singing talents. She says the teacher told her that her voice was "very mature,'" to which Brown replied, "I've been singing a long time." Brown was immediately drafted for the senior choir. Court documents also confirm Brown's academic ambitions: she reportedly told Demeny that she had "already covered the material in the integrated science course and could be successful in a high level."

At lunchtime, Brown lined up with the rest of the students in the cafeteria. Brown says that she noticed some students making fun of a girl sitting on her own. "I just told her, 'Just ignore them . . . they're just jealous, you must have something that they don't have.'" And then Brown says, she gave the girl a piece of advice: "Be who you are."

That afternoon, Brown tried on her cheerleading uniform in the Jaguars locker room for the first time. It was deep green with white sleeves, accented with glistening gold piping. The pom-poms were green in one hand, gold in the other. On her chest was the giant gold "A" for Ashwaubenon, and "JAGUARS" in a felt, athletic font. "Pretty cool," she remembers thinking. "I was like, 'Wow, I'm in a cheerleader uniform.' . . . It was like a trophy or award, like, 'This is mine?'"

On September 8, a week into the school year, Associate Principal Dirk Ribbens reviewed the first round of truancy reports. A stickler for attendance, Ribbens noticed that one student had not returned after her first day. He contacted Don Penza, the police liaison officer for the high school. Penza and Ribbens did not respond to interview requests, but according to the criminal complaint, Penza marched straight over to the student's home address. When no one answered, Ribbens contacted the student's previous high school in Nevada. What they told him was confusing: Jaimi was there, taking classes. When school officials called the student's home, they spoke to Judith, Brown's mother. Judith told Ribbens that her daughter "has a history of identity-theft type crimes."

Wendy Brown had already become undone by another deception, according to court documents. At her apartment building, police alleged that Brown had posed as the building manager and relieved a potential tenant, Teryn Cox, 21, of a $765.00 deposit. Today, Brown insists this wasn't her. Either way, records show that Brown was inside the county jail when school investigators caught up with her.

Under questioning, Brown admitted that she "wanted to get her high school degree and be a cheerleader because she had no childhood and was trying to regain a part of her life she missed." News of her confession spread through the school at roughly 300 times the speed of regular high school gossip. "[I'm] still kinda like in shock," wrote cheerleader Kelci Ashton on Facebook, on

September 18, the day Wendy Brown first appeared in court. The press had a field day. "Pom-Pom Mom Goes to Extreme," read a CBS headline. "Mom, that's my cheerleading outfit!" joked the *New York Daily News*. Newspapers as far away as England ran with the story. "Everything was just done," Brown says, tearfully. "It was devastating. I just wanted to get in a hole and die." She would never cheer at a competitive game.

In court, the judge realized that Wendy Brown was not a master criminal, but suffering from a serious mental breakdown. A court-appointed psychiatrist who evaluated Brown, Dr. Ralph Baker, agreed, diagnosing her with bipolar II disorder, post-traumatic stress disorder, and two personality disorders. According to an attorney in court, Baker concluded, "She really convinced herself that she could make all this better by enrolling in high school and starting her life over again as her 15-year-old daughter . . . Her fantasy of finishing high school and becoming a cheerleader became a delusion."

Court transcripts reveal an unusual courtroom exchange, in which the defense and prosecution team up to get Brown the help that she needed. "I think [a prison sentence] would be very, very detrimental to her," conceded Deputy District Attorney John Luetscher. "Hopefully with treatment . . . she will be able to function in society without committing crimes." Apart from the bounced check, no real harm was done, other than a deep embarrassment to the school that seems to last to this day; Ashwaubenon High School refused to comment for this story. Brown was found not guilty "by reason of mental disease or defect" to a charge of identity theft, and committed to the Winnebago mental health facility in Wisconsin for three years.

Wendy Brown became an urban legend at Ashwaubenon High School. "[The] buzz around school was just that it was hilarious that it even happened," former student Hope Edelbeck tells me. She says a powderpuff football team named themselves "Wendy Brown," and played in prison orange uniforms. But as that team of girls pretended to be Ashwaubenon High's infamous jailbird, the real Wendy Brown sat in jail, waiting three months for her transfer to Winnebago.

"I started getting mad when I was in there," Brown says. She decided to study for her GED course behind bars. This would be hard, said her tutor, without regular classes or teachers. Brown took the four-hour test six weeks after her arrest. Her tutor delivered her results to her jail cell. When Brown found out she passed, tears rolled down her cheeks.

While she was in the care of the mental institution, Brown was diagnosed with breast cancer. She went through chemotherapy under lockup, alone. On December 27, 2010, records confirm she had two serious operations to keep her alive. Slowly she recovered. She went to daily group therapy, climbed rocks, and learned to make peace with her past. She separated from her husband ("he should have been locked up, not me") and three years later, she walked free.

Today, Brown says she has come to terms with being an outcast. Away from the bustling coffee shop, she comes alive, speaking louder, laughing, and joking. She says she likes to wear a Vikings shirt around Green Bay, a city where bankers, bums, and babies all wear Packers shirts on game day. People still whisper when she is recognized, but the only ones she hides from are the former cheerleaders. Wistfully, Brown says that she has no relationship with her daughter, Jaimi, now 23. Brown says that about two years ago, Jaimi had a child too, making her a grandmother. She hopes for reconciliation, but feels that the ball is in her daughter's court.

Coach Johnson and the cheer team went on to win first- and second-place finishes in area cheer competitions, taking top honors in the 2009–10 Northern Regionals. Though Wendy passed her GED exam in jail in 2008, she had to wait to be released from the mental health institution to pick up her certificate. In 2013, she walked across the stage at a college in Wisconsin, wearing a gown, hat, and tassel. "It felt awesome," she says.

Watching in the crowd, her father snapped photographs. At their celebration dinner, Joe Mueller gave her a graduation gift, a Keurig coffeemaker. "It was just something that I always wanted to see happen . . . It makes you feel good, right? Your kid finally made it." He chuckles, and says: "It only took her 30 years."

DAN BARRY

Hit Man

FROM THE NEW YORK TIMES

THE BUICK SEDAN crawled the Providence streets. The April sky was baby blue, the air pleasant and cool. Perfect baseball weather. The man hunched in the backseat once lived for days like this.

When the maroon car stopped outside Pannone's Market on Pocasset Avenue, its backseat passenger leapt out with uncommon grace, a mask over his handsome face, a shotgun in his large hands. An armed and disguised accomplice followed close behind.

The mom-and-pop employees ducked as the nimble gunman found his target, a bookmaker who had defied Raymond L. S. Patriarca, the coal-eyed head of New England organized crime. The wayward bookie caught it from three feet away, his unused gun clattering to rest a few inches from his outstretched hand. His sidekick was dropped near a shelf of canned tomatoes, his face rearranged by buckshot.

Neighborhood children were soon pressing their noses against the storefront window as investigators examined the two bodies splayed on the blood-slick floor. The Buick was already a memory.

The killer and his co-conspirators gathered that evening in a motel a few miles away. One of them later recalled how the athletic shooter, whose apt nickname was Pro, proudly tallied his personal stats. How he was first through the door, the one who hit the bookie, the one who killed the bodyguard trying to slip away.

It figured. The habits of old ballplayers die hard.

Newspapers from Burlington, North Carolina, to Walla Walla, Washington, told the same story: Maury "Pro" Lerner could hit.

"Maury Lerner crashed a triple off the clock and rode home on Jacoby's single." "Maury Lerner doubled in two runs Sunday night to lead Boise to a 7-to-5 victory over Pocatello in the Pioneer League play." Maury Lerner singled, doubled, tripled, homered, won the game.

He could always hit. A six-foot-two prospect out of Brookline, Massachusetts, the scholarly Lerner batted .364 as a high school senior. The brief caption beneath his yearbook portrait conveyed a singular purpose ("Baseball, 2, 3, 4") and that singular nickname: Pro. It was supposedly derived from his having been called "Little Professor" as a precocious child.

Lerner claimed to have enjoyed a happy childhood, spending part of his youth in a duplex on Verndale Street, about two miles from Fenway Park. But his son, Glen Lerner, disputes this assertion of boyhood happiness. Maury's father, Glen says, never told Maury he loved him, never went to his ball games.

Maybe this explains things, he says.

Maybe.

Lerner signed with the Washington Senators at 18 and was dispatched to play entry-level ball in Erie, Pennsylvania. He batted a miserable .167 in 13 games and spent the next few years in the Marines.

But he returned in 1957 to join the Milwaukee Braves franchise in Boise, Idaho, where he smacked 158 hits in 127 games and batted an impressive .328 ("Second-sacker Maury Lerner got the vital hit, a double to right-center"). Then, up in Yakima, Washington, he hit .348 ("Lerner's drive was against the right field fence"). Then, over in the Pittsburgh Pirates organization, he hit .372 for the Wilson Tobs in North Carolina ("Lerner popped one over the short center wall").

Pittsburgh's front office was watching, just in case Bill Mazeroski at second or Dick Groat at short got injured. This middle infielder coming up, this Lerner kid, seemed respectful, earnest, even erudite. A real gentleman, except when he wasn't.

Playing in Nicaragua during the 1959–60 winter season, Lerner was hitting close to .400 and having a good time. So good, in fact, that his manager, the major leaguer Earl Torgeson, announced plans to cut him for missed curfews and other transgressions.

But then Torgeson and Lerner teamed up against some Cuban players, after Lerner complained about too many brushback pitches. Torgeson got into a fistfight with a Cuban player and re-signed. Lerner attacked a Cuban pitcher and a Cuban umpire but kept on playing. And hitting.

Frank Kostro, a future major leaguer known for his pinch-hitting, competed against Lerner that winter. "I was hitting well over .300," he says. "But I wasn't even close to the leading hitter —who was Maury Lerner."

Lerner returned to the United States with a batting title, a repu-tation for being a good but uptight teammate—and a baby wildcat he had smuggled out in a satchel, according to the book *Memories of Winter Ball*, by Lou Hernández.

He also seemed to carry a self-destructive fear of success. Family lore has it that he sabotaged a chance to move up to the Pirates after Mazeroski got hurt—it is true, at least, that Mazeroski, a fu-ture Hall of Famer, incurred a couple of injuries at the time—by picking a fight with his manager.

"One of his biggest regrets," Glen Lerner says. "Whenever he was going to get promoted, he would do something to undermine it. He didn't know how to explain it."

Maury Lerner was 24, then 25, then 26—middle-aged in minor league time. A veteran bush leaguer making about $700 a few months of the year. A onetime prospect with no prospects.

He still managed to stand out, though, by reading books, watch-ing his diet, and exercising with weights. This was at a time when almost no one in baseball concentrated on strength conditioning, according to Gene Michael, the former Yankees shortstop and general manager who played three games with Lerner on the Sa-vannah Pirates, in Georgia, in 1960.

Though the two ballplayers crossed paths only briefly more than a half-century ago—one going up, the other going down—Michael never forgot Lerner, a good fielder and a great line-drive hitter who advocated chopping down on the ball to beat out the throw to first. Over dinner one night, Lerner lectured on baseball strategy and training in ways that the younger, less experienced Michael had never heard before.

"He was way ahead of us," Michael says. "*Way* ahead of us."

No question. Pro Lerner was looking ahead. By the summer of 1961, the professional ballplayer was also trying out for a life of crime.

He was playing at the time for the Macon Peaches, a collection of has-beens and never-will-bes. One knock-around veteran had struck out in all three of his major league at-bats. Another had toiled for 16 years in the minors, got called up for one game, and didn't even get to bat.

"A bastard club," says Tony Bartirome, one of its players. "All on their way down." Including its good-hitting middle infielder.

Bartirome remembers Lerner being so well mannered that "he was like a priest, almost." Oh, and another thing: he would occasionally leave the team to take care of some personal matters.

Those personal matters might have included Lerner's arrest that summer for the armed robbery of a Boston furniture store. He was later sentenced to three years' probation.

Lerner was arrested again a few months later, charged with conspiring to commit armed robbery and carrying a firearm without a permit. According to Brookline police records, detectives interrupted Lerner and his ex-con companion in the midst of robbing an acquaintance.

Questioned by the police, Lerner repeatedly lied. And while he eventually beat the rap, the young ballplayer made an unfavorable impression. "I know the Brookline police were not fond of him," Glen Lerner says. "A Jewish troublemaker would not be well looked upon by an Irish police force."

Maury Lerner held on a little longer to his baseball dreams. He spent part of the 1962 season with the Raleigh Capitals, of the Senators organization, batting .308 and hitting eight home runs, the most of his professional career ("A two-run homer by first baseman Maury Lerner in the eighth inning won the game").

A teammate, John Kennedy, a future major leaguer, hasn't forgotten the sounds of obsession that emanated from Lerner's home in Raleigh, North Carolina, the rhythmic whacks of a fixated hitter striking a tire with a bat.

Thum, thum, thum . . .

"He couldn't care less about anything but hit, hit, hit," Kennedy says.

One time Lerner coaxed a homeless man who used to linger outside the Devereux Meadow ballpark onto the team bus. He hid the man from the manager and supplied him with enough beer to last the daylong road trip. An act of kindness, Kennedy says. "As far as I'm concerned, he was a helluva guy."

A helluva guy who was also passing worthless checks in Tennessee, stealing a television set from a hotel not far from Fenway Park, and hustling some college saps in games of pool.

Baseball scouts used to scrutinize Lerner's every move. Now agents from the FBI were the ones watching.

By this point, Lerner was hanging around with two well-known New England criminals, John Kelley, also known as Red, and George Agisotelis, also known as Billy A. Those two were central suspects in the notorious and still unsolved mail truck robbery in Plymouth, Massachusetts, in 1962, in which men dressed as police officers commandeered a Postal Service truck and made off with the then-record haul of $1.5 million in cash.

But he was also still playing baseball, holding on with a Senators affiliate in Pennsylvania with the exquisite name the York White Roses. He batted .250 in only 28 games, the reasons for his truncated 1963 season unclear, except for an internal FBI document from that time:

> *Joseph McKenney, Director of Publicity, American Baseball League, and Joseph Cronin, President of the American League, after reviewing records, advised Maurice Lerner is presently on the suspended list of the York, Pennsylvania, Baseball Team subject to moving up to a higher classification.*
>
> *Cronin stated that being on the suspended list indicates either Lerner did not report to the York team or was suspended while there for some infraction of the club's training regulations.*

There was no formal announcement, no issued news release. But Pro Lerner had given up baseball to concentrate on a new career. A name that once appeared in scouting sheets and small-town newspapers was now popping up in police intelligence reports.

Maurice Lerner, aka Pro, aka Reno. Newly wedded to Arrene Siegel. Suspect in the robberies of the Boston Five Cent Savings Bank and the Suburban National Bank. Associate of known criminals Kelley and Agisotelis. Formerly employed as a professional baseball player. Considered armed and dangerous—whether with gun or bat, it seems.

Part of the growing Lerner reputation was how Pro once applied his bat skills to his new profession by ringing a doorbell and taking a cut at the head of the man who answered. The oft-told story may be apocryphal, but word of Lerner's penchant for violence had clearly reached the front office of the Patriarca crime family, the Boston Red Sox of the underworld. And he got called up.

When some men made the ill-conceived decision to rob a bookie operation linked to a high-ranking mafioso, it was Lerner, along with Kelley, who was dispatched to straighten things out. When certain people disappeared or stopped breathing, Lerner often seemed to be, shall we say, part of the postmortem conversation.

In January 1965, the body of an inconsequential gangster named Robert Rasmussen was found in Wilmington, Massachusetts, having taken a .38 bullet to the back of his head. An informant later claimed that Rasmussen had tried to extort money from Kelley, so he was lured to Lerner's apartment with the promise of a nice score, a bookie's cash-jammed safe—only to wind up dead in a snowbank, wearing little more than a necktie.

Then there was Tommy Richards, another member of Kelley's crew, who vanished just before the 1967 trial for the mail heist in Plymouth. The well-known lawyer F. Lee Bailey, who represented Kelley, recalls that when he asked about Richards's whereabouts, he was told, "Well, Tommy won't be joining us."

Richards had a decent excuse; he was dead. Another Kelley associate later told Bailey of being present when Lerner shot Richards in the head, right after the man pleaded for his life, saying, "I never did anything to hurt any of you guys."

It was not what Richards had done, but what he might do. Kelley didn't think his friend would hold up on the stand, so, apparently, he had to go. Kelley and the other living defendants were acquitted in the Plymouth case, and the disappearance of Richards remains unsolved.

I didn't see nothing, I didn't hear nothing," said the owner of a small store close to Pannone's Market. On the clear and cool Saturday of April 20, 1968, a pair of masked gunmen had just left two dead bodies on the market's floor. Their getaway Buick was later recovered, with a sawed-off M1 carbine, two sawed-off shotguns, and two .38-caliber pistols still inside.

"You want information?" someone told an inquisitive *Providence Journal* reporter. "Call 411."

Months passed without any solid leads, although the involvement of Patriarca, the New England mob boss, was generally stipulated. Nothing moved in Providence without the say-so of "the old man," who would sit outside his small coin-vending business on Federal Hill, working his cigar as he watched the cops watch him.

"One of the most powerful crime bosses in the country," said Thomas Verdi, a Providence deputy police chief and former commander of the department's organized crime unit. "He was revered and feared by all."

But in 1969, the Patriarca operation suffered a critical security breach when one of its associates turned informant. Unfortunately for Pro Lerner, the canary was his friend and mentor Red Kelley.

A recent Brink's armored-car robbery of a half-million dollars had been too tidy to be anything other than an inside job, leading investigators to an errant Brink's employee who quickly named his accomplices. Among them was Kelley, who soon indicated his desire to exchange information for the comforts of protective custody.

Kelley told federal investigators that Lerner, the primary gunman, was bright, courageous, and homicidal: the most dangerous man he had known in his 25 years on the dark side.

Kelley kept talking. About how a Patriarca lieutenant, Luigi Manocchio, had recruited Lerner for his controlled violence, and how Lerner had recruited Kelley for his meticulous attention to escape plans. How they repeatedly scouted the daily movements of their intended victims, the wayward bookie, Rudy Marfeo, and his bodyguard, Anthony Melei. How Manocchio later shook hands after a job well executed and conveyed the message that "George" —code for Patriarca—was pleased.

FBI agents arrested Lerner early one morning at the Brookline apartment he shared with his wife and two young children. While Lerner dressed, an agent noticed a brown gun case. When law enforcement officials returned hours later with a search warrant, they discovered its contents, a pump-action shotgun and a fully loaded pearl-handled .45-caliber pistol.

As Lerner's wife took sick and went upstairs, they went downstairs to find a cellar converted into a shooting range. A silhouette target had been drawn on the bullet-pocked wall, and bits of lead peppered the floor.

The shooting of imaginary men, it seemed, had replaced the swinging of bats at imaginary balls. *Thum, thum, thum* . . .

Lerner's arrest allowed others to relax. According to FBI records, another federal informant, Richard Chicofsky, told his handlers that "that bastard Lerner got what he deserved."

"When asked what he meant by that, he replied that Lerner was a sadistic killer and that he got his kicks from watching people bleed. He told of the time that Lerner had bragged to him how he killed Billy Aggie (Agisotelis) with a .45 while he and Aggie held a casual conversation in an automobile.

"Chicofsky further stated that he feels a lot better now that Lerner is off the streets because when Lerner was around, he was never really sure when Lerner might decide to 'plank' him."

The hearings and trial for the Marfeo-Melei killings included the usual mob theatrics. One defendant screamed at a prosecutor ("I'll get you, you bastard. I'll see tears running down your face before this is over"), punched a wooden door, and broke his hand. A witness for the prosecution disappeared for a day, only to resurface with a tale of being whisked to a secret location and asked to testify against everyone except Patriarca and Lerner; as the witness left the stand, a defendant's relative threatened her life.

Through it all, Lerner was the odd man out: a Jew from Brookline, not an Italian from Providence, who sought comfort in the regular visits to the prison by a Boston rabbi.

After three days of deliberations in March 1970, a jury in Providence convicted Lerner, Patriarca, and three others of conspiracy, while Lerner was also convicted of murder. The man with a career batting average of .308 was given two life sentences. He was 34.

The former ballplayer sent word that he didn't want any more visits from the rabbi.

John Kennedy and Gene Michael. Ed Brinkman and Bernie Allen. Rich Rollins and Donn Clendenon. Tony Perez and Rusty Staub and Steve Blass and Rico Petrocelli and Tommie Agee and César Tovar and Roy White and Mel Stottlemyre. All those former teammates and opponents were still playing and even thriving in the major leagues.

And where was Maury Lerner, the hit-obsessed prospect who once sat beside them in dugouts, joined in on those long bus rides, and shared small talk around second base? Occupying a first-floor cell in an infamous corner of Rhode Island's Adult Correctional Institutions.

"One of those should-have-beens," his son says. "An American tragedy, when you think of it."

Facing life behind bars, Lerner could easily have assimilated into the hard culture of the prison's north wing, an area reserved for big-name inmates that was controlled by Gerard Ouimette, a vicious and unpredictable gangster connected to the Patriarca crime family. The rules were so lax, and Ouimette so powerful, that inmates could do pretty much anything but leave.

"I remember walking into the prison one time to work on a case, and there in an office were these big food containers full of steaks and lobster tails," Vincent Vespia, a former state police detective, recalls. "So I asked: 'What's all this for?'"

The answer: "Ouimette's having a party."

But rather than join in, Lerner removed himself, capitalizing on the uncommon deference he had earned by keeping his mouth shut about Patriarca. He was, after all, a pro.

An inveterate reader, Lerner had the second-highest IQ in the prison, and he took pride in learning a new vocabulary word every day. A fitness fanatic still, he was an early advocate for the health benefits of raw vegetables. And whenever a law enforcement official stopped by to try to draw him out, he clammed up.

"A disciplined guy; the coldest, hardest guy there," says Brian Andrews, a former detective commander for the Rhode Island State Police. "And Pro wouldn't talk. Sometimes he'd look at you and wouldn't even answer you."

Lerner "conformed strictly to the rules of the institution," a prison record indicates. He retreated to his cell when fights broke out, fulfilled his work assignments, took multiple furloughs without incident, and ably handled a work-release job at a nearby landfill. A model inmate.

In 1980, Lerner came to the rescue of a correction officer who was being choked with a cord by another inmate. He subdued the inmate and escorted the injured officer to the infirmary. A formal commendation was entered into Lerner's file, applauding him for a "heroic action" that would not be forgotten.

Gerald Tillinghast spent a lot of time with Lerner in prison.

Now 70 and out on parole, Tillinghast was a particularly feared figure in the Rhode Island underworld, the reasons for which become clear during a breakfast conversation. Over a crime scene plate of scrambled eggs slathered with ketchup, Tillinghast recalls a beef he once had with a federal informant:

"So I come up behind him, I spun him around, said what are you doing? He said it's none of my effing business. Boom. I knocked him right out, threw him down the stairs and, uh, stabbed him with an ice pick a couple of times."

He says Lerner, whom he respected, was of a different prison stripe than most.

"Take organized crime away, or any kind of crimes like that," Tillinghast says. "If you was to know him, you would never equate him with that. Never. When you get to know him? Very charismatic —if he likes you. Very seldom you'd get him laughing."

All the while, Lerner remained a family man; that is, to his own family. When appeals to overturn his conviction seemed at a dead end, Lerner moved his wife, Arrene, and their two young children, Glen and Jenni, to a small house close to the prison.

"I never met a more loyal woman in my life," Tillinghast says of Arrene. And when Pro would come into the visiting room, he says, "them kids would run to him."

Glen, who was raised to believe that his father had been framed, says he spent more time with him than most children do with their unincarcerated fathers. "I saw him five days a week, two hours a day, across a table in the visiting room," he says.

Still, it was not easy on the Lerner children. Glen says he often brawled with other kids who teased him about a father serving life for a double homicide. And his father could be controlling—"You need to do this, you need to do that"—partly because he had lost control of his own life, and partly because he wanted to steer his children away from that life.

But Glen says with admiration that domestic normality was somehow established in a profoundly abnormal situation. "My parents did an amazing job to overcome this stigma," he says, and to convey to others that "we're not who you think we are."

His father had a concrete wall installed in the backyard so Glen could practice soccer kicks, and he learned all he could about a game he never played so he could counsel his son. When furloughs allowed him brief freedom, he would attend his son's high school soccer games, cheering Glen on to star status.

"He gave us every opportunity to succeed," Glen says. "Everybody would always say to me, 'Man, I wish your dad was my dad.'"

Glen added, "I wouldn't trade him for anybody as my father."

Maury Lerner did his time: 1975, 1980, 1985. Through it all, he found distraction, and maybe even sustenance, in his former profession as a ballplayer. When he heard that a prison job counselor, Joseph Filipkowski, was the father of a promising Little Leaguer, he offered to work on the boy's mechanics. On a prison ball field, an inmate in khakis tossed Wiffle ball pitches to a 12-year-old.

The kid's doing fine, the incarcerated ex-ballplayer advised.

Lerner also became the demanding player-coach for a competitive softball team that took on all comers: correction officers, professional football players, anyone willing to play an opponent who would always have home-field advantage. The younger players listened to him, Tillinghast says, because they feared him.

"He wanted perfection," he says, adding, "God forbid you lost a game, you know what I mean?"

In some ways, Lerner still considered himself part of the professional baseball family. He once contacted a former minor league manager of his to say he had a hot prospect on his prison softball team: this kid could do it all. The former manager, by then a high-ranking Pirates executive, dispatched a scout to run the inmate through a workout.

The player turned out to be exceptionally good—at softball.

According to Tillinghast, Lerner's interaction with his players ended on the ball field. He might say hi to a teammate in the yard, but he rarely engaged in serious conversation.

"He just wanted to do his time," Tillinghast says, cleaning his teeth with a toothpick. "He did his time like 10 men. Never complained."

And after 18 years in prison, Pro Lerner finally won.

His former mentor, Red Kelley, was now acknowledging that he had embellished his testimony during the murder trial in 1970. Do not get him wrong. Things went down just as he had described, except for a few details, including that part about how he had met with Patriarca to discuss plans for the Marfeo-Melei hit. Never happened, he admitted. A corrupt FBI agent, who would later die in prison while awaiting trial on murder charges, had put him up to it.

This nettlesome matter of perjury finally persuaded the Rhode Island Supreme Court to overturn Lerner's murder conviction. So, a few days before Christmas in 1988, the old ballplayer and hit man pleaded no contest to murder and conspiracy charges, received credit for time served, and walked unshackled into the cold Providence day.

He was 53.

Lerner and his wife quickly left Rhode Island for California and then for Las Vegas—as if to get as much distance as possible from the past. Patriarca was dead and now so was a part of Lerner. He had no desire to reconnect with his former cronies, no interest in being compensated for keeping his mouth shut. He just wanted out.

"He walked away from any reminder of that life," his son, Glen, says.

By this point, both his children had attended Duke University, and his son, the soccer star, had played on Duke's 1986 national championship team and gone on to law school at Tulane. A photo from Glen's law school graduation shows his smiling parents arm in arm, his father wearing a goofy striped sweater, looking down.

A bittersweet image. A few years later, Arrene, the loyal wife who had kept the family together, died of cancer at the age of 56. Her husband was devastated.

Lerner never remarried. He continued to live in Las Vegas, where he helped out at his son's personal-injury law firm, and found some modest action at a local sports betting operation. Sometimes he took his young granddaughter for drives around Sin City, singing along with Sinatra and Ella.

Now and then, Glen Lerner would try to engage his father in a discussion about his past; more specifically, how to get out from under that past. "Why can't you forgive yourself?" the son would ask of a father who was famous for holding grudges against others —and, it seemed, himself. Even now, he wouldn't talk.

"I could look in his face, and I could see the regret," Glen says, adding: "There may have been things he did that he didn't get in trouble for."

The former athlete who once sprang so gracefully from the batter's box, bat in hand, and from a sedan, shotgun in hand, could not dodge time. A few years ago, dementia set in. He fell and broke a hip. When death came in 2013, at age 77, he left a son, a daughter, grandchildren, and so many questions.

"It's a whodunit," Glen says. "You know who did it, but why? Why?"

Maybe Lerner had gravitated toward father figures who had led him astray, his son says, sounding wishful. Maybe he was looking for someone to look up to. Maybe.

"He was very sweet at the end," Glen says. "He lost a lot of his edge."

But Maury Lerner never lost his sense of belonging to the professional baseball fraternity. Among its members, he was not known for being anything other than a loyal teammate who could hit like hell. A real pro.

In the years after prison, Lerner began calling former teammates and opponents around the country—people now in their seventies and eighties, who knew him before. He enjoyed reminiscing about the old days, the times spent in baseball's ports of call: Erie and Boise, Macon and Raleigh, Yakima and Managua.

"He called me," the former major leaguer Frank Kostro recalls. "And I says, 'Maury, where you been?'"

The old ballplayer explained as best he could.

LOUISA THOMAS

Serena Williams, Andy Murray, and a Political Wimbledon

FROM THE NEW YORKER

SERENA WILLIAMS HAS BECOME so synonymous with dominance that it can be hard not to take her for granted, her power so
obvious that it can be strangely hard to see. She is called a force of
nature, or considered superhuman, or accorded the divine right
of queens. I have done this myself; I have talked about her as if she
were a Greek goddess.

On Saturday, when she faced Angelique Kerber in the women's
final at Wimbledon, I was tempted to do it again. It was a riveting
match, a contest of contrasting styles. Kerber has become one of
the few players who can take Williams's shots and turn on them. In
the Australian Open final, in January, Kerber had beaten Williams
by using her speed to reach balls that would have been winners
against other players, and her superior strength to redirect Williams's pace and angles. In the Wimbledon final, Kerber played
another brilliant match, bending backhands around the net
post, hitting flat, reactive shots that skimmed the tape of the net,
and minimizing her errors. (She finished with only nine for the
match.) She challenged Williams throughout—but only once did
she test her. At 3–3 in the second set, Kerber earned her first break
point of the match. With a relaxed motion and gentle toss, Williams struck an ace out wide. On the next point, Williams began
with an identical movement and hit the toss in an identical spot
—but this time her serve sped down the T, another ace. Kerber
swung her arms in an exaggerated shrug of frustration. Up the ad-

vantage, Williams controlled the next point, pulling the lefty Kerber out wide to her forehand, repeatedly putting the ball behind her, and then changing directions with a backhand down the line. Kerber couldn't dig it out. From there, the match was more or less over—and the result had never really been in doubt.

Williams's 7–5, 6–3 victory earned her her 22nd major title, tying her with Steffi Graf for most in the Open era. It is her ninth Grand Slam since she turned 30, nearly five years ago. Lately, though, I have been thinking of her losses, and how we shortchange her in forgetting them. There is nothing routine about winning a major, after all—nothing automatic about an ace. As Carl Bialik wrote on FiveThirtyEight, "She earned it, and it was never guaranteed." As Williams herself put it, she is not just lucky. What is most incredible about that incredible serve of hers is not its flawless technique, or its weight or speed or spin. It's that she's more likely to hit an ace on significant points. It gets better when she's down.

What she has done has not come easy. And it is all the harder, and more extraordinary, because she is required to bear the weight of so much hope and hate, the weight of so much history.

On the morning of Andy Murray's final against Milos Raonic, the cover of the *Observer* read, "Weather Terrible, Sterling Tumbling, Politics Dismal, Euro Flops (Not Wales), Brexit Coming, Recession Looming"—and then, in giant letters, "ANDY PLEASE CHEER US UP."

Murray is a curious kind of cheerleader for the English—irascible and anti-elitist, scruffy and Scottish. Off the court, he has at times resisted the position that winning thrust him into, wary of a ravenous media and aware that he and his family would never quite be accepted in tennis's lingering culture of snobbery (nor did they want to be). On the court, he has at times gone to pieces.

But he is a marvelous tennis player, unquestionably the second best in the world right now and arguably one of the best in history. Without the overshadowing presence of Novak Djokovic—or Roger Federer or Rafael Nadal in the final—it was all the more apparent. His play throughout the tournament was steady and often spectacular; against Raonic, a 25-year-old Canadian, on Sunday, it was nearly flawless. Only three weeks ago, Raonic had raced to a set and a break lead over Murray in the final at the Queen's Club before crumbling, and, after his five-set win over Federer in the semifinals, it seemed as if the next generation might have finally arrived. (No player born in the nineties has yet to win a major.) But Murray, who turned 29 in May, showed how far the distance still is. He used his quickness to turn first-strike drives into rallies, sending up deep, high defensive lobs to prolong points. He exploited Raonic's weaker backhand with his own wicked one. And, when Raonic came to the net, Murray hit vicious, dipping passing shots. Most significantly, he had little trouble with Raonic's powerful, unreadable serve, which had, until then, carried the Canadian through the tournament. On one point, Raonic hit a 147-mile-per-hour serve into Murray's body—and lost the point. Murray not only managed to block the ball back but, with a compact swing, hit through it for a solid return. When Raonic charged the net, Murray hit a sharply angled cross-court passing shot to win the point.

After his 6–4, 7–6 (3), 7–6 (2) win, Murray broke down in tears, and for several minutes the sobbing wouldn't stop. It was, he would say, a far happier moment than his original Wimbledon win, in 2013, when he felt first the relief of so much pressure. No British man had won Wimbledon for 77 years. But he knows that he will never be able to escape the position that the public has put him in, the stage on which he must live. *Cheer us up.*

Yesterday, he did. Murray will be remembered first for his tennis. But his greater legacy may be what he has done with his platform, his willingness to speak out on social issues, especially women's rights—working with a female coach, supporting equal pay, calling himself a feminist. Sports may be an escape from politics, but there is an inescapable political dimension to sports too.

It was impossible to avoid thinking of politics at times during Wimbledon. Not during a tournament taking place outside London, just weeks after the U.K.'s vote to leave the European Union. Not when Murray acknowledged the presence of the departing prime minister, David Cameron, during his on-court interview after the match—a mention that elicited the crowd's boos. Not when Williams tweeted about the shooting of Philando Castile and was asked about the shootings in Dallas, nor when she spoke up about respect for women in sport and society. And not when the finalists included a Canadian born in Yugoslavia whose parents had fled during the Balkan conflicts.

After the women's final, the BBC played a montage of Williams reading Maya Angelou's poem "Still I Rise": "Out of the huts of history's shame / I rise . . ." She never asked for this, not for the pain or hate or chance to redeem history. But, at this Wimbledon, she has owned not only her greatness but her role as a transcendent figure in society. Still, she rises. She generates her own context. I thought of that at the end of her match, as she and Kerber lingered at the net in a long, tight hug. The picture—an African American and a blond German of Polish descent, their arms intertwined—stayed with me. There was nothing political meant by that embrace, of course. It was a gesture of admiration, affection, and respect. It was no more a political act than an ace. And yet there was something powerful to it. We sometimes project our problems onto sports. But sports can also be, in some small but real ways, where we start to work them out.

ROGER ANGELL

Almost There

FROM THE NEW YORKER

YES. THE CUBS WON, 3–2, avoiding extinction, and there will
be more baseball. Thank you, everybody. Thanks for letting it hap-
pen, all you Cubs down there—Kris Bryant, David Ross, Jon Lester,
Aroldis Chapman, etc. And back there—Ernie Banks, Hank Sauer,
Charlie Grimm. And thanks to all you Indians present and past
—Rajai Davis, Andrew Miller, CoCo Crisp, Sandy Alomar Jr., Earl
Averill, Nap Lajoie. The Cubs, trailing three games to one in this
Series, were facing winter, but now will have a day off and a sixth
game, and maybe even a glorious seventh. Baseball does this for us
again and again, extending its pleasures fractionally before it glim-
mers and goes, but, let's face it, this time a happy prolonging has
less to do with baseball than ever before. This particular October
handful has served to take our minds off a squalid and nearly endless and embarrassing election—three hours of floodlit opium or
fentanyl that can almost erase all thoughts of Donald Trump's angry slurs or Hillary Clinton's long travails. If I could do it, I would
make this World Series a best eight out of 15.

Watching the home Wrigley fans through the two soul-chilling
previous evenings was close to unbearable, as their guys put up
nothing but zeroes in their 1–0 Game 3 loss, and then a lone pair
in the 7–2 loss on Saturday. The mass silence, the gloved hands in
prayer position, the averted gazes, the mouths slack in disbelief,
the silly rally caps, and the rest made you want to put off thoughts
of the silent late trips home afterward. For me, the familiar autumn pains almost did away with the suffocating local history—the
108-year wait since the last Cubs championship, or the 71 years

since the last home Series. I was listing toward the Indians, my father's home team, but by mid-innings last night wanted only a Cubs win, to avoid the pain and gloom of a five-game dismissal. But, as we know, everything shifts when a Series goes to a sixth or seventh game. Both teams have done themselves proud, and left all their fans with important things to talk about and think about until spring, such as: why can't Jon Lester ever, ever throw to first base to hold a runner? And this sustaining glow may even take us intact to Election Day as well.

The players, to be sure, actually enjoy themselves. In the top of the third last night, the Indians starter Trevor Bauer lifted a fly ball up the foul line to right, which was somehow grabbed out there by the Cubs right fielder Jason Heyward while he hung by one arm on the wall in foul ground; Bauer gave him a sudden smile and clapped his hands in appreciation. When Aroldis Chapman, the lithe and extraordinary Cubs closer, had to bat, in the bottom of the eighth, in order to sustain his two-and-two-thirds-inning saving stint, he managed a wry, suave smile as he came up the steps with a bat in his hand for the third at-bat of his seven-year career. He put some good swings on the ball, but struck out.

There was some restitution for the Cubs home fans along the way. Kris Bryant, the National League's almost-assured MVP winner this year, had committed two ghastly errors in the same inning on the previous evening, but this time mashed a homer in the fourth inning for the Cubs' second lead in the Series. Bryant, at 24 years old, is part of the wonderful Kiddy Korps on view this fall, along with his teammates Anthony Rizzo, Carl Edwards Jr., Kyle Schwarber, and Javier Báez, and the Indians' Tyler Naquin, José Ramírez, and 22-year-old shortstop Francisco Lindor. He helps give one the impression that this is Locust Valley versus Smithtown, or Santurce versus Carolina, on an April afternoon. Báez and Lindor were in fact childhood rivals in Puerto Rico. I can't remember a more athletic infielder than Báez, who more than once threw himself at an oncoming base runner or base stealer to cut him off yards from the bag, and I was made miserable by his struggles at the plate in these latter games, when all that verve and desire demolished his swing and repeatedly sent him disconsolate back to the dugout. Lindor has been a joy, and I have him by heart now—the slinky mustache, the ready grin, the necklace, the terrier delight of it all. Terry Francona, the Indians' manager, has him batting third, and Lindor's .421 to date tops all comers. But here we must make note of those sweet swerves that only baseball provides. David Ross, the Cubs' catcher last night, drove in the third and deciding run in the fourth inning, and amputated Lindor's attempted steal in the sixth with a burning throw to the corner of the bag at second. He is 39 years old and will retire when this Series is over, so all this happened in his final game at Wrigley Field. These newer firsts and lasts seemed to brush aside the historic bits of news the announcers kept dropping on us before all this. Carlos Santana's home run in Game 4 was the first World Series round-tripper at Wrigley since Hank Greenberg's, in 1945, and back in Game 3 the roving camera picked out retired Supreme Court Justice John Paul Stevens in the stands, who at the age of 12 had witnessed Babe Ruth's called-shot home run against Charlie Root, in 1932.

There were more familiar phizzes as well—Lester, the Cubs' obdurate lefty and a longtime Red Sox regular, and the Indians' first baseman Mike Napoli, from the same Fenway bunch. Also the Cubs left fielder Ben Zobrist, a veteran of the Kansas City Royals, the Oakland A's, and the Tampa Bay Rays, a lefty hitter whose intense, bearded face when he's at the plate rests like a marble bust on the mantel of his front shoulder. Also the comforting, dadlike managers—Francona, always popping something in his mouth while he keeps his placid gaze on things, and Joe Maddon, in his horn-rims and ridiculous pom-pommed and pulled-down knitted wool winter hat. I can't see Joe Torre or Connie Mack in this eccentric-uncle getup, but I don't mind at all.

More to come. As stated, I think the Indians will win, but baseball has won already, and we're the better for it.

Contributors' Notes

Notable Sports Writing of 2016

Contributors' Notes

The New Yorker's ROGER ANGELL, a senior editor and staff writer, has contributed to the magazine since 1944 and became the fiction editor in 1956. Since 1962, he has written more than 100 "Sporting Scene" pieces. Author of numerous books, Angell is a Fellow of the American Academy of Arts and Sciences, and in 2011 he was the inaugural winner of the PEN/ESPN Lifetime Achievement Award for Literary Sports Writing. In 2014, Angell received the J. G. Taylor Spink Award from the Baseball Writers' Association of America. In 2015, he won the National Magazine Award for Essays and Criticism for his piece "This Old Man."

DAN BARRY is a columnist and reporter for the *New York Times*. He has reported from all 50 states, and his awards include a share of a Pulitzer Prize for investigative reporting. He is the author of four books: a memoir; a collection of his "About New York" columns; *Bottom of the 33rd: Hope, Redemption, and Baseball's Longest Game*, which received the 2012 PEN/ESPN Award for Literary Sports Writing; and *The Boys in the Bunkhouse: Servitude and Salvation in the Heartland*.

JON BILLMAN lives in the Upper Peninsula of Michigan. His work has appeared in, among other publications, *Esquire*, the *Paris Review*, and *Runner's World*. He is the author of the story collection *When We Were Wolves*, and is a contributing writer at *Outside*.

JOHN BRANCH is a sports reporter for the *New York Times*. His work has been part of this anthology twice before. He was awarded the 2013 Pulitzer Prize in feature writing for "Snow Fall," about a deadly avalanche. Branch lives near San Francisco.

JOHN COLAPINTO was born and raised in Toronto and has been a staff writer at *Rolling Stone* and *The New Yorker*. He is the author of the *New York*

Times nonfiction bestseller *As Nature Made Him: The Boy Who Was Raised as a Girl,* an expansion of his National Magazine Award–winning feature story "The True Story of John/Joan." He is also the author of two novels, *About the Author* and *Undone.* He is married and has an 18-year-old son.

LUKE CYPHERS has worked as a copy editor at Dow Jones & Co., as an investigative sports reporter for the *New York Daily News,* and as a senior writer and editor at *ESPN: The Magazine.* A former journalism professor at SUNY Plattsburgh and a current contributor to *Adirondack Life* magazine, he lives in upstate New York.

GEORGE DOHRMANN has worked for *Sports Illustrated,* the *Los Angeles Times,* and the *St. Paul Pioneer Press.* He won a Pulitzer Prize for Beat Reporting in 2000, and his first book, *Play Their Hearts Out: A Coach, His Star Recruit, and the Youth Basketball Machine,* won the 2011 PEN/ESPN Award for Literary Sports Writing. He lives in Ashland, Oregon.

TIM ELFRINK is an award-winning investigative reporter, the managing editor of the *Miami New Times,* and the coauthor of *Blood Sport: A-Rod and the Quest to End Baseball's Steroid Era.* Since 2008, he's written in-depth pieces on police corruption, fatal shootings, and social justice issues across South Florida. He's won the George Polk Award and has been a finalist for the Goldsmith Prize for Investigative Reporting.

SEAN FLYNN is a longtime correspondent for *GQ,* writing mostly about crime and disaster.

PATRICK HRUBY is a contributing editor at *Vice Sports* and a fellow at the University of Texas–Austin's Program in Sports and Media. He has worked for *Sports on Earth,* ESPN, and the *Washington Times* and taught journalism at Georgetown University. He holds degrees from Georgetown and Northwestern and lives in Washington, D.C., with his wife Saphira. This is his sixth appearance in *The Best American Sports Writing.*

BOMANI JONES is the host of the daily sports talk show *The Right Time* on ESPN Radio, a cohost of the ESPN sports television program *Highly Questionable,* and a panelist on the sports roundtable discussion show *Around the Horn.* As CEO of Old Soul Productions, Bomani hosts *The Evening Jones,* a weekly, one-hour, audience-driven podcast discussing a range of pop culture topics. He graduated from Clark Atlanta University in 2001 with a bachelor's degree in economics and received a master's degree in politics, economics, and business from Claremont Graduate University as well as a master's degree in economics from the University of North Carolina–Chapel Hill.

Time Magazine called PAT JORDAN's memoir *A False Spring* "one of the best and truest books about baseball, and about coming to maturity in America." He is the author of 10 other books, including *The Best Sports Writing of Pat Jordan.*

JESSE KATZ is a Los Angeles writer and the author of a memoir, *The Opposite Field.* He began his career at the *Los Angeles Times,* where he shared in two Pulitzer Prizes. As a staff writer at *Los Angeles* magazine, he received the James Beard Foundation's M. F. K. Fisher Distinguished Writing Award and the PEN Center USA's Literary Award for Journalism. In addition to *GQ,* his work has appeared in the *California Sunday Magazine, Billboard, New York, Town & Country,* and *The American Prospect.* Katz has run nine marathons, each slower than the last.

JEFF MAYSH's work has appeared in *The Atlantic, Playboy,* and *Howler.* In 2015 he was named Crime Journalist of the Year at the 58th Annual Southern California Journalism Awards. He is British-American and based in Los Angeles.

TERRENCE MCCOY is a staff writer at the *Washington Post,* covering poverty in rural and urban America. He is the recipient of numerous national awards, including the 2016 George Polk Award for a series of stories that showed how companies in an obscure industry made millions of dollars off exploitative deals with the poor and disabled. He is from Madison, Wisconsin, and lives in Washington, D.C., with his wife.

ALEXIS OKEOWO is a staff writer at *The New Yorker.* She is also a fellow at New America. Okeowo is the author of *A Moonless, Starless Sky: Ordinary Women and Men Fighting Extremism in Africa.*

RUTH PADAWER is a contributing writer at the *New York Times Magazine,* focusing on gender and social issues. She also teaches at Columbia University's Graduate School of Journalism. Her work—which has appeared in the *Guardian,* the *Times of London,* and *USA Today* and on the radio show *This American Life*—has been translated into more than a dozen languages.

S. L. PRICE has been a senior writer at *Sports Illustrated* since 1994. He has written four books, including *Playing Through the Whistle: Steel, Football, and an American Town,* which was named a Best Book of 2016 by the *Boston Globe* and *Kirkus Reviews* and was a finalist for the 2017 PEN/ESPN Award for Literary Sports Writing. This is his ninth appearance in *The Best American Sports Writing.*

DAVID REMNICK has been editor of *The New Yorker* since 1998 and a staff writer since 1992. He is the author of *Lenin's Tomb, Resurrection: The Struggle for a New Russia, King of the World* (a biography of Muhammad Ali), *The Bridge* (a biography of Barack Obama), *The Devil Problem,* and *Reporting.*

GRAYSON SCHAFFER is an editor-at-large for *Outside* based in Santa Fe. He has been with the magazine for 15 years.

DAVE SHEININ has been covering baseball and writing features and enterprise stories for the *Washington Post* since 1999. His work has been recognized with awards six times by the Associated Press Sports Editors, and in 2010 he received a first-place National Headliner Award for Sports Writing for his season-long coverage of Stephen Strasburg's rookie year. A graduate of Vanderbilt University, where he studied English and music and trained as an opera singer, he lives in Maryland with his wife and two daughters.

KURT STREETER is an ESPN senior writer focused on a wide range of sports and drawn to untold, overlooked stories. Prior to joining ESPN, he worked at the *Baltimore Sun* and the *Los Angeles Times,* where he was a metro desk feature writer and sports columnist and covered beats ranging from religion to the LAPD. An accomplished athlete, Streeter co-captained the California Berkeley men's tennis team in the late 1980s and held a pro tennis world ranking for four years. His stories about a young female boxer from East Los Angeles and an elderly boxing timekeeper appeared in the 2006 edition of *The Best American Sports Writing.* He lives in Seattle with his wife and son.

RICK TELANDER is the senior sports columnist for the *Chicago Sun-Times.* This is his eighth appearance in *The Best American Sports Writing.*

LOUISA THOMAS is the author of *Louisa: The Extraordinary Life of Mrs. Adams* and *Conscience: Two Soldiers, Two Pacifists — A Test of Will and Faith in World War I.* She is a contributor to the website of *The New Yorker.*

TERI THOMPSON is the former managing editor for sports at the *New York Daily News* and the founder of the newspaper's award-winning Sports Investigative Team. She was the recipient of the *New York Times* Fellowship for Journalists at the Columbia Law School in 1992 and is a member of the Connecticut bar. She is the coauthor of three books centered on crimes in sports: *American Icon: The Fall of Roger Clemens and the Rise of Steroids in America's Pastime, The Card: Collectors, Con Men, and the True Story of History's Most Desired Baseball Card,* and *American Huckster: How Chuck Blazer Got Rich From — and Sold Out — the Most Powerful Cabal in World Sports.*

WRIGHT THOMPSON is a senior writer for *ESPN: The Magazine.*

DON VAN NATTA JR. is a senior writer for *ESPN: The Magazine* and ESPN .com. He joined ESPN in January 2012 after 16 years as a *New York Times* correspondent based in Washington, London, Miami, and New York. A member of three Pulitzer Prize–winning teams, Van Natta is the author of *First Off the Tee* and the coauthor of *Her Way*—both *New York Times* bestsellers—and *Wonder Girl*. He's now writing a book about the modern-day NFL with his friend and colleague, Seth Wickersham. He lives in Miami with his wife, Lizette Alvarez, who is a *Times* correspondent, and their two daughters. This is his fourth appearance in *The Best American Sports Writing*.

DAVE ZIRIN is the sports editor for *The Nation*—their first in 150 years of existence—and a columnist for *SLAM* magazine and *The Progressive*. Zirin hosts the podcast *Edge of Sports* and cohosts the radio program *The Collision: Sports and Politics with Etan Thomas and Dave Zirin*. He is the author of nine books on the politics of sports. His latest is *Last Man Standing: Jim Brown and the Price of Legend*.

Notable Sports Writing of 2016

S E L E C T E D   B Y   G L E N N   S T O U T

THE BEST AMERICAN SERIES®

FIRST, BEST, AND BEST-SELLING

Available in print and e-book wherever books are sold.

Visit our website: *www.hmhco.com/bestamerican*